Mr. Raymond C. Davis
Librarian

Dear Mr. Davis

I take pleasure in contributing my mite toward the Library. Perhaps you have these volumes on the Life & Letters of Chancellor Lindsley but I think not.

and pleasant re-
collections of work
done with yours in
Bibliography,

Yours very sincerely

Carl C. Warren

135 North Spruce St.

Nashville Tenn.

June 5th 1899

In any case they
may perhaps be
of some use at
some time

I obtained them
through the kindness
of Mrs. J. B. Lindsley
of Nashville Tenn.
widow of Chancellor
Lindsley's son.

With many good
wishes always

WORKS OF

PHILIP LINDSLEY, D.D.

J. W. Dodge. Painter. Illman & Sons. Engravers.

PHILIP LINDSLEY, D.D.

J. B. LIPPINCOTT & CO. PHILADA

THE
WORKS
OF
PHILIP LINDSLEY, D.D.,

LATE PRESIDENT OF THE UNIVERSITY OF NASHVILLE.

"From his cradle,
He was a scholar, and a ripe and good one."

VOLUME I.

EDUCATIONAL DISCOURSES.

PHILADELPHIA:
J. B. LIPPINCOTT & CO.
NASHVILLE: W. T. BERRY & CO.
1859.

PREFACE.

Doctor Lindsley may undoubtedly be regarded as one of the leading spirits of his time, especially in the great cause of education, to which his life was more immediately devoted. His writings were mostly Addresses and Occasional Discourses, a considerable part of which were printed in his lifetime, and some of them passed through several editions. Since his death the wish has been expressed by many of his most intelligent friends, representing, it is believed, the general voice of the Public, that not only the productions of his pen already printed, but others which have remained till this time in manuscript, should be brought forth afresh, or for the first time through the medium of the press, to a mission of honourable usefulness. The author possessed, unquestionably, one of the most philosophical and accomplished minds in this country; and it would have been unjust not only to his memory, but to his generation and to posterity, to allow such memorials of his greatness and goodness to perish. No liberty has been taken, in the way of revision, with either the printed copies or the manuscripts, but both have been strictly followed, even to the punctuation. A second volume may be expected to follow this, within a moderate period, and after that, a Memoir of the venerable author by one of his friends.

CONTENTS OF VOL. I.

New Albany, Indiana, Feb. 1, 1853.

My dear Sir,

I have lately received, from a friend, a copy of your "Oration on the Life & Services of Daniel Webster", which I have read with the deepest interest and with unmingled satisfaction. So much so, that I cannot deny myself the grateful pleasure of expressing my obligations to the author. Next to the divine gift of such a man to our country and to the world, is a just appreciation of his merits & public services. You have done him justice — not more than sheer justice — and without a particle of extravagant eulogy or fulsome adulation. Among the many discourses pronounced on the occasion of the great Webster's death, I have seen none that meets my views nearly as well as yours. I heartily approve your opinions, teachings & warnings, as well as the exceedingly felicitous style & manner in which they are exhibited. I wish a copy of the Oration could be placed in the hands of every intelligent youth of Tennessee and of the whole republic. Again, I thank you, sincerely & fervently, for this labor of love, and most righteous tribute to the master mind of the age. With sentiments of the highest consideration, respect & regard,

I remain, as ever, most truly,

Yours, &c. &c

Philip Lindsley

Hon. Edwin H. Ewing,
Nashville, Tenn.

By the way, will you not favor us with a book a ~~book~~ of travels? or of reminiscences & impressions of matters & things as presented to your own mind & observation, during your recent rambles in the old world? You could give us something more than a mere journal of commonplace sight-seeing: And I am sure you would oblige and edify multitudes of readers besides your old friend. P.L.

Furnished for publication by request of the family of Dr. Lindsley.

INAUGURATION

OF THE

PRESIDENT OF CUMBERLAND COLLEGE.

INAUGURAL ADDRESS,

DELIVERED AT NASHVILLE, JANUARY 12, 1825.

On the subject of Education much has been said and written. Of its importance, at least, to a certain extent and for certain purposes, but one opinion has ever prevailed. Even among savages, and the ruder classes of civilized men, it has been found necessary to instruct children in the few imperfect arts and branches of knowledge with which the parents happened to be acquainted, in order to fit them for the mode of life to which they were destined. No animal is by nature so destitute and helpless as man. He is emphatically the creature of education. As a general rule, it may be affirmed of him, that he can be moulded into any form and character, and exalted to any degree of intellectual excellence, by suitable instruction and discipline. And, ordinarily, the scale of education is graduated by the wisdom and intelligence of those who, in any age or country, superintend and direct the seminaries of youth.

Many systems of education, considerably differing from each other in several important features, have been proposed to the world; and each has had its advocates and admirers. The question has often been agitated, whether a public be preferable to a private education? Much has been plausibly urged in behalf of each mode. The decision of mankind, however, has been pronounced in favour of a public system. Such was the award of Quinctilian; whose treatise on the subject is among the most ancient which have escaped the ravages of time. Of the various methods of communicating instruction in public —in schools and colleges—much diversity in theory and practice still obtains: and perfect uniformity is, perhaps, not to be expected. Partial and local, physical and moral, political and religious causes may occasion and tend to perpetuate this variety. Every system must be adapted to the genius, character and circumstances of the society for which it is designed. In most cases, however, useful hints may be borrowed from every source; while experience and talent will add something valuable to any existing system.

We cannot ascend very high into antiquity for light and information on this subject. Moses, the earliest and the only historian of the origin and primeval condition of our race, has recorded only a few striking facts and events relative to a period of more than twenty-five hundred years. These facts are, however, conclusive as to the general state and character of mankind during the primitive ages. They indubitably possessed the arts, knowledge, skill and enterprise of civilized life. The venerable father of the human family was their first instructor. Himself created in the full maturity and vigour of all his faculties, moral, intellectual and physical; and taught immediately by his Maker everything necessary for him to know; and living through a period of nearly a thousand years; he could not have failed to prove an able instructer to his posterity.

How much of literature, science and the arts may have been possessed by the antediluvian world, it is impossible for us to know, and useless to conjecture. That they had made no mean attainments is evident from the Mosaic narrative: and that their descendants, who survived the ruins of the deluge, had not lost the arts, is manifest from the sketch of their first exploits as given by the same faithful and inspired writer. Noah, indeed, remained a teacher in the new world for three hundred and fifty years. Within which period many of the cities of Chaldea, Assyria, and Phœnicia, had been founded, and were fast rising to that height of power and splendour which has made them the wonder and admiration of all succeeding ages. Egypt too, which has ever been reputed the cradle of the arts, had become a populous and flourishing kingdom, at least, in the days of Abraham. From the creation of Adam, therefore, down to the age of the great Hebrew patriarch, we behold no trace of savage life on the face of the earth. Nor for ages afterwards, in those countries which were first settled after the deluge, and which enjoyed the regular, uninterrupted instructions of the original masters and of their successors. Along the eastern and southern shores of the Mediterranean—upon the banks of the Tigris, the Euphrates and the Nile—there continued to exist, for many generations, the proudest monuments of human art and industry; and many of them exist still, upon a scale of gigantic grandeur and adamantine strength, which look down with contempt upon the puny efforts of modern ingenuity and refinement.

I intend, in these desultory remarks, to institute no comparison between the ancients and the moderns, as to the amount, utility, or excellence of their respective attainments. I am taking a rapid glance at a few prominent facts merely in reference to education. Their bearing on the subject will appear presently.

It has been generally supposed, and this is the prevailing philosophy, that the savage was the primitive state of man: and that he has been slowly advancing, from age to age, by the gradual development of his powers, until he has, at length, arrived at that degree of refinement which now characterizes civilized society. This theory is contradicted alike by reason, by revelation and by history. I hesitate not to affirm, that the world cannot produce an instance of a nation, a tribe, a family—or of an individual who has ever emerged from the rudeness of savage life without any foreign or external aid; or without the instruction and example of those who were already civilized. This is not the place to present the argument, or to attempt the induction which establishes my position. All the phenomena of the savage state can be easily explained—while, had this been the original state of mankind, his subsequent improvement could never have been accounted for consistently with scripture or history. Had men been savages at the outset, they would have been savages to this day, unless the Deity had interposed in their behalf. Man is prone to degeneracy; and when sunk to the lowest state of degradation, he remains stationary, until light from abroad dispels the darkness which envelops him. The history of all savage tribes, with which we are acquainted, confirms this statement.

The cause of the savage state has ever been the want of suitable instruction. When colonies removed from the fertile plains of Shinar to inhospitable climes—to remote islands—to dreary forests or barren deserts—it may readily be imagined that in many instances they would soon lose all knowledge of the arts which they left behind them. That such was the case we know from history. The Greeks were once comparatively rude and barbarous. If we admit that they were descended from the same stock with the Egyptians and Phœnicians, then, we must admit that they had greatly degenerated. And they acknowledged themselves debtors to the East for all their science, literature and arts. Here is one striking instance of early degeneracy, and of speedy recovery by the aid of foreign and cultivated nations.

Such has ever been the order. We can trace the stream of civilization flowing from the garden of Eden—through the antediluvian world—following the little company that issued from the ark—fertilizing the plains of Phœnicia and Egypt—at length, reaching the Grecian shores—and hence gradually advancing Westward till barbarous Rome felt its transforming power—then, interrupted, for a season, by the Northern Scythians, it seemed to linger in its march awhile about a few favoured spots, until in time it spread over the European world—and has finally crossed the Atlantic, and nearly reclaimed from savage cruelty and wretchedness a whole continent.

A portion of instruction must be communicated in order to awaken to active exertion the native energies of the human mind. Some elementary principles must be acquired from others before any individual will subject himself to the discipline of self-improvement. It is a false philosophy which takes for granted that man is ever disposed to better his condition and to cultivate his faculties. He must first be supplied with a stock to commence with. The amount to be furnished to answer the purpose of prompting to further attainments will vary with different persons, and under diverse circumstances. A child will never learn to read who has not been taught the alphabet. A savage never dreams of letters at all. The son of a Bacon, if left from infancy to himself, would grow up as destitute of science as the child of a Hottentot. But give him instruction sufficient to inspire him with a scientific taste, and then, if he have genius, he may, by his own efforts, surpass his parent.

Wherever education declines, there human nature proportionally deteriorates. Were it totally neglected in any community, not many years would elapse, before the people would become as absolutely savage as the Indian or the African. Learning cannot be inherited like money and lands. The same tedious, painful process must be repeated with every new generation. An apprenticeship must be served in order to acquire even the humblest mechanical arts—much more is it essential to literary and scientific attainments. The difficulty, in the most advanced stages of society, is to keep men up to the standard of excellence which has been already reached.

> * * * "Facilis descensus Averni:
> Sed revocare gradum, superasque evadere ad auras,
> Hoc opus, hic labor est."

The great question, therefore, is, how is useful knowledge of every kind to be retained in a State—how to be communicated or transmitted to those who are speedily to occupy our places—how to be advanced and extended in the most effectual and beneficial manner? The glory of Egypt and Western Asia—of Greece and Rome—has long since faded away: and those proud luminaries of science are forever extinguished. Whether a similar doom awaits the literary halls and academic groves which now diffuse the cheering beams of science over the Christian world, time alone can determine. We have reason to think not. The art of printing has arrested the march of the destroyer, and given stability to the inventions, discoveries and productions of genius. Still, the benefits of learning are but partially enjoyed. This is true of the nations of Christendom compared with each other—it is true of portions of the same kingdom, and of the individuals of every country, compared with one another. In ancient Egypt and Chaldea the higher sciences were monopolized exclusively by the sacerdotal order—while the body of the people were instructed only in the necessary and useful arts. When, therefore, the colleges of the former were destroyed, and the order itself abolished by the Persians, science became extinct.

In Greece, and afterwards in Rome, only a small number of the citizens ever became eminently learned: but a much larger proportion of knowledge was diffused among the people than is generally supposed. The popular assemblies, public games, national and religious festivals, theatrical entertainments, shows, pomps, processions, triumphs—which drew together the multitude frequently during the year—were, to a certain extent, schools to discipline and invigorate the faculties—and to animate courage, skill and ambition to daring enterprise. Besides, on these occasions, it was customary for the orator to harangue—for the poet, historian and philosopher to read their respective productions. The people were thus constituted a kind of literary tribunal to pronounce sentence upon the merits of their scholars, sages and poets. Hence they became familiar, in a degree, with all the polite learning of their age and country; and were distinguished for intelligence and refinement of taste. Neither the populace of London nor of Paris could vie, in these respects, with that of Athens or of Rome. But when these means of general instruction ceased, the people immediately lost their proud pre-eminence, and sunk to a level with the surrounding barbarians. From that period almost to the present, ignorance, darkness and superstition have been the lot and inheritance of the great mass of mankind, even in those countries esteemed the most highly favoured and enlightened. The Reformation and the art of printing commenced a brighter era: and learning has ever since been becoming more and more diffusive among the people; and just in proportion to its progress has been the melioration of their character and condition.

Ignorance, it is well known, is the parent of superstition and of oppression. It has been the policy, therefore, of every tyrannical government and ambitious priesthood to keep the people profoundly ignorant. Such a people can be easily imposed on. They can be converted into beasts of burden at the pleasure of any despotic master. None but the grossly ignorant can be retained long in bondage. Let the light of science and of the Bible shine upon the slave, wherever he is to be found in large numbers, and he will rend in sunder his chains, and assume that attitude which the conscious dignity of his nature claims as an inherent indefeasible right.

During the darkest ages of European barbarism, there were always some men of extraordinary learning and accomplishments—enough to preserve from total destruction the many precious monuments of ancient genius which we still possess, and which are still our purest guides and models in every department of elegant literature and the fine arts. They kept alive, indeed, the taper of science—though it burned dimly, and in a corner, and far from the view of ordinary and vulgar eyes. They preserved the materials for future use—the seed to be afterwards planted in a congenial and fruitful soil. They were the secret and unconscious guardians, under Providence, of the rights, liberties and happiness of all future generations. For two or three centuries past, the world has been reaping the benefits of their vigilance and labours. To form some idea of the amount actually gained, look at Europe in the days of Luther—look at Europe and the descendants of Europe at this moment. This mighty revolution, in the moral, political and religious state of so many millions of our race, has been effected by the instrumentality of learning—by the diffusion of knowledge among the people.

It is very questionable whether the existence in a community of a small number of learned men be, on the whole, advantageous, where the body of the people are doomed to absolute ignorance. They then constitute a privileged order—seek their own aggrandizement—and control the destinies of the State. Some such men have been, and still are, in every civilized kingdom. They may be found at the court of the Grand Turk, and in the most despotic empires of Asia. They are essential to the political machinery of their masters. But from the people, science is as effectually excluded, as if it were hermetically sealed up. Upon them its light never flashes except to blast and to consume.

A free government, like ours, cannot be maintained except by an enlightened and virtuous people. It is not enough that there be a few individuals of sufficient information to manage public affairs. To the people our rulers are immediately responsible for the faithful discharge of their official duties. But if the people be incapable of judging correctly of their conduct and measures; what security can they have for their liberties a single hour? Knowledge is power, by whomsoever possessed. If the people would retain in their own hands that power which the Constitution gives them, they must acquire that knowledge which is essential to its safe keeping and rightful exercise. Otherwise, they will soon be at the mercy of the unprincipled aspiring demagogue—who, for a time, may court and flatter them—but who will assuredly seize upon the first favorable crisis to bend their necks to his yoke and compel them to hail him as their lord and sovereign.

Give the people knowledge, therefore, and you give them power. Education must ever be the grand safeguard of our liberties—the palladium of our political institutions—of all our rights and privileges. In every country on the globe, where the mass of the people are best instructed, will be found the most liberty, the most virtue, and the most happiness. Look at North Britain, Switzerland, Holland, Sweden, and above all, at these United States. And just in proportion to the want of instruction will be found oppression, poverty, vice and wretchedness. Look at Ireland, Spain, Portugal, France, Russia, Turkey, with the whole of Asia and Africa. Had the French people, at the period of their revolution, been as enlightened as those of Scotland or America, they had never been the sport of one Catiline or Cæsar after another, until they were content to become the passive slaves of the Bourbons and the Holy Alliance. Nor would every other struggle for political emancipation, in the Old World, have proved equally unsuccessful, but for the same cause. What will be the issue of the present contests in Greece and Spanish America, remains to be seen. They may become independent; but if the people be destitute of suitable information, they will not establish or long maintain a free representative government.

It is the proud distinction of my countrymen, that, when their fathers adventured upon the novel and hazardous enterprise of self-government in 1776, they well understood the nature of the object at which they aimed, and steadily pursued that object without once exposing themselves to the chance of being flattered, or surprised, or cheated out of their liberties. They contended for the rights of man, and for their own hereditary and constitutional rights as Englishmen. It was not the shadowy phantom of ill-defined liberty—it was not the magic charm of a *word*, which could be made to mean anything or nothing, at the pleasure of those who employed it, that urged them on to resistance and to victory. Liberty, equality, independence, the rights of man, had with them a substantive and definite import. They were not the mere watchwords of cunning and ambition, of crime and desperation, bandied about from one factious upstart to another, to delude an ignorant degraded populace. Which yet might have been the case, had our people been as sottish as the infidel rabble of Paris, or the priest-ridden peasantry of Spain. Then, had independence been achieved, we had merely transferred our allegiance from a transatlantic sovereign to a domestic tyrant. From oppressed colonists, we had become heartless trembling helots. And instead of daring to advocate the cause of truth and liberty and science, a free press and a free speaker would, at this moment, have been strangers to our soil.

No greater foe to his country's dearest interests can be found than the enemy of education. Were it the purpose of any set of men to engross all the power, honours and emoluments of official stations—to become a dominant aristocracy—an order of self-constituted nobility in the midst of the Republic—their plan should be to discourage education—to frown upon every attempt to promote and extend it—to denounce colleges and schools of every kind—to put them down where they exist, and to prevent their establishment wherever desired. Their wealth would enable them to send their own sons abroad to be educated, while the great body of the people could not afford the expense, and would consequently be compelled to see their children become hewers of wood and drawers of water to their more fortunate and privileged neighbours.

Great is the mistake which is current on this subject, that colleges are designed exclusively for the rich—that none but the rich can be benefited by them—and therefore, that the State ought not to patronize or endow them. That funds for their support ought not to be drawn from the public treasury or the people's purse. Because this would be to tax the many for the advantage of a few. Nothing can be more groundless and fallacious than such a representation. No course more injurious to the people were it adopted. The direct contrary is their true policy and interest. For were a college established and maintained by an equitable tax upon the people—

who would pay the tax? Not the poor—for no tax, or next to none, is ever levied on them. Men would contribute according to their means; and the principal burthen would necessarily fall upon the rich, as in reason and justice it ought. The rich then would be taxed for the benefit of the whole community.

It is evident, as I before remarked, that the rich, at least, the very rich, could easily educate their children at distant or foreign seminaries. And it would be greatly to their advantage to do so, at any expense, were there no seminaries at home, or within every one's reach. Suppose there were no college in Tennessee—and but twenty individuals wealthy enough to send their sons to a college out of the State—it would then be in the power of a score or two of persons to monopolize all the liberal professions and all the avenues to wealth and honour in the commonwealth. But raise up colleges among yourselves, and you reduce the charges of a liberal education so considerably that hundreds and thousands can immediately avail themselves of their aid. Not only all the middling classes of citizens, but enterprising youth of the poorest families may contrive to enter the lists of honourable competition with the richest. As is done every day in the Northern and Eastern States; where, indeed, the poor, more frequently than the rich, rise to eminence by their talents and learning. Such is the peculiar genius and excellence of our republican institutions, that, moral and mental worth is the surest passport to distinction. The humblest individual, by the diligent cultivation of his faculties, may, without the aid of family or fortune, attain the most exalted stations within the reach or gift of freemen. What an encouragement to studious effort and enterprise? What an incentive to the generous aspirings and honourable ambition of our youth? Why should not the door be opened wide for their entrance upon this vast theatre of useful action and noble daring?

But, it may be said, that common elementary schools are sufficient to answer every valuable purpose—that these ought chiefly to be encouraged by the State—that the great majority of the people, after all, must be content with a comparatively limited education—that it would be absurd to think of giving to all a liberal education even were it practicable—because, if acquired, it would be superfluous or injurious, inasmuch as only a small number, at best, can hope to succeed in the learned professions or to fill the public offices.

Far be it from me to utter a syllable in opposition to primary schools. They are indispensable—and ought to be found in every neighbourhood. But the best mode of encouraging and multiplying these is carefully to foster the higher seminaries—because the latter must or ought to furnish teachers to the former. The greater the number of the liberally educated, in any country, the better the chance of obtaining suitable instructors for the inferior institutions. Wherever colleges abound, there is no difficulty in providing teachers for all the academies and schools in their vicinity. Witness the four universities of Scotland and the dozen colleges in New England. And what country can compare with these for the general diffusion of knowledge among the people? Where are common schools so numerous or so effective? Where can be found so many well educated men—so many college graduates? Were there a like proportion in Tennessee, there would be no lack of village and country schools. They would grow up of course and from necessity. As education extends, the desire and demand for it increase. Numbers will leave college every year compelled to gain a livelihood by their own exertions. Some will not have the means to prosecute the study of a profession immediately—some will not have the inclination or the proper qualifications—besides, many will despair of succeeding where the candidates are so numerous, and therefore will be glad to teach as a regular business. Thus the gradual supply to the community of persons qualified and willing to instruct, and the constantly increasing thirst for knowledge among the people, will react upon each other—the latter making room and giving employment to the former, who by their influence, example, and labours, will more and more extend and awaken the spirit of improvement. In this way too, *teaching* would soon become, what it ought to be, an honourable calling or profession. The advantages which would result to this State from such a policy, are incalculable. And the individuals who shall succeed in introducing it, will be hailed as public benefactors to the latest generations.

But there is another prevailing heresy on this subject which deserves exposure and condemnation. It is, that superior learning is necessary only for a few particular professions and situations—such as we have been contemplating. Now, I affirm, in opposition, it may be, to all the learned faculties of all the learned professions, and to all vulgar prejudices, that every individual, who wishes to rise above the level of a mere labourer at task-work, ought to endeavour to obtain a liberal education. I use the term *liberal* in a liberal sense; without necessarily including every branch of literature or science which usually constitutes a college course. The farmer, the mechanic, the manufacturer, the merchant, the sailor, the soldier, if they would be distinguished in their respective callings must be educated. Should it be objected, that well-educated youth will not *labour* for their support; that, if they become farmers or manufacturers, they will, at most, merely superintend and direct the labours of others, I answer—1st. That we, at this moment, need thousands of such men. Would not every planter who cultivates the soil by slaves, and every farmer who does the same by hired labourers, be the better, the happier, the more useful with a good education than without it? May not the same be said of the directors of printing, mercantile, and manufacturing establishments: and, indeed, of every man who is above, or aspires to be above, the meanest drudgery of manual labour? Here then are thousands in the community, who, or whose children at least, might be liberally educated without diminishing the number of actual labourers. So that any increase of seminaries, upon any plan, is not likely very soon to affect the common concerns of productive industry, except by bringing to bear upon them the salutary influence of more light and knowledge, and so far greatly to improve and meliorate the character and condition of all classes of citizens.

But, in the second place, were it possible to give, what might be styled a liberal education of a suitable kind to every child of the Republic, so far from proving detrimental to industry and enterprise, it would produce a directly contrary effect. Differences in rank, station, and fortune would still exist. The pulpit, the bar, the healing art, the army, the navy, the legislative hall, the bench of justice, and all posts of honour and emolument, would, of course, be occupied then as now by men of comparatively superior talents, learning or address. While the remainder would be compelled, according to their abilities or necessities, to do what they best could for a livelihood. Though all would be learned to a certain extent, yet there would be various gradations of excellence. The competition for honourable distinction would range on a higher scale, and among men of greater intellectual attainments, than is now the case; but in reference to the whole body of the people, the principle and the result would be the same. All would find their level, and every individual his appropriate place and sphere. Even supposing then, what is not likely soon to happen, that all were educated—and educated in the best manner, we need not apprehend that a famine would ensue from lack of industry.

In the third place, so far as the experiment has been made, we find that the educated poor do in fact become, in the same proportion, more industrious, useful and happy. I appeal to the school at Hofwyl—to history, and to the actual state of the world—to every fact which can be adduced as bearing upon the argument. Three centuries ago, it was considered dangerous for the common people anywhere to be taught even the art of reading. And a mechanic who could then read his Bible was a greater rarity than would be, in our day, a mechanic who could read Homer in his native tongue.

Man is a moral and intellectual being; and his moral and intellectual faculties ought to be cultivated, independently of the sordid motive or prospect of pecuniary gain, or of a mere livelihood. The grand question among real philanthropists will be, if it be not already, what system of discipline is best calculated to render men virtuous and happy?—Not what will render them rich and honourable and powerful? All cannot be rich. The great mass must ever remain in comparatively humble circumstances. But all may be virtuous and happy—so far, at least, as virtue and happiness can be predicated of mortals in this world. The labouring classes of the people do not labour always. They have their seasons of mirth and pleasure—of recreation and amusement. Of what character these usually are need hardly be specified. Let the tavern, the grog-shop, the court-house, the gaming table, and every *gathering* on public and festive occasions, proclaim their value and amount. Could not these people be better employed? Are they incapable of any enjoyment superior to that of the brute sensualist? Why is it, that, whenever they have a leisure hour, they become, in one way or another, the tormentors of themselves and their families? What should hinder the poor man from enjoying a literary repast just as well as the rich man? Nothing surely but the want of that previous training which would enable him to relish it. Were a literary taste once imbibed, books would be resorted to for entertainment and instruction: and these would prove, not only a more innocent, rational and beneficial source of enjoyment, but vastly cheaper than any of those which administer to the gratification of the mere animal and vicious appetites and propensities. How different an aspect would human society present were every farm-house and cottage supplied with useful books and every inmate a reader? Intelligence would then beam from every eye; and home—sacred home, would be the scene of the purest pleasures. Contentment too would smile on every countenance—with pious hope animating every bosom, and virtue gilding the pathway of life's humble pilgrimage to brighter mansions in the skies! Thus would be realized on earth the poet's golden age, and the Christian's millennial elysium. Whenever science and religion shall have gained universal dominion, then peace and happiness will crown the lot of every mortal.

Men are exceedingly prone to be blind to their own best interests. Hence the opposition to all benevolent and patriotic schemes and enterprises, at least, during their early and incipient stages; and until experience shall have established their claims to general patronage and support. Hence the illiberal prejudices against learning, and learned men, and literary institutions, still deeply rooted in many parts of the world, and of our own country too.

King Alfred, in an age which we despise as barbarous, understood this matter far better than many of the sapient monarchs and republican statesmen of the nineteenth century. "We will and command, (says he, in one of his public acts,) that all freemen of our kingdom whosoever, possessing two hides of land, shall bring up their sons in learning till they be fifteen years of age at least, that so they may be trained up to know God, to be men of understanding, and to live happily; for, of a man that is born free, and yet unliterate, we repute no otherwise than of a beast or a brainless body, and a very sot." And it is well known, that, in the University of Oxford, which he either founded or revived, ten times as many youth were educated, during a part of his illustrious reign, as at the present day. Had the spirit of Alfred animated his successors, many ages of darkness, superstition, tyranny and wretchedness had been spared to the land of our sires—and America might have been centuries in advance of her present attainments.

Admitting then that colleges are necessary, no less than common schools, the question arises, how and by whom are they to be established? Our general government does not think proper to interfere—or to make provision for this most momentous concern. It is evident, therefore, that colleges and all literary institutions must owe their origin and support to the several State legislatures, or to the munificence of public-spirited individuals. Some of the States have adopted a wise and liberal policy in this behalf. Witness Massachusetts, New York, Virginia, the Carolinas, and Georgia. Others have done something, while many have done nothing. It does not become me, a stranger, to speak of the acts of the Tennessee Legislature in relation to her colleges. Whether they could with propriety do more than they actually have done, may depend on circumstances of which I am ignorant, or not a competent judge. It is certain, however, that Cumberland College, if she attain to a rank equal to her sister institutions, must be indebted chiefly to individual enterprise and liberality. Her funds, whatever may be their ultimate value, are, at present, unproductive; consisting of landed property, which cannot be sold without a sacrifice, and which it is desirable to retain until it can be brought into a better market. The trustees of the institution, and many of its friends in this town and vicinity, have contributed handsomely towards its support. But much—very much remains yet to be accomplished. The grand experiment is about to be made, whether this college shall be organized on a permanent and respectable basis: or whether it again be destined to a temporary existence and to ultimate failure from the want of due encouragement and patronage from the wealthy citizens of West Tennessee and the adjacent States. That there are ample means in the hands and at the disposal of the good people of this vast and fertile section of our country cannot be doubted. Situated as this college is, almost on the line which separates the healthy from the unhealthy portions of the great valley of the Mississippi—as far south, probably, as it will ever be desirable to establish a seminary of the kind—and offering, as it does, inducements the most powerful to the notice and patronage of Alabama, Mississippi and Louisiana, may we not indulge the hope that the opulent citizens of this extensive region will not suffer our infant establishment to languish and die, under their eyes and at their very doors, from any paltry jealousies or illiberal sentiments and prejudices? May we not trust, that, by judicious and seasonable efforts and representations, our funds may be gradually augmented until the most sanguine wishes of the founders and patrons of this college shall be fully attained? Let us be encouraged by the success which has crowned the labours of our brethren in other States. The Theological Seminary at Andover received from a few benevolent donors several hundred thousand dollars almost at the outset. The Theological Seminary at Princeton has, by perseverance in a regular system of begging, within a period of twelve years, succeeded in erecting all the necessary edifices, in procuring a library of six thousand volumes, and in endowing all the necessary professorships. Yale College and Nassau Hall, without the smallest legislative aid, have, by a similar course, been exalted to the highest rank among the colleges of our country. The example of Transylvania University is still nearer at hand and more prominently within your view.

Let us then not despair, or remit our exertions. Every dollar obtained is an encouragement to solicit more. Reduced to the necessity of asking assistance, let us not be ashamed to beg until there shall be no further need of it. The cause is worthy of the people's charity. It is emphatically the cause of the people—and of all the people, without distinction of sect or name. For Cumberland College, though a Christian, is not a sectarian institution. Its immediate patrons and directors belong to several religious denominations. It is the property of no sect or party. It looks for support to the liberal of all persuasions—and is pledged to be equally friendly and indulgent to every class and description of citizens. No parent need apprehend danger to the religious creed of his son by any influence which shall here be exerted. With this understanding, and with this catholic declaration, we confidently appeal to the generosity of all our fellow-citizens, assuring them that their charity will not be misapplied or unworthily bestowed.

To the citizens of Nashville, a more selfish argument might be addressed, were it worthy of the object or the occasion. They will chiefly reap the immediate benefit of the pecuniary expenditure which must necessarily follow the establishment of a flourishing literary institution in their village. Every student who comes from abroad will contribute to the wealth and prosperity of this people. New Haven derives a revenue of between two and three hundred thousand dollars annually from her students. Were you, therefore, merely to consult your own pecuniary emolument in this concern, it would be greatly to your interest to advance the whole sum necessary to insure complete success to your college. It could be easily shown also, that the surrounding country, and, indeed, the whole State would be proportionably benefited by every addition to the wealth of this town. Could Nashville be made to-morrow as large and wealthy as Philadelphia, it would instantly stamp a hundred-fold value on all the property and employments in the country for many hundred miles in every direction. There is no ground therefore, in any view of the subject, for the slightest local or sectional jealousy or hostility.

I proceed to another very important branch of this very comprehensive subject. And here again I must content myself with a few general remarks. A great desideratum in the education of youth is such a system as will most effectually develop, invigorate and mature all the faculties, physical, mental and moral. The body, the mind and the heart ought to be the objects of the most assiduous care and cultivation in every seminary of learning. I need not stop here to philosophize on the connection which subsists between the body and the mind, or to show how they mutually affect and influence each other. The fact is too well known to require proof or illustration. "Sana mens in sano corpore," is an ancient adage. Among the republican Greeks and Romans of the purest ages, no pains were spared to train their youth to health, vigour and activity, while they were acquiring a learned and liberal education. Their *gymnasia* and *palæstræ* sufficiently indicate the original and primary purposes of their institution. The arts and sciences, philosophy and rhetoric, were taught by the most accomplished masters, in a way calculated to elicit all the energies of the mind, and to inspire their pupils with a generous emulation to excel. These listened, not merely to a course of lectures got up by the aid of the dead and the living—and pronounced *ex cathedra* with magisterial solemnity and soporific pathos: nor were they compelled to commit to memory the rounded periods and loose statements of a prosing text-book, but they were permitted to inquire and to reason—to interrogate their instructors—to discuss subjects—to start difficulties—to examine and to master the *pro* and *con.* of every question. Thus were their talents called forth, and tried, and sharpened, and prepared for active life. Thus was their knowledge rendered practical, exact and ever ready for use. It was *their own,* in the strictest sense of the term. It had been thoroughly canvassed, sifted and adopted upon evidence. It had been reasoned into them, and incorporated with their very nature. When, therefore, they were called to prepare an oration for the forum or the senate—when they sat down to compose a treatise on any subject, they were not compelled to recur to a thousand volumes for sentiment, metaphor, illustration or argument. They drew from their own stores. They spoke and wrote like men who were masters of their subject. And hence the originality which so pre-eminently characterizes their productions. Every piece is, in a great measure, an *unique*—It is of that continued uniform texture which bespeaks it the work of a single artist. No patchwork of various colours and qualities—the manufacture of a hundred ages and countries, as is not unfrequently the case with the modern scholar, who ventures not to write a page without the inspiring and guiding genius of some ponderous folio ever at his elbow.

Their schools, too, were all theatres of active sports and games and military tacticks. Inured to labour, to athletic exercises, to temperance, to study, to every species of bodily and mental effort from infancy, their youth entered upon the duties of manhood with every advantage, prepared to serve their country in the cabinet and in the field, in peace and in war, at home and abroad, in public and in private, with the strength of Hercules and the wisdom of Minerva.

The moderns have dispensed with this hardy training. Colleges and universities have long been consecrated to literary ease, indulgence and refinement. In them, *mind* only is attempted to be cultivated, to the entire neglect of the bodily faculties. This is a radical defect; so obvious and striking too as to admit of no apology or defence. Youth, at most public seminaries, are liable to become so delicate, so effeminate, so purely *bookish,* as to be rendered, without some subsequent change of habit, utterly unfit for any manly enterprise or employment. How frequently too, do they fall early victims to this ill-timed system of tenderness and seclusion? But this is not the worst of the case. Youth must and will have employment of some kind. They cannot study always. In our colleges they are usually suffered to devise their own ways and means of amusement. They are expected indeed, perhaps exhorted, to take exercise, and they are allowed abundance of time for the purpose. Still the whole concern is left to their own discretion. The time they have—and the question is, how do they spend it? Often in mere idle lounging, talking, smoking and sleeping. Often in sedentary games, which, whether in themselves lawful or unlawful, are always injurious to the student, because he requires recreation of a different kind. But too frequently in low degrading dissipation, in drinking and gaming, to the utter neglect of every duty, and to the utter abandonment and sacrifice of every principle of honour and virtue. I will not finish the melancholy picture which I had begun to sketch, not indeed from fancy or from books, but from facts which I have often witnessed, and which have sometimes led me almost to question the paramount utility of such institutions to the community. Still, with all their faults, I remain their decided advocate. But may they not be improved; or may not others be organized upon wiser and safer principles?

That system, which should provide complete employment of a *proper* kind, for all the time of every individual, would, in my opinion, be the best system; and might, perhaps, be fairly denominated a perfect system. And every approximation to it will, to the same extent, be an approach to perfection in this all-important concern. Keep youth busy, and you keep them out of harm's way. You render them contented, virtuous and happy.

I have said that the heart, or the moral faculties, ought to be cultivated. I am aware that a system of ethicks or moral philosophy usually constitutes a part of a college course, and the last part too. It is studied as a science—just as chemistry or astronomy is studied. But the moral powers need constant cultivation from infancy to manhood. Correct habits of thinking and acting are to be formed. Precept, lecture, exhortation, are not enough. The daily walk and conversation must be inspected, guarded, and moulded, if practicable, into the purest form. The Bible ought to be studied, and its lessons of wisdom diligently enforced and practically exemplified. I say nothing of creeds, or confessions, or systems of doctrine. I speak of the Bible—the grand charter of our holy religion—of our common Christianity. And who of the great Christian family can object to this? In the heathen schools, youth were always taught the religion of their country. Every Mussulman is required to be master of the Koran. And shall Christian youth be less favored than the Pagan and Mohammedan? Have we a book bearing the impress of heaven—confessedly embodying the purest morality ever yet known in the world—the only authentic record of the origin of our race, and of the most stupendous events which have occurred upon our globe—filled with scenes of real life the most instructive, with biographical incident the most extraordinary and pathetic, with strains of eloquence and poetry the most melting and sublime—and withal professing to be, and acknowledged to be, our only safe guide through life, and the foundation of all our hopes of a blessed immortality—shall this book be excluded from our seminaries, and withheld from our youth, at the very period too, when they most need its salutary restraints and purifying influence? And this, lest, peradventure, some speculative error, or some sectarian opinion might be imbibed? as if worse errors, and more inveterate prejudices, and the most pernicious principles, will not be sure to find their way into that heart which remains a stranger to the hallowed precepts of the sacred volume. But I intend to offer no formal argument upon this point just now. In every place of education, the Bible ought to be the daily companion of every individual; and no man ought to be suffered to teach at all who refuses to teach the Bible. "Train up a child in the way he should go, and when he is old he will not depart from it," is the doctrine of revelation, of reason, and of experience.

The benevolent and enterprising Fellenberg has done much towards remedying the existing evils attendant on a public education, and also towards making provision for the proper instruction of the poor. He has contrived, without expense to himself or others, to educate liberally hundreds of the poorest children of Switzerland, and he is still engaged in this good work. At Hofwyl the poor maintain themselves by labour. The rich pay for their privileges. And all are constantly under the eye and control of their teachers. There, the poor learn trades, or become practical farmers, at the same time that they are thoroughly instructed in every branch of useful science. The rich are trained to all manly exercises, and to various useful arts, while their minds are diligently cultivated by the most accomplished professors. M. Fellenberg appears, so far as we are enabled to judge from the several statements which have reached us, to have completely succeeded in supplying the deficiencies of the old system, and in forming an institution adapted to the character and the wants of all classes of citizens. There, the body, the mind, and the heart, receive their due proportion of care and improvement. There is no idleness, no dissipation, no extravagance, no effeminacy, no sacrifice of time, money, health or morals. All is life, vigour, animation, order, industry, emulation. Every moment is profitably improved. The employments are so judiciously varied that they never become irksome or oppressive. Every change is a relief, and partakes of the nature of recreation. The shop, the field, the garden, riding, fencing and other military exercises, musick, history, ancient and modern languages, the mechanical and the fine arts, with all the sciences physical and moral, abstract and practical, constitute the business, the amusement, and the study of this well regulated establishment.

Several of the most eminent noblemen of Russia and Germany have already sent their sons to Hofwyl, in preference to any and to all the Universities of Europe. A similar establishment would doubtless find liberal patrons among American gentlemen. A practical acquaintance with agriculture and the useful arts would, on their own account, be advantageous to every man: but, considered as a part of moral and healthful discipline, their importance is greatly enhanced. Should some, however, object to mere manual labour of any kind, as too degrading to their high descent and lofty aspiring, though resorted to chiefly as exercise and recreation, still regular active employment, in sufficient abundance and variety, may be provided even for the most fastidious; and such as they would esteem gentlemanly accomplishments, at the same time that they are acknowledged to be valuable. These, at proper seasons, and under the direction of proper authority, might occupy many an hour which would otherwise be worse spent. Neither Greek nor Mathematics would lose any thing by such interruptions. Let these general hints go for what they are worth. I am no advocate for sudden changes and innovations, nor am I invincibly attached to the beaten track of my fathers.

But since I have ventured thus far, allow me to pursue the train of speculation suggested by Fellenberg's system, as applicable to the hardy sons of our honest yeomanry and mechanics—not excluding those of the humblest poverty, wherever the germ of future excellence can be discerned. I have already shown how colleges of any kind must or may benefit the middling and poorer classes of the people; and, that, it is their special interest to wish them success. Here, however, a more direct chance for mental culture may be offered them—and for such culture as best befits their previous habits, their present circumstances, and their future prospects. As they cannot be expected to pay as liberally for their privileges as the rich, let them fare and dress according to the dimensions of their purses—let them supply any deficiency by their labour—or, when necessary, let them maintain themselves entirely by their own industry, as is done by the poor at Hofwyl. Two hundred acres of land, more or less, in the vicinity of Nashville, divided into fields and gardens, under judicious management, would afford to many a youth, not only a practical knowledge of farming and horticulture, but the means of living while he is pursuing his studies at the college. Let some dozen or twenty mechanics of good moral character, be duly authorized to open their shops for such as might prefer, or as might be better adapted to, this species of labour. Thus, many useful trades might be learned, and the whole expense of their education be defrayed, without any material loss of time—even if time, thus employed, could be accounted lost. A youth, ardent in the pursuit of knowledge, would learn more in half his time than most of the indulged sons of affluence actually acquire in the whole. And there are few industrious young men who could not earn their living, and a little more, by labouring half of their time: especially in a town where so many profitable occupations would be at their option, and where the products of the field, the garden, and the workshop, would ever find a ready market.

The most startling difficulty in the way of any plan of this kind, would be suggested, probably, by the obvious inequality and apparently invidious distinctions which would obtain among the pupils of the same institution. But does not a similar inequality exist among our citizens and youth everywhere in society? The objection, however, is merely specious. For, in the first place, none but youth (poor youth, I mean,) determined to have an education, would resort to such an institution. These would soon learn to disregard or despise the *petits maitres* who might affect to be their superiors. They would in fact be as independent as the richest. How much more truly respectable and republican would be their condition, while thus *labouring* for the food of body and mind, than that of the student who is supported in luxurious ease by the charity of individuals, or of the public? How vastly preferable to the situation of a Cambridge sizer or Oxford servitor—many of whom, nevertheless, have filled, and are filling, the highest stations in church and state? In the second place, the *esprit du corps*, which would prevail in the several ranks or classes of students, would serve to keep each other in countenance, and to render them indifferent to imaginary evils. Besides, they would be a regular component part of the establishment. They would be in the fashion. They would conform to established usage. They would have law and public sentiment in their favour. They would not form a sorry half dozen of pitiable exceptions to the reigning mode, as they would, if found in any of our present colleges. They would constitute a respectable moiety—perhaps, a large majority of the whole. And they would be respectable just in proportion to their modest, fearless, independent conformity to their actual condition. A poor youth of talents and becoming deportment, will never be long despised anywhere. But here he would occupy a post of honour, and have every motive and every encouragement to persevere, till he should be qualified to do honour to himself, his friends and his country.

Should it be thought impracticable or inexpedient to connect with this, or with any other college, such an appendage for the benefit of the poor as I have just pointed at—still, something of the kind might be attempted in another and distinct form, and it may not be unworthy of the serious consideration and patronage of individuals and of the government. The course of instruction should be adapted to the character and destination of the pupils. An education may be perfectly liberal, as I have already intimated, without always embracing the same precise order, kind or amount of studies. Much discretionary latitude will remain with the directors in this as in other matters.

And now, in reference to this topic generally, let it be remembered, that, the particulars which have been specified, need not necessarily enter into any improved system of education. The principle which we have endeavoured to illustrate, admits of an indefinite variety of modification and application. The *principle*, or, if you please, the *genius* of the system, is constant employment, under proper direction, so as most effectually to improve every faculty of the pupil, and to fit him, in the best manner, to act well his part in future life.

Let us, then, borrow some ideas from the schools at Hofwyl and Yverdun—something from the ancient Greeks and Romans—something from our own Military Academies at Norwich and West Point—something from the pages of Locke, Milton, Tanaquil Faber, Knox, and other writers—something from old and existing institutions of whatever kind—something from common sense, from experience, from the character, circumstances and wants of our youth, from the peculiar genius of our political and religious institutions; and see whether a new gymnasium or seminary may not be established, combining the excellencies and rejecting the faults of all. I seriously submit it to my fellow-citizens, whether this subject be not worthy of more than a passing thought or momentary approbation. Who is prepared to enter fully into its spirit, and to engage heart and hand in the enterprise?

Will any man, in this enlightened age of discovery, invention and improvement, pretend that we have already reached perfection in the science and the work of education—the very *beau ideal*—the *ne plus ultra* of human skill and attainment? That nothing more ought to be done, or can be done, in this vast province of illimitable extent, and of infinite concernment to the young and rising generation? Raikes and Bell and Lancaster have, in our day, revolutionized the common school system, and have wrought miracles in behalf of the poor—and, indeed, of all, during the incipient stages of a public education. Must we stop here? Can nothing be effected within the massive walls of our ancient and venerated literary cloisters, where the usages of a thousand years still predominate—where proud prescription, resting on a throne of adamant, seems to arrogate a more than popish infallibility, and to threaten a reign of interminable duration?*

* It may not be amiss to inform the reader, that several of the preceding remarks have already been given to the public, by the author,

In an address like the present, it may be expected that something should be said relative to the course of study to be adopted in our institution—something upon the requisite qualifications for admission, and something on the subject of government and discipline.

I. For admission into college, I would briefly premise, that every candidate ought to be able to read, write and spell his native tongue—(I will not say *perfectly*—for this would be requiring what is seldom or never attained to by any—but in a style much superior to what is ordinarily witnessed)—he ought to be well skilled in Geography, English Grammar and Arithmetic—and to be thoroughly grounded in the elements of the Greek and Latin languages. This should, in all cases, be the *minimum* that will be tolerated. Whether it be expedient, at present, to demand more, must depend on the state of our schools and academies. A much larger amount of mental furniture is desirable, whenever it can be supplied—and the more the better.*

---

in a series of essays published, last spring, in the Trenton Emporium, over the signature of THE HERMIT.

* A leading defect in the American system of education, is the want of good preparatory schools. This evil is felt and acknowledged, in a greater or less degree, in every part of our country. Colleges complain, and with abundant reason, that very few of their pupils come to them well taught even in the few elementary branches which their statutes require as qualifications for admission. I should be within bounds, were I to affirm, that, during my connexion with one of our most respectable colleges, not one youth in ten entered it thoroughly prepared. It cannot be supposed that the grammar schools are on a better footing in the Western than in the Middle States. The truth is, that no regular efficient system has as yet been adopted anywhere. This matter is left too much to chance, or to individual enterprise.

II. To a college course in general, and, at least, prospectively considered, no limits can be assigned. It may comprehend every branch of literature and science. But

---

Sufficient encouragement is not usually given to classical teachers to render their profession lucrative and honourable—so as to command the services of men of talents and learning. Without this inducement, such men will seldom consent to teach; except, it may be, for a season, as a matter of convenience or necessity, and as the means of rising to some other and better occupation.

In England there are several hundreds of richly endowed grammar schools—the head-masters of which receive a much larger pecuniary compensation than the Presidents of our richest colleges. The superiority of her scholarship need not therefore occasion any surprise. The cause is obvious. I am no blind admirer of the English school system —unrivalled as it has ever yet been; nor do I wish to see it introduced into this country without very considerable modifications. Still, we have nothing that deserves to be compared with it. Nor need we expect similar excellence until merit in the teacher be adequately rewarded.

If there be one vocation more important to the community than any other, or than all others, it is that of the instructer of youth. And yet it is regarded and treated, in many places, as scarcely above contempt; and its emoluments barely suffice to preserve a family from beggary. Physicians, lawyers, merchants, farmers, mechanics, may all become rich: but whoever heard of a schoolmaster's making a fortune by his profession in our country? And yet, who will pretend to say that his profession is less useful, necessary or meritorious than any other in the nation? Why then should it be less profitable or less respectable? I fearlessly put the question to any man of liberal feelings and sound judgment; and I challenge him to assign even a plausible pretext for thus degrading a teacher to the level of a drudge, or for employing none but those who are content to be drudges, and who are fit for no higher rank in society? I again repeat, regardless of all prejudices and defying all rational contradiction, that, in a Republic, where knowledge is the soul of liberty, no profession ought to be more generously cherished, honoured and rewarded, than that of the worthy instructer of youth.

Our country needs seminaries purposely to train up and qualify young men for the profession of teaching. Though the idea perhaps may be novel to some persons, yet the propriety and importance of such a

in reference to our present youth, with the qualifications just specified, it may be safely assumed, that the mathematics and ancient languages will furnish employment

---

provision will scarcely be questioned by any competent judges. The *Seminarium Philologicum* of the late celebrated Heyne at Göttingen, though a private institution in the midst of a great university, furnished to the continent of Europe, during a period of nearly half a century, many of its most eminent and successful classical professors and teachers. We have our Theological Seminaries—our Medical and our Law Schools—which receive the graduates of our colleges, and fit them for their respective professions. And whenever the *profession* of teaching shall be duly honoured and appreciated, it is not doubted but that it will receive similar attention, and be favoured with equal advantages.

At present, the great mass of our teachers are mere adventurers—either, young men, who are looking forward to some less laborious and more respectable vocation, and who, of course, have no ambition to excel in the business of teaching, and no motive to exertion but immediate and temporary relief from pecuniary embarrassment—or men, who despair of doing better, or who have failed in other pursuits—or who are wandering from place to place, teaching a year here and a year there, and gathering up what they can from the ignorance and credulity of their employers. That there are many worthy exceptions to this sweeping sentence, is cheerfully admitted. That we have some well qualified and most deserving instructers, we are proud to acknowledge—and as large a proportion probably in this section of our country as in the older States. Still, the number is comparatively small: and the whole subject demands the most serious attention of the good people of this community. We have no system—no regularly and judiciously organized schools for classical instruction; where the teachers feel themselves comfortably, honourably and permanently established; and where the pupils are duly trained and disciplined as candidates for the college or university. We have taken the liberty to name the evil; and we appeal to the good sense of the public with confidence that the time has arrived for its correction or removal. Should these remarks meet the eye of any faithful instructer in this vicinity, he will regard them as proceeding from a friend, who feels for his situation, who respects his office and character, and who will never fail to afford him all the countenance, and to render him every service that may be in his power. Every such man deserves well of his country—and is more

for the greater portion of their time while they remain under-graduates. An accurate and profound acquaintance with these is essential to every individual who aspires to the reputation of a scholar. And neither time nor pains ought to be spared to ensure such proficiency to all our pupils. If these be not learned at school or

---

justly entitled to her lasting gratitude than multitudes of those whom she most delights to honour.

In consequence of the unfortunate state of our schools generally, colleges are compelled to fix their standard of qualifications for admission so low as necessarily to remain themselves but grammar schools of a rather higher order. Had we schools of the proper character, and in sufficient numbers, then might our colleges become in fact what they assume to be in name. Then might be learned in the former, so much of the classics and mathematics, of history, chronology, antiquities and other branches, as that a college would be a fit residence for young men, and its liberal pursuits adapted to their previous attainments. Then philosophy and science and elegant literature might unfold their richest treasures to minds prepared to receive and to relish them. And, until then, we must be content to pursue the humble course which has been already marked out.

But let us not despair of ultimately reaching the very *maximum* of our wishes. Let us commence where we must—with such youth as our country can furnish. Let us diligently cultivate, improve and polish the materials at hand—in the best manner we can. Let us not seek to make children youth, and youth men, and men lawyers, physicians, clergymen or politicians, too fast. Let us keep our pupils at their proper work—and carry them as far as they can safely and surely go, and no further. Better teach them one thing well than twenty things imperfectly. Their education will then be valuable as far as it extends. Some will leave us able and willing to teach others upon our own plan. Every year, perhaps, we may advance a little—demand something more for admission—and that something in better style—send forth more and abler instructers—in return, receive still more accomplished pupils—and thus proceed, year after year, slowly but surely, until we elevate our schools and our college to a rank and standing worthy of a free, enlightened and magnanimous people.

college, the presumption is that they will never be learned at all. Whenever these are mastered, it will be comparatively easy for the inquisitive and studious youth to extend his researches and his acquisitions as far as he pleases. In this opinion all competent judges concur; although popular sentiment may, in some places, be opposed to it.

Of the value of mathematical science, on many accounts, there may be no question. But the importance of the dead languages is to some not quite so obvious. I am well aware of the objections usually urged against their study—and of the ridicule with which they have been assailed. Still, classical learning maintains its ground; and is daily acquiring credit even in our own country. It is, indeed, so interwoven with the very texture of modern science, literature and language, that it is vain to expect scholarship without it—and equally vain for ignorance or prejudice any longer to denounce it. I mean not now to attempt its eulogy or to point out its uses and advantages. I merely affirm, that the classicks must be studied—and studied until the mind be richly imbued with their beauties, and the taste refined by their influence. At school, the first steps only are taken—the mere outworks secured—while at college, the pupil advances from mere verbal and grammatical and metrical attainments, to those interior, more subtile, and more intellectual stores with which the ancient classicks so pre-eminently abound. The labour, or, if you please, the drudgery of drilling boys in the elements of Greek and Latin, belongs to the schoolmaster. To the

Classical Professor pertains the higher province of philology and criticism—not, indeed, to the neglect of the minutest principles of grammar and prosody—but, beyond these, he ranges over a larger and more variegated field—and inspired with the genius of the poets, orators, historians and philosophers of the olden time, he will make their study the delight of his pupils. He will (to adopt the words of Milton) insensibly lead them up the hill-side of classic lore, usually indeed laborious and difficult at the first ascent, but under his kindly guidance and skilful illustrations, will appear so smooth, so green, so full of goodly prospect and melodious sounds on every side, that the harp of Orpheus could not be more charming.

It is desirable, that, in a college, provision should be made for instruction in all the sciences and in every department of philosophy and literature. To the ultimate attainment of this desideratum we must direct our views. We hope to see the day, or that our successors will see it, when, in Cumberland College, or in the University of Nashville, shall be found such an array of able professors—such libraries and apparatus—such cabinets of curiosities and of natural history—such botanical gardens, astronomical observatories, and chemical laboratories, as shall ensure to the student every advantage which the oldest and noblest European institutions can boast. So that no branch of experimental or physical, of moral or political science—or of ancient or modern languages and literature, shall be neglected.

Let us aim at perfection, however slowly we may advance towards the goal of our wishes. But in this aim and in this anticipation, let not our object be mistaken. We do not look forward to the period when every individual shall study everything which the amplest means of instruction may place at his option or within his reach. Far from it. The loftiest genius and the longest life cannot compass the whole of human knowledge—nor, indeed, any comparatively large amount of what is attainable. Much less can we expect youths, between the ages of fifteen and twenty, and during a period of four years, to grasp all the science or to read all the books which a well-endowed college may happen to possess. Could the vast intellectual treasures of Oxford and Paris be instantly transferred to Nashville, together with all the living spirits which animate their learned halls, still the mental capacities of our youth would remain the same as before, and would require a similar discipline. More indeed might be learned in a given time, because more facilities for the purpose would be afforded them. And here we perceive an obvious and very considerable advantage furnished to youth thus eligibly situated. Their minds may be cultivated to the utmost extent of their ability to learn. And few know how much a child or youth may be taught by a judicious system, which, while it keeps him steadily engaged in some great department of solid learning, is yet able to present such a variety, at proper intervals, as to keep the mind ever on the stretch and eager after knowledge. Let a parent make the experiment with his son of ten years old for a single week, and only during the hours which are not spent in school. Let him make a companion of his child—converse with him familiarly—put to him questions—answer inquiries—communicate facts, the results of his reading or observation—awaken his curiosity—explain difficulties, the meaning of terms and the reasons of things—and all this in an easy playful manner, without seeming to impose a task—and he will himself be astonished at the progress which will be made. So in a college, if, besides the regular daily routine of close and diligent application to severer studies, provision be made for easy access to any species of information at all times, much will be gathered, without in the least diminishing the amount of more solid attainments. The pupils will breathe a literary atmosphere. They will be encompassed with the means and incentives to every kind of mental effort. They will be in the midst of a learned society—and every hint they receive may be improved. Books, lectures and experiments may be read, heard or witnessed—even on subjects which they cannot thoroughly investigate; from which, nevertheless, much that is useful may be acquired. It is worth while to know the elements—the extent and general nature of the sciences—and to form such an acquaintance with books, as to be able to estimate their intrinsic and relative value. Thus circumstanced, they will acquire liberal and enlarged views and feelings. Their horizon will be extended far beyond ordinary limits. They will direct their future endeavours towards a more elevated standard and rank of scholarship than they would otherwise have dreamt of. The mighty dead with whose character and works they have been conversant; and the living who have directed their youthful pursuits, will be in their eye, and stimulate them to many a noble effort, long after they bid adieu to the walls of *Alma Mater*.

But here too are dangers to be avoided. There is a fashion, already prevalent in some of our colleges, to attempt to teach their pupils everything. To hurry them from book to book—and from science to science—with such rapidity as rather to confuse the youthful mind by its variety, than to enrich it with its abundance. The rage often is to attend the greatest number of lectures, not to master the subjects of any—to hear and to see, rather than to study. We have only to cast an eye over the course prescribed in many institutions to be convinced that no more, at best, than a smattering of the whole can possibly be acquired. By aiming at impossibilities they do nothing as it should be done. The public is often imposed on by the rich bill of fare which is held forth *ad captandum*. Parents, allured and deceived by a long list of hard terms which they do not understand, send their sons to seminaries which seem to promise most; without stopping to inquire, or being able to judge, whether the promise can be fulfilled. They would readily appreciate the absurdity of any pledge, from however respectable a source, to teach their sons some dozen or score of mechanical trades within the short space of four years.

But there is a still more grievous evil attendant on this desultory system. A superficial course of reading has an obvious tendency to engender vanity and self-sufficiency. Youth are fond of novelty and variety—and rigid application to any apparently dry and difficult science or subject is readily dispensed with for the pleasures and *eclat* of universal knowledge. General reading becomes the order of the day—and those who read most, and can talk about the greatest number of books, bear away the palm from the *dull plodding* student who may chance to find in Euclid or Demosthenes full employment for his time and faculties. Against such a fashion or such a system, and against any the least tendency towards it, I beg leave, once for all, to enter my solemn protest. It is ruinous to all scholarship—and never forms humble, modest, useful citizens.

The grand aim of a college education, besides the solid basis for a future superstructure, and besides the incidental advantages to which I have adverted, ought ever to be, to impart quickness in investigation and patience in research—to give the power of grappling with difficulties, accuracy of thought, and clearness of reasoning—to form the judgment—to refine the taste—to instil delicacy of feeling, and a vivid perception of poetical beauty and moral excellence—in a word, to develop faculty, and to subject it to such training and discipline as will ensure its future growth to manly vigour and maturity.

Why then should we desire teachers in a college for more branches than the pupils can learn? If I have been happy enough to exhibit my views fairly, I have already assigned good and sufficient reasons for such a provision, so far as it has a bearing on the regular students during the appointed period of a college residence. But we look further—we contemplate a system adapted to the wants and pursuits of men after graduation. And here appears its paramount advantage. Our own *alumni* may remain here, or strangers from other institutions may come hither, to prosecute their studies to any extent desirable—to master any particular science thoroughly—to expatiate more largely over classick ground—and to avail themselves of any aid or benefit which such an establishment can afford them. There are various other ways also in which the community would be directly or indirectly benefited. A large body of learned men might here be cherished, who, if leisure were allowed them, might extend the boundaries of science, and add to the elegant and useful literature of the world. We might, in time, boast of our Linnæus, our Porson, our Heyne, our Newton, our La Place, our Stewart, our Cullen, our Blackstone, our Robertson, our Blair, our Paley, our——but there is no end to the catalogue—and no limit to the advantages which may result to individuals and the State from our university when liberally organized and endowed.

In the mean time, we are prepared to carry our pupils as far as their previous attainments will enable them to advance—and as far as they could advance in any college in our country.

III. On the subject of government it becomes me to say but little and to promise nothing. Those who have had most experience in the management of youth, know full well the difficulties which it involves, and can best sympathize with their fellow-labourers in this important concern. So much depends on the previous training of youth while under the parental roof—on the sentiments there imbibed and the habits acquired—so much on public opinion, both in the particular place where a college is situated and in the community at large—so much on those who have the supreme direction and control of its interests—that, it is not easy to mark out the course to be pursued by a faculty, prior to any experience, in circumstances which to them may be entirely novel. In general, it may be remarked, that the government of a college ought to be, as far as practicable, strictly parental. Every instructor ought to conduct towards his pupils, and to be esteemed by them, as a father or elder brother. They ought to regard him as their best friend, and to confide in him as such. Wherever this mutual confidence and affectionate intercourse do not obtain, the connexion will neither be happy nor beneficial.

In a college, established upon the ordinary plan, the youth are necessarily left much to themselves. They constitute a large family, or a small community—have their laws, rules, usages, rights and privileges—are dealt with, not as children, but as young gentlemen—the sanctions of authority, the rewards and penalties are all addressed to the sense of duty, of honour and shame. If they cannot be sufficiently controlled upon these principles, or restrained by moral and religious considerations, there remains no alternative but temporary or absolute and final dismission from the institution. How much therefore depends upon the prudent, judicious, temperate, vigilant, mild, firm, equitable and faithful administration of its government may readily be imagined. On this subject it is much easier to speculate wisely than to execute skilfully. Some men may entertain the best theory in the world, and yet be utterly unfit for practical service. They may talk sensibly enough—prescribe well—and resolve how to act in any given or supposable emergency—but when the trying crisis arrives they know not how to avail themselves of the peculiar features and circumstances of the case, or when to seize upon the favourable moment for prompt decision—or how to gain access to the heart and understanding, or in what direction to turn the popular current—or whether to exercise extraordinary lenity or extraordinary severity. They have not the presence of mind—that complete self-possession—that instantaneous and intuitive perception of what is proper and expedient—which alone can command and ensure success. They are, in a word, destitute of that natural *tact*—that instinctive sensibility to every expression of the countenance, and to every symptom which a word, a look or a movement may indicate—and which, though no art, is superior to all art, and can never be learned in any school. All the avenues to the human heart—all the springs of youthful action, and all the modes of allaying and regulating youthful passion, must be so obvious and familiar, that a man may be said, at the instant, rather to *feel* his way than to study or devise it.

The government of a college differs so widely from a military or civil government, that little aid or illustration can be borrowed from either. A General would find it easier to maintain strict discipline in an army—and his Excellency to administer the laws of a State—than either to govern a college. And although it be nearly allied to the parental, as has been stated, still the government of a family is but an epitome, or remote resemblance of that which obtains in a college—where a hundred or more youths are assembled from every quarter, and possessing every variety of character.

The characteristic vice of the present age is *impatience of control.* It is manifested everywhere—and in regard to almost every species of government from the domestic to the imperial. The spirit of insubordination—of independence—of freedom from restraint—of superiority or indifference to all authority—is cherished from infancy to manhood—and no very plausible occasion for its display is suffered to pass unimproved. Towards teachers, especially, it assumes a more than ordinary virulence, in consequence of the very absurd and erroneous sentiments which are prevalent concerning their character and office. They are commonly regarded as petty tyrants—as the abridgers of youthful pleasure—as unfeeling, little-minded, arbitrary pedants, who delight in imposing unreasonable burdens, and in inflicting undeserved punishment. This illiberal prejudice is often entertained by the parents as well as by their children. The latter frequently imbibe it from the former. It is deeply rooted in the public mind, to the serious injury even of the best regulated seminaries in our country. Its noxious fruits are more or less visible among all ages and descriptions of pupils wherever assembled and by whomsoever instructed.

Youth, therefore, not unfrequently come to college, after having *fought* their way through the preparatory schools, and acquired a reasonable share of adroitness in evading law and in *plaguing* their teachers—anticipating a system of vigilant *espionage* and rigorous discipline—and fully prepared from the first to regard the faculty as their enemies. They form a party by themselves—a distinct interest of their own—view with suspicion every measure or movement of the faculty—and resolve to contravene and to thwart their plans as far as it may be in their power. The evils and miseries of such a state of things are too palpable to need naming.

Why should it exist a single moment in any institution? Is it a natural order? Does it necessarily result from the connexion? No: it is unnatural—contrary to all good feeling and right principle. College officers, of the proper spirit and temper, (and no others ought to be employed,) will ever find their own happiness in rendering their pupils intelligent, virtuous and happy. This too is their interest. It is their pecuniary interest to promote the welfare of their pupils to the utmost of their ability. How powerful a motive this may be to stimulate their efforts, can be duly estimated by all money-making and money-loving men in the nation. Their interest, their duty, and their happiness, combine to inspire them with every tender sentiment towards the youth under their care, and with every disposition, desire and endeavour to make them comfortable, contented, cheerful—at the same time that they solicitously guard them from error and vice, and seek to imbue their minds richly with manly and useful science.

The prejudice, then, which exists against them, is groundless, ungenerous and cruel. It would be ridiculous and foolish for any set of teachers to study to render themselves odious to their pupils and to the public—or, in other words, to make themselves unhappy, and their occupation unprofitable. But the true secret of their unpopularity with the youth of their charge, may generally be traced to their conscientious fidelity. They seek to render them happy, not by indulging their propensity to idleness and dissipation, but by prompting them to industry, and by restraining them from pernicious indulgences.

"Omnis disciplina gravis est puero."

Hence the opposition and the loud clamour against them which we so often witness. Let parents then—let trustees—let the public beware how they countenance and encourage this wicked spirit which would free itself from all wholesome control—and which, if suffered to gain the ascendency, would convert any seminary into a sink of iniquity and abomination. Uphold and fortify, by every means in your power the dignity and authority of those to whom you entrust the dearest interests of your children; or you will yourselves speedily reap the bitter fruits of your own imprudence and folly. No efficient college discipline can long be maintained where the voice of the public is against it. None where parents and friends denounce and counteract it. I fain would hope, that, in me and my worthy colleagues, every well-disposed youth, who becomes a member of this college, will recognise his warmest, most devoted and affectionate friends. If so, happy for them, and happy for us, will be the connexion which is about to subsist. It shall be our study to deserve their confidence, by steadily and assiduously promoting their improvement and their welfare to the best of our humble ability.

Lastly. In entering upon an enterprise so infinitely momentous—in giving renewed existence and permanent character to an institution destined to affect the dearest interests of this community to the latest generations—it becomes us to take every step with the greatest possible circumspection, and with a solemn sense of the high responsibility under which we act. It is with unutterable emotions of anxiety, of fear and trembling, that I venture upon the honourable part assigned me in this great work. Especially, when I recollect what this institution has already been, under the masterly guidance of its distinguished founders, the indefatigable labours of its first most worthy instructors, and the faithful administration of its late lamented President, whose eminent talents, learning and virtues will long be the proud theme of grateful panegyric in these consecrated halls—and whose memory is embalmed in the hearts of his affectionate and accomplished pupils.

When I consider the value of a single individual in

reference to this life—and still more in reference to a future world—and that his character and his destiny may be fixed forever in this seminary—I involuntarily shrink from the awful charge. What then must be the sensation created by the contemplation of the hundreds and the thousands who will here imbibe those principles, and acquire those habits, which must render them blessings or curses to themselves and to the world? Who is sufficient for these things? No unassisted mortal assuredly. To God we must humbly and devoutly look —to the infinite Fountain of grace and wisdom I must continually look—to the Eternal Giver of every good and perfect gift we must all look for that support and direction which we so eminently need.

May the blessing of Almighty God rest upon this infant establishment, and crown all our exertions in its behalf with success—that we may ever have abundant reason to remember this day with joy and gratitude—and be encouraged to still greater zeal and activity in the cause which we have begun to espouse under auspices so favourable and promising!

THE

CAUSE OF EDUCATION

IN TENNESSEE.

BACCALAUREATE ADDRESS,

AT CUMBERLAND COLLEGE, 1826.

Young Gentlemen:

Your academical career is now ended; and you have just received the usual honours and testimonials of this institution. According to the opinion which too generally prevails, you have completed your studies. This, I am persuaded, is not your own opinion. You have already made a juster estimate of your own attainments; and of the vast and variegated field for future investigation which still lies before you, and which invites your assiduous cultivation. If you have learned *how* to study, and have acquired a thirst for knowledge, you will continue to study and to learn while you live. This, indeed, is the grand aim and object of all elementary education. It is to discipline the mind, to develop faculty, to mature the judgment, to refine the taste, to chasten the moral sense, to awaken and invigorate intellectual energy; and to furnish the requisite materials upon which to erect the noblest superstructure. Hitherto, you have been laying the foundation; and serving that kind of apprenticeship which may enable you to march forward by your own diligent and persevering efforts. Do not imagine, therefore, that your work is done. You have only commenced your studies. Whatever may be your future profession, pursuit, business or destination, let books, science, literature be your constant companions.

Every man, who intends to do the greatest possible good in his day and generation, will, every day, seek to acquire additional information. He will gather it from every source within his reach. His experience, his observation, his intercourse with the world, with men and things, his daily occupations, his incidental associations, the great volume of nature, ever open and spread out to his view, the intellectual treasures of a hundred generations which have passed away, the records of heavenly truth and wisdom—all will conspire to increase his stores, and to qualify him for a greater and a wider sphere of useful and virtuous exertion.

All the great and good men, who have enlightened, adorned and purified the world by their labours and their counsels, have been indefatigable in the pursuit of knowledge, up to the last moment of their existence. No matter how exalted any man's genius may be—history demonstrates, that, genius has never achieved great things without industry.

The lawyer, physician or divine, who limits his range of thought and study to the mere mechanical rules, or precedents, or forms, or prescriptions of his professional rubrick, will never become eminent in his own particular profession, nor will he ever be distinguished as a man. He may pass along with tolerable respectability, countenanced by the multitude of his brethren who are like himself, among a people not wise enough to distinguish noise from sense, or technical jargon and pedantry from learning and argument. But bring him into the presence of the master-spirits of the land or of the age, and he instantly shrinks into his native insignificance. Mere professional business of any kind, when a man never makes an excursion or voyage of discovery beyond it, always tends to narrow and contract the mind. He may be expert in small things, in petty official details, like an artisan in his workshop; but take him out of his daily routine, from off the beaten track, and he is bewildered and confused, or opinionated, obstinate and illiberal. He cannot grasp a great subject, or comprehend a new moral theorem or proposition. He will discuss the interests of an empire as he would treat the cause of a client, or the case of a patient, or a point in theology. Now all these may be important matters; and so is the manufacture of a nail and of a pin. But a man of intellect ought to aspire after higher objects, and nobler attainments, and more expanded views.

In England, even the humblest artificers and mechanics, tradesmen and farmers, in almost every town, are beginning to form associations for mental improvement. They have procured libraries—they read literary and scientific journals—attend lectures on chemistry, political economy, mechanics, natural philosophy, history, mathematics—they study and converse with each other at every spare moment or leisure hour. In a few years, they will take the lead of half the professional men in the kingdom, unless the latter condescend to follow their example. A similar spirit of enterprise and improvement has already appeared in our larger cities, and its march will be rapid, and its effects most salutary. Our youthful candidates for the learned professions, therefore, must prepare to enter the lists of honourable competition with a new and vigorous race of rival combatants for the prize of intellectual supremacy.

I know not what are to be your future professions or occupations. Every honest calling ought to be esteemed honourable. I address you as moral and intellectual beings—as the patriot citizens of a great Republic. You may be merchants, mechanics, farmers, manufacturers—and yet be eminently distinguished and eminently useful, if you will persevere in seeking after knowledge and in making a proper use of it. The Medici—Necker—Ricardo—were merchants or bankers: Franklin was a mechanic: Washington was a farmer. By far the greater part of our countrymen are and must be farmers. They must be educated; or, what is the same thing, educated men must become farmers, if they would maintain their just influence and ascendency in the State. I cannot wish for the alumni of Cumberland College, a more healthful, independent, useful, virtuous, honourable, patriotic employment, than that of agriculture. Nor is there any condition in life more favourable to the calm pursuits of science, philosophy and religion; and to all that previous training which ultimately constitutes wisdom and inflexible integrity. Should our college eventually become the grand nursery of intelligent, virtuous farmers, I shall esteem it the most highly favoured institution in our country. I have long thought that our college graduates often mistake their true path to honour and usefulness, in making choice of a learned profession, instead of converting agriculture into a learned profession, as it ought to be, and thereby obtaining an honest livelihood in the tranquil shades of the country.

I mean not, however, on the present occasion, to offer any advice as to the choice of a profession. Whatever station you may occupy, or whatever be your pursuits, never cease to gain knowledge and to do good, as God, in his providence, shall give you opportunity.

But, in the second place, as you have yourselves enjoyed superior advantages of education, it is reasonable to expect that you will be the steady, enlightened, zealous friends and advocates of education, in every degree, and to the utmost extent, which the welfare of the community may require.

I present to your patronage and support the grand cause of education, in all its purity and excellence, and without restriction as to its objects.

That learning has been often abused and perverted—that many systems of education have proved ineffectual, useless or pernicious—that most existing seminaries might be greatly improved—I freely admit. Still, these admissions detract nothing from the intrinsic value of knowledge, nor from the paramount importance of education. The native character, tendency and genuine effects of any principle, system or institution, must decide its utility, and its claims to general adoption and support; and not the partial evils which human artifice, or folly, or wickedness may render it the instrument or the occasion of introducing and propagating. Under the plea and sanction of religion and liberty, our world has been filled with tumult, convulsion, crime and suffering. Are religion and liberty therefore worthless, or injurious to mankind? Would you banish religion and liberty from the earth, because both religion and liberty have been most grossly profaned; and employed, in ten thousand ways, to deceive, oppress, and degrade mankind? Then oppose not—condemn not education. The want of it has occasioned most of the misery and crime which have been inflicted on our world under the specious names and imposing authority of religion and liberty. When or where did crafty ecclesiastics or politicians ever succeed, under the guise of religion or liberty, in cheating the people out of both, except where the people were so ignorant that they could comprehend neither the one nor the other? Without competent knowledge, or without education, there can be neither religion nor liberty. Religion implies knowledge. Its simplest principles and dictates—its plainest duties and requirements cannot be understood or performed, without previous instruction. This is true of every religion yet known—and of every religion that can be conceived—of paganism and theism—as well as of Christianity. Nor can liberty be appreciated, acquired, defended or maintained, except by those who have learned what liberty means. If religion and liberty, therefore, be, in any degree, desirable;

if they be indispensable to the happiness and perfection of our nature; if they be justly prized above all other blessings which bountiful Heaven has placed within the reach of the human family; then is the cause of education sufficiently established.

By education, we mean, such a thorough cultivation of all the faculties of our youth, as will best prepare them for the greatest usefulness and happiness. Let this definition be kept in view during the whole progress of our argument and illustrations. Those of my hearers who have reflected much on this subject will not expect any benefit or information from the discussion. They will patiently bear with me, however, while I endeavour, in a plain popular way, to secure the goodwill of this audience, generally, to a cause which may be emphatically styled the cause of the people.

Schools or Seminaries of education may be classed as follows: namely,

1. Primary or Infant Schools. 2. Common Schools. 3. Academies, or Classical or Intermediate Schools. 4. Colleges or Universities. 5. Special or Professional Schools: Such as those for Law, Divinity, Medicine, Military or Naval Science, Agriculture, Architecture, or any of the useful or liberal arts.

My remarks will be limited chiefly to Common Schools and Colleges.

But, in the outset, I beg leave to state distinctly, that, I do not ascribe omnipotence, or any uncontrollable sway to education. I do not go the length of asserting that man is absolutely and invincibly the creature of circumstances or of education. That he may be made an angel or a devil, or something between both, by any discipline or accidental associations. Still, to a certain extent, and with certain qualifications, this is true; and it is a truth of revelation, no less than a deduction from reason and experience. To exhibit at once, and in pretty bold relief, the natural province, and legitimate power of education, I refer you to an extreme case or two, and to others of every day's occurrence. Suppose a person were to grow up, from infancy to manhood, in a desert or forest, without ever seeing a human being or hearing a human voice—in what respects would such a wild man differ from other wild animals? Would he speak, or think, or reason, or discriminate between good and evil, virtue and vice, happiness and misery? Would he not resemble the bears and the wolves of which he had been the nursling, the pupil and the companion—and, like them, shun the presence and the abodes of men? Again, were the son of a Solomon or a Bacon to be trained from his birth among savages—would he not become a savage in sentiment, manners, and habits? Indeed, it requires but a rapid glance at the nations of the earth, to perceive that the great mass of the people are everywhere formed by the circumstances, associations and instruction to which they are subjected. Where these are most auspicious, human nature assumes its most attractive and dignified character. Where these are most unfavourable, human nature appears in its most abject and degraded form. This, as a general truth or fact, none will dispute. If we pass from the ten thousand varieties of national character, and the ten thousand gradations of national excellence or depravity, to individuals of the most enlightened and most highly favoured country in Christendom, we shall behold similar effects continually resulting from similar causes.

It requires a good deal of patient investigation and minute analysis to ascertain how much of good and evil may be instilled into the mind of every child, by the means just specified, even when most destitute of regular and formal education. Thus, a child could never learn to speak, or to utter articulate sounds, without instruction; or, what is the same thing, without an opportunity of imitating others. Yet every child, not destitute of the proper organs in a sound state, does learn to speak, and that, too, without being sent to school for the purpose. Thus, then, the first and most important of all arts is insensibly acquired at an age when it is usually thought superfluous or useless to commence the work of instruction. Further, of the many hundreds or thousands of dialects actually spoken by mankind, the child always learns the language of its parents and companions: and he learns it more or less perfectly according to their habitual use of it. If they pronounce it correctly, and speak it with grammatical accuracy, purity and elegance, he will speak it agreeably to the best rules of orthoepy, grammar and rhetoric, without an effort, and previously to the knowledge of any rule whatever. In the same manner, and with the same facility, a child might acquire a number of languages, as experience has fully demonstrated. Now, this simple fact proves, first, that much, very much is actually learned by every child in infancy: and secondly, that the amount and perfection of this knowledge depend entirely on the opportunities and advantages possessed. Were we to extend this analysis to other particulars or departments; to principles and habits, moral, economical, physical, intellectual, religious, we should find the infant mind yielding to a daily and almost invisible influence, which may mark its character and destiny through life.

How important then to human happiness is it, that, the first school—the infant school—the parental school—should be a good one? Here is the great nursery of human weal or woe. Now, I care not whether children ever go to a public school or not, if parents will keep a better school at home, and do their duty to their offspring. I care not whether our youth go to college or not, if parents can and will teach them more effectually by their own firesides. But, unfortunately, the great mass of parents have shown themselves but sorry instructors and faithless guides to those who ought to be dearer to them than their own life. They are themselves, in general, too ignorant, to say no more, to do much. Hence, in our day, INFANT SCHOOLS have been established in many places, to supply this radical defect. And report speaks well of them wherever they have been tried. How far it may be practicable or beneficial to introduce them into our country, except in large towns or manufactories, I shall not stop to inquire.

In order to furnish the community at large with the

next best aid to parental instruction, and as a substitute for it, after the first period of infancy, Common Schools prefer the strongest claims to our regard. We hear a great deal, at the present day, about *common schools:* and one would imagine that they had already become the favourites of the people. If so, then the cause of liberty and virtue has gained much in our land, and we need not despair of the Republic. Upon this ground we can all meet and harmoniously co-operate. In this grand enterprise, all the advocates of colleges in our country will go hand in hand with the humblest of the people, not merely in declaiming about the necessity and importance of common schools, but in organizing and putting into practical operation the best system that can be devised. I have no fears that any of the alumni of Cumberland College will ever prove recreant or backward in this good work.

Common Schools, then, are needed in Tennessee. How shall they be established? Let the people decide. What character and form shall they assume? Let every county be divided into such a number of school districts or departments as will conveniently accommodate all the inhabitants. Erect comfortable and commodious school-houses. Attach to each school-house a lot of ten acres of land, for the purpose of healthful exercise, gardening, farming and the mechanical arts. For the body requires training as well as the mind. Besides, as multitudes must live by manual labour, they ought betimes to acquire habits of industry, economy, temperance, hardihood, muscular strength, skill and dexterity. Employ teachers qualified to govern and instruct children in the best possible manner. Pay them according to their merit. Pay any sum necessary to command the services of the best and most accomplished teachers. Parsimony in this particular is not only impolitic; it is mean, it is absurd, it is ruinous. Better have no teachers, than to have incompetent, immoral, lazy, passionate or indiscreet ones; however cheaply they may be procured. Their influence will not be merely negative: it will be positive and most powerful. I have often looked with horror upon the kind of common schools and teachers to which thousands of children, during several of their best years, are cruelly and wantonly subjected in the older States. But it is or was the fashion, in many places, to hire a blockhead or a vagabond, because he would teach a child for a dollar and twenty-five cents per quarter! Now, if there be anything on earth for which a parent ought to feel disposed to pay liberally, it is for the faithful instruction of his children. Compared with this, every other interest vanishes like chaff before the wind—it is less than nothing. And yet, unless the world has suddenly grown much wiser, there is no service so grudgingly and so pitifully rewarded. The consequence is what might have been expected. Every man of cleverness and ambition will turn his back with scorn upon the country school. He will become a lawyer, a physician, a merchant, a mechanic, a farmer, or a farmer's overseer, in preference. Until school-keeping be made an honourable and a lucrative profession, suitable teachers will never be forthcoming in this free country.

But what is meant by a common school education? This question has never been answered; and it cannot be very satisfactorily answered. Some may think it enough that their children learn to read: others will insist on writing: many will be content with reading, writing and arithmetic. Others will add to the list, grammar, geography, history—perhaps, practical mathematics, physics, astronomy, mechanics, rural economy—with several other branches of science and literature, as ethics, rhetoric, political economy, geology, chemistry, mineralogy, botany:—in short, where shall the limit be fixed? Who shall prescribe the boundaries beyond which a common school education shall never extend? It is evident, upon the slightest reflection, that the phrase *common school education* is a very indefinite one. How far beyond the alphabet it may be carried, has never been ascertained. Experiments are now making in Europe, and in several sections of our own country, which are calculated to give a totally different aspect to this whole concern. It has been discovered at length, what indeed was always sufficiently obvious, that a boy need not be kept at school eight or ten years to learn to read his primer, write his name, cipher to the rule of three,—and to hate books and learning for the rest of his life. It has been discovered that boys may, in three or four years, be taught a hundred-fold more, by skilful teachers, in a skilful way, than their fathers ever dreamt of learning at all. This is the grandest discovery of our age. It will do more to meliorate the moral, physical and political condition of mankind generally, than all other means ever yet devised.

The excellence and the extent of a common school education, therefore, will ever depend on the qualifications of the teacher and the system which he pursues. No man can teach more than he knows himself. Every man can teach all that he does know. The more he knows, the more useful will he be. In the humblest school in the country, he will find some pupils to be benefited to the utmost extent of his ability to instruct them. And upon the Monitorial or Lancasterian plan, he can teach any number.

Let us then speedily have common or elementary schools so abundant and so wisely conducted, that, every son (I say nothing now of the daughters) of the commonwealth may be well and amply instructed. Let him acquire a taste for knowledge, and he will never cease to be a learner while he lives. He will then be fitted for usefulness and honour. He will always have resources within himself. He will be conscious that he is an intellectual being; and that intellectual pleasures are among the purest, noblest and least expensive that can be enjoyed.

But we must not stop here. Common schools are not enough. They will not satisfy the public necessities. The better and more efficient the common schools become, the greater will be the demand for institutions of a higher order. Multitudes of aspiring youth will pant for more intellectual treasures. They will look out for other seats of learning where they may advance still further. Will you drive them to neighbouring or distant States, and compel them to expend abroad the thousands of dollars which sound policy, to say no more, ought to induce you to keep in circulation at home? You must then establish, in every county, one or more first-rate *Classical Schools* or *Academies*, where the languages and sciences may be more extensively and systematically taught. Let some twenty or fifty acres of land be attached to each of these seminaries, for the same purposes that we have already assigned them to the common schools. Here again I must avoid details. Merely adding, however, that all this will not be sufficient. Learning is like wealth;—the more we get, the more we covet. No laws can prescribe the limit to mental, any more than to pecuniary acquisitions.

We must have one or more colleges to receive the numerous candidates for the highest literary honours and attainments. Our sister States have them: and if our youth cannot be accommodated at home, they will go where they can be better served. Now, a great College or University cannot be reared except at a great expense. It is not like an ordinary school or academy, which any enterprising individual, with moderate resources, may establish anywhere. The aid of government—the wealth of the State—or else the combined efforts and contributions of many liberal individuals—will be necessary to build up a college. Upon the University of Virginia above half a million of dollars were expended before a pupil was admitted: and fifteen thousand dollars have been appropriated annually forever to the support of Professors. And this was the work of the people's long tried champion and greatest favourite—the very oracle of orthodox republicanism—the immortal author of the Declaration of our National Independence.

I do not say that Tennessee should forthwith vote half a million of dollars, or any other sum, to a college. But she ought to make ample provision for the intellectual wants of her citizens. And she is able to do this, cost what it may. Were a judicious system of common schools and academies put into operation immediately: within half a dozen years, there would be five hundred youths in West Tennessee alone, eager to avail themselves of the benefits of a college. And should there be no college in West Tennessee, adapted to their wants and wishes, they will cross the Mountains or the Ocean in search of knowledge, and carry along with them from two to five hundred thousand dollars a year, as a tribute to the superior wisdom and intelligence of distant or foreign States. Thus, in a single year, might be withdrawn from the State more money than would suffice to create a Cambridge at our very doors. This is a consideration which every political economist ought to appreciate, and which the legal guardians of the people's welfare and prosperity ought gravely to ponder. It is assuredly no light evil to any community, when capital or income shall seek a foreign market without producing an equivalent return. Every dollar thus forced away is a dollar lost to the State.

I am well aware of the popular prejudices and apprehensions which are cherished in regard to colleges and college graduates. I know that they are frequently represented as the enemies of general improvement—as having no sympathy, or community of feeling or interest with the great mass of the people. That they constitute a class or party by themselves, and that they ought to be viewed with jealousy and suspicion by all the vigilant patriotic guardians of our liberties. If there has ever been any plausible pretext for such an opinion, it certainly exists not in our country. I have never yet heard of one liberally educated American who was not a decided friend to every well-devised plan and measure calculated to diffuse the blessings of knowledge universally. He is from experience, from conviction, from principle, from patriotism, from philanthropy, the firm, persevering and zealous advocate and promoter of education among the people. He ardently desires that every son and daughter of the Republic may be well educated. And that his deeds have nobly corresponded with his professions, let facts speak for themselves. This is logic not easily to be encountered.

And if there be any friends of popular instruction, of liberty and the rights of man, in the old world, they are to be found exclusively among the best educated. The demolition of despotism in France, and the establishment of a free representative government in its stead, were first thought of, canvassed and attempted by the most enlightened men in the kingdom: and long before the ignorant millions of that ill-fated country had ever heard the name of liberty. And it was precisely because the millions could not comprehend its import, much less appreciate its value, that, when once excited, they became ungovernable, furious, brutal, ferocious: and the consequences need no recital or comment. Had the people, however, been previously instructed in the first elements of letters and politics; had they learned how to reflect, to reason and to judge, a very different result would have been witnessed. Similar attempts have been made, by a few enlightened patriots in other parts of Europe, to meliorate the political condition of the people, which, from a similar cause, have proved equally abortive.

From the Colleges and Universities of Europe have emanated those rays of light which have caused despots to tremble on their thrones. And, at this day, those great nurseries of truth and liberty are more dreaded by the emperors, kings and princes of Russia, Austria, Prussia and Germany, than any and all other enemies put together. Hence the rigid system of police and jealous espionage exercised towards them. Strange that republicans should represent colleges as hostile to liberty, when tyrants persecute them because they are friendly to liberty. Youth cannot long be familiar with the history and institutions of Greece and Rome, without imbibing something of that enthusiasm for liberty which inspired a Demosthenes, an Epaminondas, a Phocion, a Cicero, a Brutus and a Cato. By the way, the friends of liberty ought to be the last men on earth to decry classical learning.

It was from the newly instituted colleges of Scio

and Bucharest, that, the first champions of liberty and independence issued, to animate their fellow-bondmen of Modern Greece to break the chains of their Mohammedan oppressors. And they have made every effort to establish schools, throughout their degraded country, to teach lessons of liberty to the people. God grant them success in their glorious struggle; and a generous, high-minded, patriotic, virtuous, enlightened Washington, to direct their energies in the cabinet and in the field!

Now there can be no better or stronger evidence in favour of the general beneficial tendency of learning, however obtained, than the fact, that, whenever, in ancient or modern times, endeavours have been made to procure liberty to a people, and wherever it has been acquired, those endeavours were made, and that acquisition secured, by men of superior knowledge. Such is the language of history from Moses to Bolivar. And among the most enlightened philanthropists on the continent of Europe at this moment, the grand cause of their discouragement and despair in regard to liberty, is, that the people are too ignorant to be intrusted with liberty; and hence they feel constrained to remain inactive. They fain would give instruction to the people, in order to prepare and qualify them for free and liberal institutions, would their masters permit them.

When our fathers commenced their almost hopeless controversy with the mother country; who were the kindred spirits attracted to our shores and to our aid by the native charms and legitimate claims of liberty? Not the degraded serf or feudal slave—not the illiterate farmer or mechanic—but such men as might have adorned the proudest court in Christendom—men of whom their own country was unworthy—men who understood the full import of the glorious cause to which they were ready to sacrifice titles, and honours, and fortune and life:—they were Pulaski, Steuben, De Kalb, Kosciusko, La Fayette.

And who, allow me to ask my republican auditors, or, if they please, to remind them of what, perchance, they may have forgotten—who were the prompters, the mainsprings, the leaders of our memorable revolution? The answer to the question is upon every schoolboy's tongue. He will recount a catalague of patriots, who, for profound knowledge and practical wisdom, were never surpassed in any age or country. Such were the friends of our own liberties, at a time too, when they were not only stigmatized as rebels, but were in hourly danger of being hanged as rebels. They were the master-spirits who aroused the people to resistance. They were honest men, and they united in promoting the permanent welfare of their country. Happily, the people, having been generally educated at common schools, were sufficiently informed to comprehend their rights, when those rights were ably explained to them, and wise enough to be guided by their superiors in wisdom. But had the intelligent, the learned colonists of those days combined with the English aristocracy in maintaining the ancient government in all its plans of oppression, the people would never have thought of a revolution. Had they been enlisted on the side of the British ministry, we had this day been the loyal subjects of his majesty, George the Fourth.

They too, be it remembered, zealously espoused the cause of education; well assured that the goodly fabric of liberty, which they had succeeded in rearing, would speedily tumble into ruins, or become the citadel of some future Cæsar or Catiline, unless the rising and each successive generation should be taught to maintain their rights by fully comprehending them. Hence, whenever they had opportunity, in the legislative councils of the States or of the Nation, they endeavoured to secure a legal provision for schools and colleges, either by the appropriation of public lands, or by gradually accumulating an adequate pecuniary fund for the purpose. To the general truth of this representation, I am not acquainted with a single exception among our revolutionary heroes and statesmen. All the Presidents of the United States have uniformly agreed in sentiment on this subject. And who, of the long list of worthies whom the people have delighted to honour as patriots, has ever ventured to advocate a contrary doctrine?

Franklin laboured, during his whole life, in the cause of schools, from the humblest to the highest, and finally succeeded in founding the University of Pennsylvania: although his example has been often cited to prove the inutility of all such institutions. He had himself conquered difficulties in the acquisition of science, which not one of a million would ever think of encountering. And he possessed too much good sense, and too much benevolence to wish others to be left to the mere chance of creating for themselves a path to eminence, when a great public highway might be so easily constructed for their convenience. He knew that an extraordinary exception to a general rule or law ought never to be urged against the rule itself.

Washington devoted much of his time and all the weight of his influence to the same object. And he, at last, liberally endowed a college in his native State, which still bears his name.

Jefferson, besides promoting the same great cause during the long period of his public career, consecrated the last seventeen years of his valuable life to the establishment of a University, upon the most permanent basis and of the most enlarged dimensions. And centuries hence, probably, the name of Jefferson will be more revered and distinguished as the father of the University of Virginia, than as a philosopher or statesman.

No man, it is presumed, will, at the present day, accuse a Franklin, a Washington, or a Jefferson of any lack of patriotism or republicanism. And no man need be ashamed to follow their example. May their spirit rest upon some favoured son of Tennessee; and may she have the honour of perpetuating upon the page of history, a name worthy, in all respects, to be associated with our immortal Franklin, Washington and Jefferson! This honour, I doubt not, she will have; and that our Academic Halls will hail him as a patron and benefactor, while virtue and science and liberty shall exist in our land.

As I am dealing altogether with facts, and not with

theories; and as I do not wish to go a hair's breadth beyond the simple truth, I take leave distinctly to announce to you, that, I do not affirm that all men of learning have, everywhere and under all circumstances, been the friends of liberty and of human happiness. Far from it. The position which I maintain is simply this; —that liberty and the best interests of humanity have ever been ably and successfully advocated and promoted only by men well informed; and by the best informed too of the age and country in which they flourished. And, that, among ourselves, the most enlightened citizens have ever approved themselves the most effectual guardians of the people's rights. I admit also, that so far as this argument is concerned, it matters not where or how they acquire the requisite knowledge—whether in common schools or high schools—in colleges or universities—at home or abroad—by their own unassisted efforts and enterprise, or from public institutions established by the government or by individual munificence. But until a better mode of arriving at the object can be devised, we shall continue to regard schools and colleges as indispensable. So long as the Republic shall need learned men, we shall expect schools and colleges to furnish them. They have already done the State some service: and they are destined, we trust, to do it a great deal more.

I am no blind admirer of colleges and universities. There exists not one, in Europe or America, which might not be greatly improved. The same may be said of common schools, and of all human institutions.

Shall we, therefore, put an end to every system of education, because none has hitherto been faultless? Will those who denounce colleges, pretend that common schools are less obnoxious to censure; or that they are as good as they need to be? *Reformation—improvement* —is the order of the age—and it must be obeyed. The work must be commenced and continued simultaneously in all our seminaries, great and small. The cause is one and indivisible. Colleges exert an important influence on the character of common schools: and these again constitute the foundation of colleges. Unless common schools be good, our colleges will not be good. The intermediate schools or academies will not remedy the defects of the one or the other. It is all important to begin well. If boys enter college with idle and vicious habits, they will probably continue idle and vicious. If they have been well trained at home and at school, they will be orderly, virtuous and diligent in college. The graduates of our colleges generally will be found to have received their bias to virtue or vice, under the parental roof, and from their earliest instructors and associates. If parents neglect their sons, or leave them to ignorant or profligate preceptors or companions, during childhood and early youth, they need not expect that the discipline of any college on earth will operate upon them any miraculous regenerating influence. Such boys are ruined before they enter college: although parents are generally charitable enough to blame the college for their own inexcusable folly and cruel indulgence, when their hopeless sons disappoint their unreasonable expectations. Colleges have enough to answer for: let them not be charged with sins of which they are innocent. Nor let them be required to accomplish impossibilities. Supply them with pupils, who have been thoroughly disciplined at home and at school—of a suitable age to act with reasonable discretion, and who are really desirous to acquire knowledge—and the public will hear very little of the follies and dissipation of a college life. No real friend of colleges, therefore, can ever be hostile or indifferent to good common schools.

It were well for the community, if the professed advocates of common schools were equally well disposed towards colleges. Their grand objection to them, besides those already hinted at, is briefly this:—That colleges are designed exclusively for the rich—that the poor cannot be benefited by them—and, therefore, that the poor ought not to be taxed for their support, or that the people's purse ought not to be burdened on their account.

This specious and very sage objection contains several sophisms and several falsehoods.

In the first place: Colleges, in our country, are not, never were, and never can be designed exclusively for the rich. For, in fact, many poor youths have been educated in every college of the Union during every year of their existence. But then, such poor youths must usually belong to the vicinity, or at least to the State, in which the college is situated. Neither Connecticut nor New Jersey would ever think of educating at their colleges a poor youth of Tennessee: but many hundreds of poor, very poor young men of their own States have been thus educated. Without a college at home, every poor youth is necessarily cut off from all hope or chance of any such privilege.

Again, between the rich and the poor, there is in the community another class of citizens vastly larger than both of them put together—the middling class, and the best class—all of whom might educate one or more sons at college, at an expense of from fifty to a hundred and fifty dollars per year, who could never send their sons abroad at an expense of from five hundred to a thousand dollars a year. Will the State do nothing for this large and respectable body of her citizens? The merest trifle contributed by each would place advantages within the reach of the whole, which no individual could otherwise possibly command.

But, in the second place, grant that colleges are designed exclusively for the rich. What does a wise policy dictate as the proper course to be pursued? The question is not, whether the rich shall, or shall not educate their sons at a college; but whether they *may* do it at home, or *must* do it abroad? For with money, they can do what they please. They can send their sons to Philadelphia or Paris, to Oxford or Edinburgh. Would it not be good policy then to require these rich men to build up a college, suited to their own purposes, and at their own expense; and thereby constrain or induce them to employ their funds, and to disburse their ample revenues within the State, to the unspeakable benefit of all classes of citizens, and especially of the middling and poorest, by encouraging every species of industry and enhancing the value of every description of property, to the full amount of the money thus prevented from going into the hands of foreigners? Were this matter rightly understood by the people, they would presently perceive, that, the main scope of the pretext so artfully employed to mislead them, was, after all, at bottom, nothing more than to spare the purses of the rich, to the manifest detriment of the whole community—of the rich as well as the poor—for the rich deceive themselves if they imagine that they will be the gainers in any way by such a course. It will cost a rich man ten times as much to educate one son at a distant seminary as he would be required to contribute, during his whole life, for the erection of a college, according to any equitable plan of assessment or taxation which might be adopted for the purpose.

But, in the third place,—why all this clamour and affectation of zeal in behalf of the poor? Do men legislate only for the poor? Does the government exist solely for the poor? Are the poor, and they only, elected to office? Is not some pecuniary or *landed* qualification indispensable to any man's eligibility to office? Is the public money—ay, the people's money—paid out in salaries to the poor—to poor governors, poor judges, poor senators? Are banking, insurance, manufacturing, turnpike, bridge, or canal companies incorporated from among the poor, and chiefly for the benefit of the poor? One might imagine from the noise made on the subject, that the poor were all in all to the State;

that they were the precious objects of the government's special care and protection: Since their self-constituted patrons virtually maintain, that, if they cannot all go to college, there shall be no college. Why not decree, that if the poor man cannot ride in a coach, there shall be no coaches; or that the rich shall not use them?

Now the plain simple truth is, that the poor are never taxed in our country for any purpose whatever. All taxes are levied on property. Were twenty colleges to be commenced to-morrow, the poor would not be burdened a farthing. They would, on the contrary, be immediately benefited by the demand thus created for their labour, and by the liberal wages which would be paid them.

But, in the fourth place, strictly speaking, there are no *poor* in our country. Among the white population there is no degraded *caste*. We have no *class* of poor, like the poor of Europe. We impose on ourselves by the imported terms and phraseology of transatlantic society. And hence we talk as currently about the *poor*, as would an English lord or German baron. Forgetting that the poorest man in the Republic may become rich. The richest of our citizens have been poor. The rich and the poor are frequently related to each other. The rich man may have a poor father or brother. And the poorest individual may be nearly allied to the most distinguished families in the land. Our state of society is constantly fluctuating. Rich families daily decline: poor ones daily advance. Wealth and poverty are mere accidents. They are not hereditary in particular lines, or perpetuated in particular families. It is absurd therefore to declaim or to speculate about the poor as if they were an oppressed, miserable, helpless class, like the Russian or Polish peasantry. We have all been poor. We may be poor again. When poor, we were obliged to deny ourselves many comforts, luxuries and privileges which we now enjoy; and it was mainly by this self-denial that we were enabled to improve our condition. And such must ever be the case. If the poor wish to rise above their present condition, they can do so, everywhere in our country, by industry, prudence and economy: and they will continue to do so, as long as they shall be left to their own free energies. I trust the time is far distant, when our government shall think it worth while to perpetuate pauperism amongst us by legal encouragement—by premiums in the shape of poor-rates.

The only distinction which exists among our citizens, worthy of notice, is between the educated and the uneducated. The former engross all the wealth, offices and influence in the nation; while the latter remain the victims of want, of crime, of infamy, and of punishment. I here use the term *educated* in a very wide and comprehensive sense. That individual who has learned how to labour at any honest occupation, and who knows how to manage his earnings skilfully, is educated, and well educated, compared with those who have been brought up to no business; or who are destitute of sobriety, prudence and economy. *He* may become rich and honourable; while *they* are necessarily doomed to poverty and wretchedness. Between these two descriptions of persons there is an impassable gulf. They are further removed from each other than the lord and his vassal: and the longer they live the wider will be the distance between them. Whoever has grown up in total ignorance of the means of acquiring an honest livelihood, and with vicious habits, may be regarded, in general, as helpless and hopeless. Gross ignorance, at least of everything good and useful, is the cause of all the degradation in our country. Now although there may be no effectual remedy for the evil which actually exists, yet there is a preventive—its further progress may be checked—its recurrence may be prevented. This preventive remedy is instruction, moral, intellectual, physical, religious. It is not only the cheapest—it is the only remedy. If inveterate habits cannot be changed; take care that the children form better habits, and imbibe better principles than their fathers.

Our country has expended, and continues to expend, on courts of justice and criminal prosecutions—on prisons and penitentiaries—for the punishment and safe keeping of a few veteran and incorrigible villains, vastly more money than would be required to give a suitable education to all the absolutely indigent youth in the nation. If government, therefore, instead of wasting millions in the hopeless endeavour to reform the hardened offender, would cause such children as would otherwise be neglected, to be properly disciplined and brought up, there would soon be little necessity for prisons or penitentiaries. Here is the right end to begin at—the proper starting point—the first step in the work of general reformation, without which every other will be taken in vain. Happily, wherever the experiment has been made, it has fully succeeded. Among the thousands of poor children recently trained in the free schools of the city of New York, not one has been sentenced to Bridewell. Thus far then, at least, the rich might be fairly taxed for the benefit of the poor. This would not only be real benevolence—it would be the wisest policy—the least expensive course that could be adopted. And if the State should choose to do more; let a certain proportion of the most promising boys in the common schools be annually advanced to the academy; and the best of these again to the college, at the public expense.

It is worse than idle to object to colleges because they do not educate the poor, and yet to refuse them the means of doing it. If the State please, she can organize and endow a college, so that the poor and the rich may enjoy its privileges gratis. Or she may make such provision only for the poor, and compel the rich to pay. She has it in her power to confer on the poor, in this respect, whatever favours she chooses. If any honest friend of the poor and the ignorant can devise a more liberal or judicious system for their elevation in society, it shall receive my hearty approbation and support.

Let it not be inferred from anything just said, that I am an enemy to the penitentiary system. It is, when judiciously administered, a good and necessary system, in the existing state of our society. But it may, and I doubt not, will be, in a great measure, superseded by the proper training of our youth, who would otherwise become its pitiable subjects.

Having thus, at greater length than I intended, disposed of some of the popular objections to colleges—objections which I have frequently heard advanced in Tennessee—I might proceed to show what a college ought to be. But as I have, on a former occasion, expressed my views pretty fully on this subject, I shall not repeat them now.

I must be permitted, however, to say a word in behalf of Cumberland College; especially to my young friends, who have just been adorned with her laurel, and who will be regarded as her representatives before the public, and whom she will regard as her natural and most warmly devoted friends and advocates.

You have been told, or you have witnessed the various fortune of this institution—its many and well-sustained struggles for existence—its decline and failure after a few bright days of sunshine and prosperity—its recent resuscitation under circumstances which would have discouraged and appalled men of ordinary capacity and enterprise—its conduct, character and progress during the period of nearly two years since its re-organization; and you cannot be insensible to the numerous difficulties and obstacles, which it must still encounter, before it can attain that pre-eminent rank to which she aspires. For she will not be content with humble mediocrity, nor with a mere equality with her sister institutions. She aims at vastly greater eminence and usefulness than has yet been reached by any of them. This aim will be pronounced visionary by those who do not know what constitutes the real excellence of a college, and by those who are ever disposed to predict a failure where they do not wish success.

Men frequently, too, labour under an unfortunate prejudice on this subject. They presume that colleges must be growing better as they grow older; and distance of situation greatly increases their reverence. Hence, a venerable monastic establishment, a hundred years old, and a thousand miles off, is conceived to possess advantages which young Tennessee cannot hope for in a century. Now I venture to assert, that, our infant university might be made, in five years, superior to any and to all the colleges in our country—if the people will but decree it. Let us not be imposed on by mere names. Buildings, books, apparatus, teachers, constitute the principal expensive ingredients of a university: and money can command them all, in as great abundance and perfection *here*, as in Europe or *old* America. We have the full benefit of all past experience to begin with. Whatever is excellent in existing institutions, we may adopt: whatever is superfluous, or antiquated, or faulty, we may reject. It is much easier to create a good institution than to mend a bad one. Ancient usage naturally becomes prescriptive, and ordinarily prevents innovation or improvement.

Upon the virgin soil of Tennessee, then, may be reared a seminary, which shall eclipse, in grandeur of design and felicity of execution, and in the wisdom of its arrangements and combinations, all other institutions —if her sons will but prove true to themselves and faithful to future generations. A more eligible or healthful site for such an establishment cannot be found in the Western country. *Here* is the place, and *now* is the time for generous enterprise. Here let us erect a university, so decidedly and confessedly superior in every department, that a rival or competitor need not be feared. Let us make ample provision for every species of instruction—scientific, literary, professional—which our country demands. Let education be extended to the physical and moral, as well as to the mental faculties. Let agriculture, horticulture, civil and military engineering, gymnastics, the liberal and the mechanical arts—whatever may tend to impart vigour, dignity, grace, activity, health, to the body—whatever may tend to purify the heart, improve the morals and manners, discipline the intellect, and to furnish it with copious stores of useful elementary knowledge,—obtain their appropriate place and rank, and receive merited attention in our seminary; so that parents may, with confidence, commit their sons to our care. Assured that they will be in safe and skilful hands—under a government, equitable, paternal, mild, firm, vigilant and faithful—where their every interest will be consulted, their every faculty be duly cultivated, and where every effort will be made to render them intelligent, virtuous, accomplished citizens. Does any man doubt that such an institution will ever want patronage? Make it the best in the country; and will it not command the patronage of the country? Such an establishment as we contemplate, the public mind is already prepared for, and has begun to call for. This call is imperative—it will be heard—it will be answered. We must meet it or others will.

Our college is already as good and respectable as most others; certainly inferior to none in the West. It has received the most flattering encouragement. No college, in any part of our country, has, with the same means, effected as much, or numbered as many students, in so short a period. I may add, too, without exaggeration or compliment, that, the orderly, moral, gentlemanly deportment of our students, during the past session especially, and of most of them from the beginning, would have done credit to any seminary. And that they have made extraordinary proficiency in the languages and sciences, taught by our laborious and accomplished professors, has been fully acknowledged by all who have attended their public examinations or ordinary recitations. The friends of the college, therefore, have no ground for despondency on the one hand; and we trust that they will not be so far satisfied with its actual condition on the other, as to relax their zealous efforts for its future improvement.

In this great work, there is no resting place—no point to stop at. With the increase of population, with the march of mind and the progress of universal improvement, we must keep pace. We must daily advance. PERFECTION should be our motto and our aim, however much we may ultimately fail of attaining it. Every successful step should prompt to another and a greater. When we have gained one eminence, we shall be able to descry a still higher and a more inviting; which, when reached, must serve only to enlarge our horizon, and extend our vision, and brighten our hopes, and animate our efforts, and cheer us in our labours, for the welfare of mankind.

The Trustees of Cumberland College have purchased one hundred and twenty acres of land to meet the various purposes of their contemplated university. It is proposed immediately to commence the erection of a series of buildings for the accommodation of students, instructors and stewards; consisting of five additional colleges, each sufficiently commodious for a hundred students and three assistant professors or tutors, and of seven houses for as many principal or head professors. We shall then have six colleges, and twenty-five instructors, and accommodations for six hundred pupils. To each college will be attached a refectory or boarding house, with eight or ten acres of land for gardening and exercise. The colleges will be erected at such distances from each other as to prevent the usual evils resulting from the congregation of large numbers of youth at the same place. Professors will occupy houses on the intervening lots: and there will be at least three officers resident within the walls of each college. We shall thus have six distinct and separate families, so far as regards domestic economy, internal police, and social order; while one *Senatus Academicus* will superintend and control the whole.

Gardens and mechanics' shops will be interspersed among the various edifices, in such manner as to be easily accessible to all the youth for improvement and recreation. Whenever the present ground shall be thus occupied, it will be necessary to procure fifty or a hundred acres more, for a model or experimental farm; that agriculture, the noblest of sciences and the most important of the useful arts, may be thoroughly studied and practised. At a future period, or as soon as the means can be obtained, other suitable edifices, both useful and ornamental, may be erected. The plan admits of indefinite extension; and in proportion to its enlargement, its advantages will be increased, while the expense of its maintenance will be diminished.

In order to execute our present design, only about $200,000 will be required. This sum might be furnished by the State at once; or in two, four, eight or ten years. Or it may be obtained partly by donations, and partly by loan. Any individual, for instance, bestowing $20,000 may give his name to a college or to a professorship: or any number of individuals, subscribing that sum, may give any name they please to a college or professorship. Suppose Davidson county, or even Nashville were disposed to erect a monument to the memory of her most honoured citizen; what could she do more grateful to him, more worthy of herself, more beneficial to the Republic, than to contribute the sum of $20,000 to build an edifice, on yonder hill, to be known among all future generations as JACKSON COLLEGE, founded and endowed by the citizens of Davidson county or of Nashville, in the year —— what year shall be designated? If the appeal were made to her generosity, her public spirit, her gratitude, her just pride and magnanimity, I cannot deem so lightly of her present citizens as to anticipate a refusal, which would prove her alike unworthy of a great University and of the Hero of New Orleans.

Let us calculate—we have, within the limits of our city corporation alone, not less than four thousand free white inhabitants. Were each to give five dollars, or were two thousand to give each ten dollars, or were one thousand to give twenty dollars apiece, the object would be accomplished without the aid of the county at large: and who could feel the burden? Thus, then, one college, at least, is provided for. Some others might possibly be erected by similar means, and in honour of other meritorious individuals.

The little town of Amherst, in Massachusetts, which does not contain one-half of the population, nor one-twentieth part of the wealth of Nashville, raised, by private subscription in 1821, the sum of fifty thousand dollars to commence a college within its limits.* And several other towns in our country have been equally munificent.

Let no man imagine, that, in giving money to a college, he is doling out alms to an importunate or worth-

* Another sum of $50,000 was added to the funds of Amherst College by the private subscription of its friends, during the last year (1832.) And the sum of $100,000 was raised for the benefit of Yale College by her alumni during the same year.

less beggar. He does honour to himself by the act; and the institution honours him by accepting his bounty; and is able to confer on him and his family a greater and more durable honour than mere selfish wealth can ever procure. The otherwise obscure names of Harvard, Yale, Dartmouth, Bowdoin, Williams, Brown, Bartlett, Phillips, Dickinson, Rutgers, will be immortalized by the seminaries to which they have been benefactors, and which will bear their names forever. If honour, real honour, lasting honour, be worth seeking; here is the road to it.

If, however, nothing can be obtained from our legislature, or from our good city or county, or from individuals, we may borrow the whole sum of two hundred thousand dollars, at an interest not exceeding six per cent.—creating a transferable six per cent. stock—and, in twenty years, we could easily pay off both principal and interest, at the present rate of charges for tuition and room-rent. It would be merely necessary, in order to procure the loan, that the State should guaranty the payment, or that responsible individuals should underwrite for us. And we can pledge ample means either to the State or to individuals, to secure the one or the other, from all hazard of eventual loss; as I am prepared to demonstrate, at the proper time to all competent judges. Now it would be vastly preferable that the money should be gratuitously furnished, because (to specify no other advantages) the expenses of an education at our university might be diminished one-half immediately; and thus would the portals of science be opened wide to the great majority of our people.

But the funds must and will be forthcoming from some quarter. We are not to be deterred or frightened from our purpose by any obstacles, real or imaginary. We have very deliberately counted the cost: and ONWARD is engraven upon our banners and upon our hearts.

Who, let me ask—I put the question to this assembly—to the good people of Tennessee—who will oppose our projected institution, designed, as it is, exclusively for the benefit of this people? I will tell you. It will be opposed by the faint-hearted, the cowardly, the ignorant, the covetous; and by all the enemies of light, truth, virtue and human happiness. It will be opposed by that description of selfish, arrogant, self-sufficient, *would be* lords and Solomons, who exist in every petty village, and who always oppose whatever does not originate from themselves, or which is not submitted to their own *wise* management and control. It will be opposed by those who can, by any artifice or misrepresentation, convert the scheme into a political hobby to ride into office. It will be opposed by those who despair of getting out of it a job—a bargain—a money-making speculation—some paltry private gain or advantage. But it will never be opposed by one honest man, by one honourable man, by one enlightened man, by one patriotic man, by one benevolent man, by one great or good man.

Here then, before the venerable fathers, who first planted the standard of civilization and Christianity in this recent wilderness, shall have left the scene of their early toils and sufferings forever, let the banks of the Cumberland be adorned with the majestic temples of science and with the academic groves, which may proudly vie with those which have conferred immortality on the Cam and the Isis.

ALMA MATER confidently appeals to her own ingenuous alumni; and claims of them chivalrous fealty, and honourable service, and lasting attachment, and generous support. She will not appeal to them in vain. And may she, as I doubt not she will, a thousand generations after all her enemies shall be forgotten, be the ornament, the pride, and the glory of Tennessee!

Having thus earnestly pressed upon your notice the great cause of education, and the cause of our own infant university in particular, as worthy of peculiar regard and beneficence; I may briefly add, in this connexion, that every scheme and enterprise, calculated, in any degree, to promote human happiness, will also claim your countenance and support. You must be the leaders—where others better qualified do not offer—in every good work. I do not recommend to you merely those magnificent and imposing projects for the melioration of the condition of mankind, which are sufficiently popular to command general respect; but, besides these, I recommend to you those humbler, less dazzling, less conspicuous, and, frequently, more disinterested modes of doing good, which occur every day, in every village, and in almost every family. Now, to be able to do good, in any of the modes suggested or contemplated, remember, that, industry in acquiring knowledge or wealth will not alone suffice. Nor will it be sufficient to abstain from degrading vice—from intemperance and gambling—from every species of youthful irregularity and ruinous dissipation. You must study prudence and economy in the management of both time and money. A man, extravagant in his ordinary expenses, fond of show and ostentation, eager to be at the head of the fashionable world or in the pursuit of fashionable pleasures and follies, is not likely to be generous. He will never become a Howard or a Franklin. The man of plain and simple habits, who avoids all needless display and luxury, who is content with what is useful and comfortable, is the man who has the most to bestow on objects of charity, benevolence and public utility.

Go then, Young Gentlemen, and prosecute with persevering ardour, the new course of study and discipline, which is to qualify you to enter, in due time, upon the great theatre of active, useful, honourable life. Be not in haste to engage in those various liberal professions, to which most or all of you, perhaps, intend hereafter to devote your faculties. Wait, with patience, the full development of your mental powers; and continue long to collect, with untiring assiduity, from every source, the treasures of knowledge which are necessary to fit you for eminence in any profession; and for the noblest career of usefulness to your country, and for the most exalted stations within her gift. Despise not—neglect not any department of human learning, whenever and wherever it can be consistently cultivated. No man ever denounces, as useless or superfluous, any science or language with which he is himself acquainted. The ignorant only, condemn: and they condemn what they do not understand, and because they do not understand it. Whenever, therefore, you hear a man declaiming against any literary or scientific pursuit, you may rest assured that he knows nothing of the matter: and you will need no better evidence of his total incompetency to sit in judgment upon the case. Of all the learned men of whatever age, country or profession, who have benefited our world by their labours—who have been most distinguished and most successful? Precisely those who have judiciously put under contribution, to the greatest extent, every corner and recess of the grand temple of science, which it was possible for them to explore. There is such an intimate connexion between the sciences, such a perfect harmony of parts in the great whole of human knowledge, that all may frequently, like the rays of the sun, be brought to bear intensely on a single point; or, at pleasure, be spread over an immense surface, diffusing light and heat and joy to the utmost verge of civilized society.

Study, then, to improve all your time in the most profitable manner. Let your amusements be rational, virtuous, seasonable, manly, and invigorating to body and mind. Let order, and method, and system be adopted and rigorously maintained. Study hard while you profess to study. Relax at suitable intervals, only to return with redoubled ardour to your books. Thus, health, serenity of mind, elasticity of spirits, present enjoyment, future usefulness and honour will all be promoted and secured.

Be not, however, the blind idolaters of genius or of science. Both may exist where not one lovely or commendable trait of character can be found. The loftiest intellect, without virtue, is but archangel ruined. In God only, do we behold the perfection of understanding, of wisdom, of knowledge, of holiness. And HE is that perfect standard which we are commanded to aim at. Religion, which requires us to be like God, constitutes the whole of moral excellence. And in proportion as religion influences the heart and life, will be the moral worth of any individual. There can be no principle of integrity, of truth, of kindness, of justice, independently of religion. No human laws, usages, institutions or opinions can, of themselves, ever render any man perfectly honest in all his dealings and transactions with his fellow-men. He has it continually in his power, *with a fair reputation too*, to mislead, deceive, defraud—and, in a thousand ways, to practise imposition. And he is continually tempted to do this, in a country where influence, office, money are the objects of universal desire and ambition, and where *success* is regarded as the criterion of merit and talent. He may not be a thief or a robber in the eye of the law, or according to the ordinary judgment of men; and yet he may be habitually more criminal than either, in the eye of infinite purity and justice; and would be so pronounced by any tribunal of perfectly honest men, who could take cognizance of all the motives, facts and circumstances. That man, who will take any undue advantage of another in a bargain, or in any mode whatever, would steal or rob just as soon, if he could do it with equal honour and safety. Nothing does, nothing can, nothing ever will restrain any mortal from any indulgence, pursuit, gain or abomination which he covets, and to which no disgrace is attached, except the fear of God—or, what is the same thing, RELIGIOUS PRINCIPLE. The most ignorant pagans, as well as the most enlightened sages on earth, are restrained by this fear, or by this principle, whether they are conscious of it or not. I mean so far as they act from *principle* at all—and without reference to human laws or opinions. The salutary and restraining influence of religion extends, in fact, throughout the world. It is daily felt in all the relations of life. It is apparent in the whole texture and organization of human society. All the peace, comfort, virtue and felicity in the world, or which have ever been in the world, flow, and have flowed, from religion. In proportion as pure religion prevails, in the same proportion do we behold human nature approximating the purity, happiness, dignity and glory of angels. And in proportion as it is anywhere neglected, opposed, despised, in the same degree do vice, ignorance and misery abound. This is a *fact* obvious to every man's observation.

It is absurd for any man to pretend to reject religion altogether, because he is, in spite of himself, religious or superstitious, in some form or other, whether his views be right or wrong. It is madness and cruelty, because, were it possible for him to banish religion from our world, he would put an end to civil government, to social order and to social existence.

I shall not attempt to tell you what religion implies or inculcates; nor, of the many religions in the world, which is the best. The worst is better than none. I have no fear that any religion whatever will be preferred to the Christian. I have no fear that any man, who honestly and soberly examines the records and the charter of our religion, will ever fail to acknowledge its paramount claims, and to practise, at least to approve, its precepts. And this is all that I now urge. Study the Bible faithfully and prayerfully, and you will learn what true religion is. All who do this, with a proper temper and spirit, will agree in essential points of doctrine, as well as in the essential rules of conduct. All who diligently study the Bible—from the Roman Catholic to the Quaker—will think and act alike in all things which are important, and they will never contend about unimportant forms or questions. Were the Bible resorted to for our theology and our ethics, instead of human teachers or systems, all bigotry, fanaticism, uncharitableness and persecution would disappear from the Christian world. Ignorance of the Bible is the prolific source, not only of error and superstition, but of all that demon spirit of party and sectarism which rages among those who profess the same faith, and which keeps asunder brethren of the same family.

It assuredly ill becomes those who are liberally educated to be illiberal and intolerant on the subject of religion, or to manifest illiberal hostility against it. Nor would such an anomaly ever be witnessed, were our scholars to study the Bible as carefully and profoundly as they study, or profess to study human science and philosophy. Simply as an integral part of a liberal education, it demands the most thorough investigation. What right have men to dispute and dogmatize about religion, when, in truth, they know little or nothing of the Bible, which alone can teach it? Who is the self-sufficient bigot, that deals out anathemas against all who do not adopt the same peculiar phraseology and the same ceremonial with himself? Who is the sneering captious skeptic, who is ever railing at the hypocrisy, the credulity, the superstition, the weakness, or the inconsistency of Christians—as if these were the genuine fruits of Christianity, or constituted any part of its character? Who is it that deliberately intrenches himself within the strongholds of his own understanding, and affects to yield to the dictates and discoveries of reason, and to do homage to the dignity of human nature at the expense of revelation? Who is it that denounces the Bible as containing unintelligible mysteries and dogmas —as imposing rules and precepts too strict and severe for frail humanity—as presenting sanctions, and threatening penalties, revolting to infinite justice and goodness? They are to a man, ignorant of the Bible, and of the heavenly spirit which pervades it. They must be sent to school, before they can be reasoned with.

Happily, the reign of atheism has passed away. And the fopperies of infidelity are no longer in fashion. Men of sense are ashamed to avow the one, or to exhibit the other. Multitudes, however, at the present day,—and those too, frequently, among the most intelligent and influential members of society—appear desirous to stand on neutral ground. Not aware, perhaps, that the thing is impossible. They neither oppose nor profess the Christian religion. They give themselves very little concern about the matter. They live under its general influence, and participate in its general charities, and seem to fancy themselves exempt from its more immediate and authoritative control; so long as they do not submit to the discipline of any particular church. As if it were at their option to obey or to disobey the divine command—to be religious or irreligious—to admit or reject as much or little of religion's precepts as may comport with their inclination or imaginary interest. Now, this is most egregious trifling with reason and duty—with themselves and their Maker. Young persons easily yield to these delusions, and are apt to think that religion is not designed for them, and that it ill becomes them. Or that it will render them miserable, or singular, or unfit for the business and concerns of the world. I pass, however, all this sophistry, all these prejudices, misapprehensions and difficulties, and again refer you to the Bible for instruction.

If man was made to be religious—and that he was, universal experience proves beyond the possibility of a doubt; if, without religion, he is both worthless and wretched—and that he is, the same experience as fully demonstrates; then is religion necessary, and equally necessary to all men. It is equally binding on all men—

on the lawyer, the physician, the statesman, the soldier, the youthful student—as on the clergyman, the saint, or the sage of fourscore. It does not consist in particular acts or ceremonies, nor is it restricted, in its operations and influence, to particular times, places and occasions. It regulates the temper, reigns in the heart, and keeps alive the spirit of devotion, of purity and love, wherever we go, or whatever may be our worldly vocation. In every human pursuit or station, religion supplies the only true principle of action, and points out the only legitimate ways and means of success. Happy the man, who, in every undertaking, in every purpose, and during all his exertions and trials, can devoutly look to God for direction, for assistance, for wisdom, for a paternal blessing.

Finally, be courageous. Dare to be honest, just, magnanimous, true to your God, to your country, to yourselves, and to the world. Dare to do to others as you would have them do to you. Most men are cowards. They are afraid to speak and to act, when duty calls, and as duty requires. I recommend courage as a great and a rare virtue. Few men will suffer themselves to be called cowards; and yet they betray their cowardice by the very course they take to avenge the insult. A man may intrepidly face the cannon's mouth, and be an arrant coward after all. There is a higher, a nobler courage, than was ever displayed in the heat of battle, or on the field of carnage.

There is a moral courage, which enables a man to triumph over foes more formidable than were ever marshalled by any Cæsar. A courage which impels him to do his duty—to hold fast his integrity—to maintain a conscience void of offence toward God and toward men—at every hazard and sacrifice—in defiance of the world, and of the prince of the world. Such was the courage of Moses, of Joseph, of Daniel, of Aristides, of Phocion, of Regulus, of Paul, of Luther, of Washington. Such is the courage which sustains every good man, amidst the temptations, allurements, honours, conflicts, opposition, ridicule, malice, cruelty, persecution, which beset and threaten him at every stage of his progress through life. It is not a noisy, obtrusive, blustering, boastful courage, which pushes itself into notice when there is no real danger, but which shrinks away when the enemy is at the door. It is calm, self-possessed, meek, gentle, peaceful, unostentatious, modest, retiring; but when the fearful hour arrives, then you shall behold the majesty of genuine Christian courage, in all her native energy and grandeur, breathing the spirit of angelic purity, and grasping victory from the fiery furnace or the lions' den; when not one of all the millions of this world's heroes would have ventured to share her fortune.

I fear God, and I have no other fear—is the sublimest sentiment ever felt or uttered by mortal man.

May each of you, beloved youth, living and dying, be enabled, in sincerity, before the Searcher of hearts, to exclaim,—I FEAR GOD, AND I HAVE NO OTHER FEAR.

BACCALAUREATE ADDRESS.

[CUMBERLAND COLLEGE, OCTOBER 3, 1827.]

BACCALAUREATE ADDRESS,

AT CUMBERLAND COLLEGE, 1827.

It may be expected that youth, who have been well instructed in the elements of science, will continue to study and to advance in knowledge while they live. But it is not enough to know more than others, or to be satisfied with a constantly increasing store of intellectual treasures. A higher, a purer, a nobler end must be kept steadily in view, than any selfish gratification or interest whatever. "For unto whomsoever much is given, of him shall be much required: and to whom men have committed much, of him they will ask the more."

Such are the language and doctrine of universal equity and reason, as well as of divine revelation. Human responsibility is everywhere graduated according to the talents, knowledge, privileges, means, opportunities, power, influence, actually possessed, or fairly attainable by honest effort and industry. To whom much is given—whether of genius and the means of ample cultivation, or of wealth and the usual facilities for the proper use of it—of him will much be required.

To you, Young Gentlemen, your country and the world will look—they have a right to look—for superior virtue and wisdom, for greater light and knowledge, for more vigorous, more persevering, and more successful efforts in the cause of human happiness, than from the great mass of youth in ordinary circumstances. It is already incumbent on you to ponder well and seriously how you ought to live and act, so as to confer the greatest benefits on your fellow-men. For, the doing of good to others, according to the measure of your ability, is the only return which you can render to God for his distinguishing favours to you. This is precisely the return which he demands. This is the scriptural and the only rational test and evidence of real gratitude to God. No man can show his gratitude in any other way. To offer up to the beneficent Deity, for his daily bounty, mere verbal thanks—however frequent, loud, long-continued, or apparently devout and fervent—and to do nothing more—is sheer hypocrisy or fanaticism. No artifice or cunning can elude or make void the great law of heaven and earth, that, of him to whom much is given, much shall be required. Nor can this law ever be transgressed with impunity. If men receive much, and make no suitable return, they necessarily incur, and sooner or later, suffer the penalty of their disobedience. The providence of God will not—does not—permit them to escape. Their inordinate wishes, their unhallowed desires, may be gratified; their selfish schemes may be executed; they may achieve or gain all that they seek or aim at; they may even reach the loftiest pinnacle to which human ambition ever dared to aspire—and what then? With what emphasis may it not be said of all such—"and HE gave them their request, but sent leanness into their soul!"

Success is no decisive proof of divine favour, or of individual enjoyment. Could every covetous man become a Crœsus, or every ambitious man an Alexander, or every vain man a Voltaire; it does not follow that happiness would, in any degree, accompany, or result from, the possession of riches, power, fame, genius or learning. These become real blessings only as they are legitimately acquired, and faithfully employed for the benefit of others as well as of ourselves.

To be good, and to do good, are nearly convertible terms, and necessarily imply each other. The man who wishes to do good, must himself become good. And again, every good man will do good. All your resolutions to do good will avail nothing, until you first resolve to be good. This will prove a very difficult or a very easy task, according to the standard by which you estimate goodness. There is a superficial counterfeit kind of virtue or goodness which passes very current in the world, and which is of easy acquisition. I shall not stop to describe it. Fashionable life and fashionable reading may be consulted for its true character and value.

Genuine goodness or virtue consists in perfect obedience to the divine law. I offer no proof of this position; because, if there be a divine law, none will deny that it is our duty to obey it. I now take for granted that there is a divine law; and that this law is recorded and explained in the Bible. By goodness or virtue then,

I mean such moral excellence as the Bible requires and inculcates. Whether men generally obey the divine law at all, or to any considerable extent—whether any obey it perfectly, or whether any can do this—I leave to the decision of those who are best acquainted with the Bible and with the human heart. That the law is holy, just and good; that it ought therefore to be obeyed; and that it is exceedingly difficult for man, constituted and circumstanced as he is, fully to obey it, will not be questioned by those men who are universally acknowledged to be the wisest and most virtuous of mankind. While, on the other hand, those men who proclaim it to be a very easy matter to be good enough, or to do all that is required of them, are precisely such as are not most remarkable for kindness and purity of heart or conduct.

The same law which says—"Thou shalt not kill—Thou shalt not steal,"—also says—"Thou shalt not take the name of the Lord thy God in vain. Thou shalt not covet anything that is thy neighbour's. Thou shalt love the Lord thy God with all thy heart—and thy neighbour as thyself." Nay further—"Love your enemies, bless them that curse you; do good to them that hate you, and pray for them which despitefully use you and persecute you. If ye forgive not men their trespasses, neither will your [heavenly] Father forgive your trespasses. And as ye would that men should do to you, do ye also to them likewise." Such is a specimen of the spirit and extent of the divine law—of the morality of the Bible—of the celestial purity and charitable constitution of the Christian religion.

In the Bible you will learn, both, what you are commanded to become, and what you are commanded to perform. And truly, the path of virtue and duty is steep and arduous. But it is a law of our nature that nothing valuable can be acquired without labour. The highest virtue—and consequently the highest honour and happiness—can be attained only by constant persevering vigilance and effort, agreeably to the divine will, and when crowned with the divine blessing. Commence the great business of life then, in the fear of the Lord. This is the beginning of wisdom. Refer every purpose and every action to the will of God: and ever have in view, not your own interest and gratification merely, but the happiness and comfort of those around you.

Wherever you reside, *there* study to do all the good in your power. I say *study*,—for much laborious investigation, much anxious reflection, much hard-earned information may be necessary to enable the soundest judgment, frequently, to decide on the best plans and means of attaining the most benevolent objects. It is not enough to be willing to do good, or to desire to do good—we must spare no pains to acquire all the knowledge that may aid us in doing it in the best manner and to the greatest extent. *Indolent* benevolence—if its existence be possible—or ill-directed, misapplied benevolence may do as much injury as avowed selfishness or misanthropy itself.

Young persons are apt to fancy that they would like to do good on a grand scale—to be great benefactors—

to immortalize their names—to fill the world with the fame of their disinterested, patriotic, noble, philanthropic achievements—to become the Luther, the Columbus, the Howard, the Franklin, or the Washington of the age. This however may be a very selfish, pitiful ambition—a mere coveting of the renown, the glory, or the more substantial rewards, which such men, sooner or later, receive from the equity and gratitude of mankind. I mean not to discourage you from aiming high—very high—even at the loftiest mark. "Be ye perfect, even as your Father which is in heaven is perfect." But do not mistake your own views and motives. Every eminent man, who has been good as well as great, has served a long and laborious apprenticeship (and most probably) in a comparatively humble and narrow sphere. He has been content to do good every day to the extent of his means and opportunities, without ever dreaming of the honours and the homage which awaited him. Present duty, not future distinction, was the moving principle and spring of action. Unhallowed ambition may indeed conduct its votary to a throne: and the world shall call him great: but the world—the impartial world—will never pronounce him good.

Your field of labour may, at first, be very limited. Cultivate it diligently, and it will gradually enlarge. Be faithful in a few things: more will presently be intrusted to your care. Your sphere of duty will widen on every side, just in proportion to your industry and fidelity. And although your deeds may never be celebrated in the records of this world's immortality,—still your reward will be sure, as well as adequate and satisfactory.

So long as ignorance and poverty, vice and misery exist in our land and in the world, so long at least, will be found an ample province for humane and beneficent enterprise. In every hamlet and village—in every inhabited section of our country—there is much to be done for suffering and degraded humanity. I am not going to enter into much detail on this fruitful topic. I will barely specify two or three evils to which youth are peculiarly exposed—which everywhere prevail to an alarming extent—which it becomes us all most sedulously to avoid ourselves, and to do what we can through life to preserve others from their destructive influence.

Hitherto, mankind have been disputing and contending chiefly about errors and heresies of a purely speculative character: as if virtue, and happiness, and heaven depended on the use of certain words and phrases; or upon the implicit acknowledgment of certain propositions and doctrines, which, in their very nature, perhaps, involve considerations absolutely beyond the province of human reason—while practical truth has been comparatively overlooked. Now, practical truth, or truth which directly and necessarily influences human conduct, is the only species of truth with which the philanthropist is immediately concerned. Casuists, theologians, metaphysicians, may argue and speculate (in the same manner as they frequently have done) forever, without contributing one iota to human improvement and happiness: while the humblest individual, who points out to his neighbour a mode of obtaining an honest livelihood, ought to be esteemed a greater benefactor than all of them put together. But the reign of mysterious absurdity and unmeaning *verbiage*, we trust, will have an end—and that men will be induced to direct their energies to the melioration of the character and condition of their fellow-men. Many sentiments and usages which have been sanctioned by the authority and wisdom of ages, and the propriety of which, none perhaps, at the present day, will venture to call in question, are destined hereafter, we believe, to be renounced and condemned as erroneous and immoral.

The progress of practical moral truth is extremely slow. Thus, for instance, the claims of mankind generally upon Christian benevolence were not recognized, in any considerable degree, prior to the commencement of the present century, nor are they even yet, except to a very partial and limited extent: and the slave trade itself was not denounced until within the memory of the living generation. The habits of society cannot be easily changed; and it is but seldom that any one dares to oppose them.

Whatever is, is right, is a maxim of no small influence in *fact*, even where its correctness would not be acknowledged in *terms*.

"We must take society as it *is*, not as it *should be*," is the usual apology for whatever evils happen to be tolerated in the community.

"We must enact laws to encourage the manufacture

of domestic spirits, (pleads the politician,) for though the people may be ruined in soul, body and estate, by the excessive use of this physical and moral poison, yet we must legislate for men as they *are*, not as they *might* be."

"If I do not sell the liquor that intoxicates my neighbour, some one else will"—says the publican, while he deliberately pockets the price of his brother's infamy and perdition.

In these instances, I advert to only one mode of the operation of only one false principle or assumption—and who can calculate the misery which it every day diffuses throughout the entire population of our country? Who can estimate the evil of intemperance?

Whence is it that our prisons and penitentiaries—erected at a cost of many millions of dollars—are crowded with convicts, supported at an annual charge to the public of millions more? Whence is it that our poor houses and poor rates, private charities and benevolent associations, are unable to satisfy the daily increasing demands of clamorous pauperism? Let the officers and the records of all these institutions—let the dispensers of a nation's justice and of a nation's alms—answer the inquiry. They will tell you that three-fourths, nay frequently, that nine-tenths of these criminals and paupers have been ruined by intemperance.

It has been computed from authentic data, and published to the world, that, during the last year, more than ten thousand of our citizens were cut off, in the midst of their days, by this one fell scourge. That, at least, fifty thousand more were destroyed by diseases occasioned by intemperance. And that there are three hundred thousand drunkards now living, or rather dying, in our country.

It is moreover ascertained that, at least, fifty millions of gallons of distilled liquors, foreign and domestic, are annually consumed by our people. Suppose the average price to the consumer to be fifty cents per gallon, then the amount expended annually on this object will be twenty-five millions of dollars. And the pauperism occasioned thereby is estimated to cost some ten or fifteen millions more.

Taking the population of the United States at twelve millions, and that of Tennessee at six hundred thousand, then will Tennessee, at the same rate of consumption, expend $1,250,000 a year for ardent spirits alone; and, in ten years, $12,500,000, without allowing for any increase whatever in numbers, and without reckoning the interest of the money thus annually expended. How far, permit me to ask in passing, might such a sum go towards providing the ways and means of educating our children?—of creating a permanent school fund for the benefit of every family in the commonwealth?

That I may not be thought to have presented an exaggerated statement relative to Tennessee, I will add, that, it has been recently communicated to the public, from very high authority, that the annual expenditure for intoxicating liquors in Massachusetts exceeds $1,300,000 for a population of only 550,000. I am willing to believe that we are not quite so bad in this respect as our Eastern brethren, and hence the estimate just given is much more favourable.

Drunkenness however, it cannot be denied, is sapping the foundation of morals—is filling the country with miscreants and vagabonds, with beggars and felons—is imposing burdens on the rich and ruining the poor—is impairing public virtue and destroying domestic peace—is not only diminishing the enjoyments of this life, but jeoparding the hopes of a better—is already an evil more tremendous and threatening than war, or famine, or pestilence, or than all combined—and is continually increasing in a ratio which baffles calculation, and which, in a few years, may defy all control.

Is there not scope here for the most active and intrepid benevolence? Who will deliver his country from the deadly grasp of this many-headed monster? Who will devise a remedy for this most fatal disease which is already preying upon the vitals of the Republic?

Many remedies have been proposed — the merits of which I shall not stop to investigate. I pass all medical prescriptions. I say nothing of the expediency of legislative interference. Nor shall I expatiate on the benefits that might be expected from the extensive and general cultivation of the vine. I merely hint at the principal remedy which *we* can immediately apply—and which each of us can apply—and which is strictly of the moral and preventive character. By our example, our counsel, our instructions, we may do much. We can ourselves abstain altogether from the use of ardent spirits—banish them from our tables, from our houses, from our farms, from our labourers, from every place over which we exercise control. This we *can* do. And this, every motive and consideration of patriotism, benevolence, and Christian duty should constrain us to do while we live. If all virtuous reflecting men, all honourable influential men, all college graduates, all reverend clergymen, would do this, the evil would be effectually checked, and it would rapidly diminish.

How much of this very evil indeed is fairly attributable to the countenance which such men have given to it? They have made it customary and fashionable to *drink* on all joyous and festive occasions—to *treat* each other at every social visit—and thus to be continually presenting temptation, in the most alluring form, especially to the young and inexperienced. For to them nothing usually is so difficult to resist as the claims or prescriptions of fashion. Here then the evil must be arrested. The fashion must be changed. Ardent spirits of every description must be forever proscribed, and exiled from good company. In reference to this most insidious and direful bane of human peace and virtue, the motto of every young man, who aims at being good or great, should be—"touch not, taste not, handle not." With this enemy hold no parley—make no treaty, truce or compromise. To hesitate, to listen, to tamper, is to yield the victory; and, perhaps, to yield it forever.

I urge this point with all possible earnestness, because it is so completely overlooked by the young, and because a failure here is blasting to all their hopes. It will be death to all their golden dreams and prospects of earthly bliss and earthly honour. It will make few their days: and will render those few a burden and a curse to themselves, to their friends, and to the world. I urge it with affectionate importunity, because I have seen issue from colleges, consecrated to science, to virtue, and to piety, most melancholy and heart-rending examples of all the misery of which youthful intemperance, in its various forms, is capable. Ah, my young friends, did you know the grief—the torture—which you may inflict in the bosoms of those who love you most, and who would esteem no sacrifice too great to save you from the snares which beset your path, you would dash from your lips the proffered cup, and spurn with indignation from your sight, the wretch who would seduce you from wisdom's ways.

Why is it that the scenes of intemperate mirth and revelry—the haunts of folly and dissipation—nay the very sinks of iniquity and abomination—are so often sought and frequented? Where shall we find an adequate, or even a specious apology for such madness? Why is it that the dictates and counsels of wisdom are so often contemned by youth, when associated for the noblest purposes—when engaged in the most exalted and grateful pursuits—when professedly submitting to that course of discipline and culture which will prepare them to lead the way in honour's high career, and to ascend the loftiest steeps of human greatness?—To say nothing of other and nobler ends to which well directed and sanctified learning is ever subservient. Surely, if there be anything in human prospects alluring and encouraging; anything in itself calculated to impart stability to character; anything to deter from gross and destructive vice; anything to prompt to enterprise and exertion; the privileged student or graduate of a college is the individual, above all others, who should be the farthest removed from all that is grovelling and mean and licentious. It is he, if any one on earth, whom we should expect to see asserting the dignity of his nature, and manfully contending for the noblest prize within the grasp of mortality.

I proceed to the consideration or exposure of another evil—which, like intemperance, may aptly be denominated LEGION—for it is the cause or fountain of many evils. I mean *the tyranny of custom or fashion.* We have seen that intemperance occasions most of the crime, and poverty and wretchedness in our country; and that no small portion of this very intemperance is the natural result of the general and fashionable use of inebriating liquors.

But the despotism of fashion extends far and wide—pervades all departments of human thought and action—controls opinion—determines principles—regulates manners and conduct—and moulds the passions and affections at pleasure.

I need not advert to its resistless sway over the whole mass of human expenditure, beyond the bare necessaries of existence—over the dress, the equipage, the furniture, the table, the entertainments, the amusements, the education, the accomplishments, of the whole civilized world—for here its absolute dominion has never been questioned. And how dreadful the bondage is—how excruciating the tortures of the hapless victims—may be witnessed every day by any man who will open his eyes upon what is passing around him—upon the anxious struggle, the sacrifice of peace and comfort, made by the several classes of the people in order to reach or surpass those who are looked up to as *fashionable* and *honourable*. Very rich men may indulge their vanity and ostentation and caprice, without any pecuniary embarrassment or inconvenience. Not so with the host of inconsiderate imitators, of smaller fortunes, or of no fortune at all. A rich man, it is true, ought not, in regulating his personal or family expenses, merely to consult the extent of his own means. He ought, in duty, to consider what his poorer neighbours can afford; because they will be sure to follow his example; and that, too, precisely in things the least useful, or entirely superfluous, or positively injurious to health and morals, as well as to property. For the fact is, however absurd, that, when any amusement, vice or pleasure becomes fashionable, then will thousands throw away their scanty and hard-earned pittance, in order to participate in the indulgences, the follies and the extravagancies of the *great*, and to dissipate and *show off* among those whom they foolishly account their *betters*. "Pride (says Franklin) is a beggar quite as clamorous as want, but infinitely more insatiable."

Thus is it also in regard to opinions which govern the world. There is, for instance, "the Law of Honour"—as distinct from the law of the land, and from the law of God. "It is a system of rules constructed by people of fashion"—and for their own special benefit and convenience,—without the slightest recognition of the duties which they owe to their Maker,—or to the mass of the people, who are heartily despised as their inferiors.

"For which reason (says Paley) profaneness, neglect of public worship or private devotion, cruelty to servants, rigorous treatment of tenants or other dependents, want of charity to the poor, injuries done to tradesmen by insolvency or delay of payment, with numberless examples of the same kind, are accounted no breaches of honour, because a man is not a less agreeable companion for these vices, nor the worse to deal with, in those concerns which are usually transacted between one gentleman and another. Again—the Law of Honour, being constituted by men occupied in the pursuit of pleasure, will be found, in most instances, favourable to the licentious indulgence of the natural passions." Thus it allows of drunkenness, prodigality, duelling, revenge, gaming, and almost every species of sensuality and dissipation, provided the fashionable mode be duly observed.

This Law of Honour, with many other equally precious institutions, we have inherited from our European ancestry. And although we acknowledge among ourselves neither nobility nor gentry—with whom, and for whom exclusively, this law originated, and by whom it is still sustained in the old world—yet so ambitious are we of whatever savours of *high life*, that, without family, or estate, or royal favour, or legal immunities, we have introduced all the pompous phraseology and all the aristocratic usages of that very country whose right to govern us we have long since disclaimed and forever renounced.

The subject, indeed, assumes an aspect sufficiently ludicrous to be left to the ridicule and contempt of men of sense; were it not for the serious interests which it involves, and the blind infatuation of our countrymen in regard to it. Already we have among us an order of men—a very large one too—styled gentlemen; as contradistinguished from the rest of the people. What it is that constitutes a *gentleman,* in ordinary parlance, I shall not attempt to define. Perhaps *wealth,* or the appearance of it, may be assumed as the main or indispensable requisite. At any rate, we every day see money transforming clowns and fools and blockheads—and even not a few rogues and knaves—into marvellous fine gentlemen.

Our concern at present, however, is simply with this code of honour—this English, European, aristocratic code—which our American gentlemen have adopted as their own.

Like their transatlantic superiors—I have a right to the term *superiors,* however offensive; for in this matter at least, they are servile copyists, mere humble and *despised* imitators of what they can never effectually reach—like their transatlantic superiors then, they affect to be entirely above—and too often prove themselves to be above—the laws of their country. With these laws, indeed, they have no concern, except, it may be, to aid in manufacturing them for the benefit of the meaner sort. And as to penal statutes—prisons, gibbets—these were all contrived for the vulgar—for poor beggarly plebeians. A gentleman, of the *true water*, has no fear of them, and no need of them. His pistol or dagger will answer every purpose of judge, jury and executioner. He habitually walks abroad in all the conscious dignity of irresponsible freedom and independence. And even our little masters—the hopeful sons of most gallant sires—long before they ought to be trusted out of their mothers' sight, sally forth to do valiant deeds in the village streets or village school; and show their spirit and their breeding by the seasonable display of that most knightly—most gentlemanly weapon—the DIRK.

Again—Our gentleman is a perfect pink of honesty and fair dealing. He will not steal your horse or your purse; he will not counterfeit the coin of his country, or forge a note upon his neighbour;—this would be vulgar, and consequently, infamous. Whether he is always equally scrupulous about appropriating to his own use the property of others, under some one or other of the ten thousand specious, genteel, fashionable forms and pretexts, with which *honourable* men are sufficiently familiar—I respectfully submit to the decision of those most competent to judge.

His *veracity* is never to be questioned with impunity. He will not violate his promise or his word, nor injure your reputation, if you happen to pass for a gentleman, or belong to *society*. No, no—upon these points he is exquisitely tender, delicate and guarded. But he may unblushingly, and greatly to his honour, resort to all manner of artifice and deceit, of falsehood and perjury, in order to win and to betray the confidence of unsuspecting female innocence: and thus blast forever the prospects, the character, the happiness of an honest family, in every just sense of the term, incomparably his superior.

There is, too, the *gentleman* gamester; as well as the hardened, crafty, unprincipled gambler. The *practice* of gaming, I believe, is countenanced throughout the world of fashion; while, the *vice* of low, vulgar, petty gambling is universally censured and denounced, as ruinous to the morals and industry of the common people. Between the *practice* and the *vice*, as exhibited in the drawing-room and the alehouse, I leave it to the casuist and the lawyer to point out the moral distinction and to calculate the difference. Of the horrible effects of gambling, as witnessed in most of the European capitals and in the larger cities of our own country, it would be impossible, by any language, to convey an adequate idea.

It will not be inferred from anything already said, that I lay to the charge of all persons who are regarded as gentlemen, the whole or any part of the sins and follies just hinted at. I imagine, however, that I shall not be misunderstood. There are gentlemen who would do none of these things—who bear themselves more loftily—whose moral tone and spirit, whose wisdom and virtue shed a lustre upon talent and station—but who, after all, are subject to the *law of honour*, in some of its worst claims and features.—Who dare not exhibit the courage and the independence which in heart they approve and admire.

Such a gentleman would shudder at the thought of murder or assassination—nay he would scorn to appear discourteous or unkind—he may be most humane, tender, gentle, amiable and benevolent in temper and practice—but he will, when the law of honour requires, call you out, bid you defend yourself, and shoot you or submit to be shot, with as much apparent coolness and indifference, as if he were the sovereign arbiter of life and death. He *must* do this or lose *caste*—forfeit his standing in *society*—and be sneered at as a coward or a *saint*. And who could brook the disgrace of being reputed "to obey God rather than men"? Who could forgive an injury or an insult, whether real or imaginary, great or small, accidental or designed, with true Christian meekness and magnanimity? Or who could pass unnoticed an offence, however trivial or ideal or constructive, when his peers proclaim that blood alone can expiate the offender's guilt, or satisfy the behests of this inexorable law?

I upbraid not individuals. They merely participate in the bondage and the infatuation of general sentiment and custom. So long as the infatuation and bondage obtain, so long are all men of *honour* duellists *virtually*, whether they ever fight a duel or not. Because all acknowledge the same principles, and countenance the practice. I advert to it, not in the spirit of the cynic or illiberal censor—not for the purpose of personal rebuke or crimination or reproach—nor as a convenient topic for harsh invective or loose declamation. But because it is a great and growing evil—a national evil—the plague and disgrace of the Christian world:—and with a view to its correction and removal.

Cannot the *code* of *honour*, which compels honourable men to fight duels, be repealed or abrogated? In its favour or defence, I have never read or heard one argument, or the shadow of an argument, advanced from any quarter or by any individual. It is, on the contrary, universally condemned by duellists themselves—whether successful or unfortunate—in the hour of victory or of death—frequently before, and always after the fatal meeting. They generally speak of it in terms of reprobation, and lament the tyranny of custom, which drives them, however reluctant and at whatever sacrifice, to mortal combat—merely to satisfy the wanton, the capricious, the abominable, the fiend-like demands of an arbitrary tribunal—which is nowhere visible or tangible,—which can hardly be said to have a local habitation or a name, and which, nevertheless, is universally and implicitly obeyed, in open and reckless defiance of all that is good, and just, and kind, and merciful, and holy, and dreadful, in earth or heaven!

Is this a custom or a law which is, in its own nature, everlasting and unalterable?—which is never to pass away into the darkness and oblivion which have long since shrouded most other Gothic absurdities and enormities? As the law now stands, a man *must*, in certain cases, give or accept a challenge, or men of honour will not countenance or acknowledge him as a gentleman. Such is the law, and such is the penalty. Now, let me ask, cannot these same men of honour, whoever they are or wherever to be found, put down this law, extirpate this relic of feudal barbarism, and decree that no gentleman shall henceforth fight a duel, under precisely the same penal sanctions—namely, the forfeiture of his place in society as a gentleman or man of honour? Could they not as easily abolish the law as they now sustain it? Especially, as they all agree in denouncing it, and as the rest of the world would heartily approve the measure. I verily believe that it is in the power of some twenty individuals, in each of these States, by acting in concert and with decision, to render it as ungentlemanly, as dishonourable, as infamous, to fight a duel, as it now is to commit any felony whatever. The object is at least worth the experiment.

If it were ever expedient to summon a national council or convention, to devise plans of deliverance from oppression, or to seek a redress of grievances, then is it now expedient; for we are literally perishing under a moral slavery the most ruinous, burdensome and degrading. And the man, or the men, who shall succeed in rescuing the Republic from the despotism of opinion —who shall break down the dominion of intemperance, of gambling, of duelling—will deserve higher honour than has been awarded to the sages, heroes and martyrs of our glorious revolution.

Having thus glanced at some of the obliquities and the general character of the dominant system, it may be proper to add, that, I do not mean to censure anything that contributes to the comfort and well-being of society. Many things fashionable may be very good and useful. They are so, however, not because they are fashionable, but in spite of fashion. The extremes of luxury and extravagance on the one hand; of meanness and avarice on the other, are to be equally avoided. Amiable manners—genuine politeness—an easy, graceful air and carriage—unaffected refinement and delicate courtesy—are very desirable and are justly prized. Hence it is that they are more frequently counterfeited than actually possessed. Good manners—civility—urbanity—it has been well remarked—may be regarded as the homage which hypocrisy frequently pays to virtue. A man may be, in all his exterior, a perfect gentleman; and yet prove a heartless rake or villain after all. Real good-will to others—kindness felt and cherished—an honest, habitual desire and purpose to be useful—must lay the foundation for the most solid, valuable and durable politeness. I would recommend the school and the writings of St. Paul, as infinitely preferable, in forming the gentleman, Christian and scholar, to all the *Maxims* and *Letters* of all the Rochefoucaulds and Chesterfields, dead or living, who have ever written or dogmatized on the subject.

The principal remedy for the worst evils which prevail amongst us is *education.*—The proper, thorough, Christian education of all the people from infancy to manhood. An education which commences at the earliest possible period—which is faithful in the discipline and improvement of all the faculties, moral, physical and intellectual—which keeps steadily in view every virtue which can adorn and elevate the character of man—and which regards each individual, not only as a constituent part of the great national family, but as a candidate for a holy and a happy immortality in heaven. "Train up a child in the way he should go, and when he is old, he will not depart from it." This I believe as fully as I believe any other part of divine revelation. God's blessing will crown with success the honest efforts of those who conscientiously and faithfully obey his commands, or employ the means which himself has ordained. The children of the Republic must be rightly and thoroughly disciplined, before we can hope to see a community of temperate, industrious, economical, peaceful, virtuous, happy citizens.

The genuine American System has not yet been practically developed. True, its spirit pervades the *Declaration* of *Independence*—that imperishable document of human rights, to the support of which our fathers, in '76, pledged their lives, their fortunes and their sacred honour. True, it breathes throughout the *Constitution*, which our venerable sages, in '89, solemnly adopted as the sacred charter of American liberty. But our practice must yet be made to accord with our theory.

In this concern, as in many others, we are still subject to the dogmas and usages of European masters. We *speak*, indeed, of the majesty of the sovereign people; but we *act* towards them, at least in the matter of education, as do English lords and esquires to their vassals and dependants. English gentlemen are as proud of their liberty as Americans can be; but then it is the liberty of English *gentlemen*, not the liberty of the multitude, that they boast of or care for. In reference to the education of the labouring or operative mass of the people, the simple and sole question usually is, what will suffice them in their character and condition of labourers or *operatives?*—not, what will enable them to rise above their humble, degraded and servile condition? Hence it has become, or rather continued, customary for even sensible and well-meaning men among us, to maintain the same aristocratic doctrine; and to tell the very people who constitute the bone and sinew of the Republic, that they, the plain, honest, labouring farmers and mechanics, have no need of learning, beyond a mere *common education*,—which, according to their interpretation of the phrase, implies no more than to read, write and keep accounts. Now, is not this virtually to doom the great body of the people forever to an inferior condition?—To keep them perpetually disqualified to claim the privileges, to exercise the rights, to attain the dignities of freemen, equally with those who are better educated?*

* The people are moreover told that a *liberal* education is not only useless, or injurious, but very expensive. True, it does cost something. The question is, does it cost more than it is worth? I answer, no. A good education is preferable to any fortune which any parent can bestow on his son in lieu of it. And parents in general can afford to educate their children in the best manner—certainly in a much better manner than is now customary. I have never known an honest, sober,

But it is not merely to elevate one class of men to a political equality with another, nor is it mainly to qualify men for public offices, still less for professional eminence, that I thus earnestly and repeatedly plead the cause of education. It is chiefly to make better and happier and more useful men, in all the walks and departments, in all the pursuits and avocations, public and private, of human society. Well informed men cannot be easily imposed on by any species of charlatanry, fraud, quackery, fanaticism, superstition, hypocrisy — by lawyers, priests, physicians or demagogues. As knowledge shall be diffused, professional services generally will be less needed. Crimes will diminish. Prisons and penitentiaries, jails and bridewells,—those hot beds of depravity and abomination — those seminaries of all manner of iniquity — where every wicked propensity is indulged, and every diabolical purpose matured, and every scheme of villany and outrage most cunningly devised and prepared for execution — where no culprit was ever yet reformed — where even the juvenile novice is soon transformed into a hardened, shameless, daring, reckless cut-throat—those lazar-houses of sin and pestilence and

---

industrious man who could not give his children a *good* common education—provided good schools, or properly qualified teachers were established or could be procured within a reasonable distance. And among our respectable farmers and mechanics, there are not many who could not send their sons to college if they chose. And they would do so, were they taught to prize knowledge more highly than lands and negroes, or than the follies and glitter of fashion, or than the gratifications of low grovelling dissipation. And after all, the complaint of the expensiveness of an education comes with an ill grace from those who will do nothing towards cheapening it.

death—at once the curse and the disgrace of our country—which were established, and are now supported, at an expense a hundred-fold greater than that of all the colleges and schools in the nation—will gradually become tenantless.

Degraded and degrading pauperism will vanish—with crime—under the genial influence of virtue in union with science. Every man, however humble his lot, will be able to command and to enjoy an intellectual feast at every leisure moment: and even while busily employed in his daily labours for a subsistence, the great world of mind and matter—the grand volume of nature, in all her varied beauty and loveliness, is ever present to his view and admiration.

Let knowledge be as free as the air which we breathe—let it illumine the cottage as well as the palace—let it adorn, elevate and dignify every human being—must be the language and the wish of every enlightened philanthropist.

The *American System* is now on trial before the world. It remains to be seen, whether twelve millions of people—or fifty millions—and we shall soon be fifty millions—can exercise the rights and powers of sovereignty—can govern themselves—live in peace and safety, liberty and equality. And if so, to solve the problem of universal freedom and self-government. For the American system will, if successful, become the system of the world. I believe it will succeed. The grand instrument, under God, of maintaining and carrying it to perfection is, must ever be, education. The education too of the very people, who, at present, in almost every part of the earth, are scarcely regarded as possessing any rights, or as worthy of the slightest political consideration, or as capable of any more refined mental enjoyments than the savage or the brute. Labour, while you live, to build up this truly American system, and thus to promote the best interests of all the people—and of mankind universally.

And now, at parting, accept a word of honest and kindly counsel.

"The first and most instructive lesson, which man can receive, (says one of your college text books,) when he is capable of reflection, is to *think for himself;* the second, without which the first would be comparatively of little value, is to reject, *in himself*, that infallibility, which he rejects in *others*."

Resolve, at your outset in life, to be independent. To think, examine, judge and decide for yourselves, upon all matters, practical and speculative. Adopt none of the prevailing maxims and principles of the world, without a thorough and candid scrutiny. Yield not an implicit or an indolent faith to any creed or code—political, religious, philosophical or fashionable. Use the reason which God has given you, in the search of truth and duty and wisdom. Canvass, with candor, every doctrine which claims your acceptance or assent, of whatever school, or by whatever authority it may be upheld. Avoid all irritating and unprofitable disputes and controversies—especially concerning the tenets and mysteries of religion. But should you engage in a discussion in order to find out truth, do not presume, as is too generally the case, that you are certainly possessed of it beforehand. "Seest thou a man wise in his own conceit? there is more hope of a fool than of him." Modesty, patience and humility will become you in every investigation; and at every stage of your progress through life. When, however, you shall have ascertained what is true—what is right—what is suited to your circumstances—what will contribute to your happiness—dare to choose the good and to refuse the evil.

Never submit to the tyranny of custom. Keep aloof from every species of fashionable folly, dissipation, amusement, extravagance or pleasure—which, in the first place, you do not or ought not to approve—or which, in the second place, you cannot afford. Resist all solicitations to intemperance, to gambling, to ruinous vice of every name and description. "My son, if sinners entice thee, consent thou not." "He that walketh with wise men shall be wise; but a companion of fools shall be destroyed." In all your personal or other expenditures, consult health and comfort—the extent of your own pecuniary resources and the general good of society. Remember the adage of the wise man, that, "the borrower is servant to the lender." That frugality, which arises from order and economy, is the parent of liberality of sentiment and generosity of conduct. Had Arnold abstained from fashionable vices, and been content to live within the limits of his income, he had not been *damned to everlasting fame* as a traitor to his country.

Shun idleness as a most insidious and dangerous foe.

Be diligent in business and study. Search after knowledge as for hid treasures. Labour patiently and perseveringly, and relax not while life endures. Genius never achieves miracles—except by hard and long continued application. The talents of a Solomon would avail you nothing without industry. Every truly great man, whatever may have been his early advantages of education, has been, and is, *self-made.* He may, indeed, build upon a goodly foundation—and he regards his college discipline merely as a foundation—but he is himself the builder. The superstructure is all his own: and it is the work of years, perhaps of a long life. He is the maker—the creator of his own fortune, fame and eminence. And such must you be, if ever you rise above the crowded ranks of humble mediocrity.

Cherish and maintain a sacred, scrupulous, inviolable and universal regard to truth and integrity, in all your intercourse, conversation and dealings with your fellow-men.

Take not the holy name of God in vain. Regard the practice of profane swearing as ungentlemanly and vulgar, as it is unlawful and wicked. Treat all religious institutions with decorous reverence.

Be tolerant, liberal and charitable in your sentiments and conduct. Never condemn, denounce or censure any denomination, class, sect or party in the *gross.* You will find good men and bad, wise and simple, among them all. The spirit of bigotry, intolerance and persecution is ever a spirit of ignorance or malignity or both. Abuse no man for his opinions—much less for his religious creed—and never ascribe to his opinions or creed any consequences which he himself disclaims. As a tree is known by its fruit, so a man may be known by his actions—and of these we may, when necessary for the welfare of ourselves or of society, lawfully judge. But remember, that no heresy, of which you can be guilty, is so criminal before the majesty of high Heaven, as the practical heresy of uncharitableness.

Be courteous and kind to all. Flatter none. Deserve the esteem of the virtuous. Court not, by undue compliances, the favour of any. Humour not the follies and caprices of the high or the low—of the many or the few—of the rich or the poor. Seek to enlighten, improve and benefit the whole, by your example, your counsel, your influence, your learning and your property. And eventually, the world will make a just estimate of your talents and of your merits. While, in the mean time, you will enjoy more real satisfaction than any undeserved temporary popularity or applause could possibly yield.

Your connexion, Young Gentlemen, with this University, as students, is this day dissolved. The affectionate attachment of dutiful and generous *alumni* towards their *Alma Mater*, we trust, will never be dissolved, but will increase with the lapse of time, however distant may be your residence, or whatever may be your future pursuits. But the long looked for happy hour has, at length, arrived, which frees you from college restraints, and which sunders the ties of all college relations and associations. That you are not insensible to the painful emotions which a final separation from intimate and beloved companions must awaken in every amiable bosom, we have had abundant evidence.

That, on other accounts, youth should be eager to depart from the scene of juvenile effort, emulation and discipline—however beneficial it may have been to them—experience tells us is natural and common. That they should contemplate with joyous anticipations, the period, when they may be permitted to gather the flowers which fancy strews along the path-way of future life, and to enter upon the proud theatre of manly enterprize and generous ambition, is not to be wondered at—nor shall it receive from us any cynical rebuke or condemnation.

But there is an aspect, under which this subject presents itself to the eye and the heart of those who feel the deepest interest in their welfare, solemn and awful and melancholy and distressing beyond the power of language to portray. It is the thought, that, in the midst of all this buoyancy of spirit and of hope—of all this earthly attractiveness and fascination—of all these bright and cheering prospects—of all these dreams of virtuous exertion and honourable distinctions—of all those pleasures, joys and rewards which seem to stretch along to the remotest verge of the horizon of youthful imagination—and which cluster around his every view in the richest groups and most varied profusion, as if to chide his delay and backwardness to improve the passing moment, and to seize the proffered bounty of nature, thus pressed upon his acceptance—oh, it is the thought, that, at this very moment of purest sunshine, when all creation seems to smile, and to hail with ecstasy the commencement of that youthful career which promises so much glory and happiness—it is the dreadful thought, that, DEATH may be secretly lurking in the midst of the happy company, and insidiously making his approach to the vitals of some unsuspecting youth, on whose countenance plays the almost heavenly smile of assured confidence and unmingled delight in the fair scenes which a long life is yet to realize! Ah, my friends, would to God, there existed no reason for this heart-rending—and, to all human nature's proudest, noblest schemes—most revolting, tantalizing, overwhelming thought!

But when did a class of youth bid farewell to any seat of science, to whom the thought would have been unseasonable? or from whose number, one and another have not been summoned to judgment, within a few short years or months after their departure?

Rejoice, therefore, with trembling, in the view of that resplendent, but most deceiving world into which you are about to enter. Remember that you, like the gifted alumni of other institutions, may be cut down in the midst of the most brilliant and successful career—or in the first stages of pious and benevolent effort—or before you can even begin the work on which your hearts are all intent. In their destiny, read what may be yours. Let the dead speak and warn you to be wise. Let death be provided for first, and above all things, then peace and joy shall crown your earthly lot, be its complexion what it may. Then the world shall appear in its true colours: and though it may doom you to many trials, labours and disappointments, yet you can ever look, with a holy calmness and delight, beyond this tempestuous ocean, to that tranquil haven—to that blessed country—where the wicked cease from troubling, and where the weary be at rest.

Let the Bible be the companion of your future lives and studies. Read it daily, and with humble prayer for the illuminating influences of that blessed Spirit who first inspired and revealed it. It will be a lamp to your feet, and a light to your path, and a joy to your hearts, in all your wanderings through life's checkered scenery, and through death's dark valley. It will teach you how to value, and how to improve time, talent, learning and wealth—how to be honest—how to be religious—how to be useful—how to be happy—how to live—and how to die.

May the Almighty bless you with long life, health, peace and prosperity—grant you the renewing, sanctifying and saving influences of his Holy Spirit—make you eminently useful in your day and generation. And whether we ever meet again on earth or not, may we all meet in heaven at last, and rejoice together in heaven while eternity endures; through infinite riches of free grace in Christ Jesus the righteous, who is over all, God blessed forever! Amen.

BACCALAUREATE ADDRESS.

[CUMBERLAND COLLEGE, OCTOBER 7, 1829.]

BACCALAUREATE ADDRESS,

AT CUMBERLAND COLLEGE, 1829

THE people oppose, for a season, plans and institutions designed to promote their own welfare, through sheer ignorance. When disabused of prejudice, and fully instructed in regard to their genuine character and tendency, they usually become their warm and devoted friends. This is a solid ground of encouragement to persevere in any useful enterprise, until the people be fully informed respecting it, for *then* their support may be confidently relied on. The ever-memorable epoch of our own glorious revolution may aptly illustrate this position, and the general intelligence of our countrymen. No country could ever boast of a larger number of enlightened, gifted, noble, high-minded patriots than were, at that alarming crisis, found ready to hazard all things in defence of their constitutional and inherited rights as free-born Englishmen. But they would have struggled in vain, had not the entire mass of the people been

---

NOTE.—The reader is requested to keep in mind that the following "Plea for the University of Nashville" was delivered in 1829. No alteration, in facts or dates, has been made to suit the changes which have since occurred.

easily taught to comprehend them also, and to enlist with determined ardour in the common cause. Three millions of people were never before in a condition to act so honourably and promptly in a good cause. The master spirits in that grand drama had but to sound the alarm, and give the impulse; and every man was at his post, and ready to conquer or to die. I doubt whether, at this moment, our country possesses half the number of truly great men, in proportion to her population, which adorned and directed her counsels in the cabinet and in the field, from '70 to '89;—or a people half as enlightened, taking the whole mass into view, as they were at the period referred to. Intellectual and moral improvement has not kept pace with the increase of our numbers and resources. This is the decided opinion of the most competent judges, and our history amply confirms it.

These general remarks apply to our literary institutions—to our colleges and universities—with even greater force and pertinence than to most other objects and enterprises which are often doomed to a temporary unpopularity. Look at the rise and early history of our most ancient seats of science—at Harvard, William and Mary, Yale, and Nassau-Hall, for instance. In their infancy, and for many years subsequently, they had to maintain a constant struggle for existence. The body of the people regarded them, for a long time, with suspicion, envy, jealousy and apprehension—as destined for the rich and honourable—as likely to raise up and to perpetuate a learned and powerful aristocracy—as anything, in short, rather than what they professed and claimed to be. But their friends persevered—"Onward" was their motto—in spite of popular clamour on the one hand, and the cold indifference and sometimes direct opposition of the royal government on the other. They conquered—succeeded—and triumphed gloriously. And these very institutions became the principal nurseries of our revolutionary heroes and statesmen. By furnishing well qualified instructors for common schools, they diffused the light of science and truth over the continent, and enabled the people to discern and to appreciate their own perilous condition and jeoparded franchises.

The history of those colonial pioneers in the cause of learning, virtue and liberty, is pregnant with instruction to all men who entertain doubts or fears or prejudices in regard to the character, influence and bearing of similar establishments. Within sight of the oldest, and still most celebrated university of our country, commenced the mighty contest which created a nation of freemen. And her gallant sons poured out their blood like water upon the battle field. They roused by their eloquence every patriotic energy of their countrymen, and were ever foremost to hazard and to sacrifice fortune and life for the general weal. Then was the golden opportunity for college-bred gentlemen to have secured for themselves stars and garters and mitres and estates, by rallying round the royal standard, in support of legitimacy and aristocracy, of the priest and king; and to have placed their feet proudly upon the necks of the vulgar and illiterate. So base a sycophant, so traitorous a tory, so aspiring a *would be* lord, never disgraced a college catalogue. Not one proved recreant to the cause of popular rights and liberty. Whatever their calling or profession—lawyers, physicians, clergymen, merchants, farmers—all the sons of *Alma Mater*—were found in the ranks of hostility to Britain's claims and to Britain's legions.

Nor ought it ever to be forgotten that, throughout the original thirteen confederated colonies, afterwards States, the best educated and most enlightened individuals were decided Whigs;—and in their wisdom, intelligence, patriotism and integrity, the people reposed unlimited confidence. And they were not deceived. These were the men who directed the revolutionary conflict: and these too were the men who formed the Constitution, under which we now live in peace, prosperity and happiness, unparalleled in the history of our world.

In this new world, west of the mountains, various attempts have been made, and are making, to establish the higher seminaries of learning for the benefit of the rising and of future generations. These attempts have hitherto proved abortive, or are yet in a state of incipient and doubtful progress. I hazard nothing in asserting that no such institution in the Western States has as yet been placed on a foundation at all likely to ensure its permanent existence and prosperity. Colleges and universities, in numbers sufficiently imposing, have been gratuitously chartered by the Legislatures of different States:—as if a mere nominal charter were all that was necessary to constitute a college! Many, no doubt, have been deceived, and continue to be deceived, by the *name;* while, of the substance, they remain as destitute as before. Scarcely any portion of the civilized Christian world is so poorly provided with the means of a liberal education as are the five millions of Americans within the great valley of the Mississippi.

A dozen or more colleges and universities* have been chartered in Ohio and Kentucky, and we have five in Tennessee. Not more than three or four of the whole number can, in reason, be pronounced equal to good second-rate grammar schools. A few enlightened individuals have constantly aimed at higher and nobler results; but generally they have failed in their anticipations, and been thwarted in their purposes. Colleges rise up like mushrooms in our luxuriant soil. They are duly lauded and puffed for a day; and then they sink to be heard of no more. Do our wise men fancy, that, by the magic of a technical parchment, they can instantly convert a school or academy, with its master and usher, into a college—where the liberal arts and sciences shall be adequately and thoroughly taught? If so, why not transform at once every grammar school in the State into a college; and thus bring the means of a liberal education to the door of every poor man's cottage? Already, Western colleges, thus established, have become the objects of ridicule and contempt in every enlightened corner of the land.

The levelling system, which is so popular and capti-

* Fourteen, precisely, have been chartered in Ohio and Kentucky—and all, except two, are in *a sort of* operation.

vating with the multitude, may be made to operate in two ways, with equal success—either by nullifying altogether every institution which implies or claims more than ordinary privileges and distinction; or by exalting to equal rank everything of a similar generic character. Thus, colleges and universities, as implying odious preeminence, may be prevented from growing up among us: or every petty village school may be dignified with the name and legal attributes of a college—be empowered to confer academical degrees—and to doctorate every stripling sciolist in the commonwealth. Pretty much the same result would ensue from either of these sapient schemes; and the latter seems to have found most favour in the Western country. Democratic and republican as we are, our citizens are strangely partial to great names. Esquire, Honourable, Excellency, Major, Colonel, General, Doctor, are as much coveted and as eagerly sought after in this country, as are titles of nobility in Europe. And foreign *titled* gentry, when they condescend to visit us, are regarded and treated as a superior race. The wealthiest and proudest man in the United States would feel himself and family wondrously honoured and *renowned*, could he be so fortunate as to marry his daughter to an English earl or even baronet! This spirit, so utterly at variance with our Constitution and avowed political doctrines, is sufficiently contemptible to be left, without serious comment, to the ridicule which it merits, were it not for some of its deleterious practical effects on society. And among these is the evil in question. Our people, at first, oppose all distinctions whatever as odious and aristocratical; and then, presently, seek with avidity such as remain accessible. At first, they denounce colleges; and then choose to have a college in every district or county, or for every sect and party—and to boast of a college education, and to sport with high sounding literary titles; as if these imparted sense or wisdom or knowledge. How long this puerile vanity will continue in vogue, it is not easy to foresee.

At least, two small items may always be regarded as indispensable to the prosperity of any American college or university. Namely: 1st. An intelligent, upright, liberal, devoted, efficient, harmonious and enterprising Board of Trustees,—who understand its interests, and are ever ready to discharge their sacred and responsible duties, with untiring zeal, fidelity and perseverance. *In this one grand essential, our University, happily, has nothing to desiderate.*

2d. Adequate pecuniary funds. A university is necessarily an expensive concern. Genius, learning, wisdom, industry, and the most disinterested ardour in the cause, can achieve nothing without the *golden* lever. Money alone can erect the buildings, procure the library, apparatus, cabinets of Natural History, and all the other requisite fixtures. And when all these are duly provided, money is still necessary to command the services of talented instructors. A regular and certain revenue, independent of the precarious and ever-varying income from tuition fees, is essential to its successful operation. No respectable college in the United States depends, at this moment, exclusively on the tuition fees derived from students, for the means of paying its professors. Every such institution has an independent income from other sources—from the State Treasury—or from productive funds, furnished originally by individual munificence or by the government.

Harvard University has an annual revenue of about thirty thousand dollars, exclusive of tuition charges. And all the other New England colleges have similar endowments, to a greater or less extent.

The State of New York has, within a few years past, appropriated in cash for the benefit of Columbia College in her Metropolis, $86,225.—Of Union College, $389,250.—Of Hamilton College, $106,800.—"Besides lands, value unknown." And these large sums, amounting to $582,275, were granted, not to give incipient existence to, but to enlarge and to help forward those institutions—the pride and the glory of that truly munificent and enlightened commonwealth—which has also expended millions on common schools, academies, medical colleges, penitentiaries, and internal improvements.

William and Mary College in Virginia, has productive funds to the amount of $120,000. Washington College, at Lexington, in the same State, has a perpetual income of $3000 from the liberality of its illustrious founder, whose name it bears; besides a recent legacy of an estate valued at $100,000. While the *University of Virginia,* the last, and not the least of the patriotic achievements of the people's greatest favourite—the gifted, philosophic and republican Jefferson—is entitled to a perpetual annuity from the Virginia Literary Fund of $15,000—in addition to the half million expended on its beautiful edifices and various furniture.

The University of North Carolina is known to be one of the richest in America. South Carolina College receives an annual grant from the legislature of twelve or fifteen thousand dollars. Its buildings, library, apparatus, &c. were all furnished by the State, and are of the first order.

The University of Georgia has been equally favoured. In 1821, a bill passed the Assembly of Georgia, appropriating $25,000 for the erection of a new college edifice, and a permanent annual endowment of $8000, for the support of the institution. And the University of Alabama is about to go into operation with a productive fund of at least half a million of dollars.

In this brief notice, I have not attempted details. I have had in view chiefly the permanent means of support, possessed by some of our principal seminaries. As to the entire amount expended on any one of our older colleges, from its rise to the present time, it would be difficult, perhaps impossible, to form an estimate. But concerning its present actual revenue there can be no mistake. And this was the single fact which I wished prominently to exhibit, in order to demonstrate the fallacy of the prevalent notion—that a college needs only to be started—to be set agoing, with a few rude materials, and two or three teachers—and that then it must needs sustain itself. I repeat, no such instance of good fortune exists in all our country. Nor will such a result ever be dreamed of by any person acquainted with the history and statistics of colleges.

In enterprising the establishment of a University at Nashville, the honest purpose was fondly cherished from the beginning, to render it *in fact* all that the name imports. Its friends desired to lay its foundations deep and broad. They felt that they were going to build for posterity as well as for the living. That kind of ephemeral popularity, which is so cheaply purchased, and which is never worth the cheapest purchase, they neither sought nor coveted. They did not expect to see the gilded domes and lofty turrets of their University suddenly rising in splendour, and dazzling the eye of every beholder. They knew that they could, at best, achieve little more than the commencement of a work, which must be fostered and enlarged and matured in the progress, perhaps, of ages to come. They did, indeed, confidently expect to accomplish more than they have done; because they believed that they had at command vastly larger pecuniary resources than they have been permitted to realize. How or wherefore they have been deprived of these necessary means, it is not for me, on this occasion, to account. Or what may be the consequence of this failure and disappointment, it is not for me to predict.

I did once flatter myself that the people of Tennessee would rally round this infant seat of science, and take a just pride in its growth and prosperity. I did suppose that they would cherish an institution of their own—

established in their own flourishing Metropolis—in the midst of their own territory, and of their own peculiar manners, customs, climate, habits, and all those other nameless indescribable somethings which constitute *home*—rather than continue to be tributary to distant or foreign countries for the education of their sons, at an enormous expense, and at other hazards infinitely more momentous than any pecuniary sacrifice. I did suppose that the good sense of the community would soon perceive that a University cannot be in every town—that it must have some one permanent location—and that, when once fixed and in operation, all petty local jealousies and rivalries would die away.—And that the University of Nashville would command the favour and patronage of the public, because it would be their own, and not a foreign University.

In casting my eye over the Map of Tennessee, it struck me from the first that this was precisely the place destined by Providence for a great University, if ever such an institution were to exist in the State. And in this opinion I am fully confirmed by several years' observation and experience. I am entirely satisfied that it is physically impossible to maintain a *University* (I am not now speaking of an ordinary college) in any other town in the State. And for this single good reason, were there no other: namely—A Medical School, which may be regarded as an essential and as the most important department of a real university, can never be sustained except in a large town or city—and the larger the better. Nashville is the only place where a Medical

School would even be thought of: and physicians know full well that such is the fact. If Tennessee then is to have such a school, it *must* be established in Nashville.

How long will Tennessee continue to send her youth to Philadelphia, or Cincinnati, or Lexington, to learn the healing art? Or how long will she tolerate that murderous quackery which her untaught striplings are continually obtruding upon an ignorant and easily deceived people? Is it intended that none but rich men's sons, who can afford to spend years at our Eastern cities, shall aspire to this profession? Or will she permit the poor and friendless to form themselves for this responsible service, as best they can: and to blunder along into successful and lucrative practice, by experimenting upon the living subject instead of the dead, until they acquire that knowledge and skill, which ought to have been learned at school before they ventured to prescribe or to operate at all? In this profession, more than in any other, it behooves the legal authorities of the land to interpose; and to provide for the due qualifications and fidelity of its members.—Because the people cannot judge for themselves. When the aid of a Physician or Surgeon is needed in any critical emergency—the *Doctor* is sent for, as a matter of course, and implicitly confided in: and if the patient be killed, or maimed, or disabled for life—who is responsible for the injury inflicted? How many are thus killed every year in our country and in this State by such empiricks, can never be known. I take it for granted, however, that every half-educated young physician, who succeeds at last in getting a *re-*

putable share of practice, must have rid the world, rather prematurely, of some dozen or twenty individuals at the least, in order to qualify himself for his profession.

In most countries on the continent of Europe, especially in France and Germany, candidates for the medical profession are required by law to study at least four years, winter and summer, at some regular well endowed Medical College or University. And each pupil is obliged to dissect from four to twelve subjects, provided by government for the purpose, and then to sustain a most rigid public examination, before a diploma, or a license to commence practice even in the most obscure country village, can be obtained. "In Italy, a study of six years is necessary to obtain a degree for higher surgery:—The practice of dissection, and the performance of the principal operations on the dead body, are indispensable; and an abundant supply of subjects is afforded the student in the prosecution of his pursuits."

In our country, the utmost that is expected in order to procure an M. D. is attendance for two sessions, of three or four months each, upon a course of lectures at a Medical School, and a short apprenticeship with some practising physician. And even this brief attendance at the lecture room is frequently dispensed with: and scores of young men are licensed to practise medicine in half the time that would be indispensable to learn any mechanical trade whatever. It is easier, at this moment, in Tennessee, for a young man to be qualified according to law, to practise medicine, or any other learned profession, than to be duly qualified to shoe a horse or to build a dray. How long—I repeat the demand—are our people to be thus cheated, trifled with, and oppressed? Tyranny, the most cruel and arbitrary, may be exercised just as easily by a republican legislature, or by an infatuated populace, as by an hereditary despot. And when inflicted, it matters little to the unfortunate sufferer, by what name, or under what form.

Whether a University is of any use in training lawyers, I shall not inquire. In point of numbers, we shall always have a reasonable supply, learned or unlearned, honest or dishonest—because the nature of our political fabric, of our civil jurisprudence, and of all our legal usages demands them; and because all our important civil offices, from the Presidential Chair downwards, are filled by them. They will abound and flourish just in proportion to the general ignorance and degradation of the mass of the people. If this be an evil, the only check upon it, and the only remedy for it, will be the diffusion of knowledge among the people. Enlighten and elevate the people, and they will have less occasion and less disposition to resort to the glorious uncertainty of the law. There are probably six hundred lawyers, of one sort or another in Tennessee, who receive some six hundred thousand dollars, more or less, of the people's money annually, to aid in procuring them legal justice—which is often no justice at all, and which always costs more than it is worth. If to this be added the whole array of judges, justices, courts, sheriffs, constables, prisons, &c. our system of law and equity will be found sufficiently onerous—and infinitely more expensive and vexatious than the summary process of the Turkish Cadi, and not half as certain or equitable at the last.

I cherish no unkindly sentiments towards lawyers. So long as the Gothic-Saxo-Norman-English system of common, statute and bench-made law, which has been represented as an interminable, overgrowing, incomprehensible, labyrinthian mystery of torture and extortion —which Burke deliberately denounced, which Brougham is diligently labouring to reform, and which Bentham intrepidly threatens to annihilate:—or, (to speak the language of Blackstone and others,) so long as this intricate and beautiful science, the very perfection of written reason, to the lucid development of which the most indefatigable and distinguished sages have nobly consecrated their talents and their lives—so long as this much lauded and much vituperated system, whether it be law, science, mystery, or all combined, to which every known epithet of praise and censure has been and continues to be applied, and of which it is impossible for the uninitiated, like myself, to form any conception, except from its practical effects—so long as such a system, whatever may be its qualities or tendencies, shall find favour in our land, *lawyers* will be the oracles of truth, wisdom and justice to the people. Lawyers too, there must be, under any form of government or system of jurisprudence. And a truly accomplished, liberal, upright, high-minded lawyer will ever prove a most valuable blessing and the brightest ornament to any community. Of many such eminently gifted and illustrious jurists and advocates, our country may proudly boast. It is for the people to decide, whether they will consent to be the passive slaves and dupes of mere pettifogging smatterers, by becoming themselves sufficiently intelligent to detect and to discountenance every species of knavish quackery.

As to divines, whether they ought to be learned or not, is a question which others may decide according to their own fancy. If people choose to have *inspired* men for their spiritual guides, the less of human science with which they may chance to be encumbered, the better—at least, the more apparent and striking will be the evidences of their inspiration. Fools will always be imposed on by the cunning under some pretext or other. And all well informed men know what priestcraft achieved in the dark ages, when not one in a thousand of the laity could read, and when the Bible was restricted to the cloister, where it often remained a sealed book even to the privileged inmates and to its authorized interpreters.

I leave out of the case then, at present, both lawyers and clergymen—merely hinting mine own opinion by the way, that neither the one nor the other would be the worse for a thorough scientific education, whether acquired at a university or elsewhere.

But our farmers ought, beyond all question, to be liberally educated; that is, they ought to have the best education that is attainable. I do not say that *every* farmer ought to go to college, or to become a proficient in Greek and Latin. I speak of them as a class: and by a liberal education, I mean such a course of intellectual discipline as will fit them to sustain the rank which they ought to hold in this Republic. They are by right the sovereigns of the land, because they constitute an overwhelming majority. Why do they not then, in fact, rule the land? Because, and only because, they are too ignorant. And thus they sink into comparative insignificance: and suffer themselves to be used as the mere instruments of creating their own masters, who care as little for their real welfare as if they were born to be beasts of burden. Were it possible, I would visit every farmer in Tennessee, who is not already awake, and endeavour to arouse him from his fatal lethargy, by every consideration which can render life and liberty desirable; and urge him to reclaim his abandoned rights and his lost dignity, by giving to his sons that measure of instruction which will qualify them to assert and to maintain their just superiority in the councils of the State and of the Nation, like men proudly conscious of their intellectual as well as physical power.

The same general remarks apply to mechanics and to all the labouring classes, in proportion to their numbers. An education, even of the highest order, may be as valuable to them as to others. In our free country, a farmer or mechanic, with equal talents and intelligence, would be more likely to become a popular favourite, than either a lawyer or the well-bred heir of an opulent patrician family. Suppose a farmer could speak as well, write as well, appear as well versed in history, geography, statistics, jurisprudence, politics, and other matters of general and local interest, as the lawyer—would he not stand a better chance of being elevated to the highest, most honourable, and most lucrative offices?

The grand heresy on the subject of education seems to have arisen from the usage which obtained at an early period in modern European society, and which many centuries have sanctioned and confirmed—namely: that a learned or liberal education was and is deemed important only for a liberal profession, or for gentlemen of wealth and leisure. Hence the church, the bar, and the medical art have nearly monopolized the learning of the world. Our people reason and act in accordance with the same absurd and aristocratic system. The *cui bono* is upon every tongue. "What *good*, it is asked, will college learning do my son? He is to be a farmer, a mechanic, a merchant." Now, I would answer such a question, in the first place, directly, thus: "A college education, or the best, most thorough and most extensive education that can be acquired, will be of immense benefit to your son, simply as a farmer, mechanic, merchant, manufacturer, sailor or soldier." And I would patiently endeavour to show him how, and in what respects; but I will not attempt to illustrate such truisms at present. But, in the second place, I would reply to my plain friend's interrogatory, thus: "Educate your son in the best manner possible, because you expect him to be a MAN, and not a *horse* or an *ox*. You cannot tell what good he may achieve, or what important offices he may discharge in his day. For aught you know, he may, if you do your duty by him, become the

President of the United States. At any rate, he has reason and understanding, which ought to be cultivated for their own sake. Should he eventually live in the most humble retirement, and subsist by the hardest manual labour, still he may enjoy an occasional intellectual feast of the purest and most exhilarating kind." If all our labouring fellow-citizens could relish books and should have access to them, what a boundless field of innocent recreation and profitable entertainment would not be always at hand and within their reach? What a flood of cheering light and happiness would not be shed upon the dark path, and poured into the bitter cup, of millions of rational immortal beings; who, at present, rank but little above the brute in their pursuits, habits and enjoyments?

In reference to elementary education, a parent ought never to inqure what his child is to be—whether a farmer or a lawyer—but should educate him in the best manner practicable, and endeavour to inspire him with sentiments of virtue and independence, which would preserve him from the vulgar pride of being ashamed to earn his living by honest industry. Besides, learning is itself a treasure—an estate—of which no adverse fortune can ever deprive its possessor. It will accompany, and console, and support him to the world's end, and to the close of life.

Our farmers and labouring classes have as much leisure for miscellaneous reading and study as the professional—or even as the wealthy or fashionable *idlers* who do nothing. Paradoxical as this may seem, it is notoriously the fact. Even in England, where this leisure is not half so great as the poorest of our people habitually enjoy, it has been discovered that the most ignorant and debased and hard-worked manufacturing operatives have abundant time for much intellectual cultivation.

Poverty, indeed, in a strict sense, is not necessarily the lot of any American. It is true, we hear a great deal about the poor: and one might infer from newspaper essays and demagogue speeches, that the poor were, or ought to be, the only objects of legislative care and public sympathy.—That they were a numerous, oppressed, unfortunate race, and that the rich were their natural and worst enemies. Hence the unceasing clamour and declamation against the rich from certain quarters—as if every man who gets wealth must of necessity grind the poor, and prosper at their expense. Whereas, there are no poor, that is, no poor classes—no serfs or villains—no degraded *caste* of paupers, except the slaves, in all our happy country. Our Constitution and laws secure to every man the fruits of his own industry and talents. Our rich men have all been poor. What was the condition of the rich men of Tennessee, ten, twenty, thirty or forty years ago? Have they not all, or nearly all, risen from the humbler conditions of life—and many from the lowest poverty? And are they *therefore* unworthy or dangerous citizens? Do they not deserve well of the *State* for having thus meliorated their own condition and added to its wealth, prosperity and reputation? Are they now to be regarded with envy, jealousy, and suspicion, after having given such decisive proof of superior industry, economy, perseverance, enterprise or sagacity? What would have been the present aspect of Tennessee if every man had remained in his primitive poverty? Or how could the poor be benefited if the rich were suddenly stripped of all their possessions? Where is it that the poor man fares best and prospers most? Is it among the rich or the indigent?

On the other hand, are not the abject, incorrigible poor always idle, vicious, intemperate, reckless—and therefore an incumbrance and a burden to the community? Show me a poor man, in the enjoyment of health, who never seeks to improve his condition, and I will show you a man fit or fitting for the penitentiary or the gallows. Your thrifty, prudent, money-making people are universally the best members of society. To all general rules there will be exceptions. I do not mean to assert that every wretchedly poor man is a criminal. He may be unfortunate, and a just object of charity. A rich man, too, may be a knave, and a petty tyrant. I beg to be understood as speaking generally on this subject, and in reference to the great body of the people. As society advances in a new country, the distance between those who have amassed fortunes and those who are born poor or who remain stationary in their original poverty, becomes more marked and striking. And the poor seem, or rather fancy themselves, fixed in their humble condition, and are often in despair of any amelioration. What can be done for them? I will tell you.

Give them an education. Provide for them the means of instruction to as great an extent and amount as possible. A well educated poor youth will always rise to honourable distinction. One successful instance will stimulate others to try the same course. And thus a spirit of emulation—an ambition to excel—will be diffused throughout the ranks of our poor fellow-citizens, which will speedily elevate them to a respectable standing, and qualify them to reach the highest posts of honour and fortune. This is a matter of every day occurrence in the Eastern and Middle States. There, the labouring farmer or mechanic, who would be thought a very poor man in Tennessee, and who labours more intensely than a Tennessee slave, strives by every effort and sacrifice to procure for one or more of his sons a liberal education. The son, thus educated, as soon as he leaves college, is able to provide for himself, by teaching school perhaps, until he studies a profession—assists in educating his younger brothers—and, by and by, appears among the distinguished lawyers, physicians, divines, professors, legislators or judges of his country. The good old father and mother are then amply rewarded for all their toils and self-denial, by a grateful, honourable and affluent posterity; who cause their sun to set in peace, and their gray hairs to descend with joy and hope to the grave.

I have witnessed hundreds of such cases. Now nothing of this kind could take place were it not for the well endowed colleges with which that portion of our country is favoured. Colleges are there, as they will be everywhere, the genuine levellers of all distinctions created by mere wealth. They open their doors wide, and dispense their honours to merit, whether in the garb of penury or affluence. And real merit will presently find or *create* a path to just pre-eminence. The poor man's son, who knows that he must live by his wits, often outstrips, in the same career, the rich man's son—because the latter trusts to his expected patrimony, and therefore despises labour and exertion. Visit any Eastern college, and you will find nearly all the industrious successful students belonging to the middling and poorer classes. Look again at the thousands who are reputably practising the learned professions, and you will be told that they have nobly risen from the humblest walks of life. They were once your poor, (perhaps despised,) studious college lads, who had no money to spend in the mad frolics and ruinous dissipation, in which the sons of fortune and family sought notoriety and academic *renown;* but who have long since dwindled into comparative insignificance, or sunk into a premature grave.

How absurd then to depreciate and denounce colleges as being hostile to the poor or beneficial only to the rich. The truth is, the rich always build, endow and sustain them, while the comparatively poor reap the principal advantage. Were our opulent citizens desirous to erect themselves into a distinct and superior *order*—a moneyed aristocracy—they could not devise a surer method of compassing so foul a design, than by discouraging and frowning upon every scheme for the dissemination of knowledge. Let them put down or prevent the establishment and growth of the higher seminaries—of colleges and universities—and they might then monopolize all the intelligence and power of the State; because they could easily educate their own sons abroad at any expense, and thus fit them for the learned professions and for all the higher offices of the Republic. Will the people tamely submit to so gross a usurpation, and suffer themselves to be cozened out of their dearest birthright and most valuable privileges?

There are, we will suppose, five thousand rich, or comparatively rich families, more or less, in Tennessee, who are able and willing to give their sons a liberal education somewhere. Shall they be induced or required to establish seminaries of the proper character, at their own expense, here at home, and for their own accommodation? Or shall they be discouraged or prevented from doing this; and thus be tempted or constrained to send their sons to Massachusetts, Connecticut or New York, and to pay those States an annual tribute of several hundred thousand dollars? Would not our poor labouring people be directly and greatly benefited by the expenditure of this money among ourselves?

How *could* the poor, let me ask, in any possible way, be injured or oppressed? They are not expected to advance a farthing of the funds. What they have not, they cannot give. The State could not extort from them, in the shape of taxes, what they do not possess. The poor then, and all their noisy pretended friends may hold their peace, and quiet their patriotic alarms on this subject. They may rest assured that their *empty* purse will not be made the *lighter* by any literary scheme which may be projected. Colleges have always been reared by the rich; and, no doubt, for the selfish purpose of serving their own interests—while universal experience demonstrates that the poor, after all, reap the benefits in a ten-fold proportion. This is true, to a considerable extent, even in England—still more in Scotland and Germany—and most of all in the portions of our own country where such institutions exist. Such will be the result here. Even our own University, embarrassed as it has ever been for want of means, has already educated several indigent youths *gratis*. And this is more than is ever done at the Eastern seminaries. For there the poor must pay as well as the rich—except such as are supported by some charitable fund or association. But *there* an education is esteemed a fortune. And the father who can struggle along so as to carry his son through college, is content to leave him to his own exertions without further care or provision. Let the *rich* then, from whatever motive, build up and endow colleges; and spend their money at home. We shall soon see how the poor will contrive to avail themselves of the advantages thus presented to their view and within their reach.

But again, between the rich and the poor, there is in the community another class of citizens, vastly larger than both of them put together—namely, the middling class, and the best class—all of whom might educate one or more sons at college, at an expense of from fifty to a hundred and fifty dollars per year, who could never send their sons abroad at an expense of from five hundred to a thousand a year. Will the State do nothing for this large and respectable body of her citizens? Will the people themselves continue blind and deaf to the soundest principles of policy, to the loudest calls of duty, and to the most sacred claims of posterity? The merest trifle contributed by each would place advantages within the reach of the whole, which no individual could otherwise possibly command. Let it be remembered, moreover, that the rich or their children may become poor—that the poor may become rich—that the intermediate class may change places with both or either—and consequently that the permanent interests of all must be identical.

In this connexion, I may further remark, that government can always make provision, if it please, for the gratuitous instruction of the poor at any college under its control, or of which it may choose to become the benefactor. Suppose the professors were paid from the public treasury, upon the express condition, that all indigent youths, suitably qualified, should be taught without charge; and that fees should be demandable only from the rich, or from those able to pay. Such an arrangement would be equitable, benevolent, and beneficial to all the parties concerned. Should our worthy, enlightened and patriotic legislature see fit, in their wisdom, to vote a permanent annuity to the colleges at Knoxville and Nashville, sufficient to maintain the whole or a part of their instructors, upon condition that the poor meritorious youth of Tennessee, after having passed reputably through the inferior schools, should be privileged to complete their studies at those institutions free of expense—they would confer a favour on the cause of learning and upon the commonwealth, the value of which would augment with the lapse of ages: and posterity would revert to this as the brightest and most auspicious epoch in their history.

In this way too, the State would soon be supplied with accomplished schoolmasters. For, be it known and remembered, that nowhere on earth does there exist a good and efficient system of common schools, except where colleges and universities are most generously cherished; and where the largest number of poor youths are found among their *alumni*. These become teachers of necessity. This is matter of fact—of universal experience—and the most ingenious special pleader in behalf of popular education cannot cite an exception to the rule. The truth is, the cause of colleges and of schools of all sorts is one and indivisible. And he who should attempt to establish *good* common schools without colleges, would be compelled to import a monthly cargo of foreign teachers, or stand before the public a convicted Utopian visionary.

Men of talents and of adequate literary qualifications will never become teachers of choice, except where the profession is both lucrative and honourable. No occupation is deemed more vexatious, and none is so utterly thankless. But men will teach school rather than starve: and when our colleges shall send forth their *poor* graduates who must immediately do something for a livelihood, they will of course be willing to teach. They will look out for academies or classical schools in the first instance:—and here they may train many perhaps, poor like themselves, who will teach common schools. Thus, in time, the market will be supplied. All the schools will co-operate in the production of this supply. They will mutually aid and sustain each other. The most gifted and enterprising lads in the lowest schools will contrive, no matter how poor, to advance to the higher; and eventually by the beneficence of the State as already proposed, they will gain admission into the college. And thus the whole intellectual machinery will be fairly at work; and, by the State purse, may be duly kept in operation forever. It will not then be necessary to send our governors over half the continent in search of civil engineers whenever a turnpike road is to be formed or a canal to be dug—nor our agents all over New England in quest of academical instructors whenever a college or high school for boys or girls is to be established—nor to depend on the East for our lawyers, physicians, divines, statesmen, judges, editors, bank-clerks, musicians, *genteel* beggars, and castle-builders of every name and degree. Some of these we shall then have the sense to do without, and the others we shall manufacture at home—and thus save both our cash and our credit.

Some very obvious truths need to be often inculcated and reiterated, before they obtain a general currency, or produce any practical effects. The people will decide correctly about their own interests when fully instructed. And in regard to schools and colleges, they would long since have pronounced an enlightened judgment, had half the pains been taken to inform, which have been employed to blind, prejudice and mislead them. Should the orthodox advocates of education succeed, in their frequent attempts, in sundry ways, in gaining a few disciples to the true faith, some progress will of course be made in the work of general conversion. I think it would be easy to convince any honest man, learned or unlearned, rich or poor, of the truth, sound policy, and radical importance of all the positions usually assumed on this subject. And I cherish the hope that all college graduates (always excepting *pro tempore* renegade candidates upon the *stump*,) will be the staunch, resolute, intrepid, zealous friends of the college cause, and of their own *Alma Mater* in particular. That they will be friendly to common schools—to the universal diffusion of knowledge among the people—is a matter of course. For who ever heard of a liberally educated man who was not the hearty devoted supporter of every judicious common school system? Such an anomaly our country has not yet produced. Our most illustrious patriots and sages have been the founders of colleges, and apostles in the cause of universal education.

It is no uncommon thing, in our country, for men of considerable influence to boast that they have never seen the inside of a college—that, like Franklin and Washington, they have advanced in knowledge and reputation by their own unassisted efforts; and consequently, that colleges are good for nothing, or at best fitted only for the training of drones and blockheads. Now, besides the extreme modesty of recording their own names upon the same tablets with Franklin and Washington, they might be reminded that those truly great men never uttered such a boast, and never decried such institutions. Franklin was the father of the University of Pennsylvania, and Washington endowed a college in his native State. No man, therefore, will ever give any very convincing evidence that he resembles Franklin or Washington, by a supercilious affectation of contempt for colleges, or by a narrow, invidious, systematic, malignant hostility towards them.

We are exceedingly prone to boast of our own country as the most enlightened, free and virtuous in the world. The English entertain the same fancy in regard to their country. Both probably are, in some respects, greatly mistaken. More persons can be found in England, and in several of our States, who cannot read and write, than in many of the kingdoms on the continent of Europe. A well instructed people cannot be enslaved, be the nominal form of their government what it may. A grossly ignorant people will be slaves, even under the purest republican system. A man who will sell his vote for money or grog, or who can be wheedled out of it by the arts or eloquence of the demagogue, is not a freeman. And there are thousands of such persons in England and in America. These are, to all intents and purposes, bondmen—the mere pliant tools and instruments of crafty and aspiring Catilines and Mirabeaus—and would assist in placing them on a throne, just as readily as in elevating them to the humblest post of power and distinction. Let a large majority of our people become thus ignorant and degraded—and the most desperate and daring adventurer, or the most obsequious pander to the popular humour, will assume the imperial purple, and laugh to scorn all our simple constitutional paper guards and checks and rights and liberties.

In Scotland, Holland, Denmark, Sweden, Prussia, several of the Swiss Cantons, and Germany generally, there are more universities, athenæa, gymnasia, lyceums, higher, intermediate and common schools, proportionally, than in any other region of the globe—except New England and New York. In them it is rare to meet with an individual who cannot read and write: and it is equally rare to meet with a pauper or a criminal. The mass of the people are represented, by all impartial travellers, as being more intelligent, virtuous, privileged and happy than any other population in Europe. The lower orders, especially in some of the smaller German States, are regarded as among the most favoured in the world. Several Americans of distinguished talents and learning, who have resided for years in those countries, testify to the same general fact. One, with whom I am well acquainted, who recently spent two years at Berlin, declares that he never met even a poor boy selling matches in the streets of that royal metropolis, (and he made repeated experiments of the kind,) who could not read, and readily answer any common question on the historical parts of the Old and New Testaments—so thorough and universal is the common school system in that kingdom. Even in Austria, despotic as is the government, there are schools in every village, the masters of which are paid from the imperial treasury. "No one is allowed to marry who cannot read, write, and show some acquaintance with arithmetic. And, under a heavy penalty, no master can employ a common workman who is not able to read and write. Small works on moral subjects, written with great care, are circulated among the lower classes. Hence crimes are extremely rare; and in the course of a twelvemonth scarcely two executions take place even at Vienna"—with a population half as large as that of Tennessee, and with a most vigilant and energetic police, which never suffers a criminal to escape the legal penalty.

In the above named kingdoms, provision is made by law for the competent instruction of all the poor children of both sexes without exception. In several of them also, seminaries are established for the sole purpose of educating teachers. Hence the body of the common people are vastly superior to the same classes in every other part of Europe where the government has not interposed in their behalf. Now, if the peasantry, the labouring and poorer orders, are found to be intelligent, moral, temperate, frugal, industrious, contented and cheerful—with no haughty, feudal, baronial lords to harass, molest or oppress them, as in Russia and Poland —assured that they are exposed to neither extortion, robbery nor murder—that the strong arm of power is ever at hand, not to injure or distress, but to shield and defend them from injustice, danger and violence—protected, in short, in the secure enjoyment of all their natural *civil* rights, even though, like the clergy in Tennessee, they may be destitute of every *political* franchise —we cannot pronounce their condition so very deplorable as to be without a parallel in countries presumed to be much more highly favoured. For example—English travellers themselves seldom fail to point out the striking contrast which a happy, joyous, peaceful assemblage of German cotters on the village green, dancing to the music of their own favourite flute and violin, presents to the ignorant, boisterous, swaggering, drunken, fighting, venal mob, which they oftentimes encounter at home at the hustings, the race-course, the stated fairs, and other occasions of popular meetings and amusements. It is just possible too, that *we* might have reason to blush were a similar comparison instituted in relation to the same matters. Even the periodical celebrations of our national independence are not always characterized by the most musical concords or fraternal harmony. Our election days, moreover, are not universally the brightest and happiest among the *dies festi* of the calendar. Perhaps letters or music, or both combined, might exert a salutary and humanizing influence, auspicious both to our comfort and to our reputation. Let us make the trial.

If education can effect such marvels in countries where the people have little or no agency in their own government, what might it not achieve in a Republic where every man constitutes an integral part of the sovereignty? Were the Russian and Polish serfs as well instructed as the German peasants, could they be retained in a state of vassalage — *adscripti glebæ* — scarcely preferable to the worst species of West India servitude? But the schoolmaster has not yet been abroad among the millions, even in the chivalrous but ill-starred land of our own illustrious Pulaski and Kosciusko. It matters little, therefore, to the Polish boor whether his master's master be Muscovite, Austrian, Prussian, or native. His own lot changes not with the change of rulers. He has nothing to gain or lose in any political revolution—except that, in every conflict, his own blood may be shed, and his miseries and life be terminated together.

In poor old Scotland, there are four ancient respectable universities, with the character of which every body is acquainted. These furnish teachers to her excellent parochial schools.

In the Netherlands there are six universities. Their several incomes, during the year 1828, were as follows: Louvain, $48,000. — Liege, $28,000. — Ghent, $28,000. — Leyden, $32,000. — Utrecht, $28,000. — Groningen, $28,000. Each has a large Library, a Botanic Garden, a Cabinet of Natural History, a Chemical Laboratory, a Hospital, an Anatomical Museum, and a Hall for Dissections.

In Germany, there are twenty-two (once, forty) flourishing universities—having each from thirty to ninety distinguished professors and instructors—with immense libraries and every other useful and desirable appendage. To several of these, American graduates have often resorted to complete their education. In the twenty-two institutions just referred to, there were, in 1825, no less than 1059 instructors, nearly all of whom had once been poor youths—and 16,432 students, more than half said to be poor and destined to become schoolmasters.

In France, the system of education for the higher and middling classes, has been recently pronounced the best in the world, by impartial and enlightened judges, both British and American. And the most efficient measures are taking by the government to instruct the lower classes—which have hitherto been deplorably neglected.

This mere glance at a portion of the old world and of our own Eastern States, may suffice to teach us our inferiority in every gradation and department of education. —That neither our poor nor our rich people are equally privileged in this respect—that the cause of universities and common schools is identical—that they prosper together or not at all—at least, that the latter never *have* flourished where the former were overlooked.

I feel no disposition to undervalue my country, or her institutions, whether political or literary. But I do think it time to have done with that puerile vanity which leads to incessant boasting and self-laudation—as if perfection were stamped upon everything American. While we cherish this arrogant, supercilious, overweening, self-sufficient spirit, we shall never seek nor desire improvement—because we fancy that the very acme of human excellence has been attained. The first step towards any ameliorating process is a consciousness of our need of it. Let us dare to look at what is wrong, vicious, defective, pernicious—at the very worst of our case—and then intrepidly apply ourselves to the remedy, to the work of correction and reform, with steady perseverance, and resolute determination to exterminate evil, and to advance the cause of truth, virtue, knowledge, freedom and happiness among all the people throughout our land.

The grand inquiry of the present enterprising and philanthropic age is—how shall the human race be made better, wiser, happier? Governments are beginning to manifest a deep interest in this momentous theme. Statesmen, as well as philosophers, are studying and devising the ways and means to ameliorate the character and condition of the great mass of the people. All agree that *education* is the instrument to be employed in the work; however much they may differ as to the kind or degree adapted to the purpose.

Poverty, oppression, crime, are the great *evils* to be eradicated or diminished. We have shown how the two first will disappear under the magic influence of the talented and faithful schoolmaster. And no truth or principle has, perhaps, been more universally admitted by men competent to judge, than that education is the most effectual, if not the only preventive of crime. Education, I mean, physical, moral, intellectual, religious: Which trains youth to habits of industry and morality, as well as to mental effort and discipline: Which instructs them in some useful and honest occupation to live by, as well as imbues their minds with virtuous principles, a taste for knowledge and a thirst for continued improvement.

Our legislatures, in several of the States, are already acting upon this principle: although they seem, in some instances, to have begun at the wrong end, and with the most unpromising and undeserving materials. They have established, or are establishing penitentiaries for the very laudable purpose, as they doubtless believe, of *reforming* lazy, vicious, ignorant, hardened felons—by adopting precisely the system which would have preserved them from *crime* and *infamy*, had it been resorted to at an earlier period. That is, in these expensive, commodious, well regulated penitentiaries, or rather universities, the convicts are most thoroughly *educated*. They are taught useful and lucrative trades, so that they can, *if they will*, in due time, earn an *honest* livelihood. They learn to read, write and cipher—and often acquire other branches of science and literature according to their diligence and ability. They also receive moral and religious instruction—study the Bible—commit to memory its salutary truths and precepts—and have the gospel statedly preached to them by pious and devoted chaplains. They are kept from all vitiating associations among themselves—are lodged in solitary cells at night—are prohibited the use of inebriating liquors altogether, however intemperate they may have previously been: in short, they are most thoroughly guarded, watched, employed, disciplined, instructed, secluded from every temptation to vice, and cut off from all opportunity of indulgence. So that, at the period of *graduation*, they issue from these great *State Schools* better qualified for active, useful and respectable life than the mass of the *common* people generally in this country. Whether they actually become virtuous, useful and respectable, is another matter. Such, however, is the end aimed at by the system.

Thus, then, the State incurs the enormous expense of making provision for the most complete and appropriate, if not the most *liberal* education of its rogues and vagabonds, while it oftentimes wholly neglects its unoffending and unbefriended children and youth—who are growing up in ignorance and vice—and who will not be recognized as worthy of its fostering smiles and cares and patronage, until after they shall have been condemned as malefactors! And then they are admitted *gratis* into the colleges and universities which the State most delights to honour and to cherish. The *new* penitentiaries in Connecticut and New York are excellent models for literary institutions—and *mutatis mutandis*, among the very best with which I am acquainted. If all the schools in our country, small and great, were made, as far as practicable, in their principal features, to resemble them, I should have no fear of their complete success in training up a generation to which crime and pauperism would be comparatively unknown.

Give to the colleges at Nashville and Knoxville an

organization similar to the Auburn Prison—so far, I mean, as regards the safe keeping, moral discipline, healthful exercise and constant employment of their inmates, and their absolute occlusion from all external evil influences—and bestow upon each of them only a moiety of the sum which Pennsylvania has already expended upon the outer yard walls of but one of her incipient penitentiaries—(said walls have cost $200,000,) —and they shall render the State more service in twenty years, than all the prisons of Pennsylvania will achieve in a thousand ages, or than a score of penitentiaries would effect in Tennessee to the end of time. And yet, probably, before the lapse of fifty years, half a million of dollars will be expended, and with the best intentions too, by this State, agreeably to the prevailing fashion, upon such establishments, for the comfortable accommodation of a few hundred criminals, who have forfeited all claim to public indulgence, and certainly to the public purse. Who deserve to be punished, not rewarded. And whose punishment ought not, at the same time, to *punish* an innocent community by its expensiveness. Criminals ought always, as a matter of equity and policy, to be dealt with in a way that would occasion the least possible expense to the people. In our country, on the other hand, the wit of man has been exercised to devise the most expensive mode. Criminals too have become the objects of universal sympathy: and *reformation* is all the rage. As if reformation were the only end in view in subjecting criminals to the penalty of violated laws.

Reformation is very desirable—but this is, by no means, the sole or primary end of punishment. But if it were, penitentiaries are not likely to effect it. And if they could, the people ought not to be saddled with the expense. All that class of offenders, who would be sentenced to a penitentiary, ought to be banished forever from the State and from the United States—or transported to some Botany Bay. Two objects, at least, would be gained by the latter course. The State would be freed from the burden of maintaining them, and from all danger of further annoyance or injury by their example or misconduct. And possibly a third advantage would accrue to the culprits themselves—namely, their eventual reformation. This is the only reformatory process which experience has as yet fully tested—and this *has* succeeded. Thousands of *Old Bailey* convicts have become good citizens in America, South Africa, and New Holland—who certainly would have been hanged in a year, had they remained at large in England. I am aware of the objections to banishment or deportation as a mode of punishment to be adopted in our country, either by any single State or by all the States in concert; but I am confident that they can be easily and thoroughly obviated. For example—Constitutional difficulties could be removed in a constitutional way—by the power that formed the Constitution. And all the States might agree in adopting a uniform system on the subject.

I imagine our people have very little idea of the expense of prisons, or they would not be so enamoured of them. In point of expense, colleges are as nothing in the comparison—a mere drop to the ocean. If we could ascertain the entire amount of money expended in the erection and maintenance of prisons of all sorts, and for the arrest, conviction and support of their inmates, throughout the United States, during the last fifty years, no argument or commentary would be necessary on the subject. It has been estimated that the annual pecuniary loss to the people of the United States by *crime* is not less than from eight to ten millions of dollars. The several annual reports of the Prison Discipline Society have shed a flood of light on this dark subject—have exhibited facts and details in regard to expenditures, connected with defective or pernicious systems of management and police, of the most astounding and appalling character. I have neither time nor space for quotations. In general, it may be remarked, that our prisons yield no adequate return to the community—that they have little or no tendency to diminish crime, or to benefit either the criminal or the public—that most of them are abominable nuisances and mere sinks of iniquity and corruption, without a single commendable feature or redeeming quality—that it is even doubtful whether the best of them can, during any series of ten or twenty years, defray their own current expenses by the labour of the convicts, especially if the cost of the original outfit and all incidental charges be fairly taken into the account—and that the ultimate reformation of the criminal must be regarded as the mere day-dream of credulous philanthropy.

It is true that uncommonly favourable localities for certain kinds of profitable labour—chiefly in granite and marble—in large cities or upon navigable waters—have given extraordinary advantages to two or three Eastern penitentiaries: and their directors have reported a considerable excess of proceeds above the annual expenses. Whether the interest of the outlay was included in the items of expenditure does not appear. It is presumed not.

If any method has been or can be devised by which criminals may be made, not only to maintain themselves, but to contribute something to the public funds by their labour, it certainly would be wise and politic thus to employ them, and thereby compel them to render substantial satisfaction for the injuries which they have perpetrated. But society is under no legal or moral obligation to burden itself with their gratuitous support. This would be in effect to punish the innocent in order to spare the guilty. Could the public, however, be really profited by the labour of convicts, there would be no inducement, on the score of expense merely, either to hang or transport them. Even the murderer would be as effectually dead to the world, if immured for life at hard labour, as if he had been actually executed—while some remuneration might be gained from his industry.

Still, the idea of reforming notorious criminals in a penitentiary, and of turning them loose again in the same community where they are well known, with a mark of infamy upon their foreheads, and the consciousness of it in their hearts, does seem chimerical and visionary in the extreme. If such unhappy and disgraced offenders are ever again to assume the character and dignity and feelings of men, it must be in a strange country and among new associates; or among companions of their own *caste*, where none would have the right or the effrontery to upbraid or to contemn his fellow. It is true, some fifty or sixty individuals, who have left the Auburn Prison, are reported as *reformed*. But time sufficient to test the fact has not yet elapsed. Besides, most of them are stated to have become religious. If so, their reformation was owing to the chaplain, to the Bible, to religious instruction, and not exclusively to the prison discipline — unless religious instruction be a prominent part of it. That religion may effect such a change will not be doubted; because it inculcates and inspires genuine humility. That kind of humility which disposes a guilty man to submit, without a murmur, to any obloquy, neglect, indignity or scorn to which he may be obnoxious. But without such an influence, I question whether it be in human nature, that a man should issue from his prison cell, and take his place in society as an honest, orderly, respectable citizen. Who would regard or treat him as honest and respectable—or employ and trust him as such?

If, after all, however, in reference to this momentous subject, there be no alternative but a choice of evils—if we *must* choose among the existing systems of prison discipline—I do not hesitate to pronounce the penitentiary system, as it is now in operation in New York and Connecticut, vastly preferable to every other which has been tried; while the common county jail system is the very worst in our country. What that of Pennsylvania will prove to be, future experiment must decide.

My object in adverting to this apparently not very relevant, and certainly not the most grateful topic, was:

1. To notice the fact, that *education* is the only instrument relied on by our statesmen, politicians and sages for any salutary revolution in the character and habits of all classes and ages of criminals in our most approved penitentiaries and houses of refuge. And hence *a fortiori* to deduce the value and importance of the very same instrument in preventing crime, by suitably educating the young, that they may grow up honest, industrious, intelligent and virtuous citizens.

2. To show that the expense of training up the young is vastly less than must be incurred by the support of a few adult criminals, as our prisons generally have hitherto been constructed and managed. And that a State had better expend its treasures upon her innocent offspring than to be at unreasonable pains or expense about incorrigible, hopeless, worthless offenders.

3. To direct attention to a few of our best regulated penitentiaries as models for schools and colleges. From my own humble experience in the business of education, and from all the information which I have been able to procure on the subject, I do believe that the only efficient system for the complete attainment of every desirable end, is *that* which keeps youth constantly em-

ployed, body and mind, and which exercises unceasing vigilance and absolute control day and night—which excludes all vicious and vitiating associates and practices—which superintends all the amusements and social intercourse of the pupils—and which consequently requires strong walls and numerous guards; or a large body of faithful, prudent, devoted *Mentors* to counsel, direct, restrain and instruct them at all times, in all places, and under all circumstances.

Such a purely *domestic* system I never expect to see in practical operation—at least, not to the extent most likely to insure the happiest results. The expense would be objected to by a people who can afford money for every fashionable folly and extravagance. And its strictness, however parental and salutary, would be complained of by a people who scarcely subject their children to any restraint whatever. We must do the best we can then in the circumstances in which our lot is cast. I am not the advocate of existing usages because of their antiquity or authority. Nor am I fond of innovations merely for the sake of novelty and experiment. I am disposed to be reasonable in all things, and to make the best of a bad or indifferent system. Colleges and Universities have never been perfect, nor as good as they might and ought to have been. The same may be said of common schools, and of the higher schools. They may all be greatly improved, even without any remarkable or radical change in their organization. Their character and utility must depend on the personal qualifications, fidelity and efforts of their instructors and directors, more than on any or all other circumstances. A college, of the old sort, may be beneficial or noxious to the community, according as it is judiciously or injudiciously managed. And since, in our country, the supreme and absolute control of such institutions is usually committed to a Board of Trustees, they of course are directly responsible to the public for their proper government and instruction.

A principal cause of the excessive multiplication and dwarfish dimensions of Western colleges is, no doubt, the diversity of religious denominations among us. Almost every sect will have its college, and generally one at least in each State. Of the score of colleges in Ohio, Kentucky and Tennessee, all are sectarian except two or three; and of course few of them are what they might and should be; and the greater part of them are mere impositions on the public. This is a grievous and growing evil. Why colleges should be sectarian, any more than penitentiaries, or than bank, road or canal corporations, is not very obvious. Colleges are designed for the instruction of youth in the learned languages—in polite literature—in the liberal arts and sciences—and not in the dogmatical theology of any sect or party. Why then should they be baptized with sectarian names? Are they to inculcate sectarian Greek, sectarian mathematics, sectarian logic, history, rhetoric, philosophy? Must every State be divided and subdivided into as many college associations as there are religious sects within its limits? And thus, by their mutual jealousy and distrust, effectually prevent the usefulness and prosperity of any one institution? Why does any sect covet the exclusive control of a college, if it be not to promote party and sectarian purposes?

I am aware that as soon as any sect succeeds in obtaining a charter for a *something* called a college, they become, all of a sudden, wondrously liberal and catholic. They forthwith proclaim to the public that their college is the best in the world—and withal, perfectly free from the odious taint of sectarianism. That youth of all religions may come to it without the slightest risk of being proselyted to the faith of the governing sect. This is very modest and very specious, and very hollow, and very hypocritical. They hold out false colours to allure and to deceive the incautious. Their college *is* sectarian, and they know it. It is established by a party—governed by a party—taught by a party—and designed to promote the ends of a party. Else why is it under the absolute and perpetual management and control of a party? They very eagerly and very naturally desire the patronage of other sects, for the double purpose of receiving pecuniary aid, and of adding to their numbers and strength from the ranks of other denominations.

Let any religious sect whatever obtain the absolute direction of a college—located in a small village or retired part of the country—where their religious influence is paramount, perhaps exclusive—where the youth must necessarily attend upon such religious instructions and exercises and ceremonies as they shall prescribe—where, in fact, they can witness no other—where every sermon and prayer and form, where all private conversation and ministerial services proceed from, or are directed by, the one sect—and, is it possible that youth, at the most susceptible period of their lives, should not be operated on by such daily influences, during a period of two, four or six years? How long will the people be gulled by such barefaced impudence —by such unreasonable and monstrous pretensions?

I do not object to any sect's being allowed the privilege of erecting and maintaining, at their own expense, as many schools, colleges and theological seminaries as they please. But, then, their sectarian views should be openly and distinctly avowed. Their purpose should be specified in their charters: and the legislature should protect the people from imposition by the very act which invests them with corporate powers. Hitherto, almost every legislature has pursued an opposite policy, and has aided the work of deception, by enacting that, in the said sectarian institution, youth of all sects should be entitled to equal privileges. Thus the sectarian manufactory goes into operation under the smiles, patronage and recommendation of the people's representatives. Its friends puff it off, and laud it as the people's school, and plead their liberal charter as the talisman that is to guard the people against every insidious attempt at proselytism; and urge the people to contribute their money to build up their promising and most catholic seminary. The bait is seized—the people are cheated —and the sect has its college. Students of all denominations frequent it. And no man of sense and reflection can doubt the consequences.

There are sects in our country who have succeeded in this way, who never permit their own children to attend any schools but such as they exclusively control, who profess the greatest liberality to the public on all occasions, and who boast among themselves of the converts which they have made from their dissenting pupils. I could specify names and places, and adduce proof positive of all the facts asserted, were it necessary. Let the people see to it, or the remedy will soon be beyond their reach.

A *public* college—that is, a literary and scientific college designed for the public generally—ought to be independent of all religious sectarian bias, or tendency, or influence. And it ought, when practicable, to be situated in a town or city where the several sects, composing the body of the people, have their own places of public worship, to which their sons may have free access; and where the public eye may be constantly fixed on the conduct of the Trustees and Faculty. And where every artful attempt at proselytism would be instantly detected and exposed. Some men are so constituted that they cannot help being partisans and bigots. Such men are not fit to be the instructors of youth, except where it is intended that the dogmas of a sect shall be inculcated.

Science and philosophy ought to know no party in Church or State. They are degraded by every such connexion. Christianity, indeed, if rightly interpreted, breathes a pure angelic charity, and is as much a stranger to the strife, and intrigue, and rancour, and intolerance, and pharisaism of party, as science and philosophy can be. But so long as men are not content to be honest Christians, but will be zealous Presbyterians, Episcopalians, Methodists, Baptists, Quakers or Romanists, we must so organize our *public* seminaries of learning, as that all may intrust their sons to them without fear of danger to their religious faith.

It has been objected to Nashville, as the site of a University for the purposes of general education:—1. That it is the centre of too much dissipation, extravagance and vice. That a residence here might endanger the morals and virtue of youth, and lead them to ruinous indulgence and prodigality. This is a specious objection—but it is merely specious. Small towns and villages are generally more objectionable, in these respects, than cities containing from five to fifty thousand inhabitants. Experience has fully proved in Europe, and in the older States of this Union, that large towns or cities are greatly preferable to small ones for such institutions. All the capitals and most of the second-rate cities of Europe have their universities. And wherever they have been established in small towns, the students are proverbially more riotous and ungovernable in their conduct, more boorish and savage in their manners, and more dissolute and licentious in their habits.

A large town, moreover, always affords greater advantages and facilities for the acquisition of liberal knowledge than a small village. It has, comparatively, more literary and scientific men—more individuals skilled in various languages—more eminent professional characters—larger libraries—more ample cabinets and collections of natural curiosities and specimens of the arts—a more enlightened and refined society to polish and restrain youth from vulgar practices and indulgences—a greater variety of churches and other religious institutions to enlarge the mind and prevent the growth of bigotry and sectarism—and, in general, a more powerful and salutary moral influence is exerted and felt than in a small provincial town or country village. The empire of public opinion is recognized and respected. A vigilant and energetic police is ever at hand also to check the sallies and control the *renowning* propensities of the thoughtless, the turbulent, the idle, the reckless and the self-sufficient.

These and similar privileges an enlightened judicious parent will not fail to appreciate. And in all these respects, Nashville will be every year improving. It has greatly improved within the last eight or ten years, as every citizen, who has resided here long enough to judge, will testify. I *know* that, in Nashville, unpropitious as have been certain local and temporary circumstances, youth may be trained as safely and governed as thoroughly as in any town beyond the mountains. Youth often enter college *spoiled:* and the Faculty cannot cure or reform them. But, in no instance yet, has a virtuous, orderly, well-behaved youth been made *worse* at our institution. If they come to the University, with inveterate habits of idleness, vice or insubordination, nothing more can be expected of its government than that it speedily get rid of them. And this it has seldom—without fear, partiality or favour—failed to accomplish. The *good* have not been injured; nor are they a whit more obnoxious to evil influences *here* than in any town in Connecticut or New York. The *wicked*, if they cannot be reclaimed, are, as a matter of course, presently sent home to their parents and friends.

The good people of the Southern States generally, labour under a singular delusion in regard to the benefits which their sons are supposed to enjoy at Eastern seminaries. They have heard much of the steady habits, excellent morals, and religious character of the East; and they presume that their sons, while there, will be precluded from all exposure to vicious temptation. This is a most egregious mistake. The Southern youth, at Eastern colleges, are more exposed to all manner of expensive and ruinous dissipation than they would be at home. They invariably associate together—are always presumed to have plenty of money—are solicited from every quarter to spend it freely—are trusted without hesitation to any amount by those most interested in misleading and in fleecing them—are courted and flattered, and made to believe that they are superior to the natives, whose manners, customs and maxims they affect to despise—are actuated and bound to each other by the lofty and fastidious spirit of provincial clanship, and manifest, to a most ludicrous extent, all the pride and arrogance of aristocratic exclusiveness. Residing among strangers with whom they are never domesticated, and whose peculiarities they are accustomed to ridicule—far removed from the observation and controlling influence of that society to whose tribunal alone they feel ultimately amenable—they assume the port and bearing of independent lordlings and honourable regulators of both town and college—and, provided they manage to escape imprisonment and expulsion, they care not a rush about minor considerations or temporary consequences. In due time, after squandering, in this hopeful career, some two or three thousand dollars each per annum, they usually succeed in obtaining—what would seem to have been the sole object of their *literary* ambition—a Bachelor's diploma, certifying to the world that they are accomplished in all the liberal arts and sciences, and "adorned with every virtue under heaven." With this precious trophy of their academic achievements, they return home to gladden the hearts of doting parents, and to receive the gratulations of kindred and friends—but with heads as empty as their purses—and oftentimes with broken constitutions and dissolute habits which totally unfit them for any useful vocation or honourable profession.

This is no exaggerated representation. That there are exceptions, is readily granted. But, like the great prizes in a lottery, they are so few in comparison with the blanks, that nice calculators, who are skilled in the doctrine of chances, would not choose to hazard much upon the issue in either case. On the contrary, at Nashville, no youth from any section of the slave-holding States, will ever dream that he is superior to the common law of public sentiment—that he is above the reach of disgrace from the repulsive and frowning aspect of the society in which he lives—or that his present comfort and future respectability will not depend on the opinion which the good, the wise, the intelligent and the influential may form of his talents, industry, morals and gentlemanly deportment while a college student. In the metropolis of Tennessee, every son of Tennessee will look *up* with deference to the better class of citizens as models for imitation; while at an Eastern village he might look *down* with contempt upon the whole population. And the sneer of a companion at the *Yankees* is, at any time, sufficient to efface from his mind any salutary impression from the rebukes of authority or the counsels of wisdom.

2. Nashville has been objected to on the score of expense—and with as little reason as every other. The truth is, that the cost of an education here is less by fifty and even a hundred per cent.—all advantages considered—than at any *respectable* Northern or Southern college whatever. The price of board is one dollar and seventy-five cents per week, and the other charges are not so high as at many of our female and classical schools. One hundred and twenty dollars defray the entire college bills for all purposes (including board) during the academic year of forty-two weeks. Contingent expenses of every kind must be regulated, of course, by parental discretion. The most rigid economy is recommended and encouraged, and, as far as practicable, enforced. It is obvious that all articles imported from abroad must be cheaper in a commercial emporium than at any remote town in the country. Candidates for the gospel ministry are, without distinction of sect or name, admitted to all the privileges of the university at half

the ordinary charges. Poor young men, who desire to help themselves, either by teaching in the public schools or in private families, or by labouring on the college-farm or in the workshops of our mechanics, may earn more here than at any "Manual Labour" establishment in the country. Every possible facility is given to this species of commendable but voluntary enterprise: and no manner of disgrace attaches to the individuals who thus manfully strive to educate themselves. Every product of the garden, the field and the workshop commands a ready and profitable market. If it be possible for a youth to *work* his way through college in any part of the world, he can do it *here* with equal certainty and under peculiar advantages. In salubrity also, Nashville is unrivalled: and consequently, students are rarely subjected to any extra expense for physicians or nurses on account of ill-health.*

I have chosen to dilate on these matters, trivial as some of them may appear, because they have been grossly, if not wilfully magnified and misrepresented; and to show that there is no reasonable objection to Nashville as a favoured and popular site for a great and

* Of the salubrity of Nashville—having resided here eight years (I write this note in November, 1832)—I may be allowed to speak with reasonable assurance. If there be a healthier place on the globe than Nashville, I have yet to learn where it may be found. The youth of Canada or Vermont would be as safe here as at home. No *acclimating* process is necessary to adapt any constitution to our seasons. Our town is composed of citizens from every part of Christendom. We have had students at the University from New York, New Jersey, Pennsylvania, Maryland, Virginia, Kentucky and most of the Southern States: and all have enjoyed uniform good health.

flourishing university. And also, to remind its real friends, that the difficulties hitherto encountered and still to be encountered, so far from discouraging future efforts to advance the institution, ought rather to stimulate to greater, and more efficient, and more determined exertions and sacrifices to insure its ultimate and complete success.

Lord Bacon somewhere observes, that heroic desires contribute greatly to health. If a man would succeed, let him aim at *great* things; and, by the blessing of God, he will accomplish great things.

Little or nothing has been achieved in this country, because only a *little* has been attempted. None of our citizens have aspired to *great* things, and therefore even their humble efforts have proved abortive. If we would succeed in building up a seminary deserving the name of a University, we must, at the outset, form a just conception of the immense magnitude and importance of the enterprise; and then set about the work with cool deliberate purpose and systematic skill. If the State will not furnish the means or suffer us to use the ample means originally provided by Congress, individual munificence must be relied on, as it has been in many other places: and we must persevere, as importunate beggars, until the public yield a due supply of their treasures to effect the object—even though it be obtained by the dollar from house to house. This is the way that all our benevolent associations procure their tens of thousands annually to carry on their mighty plans of universal improvement. In this way too, the various religious sects are erecting and endowing colleges in every part of our country. Let a religious body resolve to-day to establish a college anywhere; and, in a few months, you shall hear that they have some fifty or a hundred thousand dollars to commence with. And yet this is *the* land which proudly boasts of religious liberty and equal rights, and which eschews all bigotry, intolerance and persecution. Cannot liberal and enlightened men of all sects and parties unite for the purpose of rearing one institution which shall never be under the control of any sect or party?

Such is the acknowledged character—such are the pretensions and claims of our University. It is not sectarian; and hence the *partisans* of all sects stand aloof from it. They are not satisfied with neutrality, nor with equality of influence and privilege. They must have all or nothing. Such men too, often succeed, by obstinate hostility and artful misrepresentation, in gaining, at length, the entire and absolute mastery of the very institution which had been the object of their unrelenting malignant persecution. Will the guardians of the people's rights and liberties consent to witness so mortifying a result in the present instance? Will they, by neglect or covetousness, permit this truly catholic establishment, which of right belongs to the people—to all the people without distinction of sect or name—to become the engine of any party whatever?

Generous and high-minded men are never suspicious: and, unfortunately, they seldom take that prominent and active part in public affairs to which their superior talents and virtues justly entitle them. They suffer busy, meddling, intriguing, selfish spirits to operate upon the popular mind, and to control the most important enterprises and institutions in Church and State, agreeably to their own sinister and partial views. The great, the wise, the good are generally overlooked, because they have too much modesty and self-respect to obtrude themselves upon the public notice or to solicit public confidence. Hence it is that such men often pass their days in comparative obscurity: and it is only in seasons of extraordinary emergency or extreme peril that they are summoned, by the spontaneous voice of the community, to assume the station and to exert the influence for which none others are then deemed equal. They do wisely, perhaps, in keeping aloof from the political arena—from all the petty strifes and virulent controversies of the *ins* and the *outs*—where success would be no adequate reward for any moral or even personal sacrifice —when a Clodius or a Wilkes would be more likely to win the day than a Phocion or a Hampden—and while a Cincinnatus or an Aristides might indulge their rural or philosophical propensities at home to their heart's content, without fear of being forced into notoriety by the sovereign people. But why should they desert or renounce the cause of science, of education, of morals, of human happiness? May they not, without self-reproach—nay, with conscious integrity and with the noblest devotion to the public weal—stand forth the friends and advocates of learning? Here is a sphere fitted for their unostentatious and benevolent exertions.

Our schools and colleges demand their aid. Have they fortune, have they leisure, have they patriotism, have they superior intelligence, talent, philanthropy—and will they, can they, refuse to cherish and to promote the infant seminaries of youthful instruction which are struggling for existence under their eyes and at their very doors—to which their seasonable countenance and patronage would assure complete and permanent prosperity—and which, by their indifference and inaction, may be checked and impeded—and, perhaps, be blasted forever?

The crisis has now been reached, which, it may be presumed, will frighten from our ranks all the timid, irresolute and faint-hearted; but which will nerve with new vigour and energy every bold, intrepid, magnanimous spirit, and put to a decisive test the moral stamina and genuine character of every man who pretends attachment and devotion to the noblest cause which can claim his every talent and the most invincible perseverance. Should this trying crisis be successfully passed, the victory is sure—the University will rise and triumph, and diffuse joy and blessings to thousands of the present, and to millions of future generations.*

* That the purport of the foregoing discourse may not be misapprehended, it is proper to apprise the reader, that, simply as a college for undergraduates, the University of Nashville is not inferior to other American colleges. As thorough and extensive an education may be acquired here as at any similar institution whatever. The qualifications for admission into the several classes and for graduation are nowhere exceeded. The chemical laboratory, the apparatus for every branch of experimental science, and the museum of natural history are

[The candidates, having been admitted to their degrees, were addressed as follows.]

1. To you, Young Gentlemen, who have just received the first public honours of this institution, I have but a word to say. It has been my constant study and aim, in the freedom of our colloquial intercourse in the lecture room, to imbue your minds with correct sentiments on most moral and practical topics.—And especially to teach you how to investigate and reason, that you may discover truth, and, in all cases, judge for yourselves; and never yield a blind or implicit faith to the dogmata of any sage, dead or living. You have commenced a course of study which is to terminate but with your lives. Your education, so far from being completed, is only begun. Hereafter, you must be your own instructors; as all must be who hope to attain intellectual eminence. You have mastered a few elementary principles, which will enable you, by persevering industry, to advance slowly it may be, but surely, up the rugged hill-

second to none in the Eastern States. The mineralogical cabinet especially—the specimens of which Prof. Troost (a pupil of the celebrated Häuy) has been collecting from every part of the world during twenty years past—would be creditable to any European university. The college library contains two thousand volumes: and other libraries, to which the Faculty and students have access, contain seven or eight thousand more. Still, provision has been made only for undergraduates, and for these only in limited numbers. We need funds for the permanent support of twenty professors, edifices for the accommodation of five hundred students, a library of fifty thousand volumes, a botanical garden, astronomical observatory, &c.—besides the *professional* and other departments which ought to belong to a university, worthy of the resources, the population and the republican dignity of Tennessee.

side of science, till, at length, you gain honourable admittance within the portals of the fair temple itself. Never forget that you are students; and that much may be learned every day, by a skilful and orderly arrangement of your various pursuits, from men and books, and from the grand volume of nature which is everywhere spread open to your view and admiration.

2. In the next place, study to devote all your attainments and faculties to the promotion of the best interests of society, of your country, and of mankind. This must be done frequently by a difficult, tedious, and discouraging process. If you would accomplish great good in your day, you must consent to labour patiently, and to attend to a multiplicity of apparently trivial concerns. Society is often most benefited by men who can enter into minute details—who can devise, encourage and aid judicious schemes to enlighten the minds, and to meliorate the condition and morals of those around them. Therefore, never imagine any object, however humble, beneath you, if calculated to be useful to ever so small a portion of your fellow-citizens. Franklin, when, at the height of his fame, never lost sight of the poor mechanic, nor ceased to suggest plans for his improvement. It will be expected of you, as having enjoyed superior means of education, to be yourselves the friends of education, in every degree and to the greatest practicable extent. Should you ever occupy seats in the legislative halls of your country, remember that the cause of education is paramount to all others; and that if this be thoroughly provided for, it will nearly supersede the neces-

sity of all other legislation. If you shall ever be appointed trustees of a great literary institution—an office which ought to be deemed more dignified, as it is vastly more important, than any which this commonwealth can confer—promote its interests with more zeal and fidelity than you would your own; and guard its reputation with the same sensitive jealousy that you would protect the vestal honour of a sister.

3. Be temperate: and seek to promote temperance among all over whom you may have influence. Intemperance, next to ignorance, is acknowledged to be the greatest evil which afflicts our country. It is the direct cause of most of the crime, disease, pauperism and wretchedness which prevail among us. The only effectual remedy for it has, at length, been discovered. It is total and universal abstinence from spirituous liquors. The moderate and temperate use of ardent spirits has been, for years past, the occasion of all the intemperance in our land. The man who drinks *temperately* has already entered the broad road to ruin: besides, he may, by his *sober* example, make all his sons drunkards; and thus become a curse to society and to his own posterity. The time has arrived, when, in some parts of our country, no persons who have any regard either to conscience or public opinion, dare engage in the business of manufacturing, importing or vending distilled liquors in any form. And, I doubt not, that, before many years elapse, such will be the doctrine and practice throughout this and all other Christian lands. Temperance Societies have already achieved a more glorious and salutary

moral revolution, within the last five years, than any human institution or agency had ever before effected for the welfare of mankind in half a century.

4. Endeavour, by honest industry in some useful calling or profession, to render yourselves independent. Virtue depends, much more than is generally supposed, upon pecuniary independence. In our happy land, every healthy man may become thus independent in his circumstances, if he please. I do not mean that every man must acquire what is called an independent fortune. He is truly independent, who habitually lives within his income, whatever that may be, or however honestly procured or earned. In this sense, the humblest labourer may be independent. Franklin, again, is high authority; and his own practice furnishes the best possible illustration of his excellent maxims. "If a man (said he) would preserve both integrity and independence free from temptation, let him keep out of debt." The Proverbs of Solomon are full of practical wisdom on this topic, and deserve the serious study of every person just entering upon the theatre of public life. The tyranny of fashion must be manfully resisted: and all its capricious and oppressive mandates and requirements must be disregarded from the outset, by the young man who would rise, by his own efforts, to meritorious distinction in the world. Lord Thurlow, himself an illustrious example of his own rule, used to say, that the surest cause of success to a Barrister was "parts and poverty." And I will add, that, with parts and poverty, persevering application, consistent frugality, temperance

and integrity,—honour and eminence may be attained in any profession by the humblest individual.

5. Maintain a scrupulous regard to truth—on all occasions—in small things as well as in great—in your sprightliest conversations, no less than in your graver and more deliberate statements and asseverations. Habit is everything: and truth is too sacred ever to be trifled with. Never dispute merely for the sake of victory; but honestly search after truth with the calm docility of a pupil, not with the pride and arrogance of the determined champion.

6. Discountenance and abstain from the practice of duelling. And never carry about your persons deadly weapons of any sort, lest, in some moment of angry excitement, you be tempted to use them to the fatal injury of others and to the destruction of your own peace and happiness.

7. Avoid all games of chance as you would pestilence and death.

8. Guard against infidel sentiments. They will be found as cheerless, as they have been proved to be unphilosophical and noxious.

9. Cultivate a spirit of liberality, kindness and charity towards all men, of whatever nation, creed, sect or party. Never fancy yourselves infallible in regard to those profound mysteries in speculative religion and philosophy which have hitherto baffled the wisdom of the strongest intellects, and which have converted the weak and obstinate into fanatics, bigots and persecutors. While you assert, with amiable firmness, what you be-

lieve on satisfactory evidence, and while you adhere to such forms and ceremonies as you deliberately prefer—concede to all other men the same right, and allow them to be as honest as yourselves. That pretending Christian, who denounces any other or all other Christian sects except his own, who condemns their system, asperses their motives and questions their integrity, gives ample evidence of his own narrow sectarian intolerance, and hostility to the plainest principles of the gospel which he professes. The differences which obtain among the various Christian denominations are, in general, of no great magnitude or importance; and ought never to be made the ground of ridicule or abuse, much less of hatred and invidious or malicious calumny and persecution. Stand firm to the church of your election, or in which you have been educated; but never suffer one unkindly sentiment towards other churches to enter your bosoms. I have found excellent, enlightened, and truly Christian individuals in every sect with which I am acquainted—and my personal acquaintance extends to more than twenty different sects, whose public worship I have witnessed and all whose peculiar modes I have carefully noted—and I have also met with knaves and hypocrites in my own as well as in some other churches.

You are not to judge of Christianity from the unworthy conduct of its professors. You have a surer guide—the constitution—the charter—the entire system of our holy religion—as it descended pure and unadulterated from the Father of lights and the Fountain of truth and righteousness. Let this sacred book—the volume of inspiration—the Bible—be the companion of your whole earthly pilgrimage, and the object of your daily and unprejudiced study. How beautiful is that religion which pervades all the precepts and lessons and example and conduct of its divine Author? And how different from that which is but too often inculcated by selfish, ignorant, deceiving, or self-deceived, pharisaical, ambitious ecclesiastics or spiritual demagogues of every name? The gospel breathes peace and good-will, forbearance, long-suffering, patience, forgiveness, mercy, and love towards all men; and can therefore never be made to sanction angry dissensions, and bitter controversies, and inquisitorial cruelties, and malignant revenge, and secret jealousies, and open violence, and uncharitable constructions, and exclusive sectarian pretensions. The gospel enjoins and inspires angelic purity of heart and motive and life and conversation: and can never countenance licentiousness or moral obliquity in any form or degree. And that individual whose conduct does not accord with the letter and spirit of the gospel, in all its leading features, is not a genuine Christian, however orthodox may be his creed, or however valiantly he may contend for the true faith.

I caution you, therefore, to avoid the common error of ingenious and intelligent youth, and of many distinguished professional and scientific men of the ripest years, who pronounce hastily and unfavourably of the Christian religion; because so many of its advocates have been a disgrace to it, as well as to reason and humanity; and because so many abominations have been perpetrated in its name, and apparently under its authority. Go to the record, and examine for yourselves what this religion is, and what its professors ought to be. And remember that you have an interest in the result, deep and everlasting as the foundations of eternity. This religion, if true, speaks the same language, imposes the same duties, prohibits the same indulgences, holds out the same promises, rewards, threatenings and penalties to all men, without distinction, to whom it ever has been, is now, or ever will be promulgated. Its laws are binding equally on clergymen and laymen, on believers and unbelievers, on rich and poor, learned and unlearned—on you and me—and no more on me than on you. Therefore, whatever the gospel commands or requires must be obeyed and fulfilled, at the peril of all the misery and despair which it threatens. It promises to the believing and obedient all the peace and happiness which man is capable of realizing in this world, together with joy unspeakable and full of glory in the Paradise of God, when this fleeting scene shall have passed away forever.

You will not have travelled far on the journey of life, before you will perceive the want of heavenly consolation and support. The current of this world's affairs is seldom smooth and unruffled. Calamity arrives when least expected; and in a form and from a source never anticipated. Friendship fails or is treacherous precisely when most relied on or when most needed. Popular favour is as transient and variable as the passing breeze. Wealth vanishes when most idolized. Every endearing tie, every human support, every earthly good, may be sundered or torn away. Even the treasures of literature and science, to the acquisition of which years of ardent and painful labour have been devoted, may, at length, appear almost valueless and insipid—as they did to Raleigh, Grotius, Pascal, Selden, Locke, Newton—at the approach of death, or in comparison with the momentous truths and cheering promises of the Sacred Scriptures, which bring life and immortality to light.

Such is the course of universal experience. And if the picture seem dark and repulsive, and inappropriate to this joyous occasion, when you are fondly dreaming of long life and uninterrupted felicity and honour—be assured that I have no desire to cast a single shade upon the bright perspective which youthful fancy delights to contemplate. For I have been as young, as imaginative and as sanguine as any of you: and although I do not yet rank in years with the elders of the land, I have lived long enough to inscribe "vanity of vanities" upon all sublunary good; and to be satisfied that something more than this poor dazzling world can yield is essential to the aspirings of an immortal mind. I would, therefore, in all sincerity and kindness, tender to you the humble boon of my own experience, and exhort you to be wise betimes, and to provide for the day of trial and suffering and desertion and anguish, that it steal not upon you unawares, and that you may draw consolation from a heavenly fountain; and be enabled to submit with a Christian's hope and a Christian's spirit to every dispensation of Providence; and thus finally to triumph over every temptation and every foe, till you reach, at last, the blessed, peaceful, hallowed mansions, where the wicked cease from troubling and where the weary will be at rest forever!

BACCALAUREATE ADDRESS.

[CUMBERLAND COLLEGE, OCTOBER 5, 1831.]

BACCALAUREATE ADDRESS,

AT CUMBERLAND COLLEGE, 1831.

YOUNG GENTLEMEN:

To say that your education is now *finished*—as the fashionable phrase is, in reference to youth on leaving college—would be an egregious abuse of language. You are presumed merely to have mastered the elements—the alphabet, as it were—of a few valuable sciences and branches of literature; and to have learned *how* to study. With this scanty furniture, and intellectual discipline, you are about to commence a course of more thorough, varied and extensive research, which is to terminate but with your lives. We take it for granted, that this sentiment is deeply engraven upon your hearts. We have laboured, as you will testify, to render it familiar to your minds, as a truth or first principle, not to be questioned. As students—as learners then—you have barely approached the threshold of that proud temple of intellectual grandeur, which it will be the business of future life to strive, by every honourable and manly effort, to enter and to possess as your own.

Mere persevering application to books, or universal reading, however, will not suffice to ensure a useful, brilliant or successful career. A habit of reflection—of profound inquiry—of calm, dispassionate, unprejudiced investigation—of logical discrimination and rigid demonstration—must be acquired. I do not say that you must first doubt in regard to all received principles and doctrines, before you yield assent to any. What is usually denominated a skeptical turn of mind has seldom, if ever, been found to be either very generous, or very modest, or very docile, or very sagacious, or very beneficial to mankind. It is no proof of genius, or mental vigour, or manly independence. I warn you therefore against that spirit of vulgar vanity and refined pyrrhonism which affects to exalt itself above the wisdom, and the faith, and the philosophy, and the common sense, of the most enlightened sages and the most devoted benefactors of our race. But *truth* dreads no scrutiny. She courts no concealment and no disguise; and needs no arbitrary or extrinsic support. She prefers her claims to credence and acceptance openly and boldly, and disdains all casuistic sophistry and all prescriptive dominion. Fear not then, with the genuine temper of sincere learnors, to examine into the nature and foundations of any system or of any doctrine, however important, or however venerated, or however sanctioned, which may be presented to your consideration. If it be true and valuable, you will be amply rewarded for your pains in the investigation, by the strong conviction which will fasten upon your minds, and which will induce you cheerfully to acknowledge and manfully to defend it.

It would be absurd to accept even the Newtonian

philosophy upon the mere *dicta* of Newton, when you have it in your power to judge of all the proofs and evidence which led him to its adoption. It would be absurd to take upon trust any mathematical result whatever—any proposition of Euclid, for example—when all the steps of the demonstration are at your command.

A summary catechism of mere facts and doctrines is never put into the hands of youth with a view to make them proficients in science. Youth might in this way, learn to prate like parrots, about the most abstruse principles of science, and yet be totally ignorant of the basis upon which they rest. Error, as well as truth, may be inculcated upon such a plan. A child may be taught to say that the three angles of a triangle are equal to two right angles—and this would be true. He might, however, with equal ease, be taught to say that the three angles of a triangle are equal to a dozen right angles. In both cases, the party might continue through life to repeat as *truth* the lesson of his master: and, in both cases, he would be equally ignorant; that is, equally incapable of giving a reason for his belief. The absurdity of such a procedure, in reference to the exact and experimental sciences, is sufficiently obvious. And Bacon and Newton have long since exploded the scholastic dogmatism of Aristotle and Ptolemy.

The vast region of moral truth demands the same patient, rigid, inductive process, in order to arrive at satisfactory results. But here, unhappily, the world has hitherto been accustomed to an indolent passive obedience to the prevailing system—without presuming to question the *why* or the *wherefore.* Master spirits there have been, in almost every age, who have nobly stood forth as the energetic and benevolent champions of the intellectual, moral, political, and religious rights of the people. But their enlightened sentiments have not yet obtained complete currency in any country; and in most countries they still remain locked up in the minds of the initiated reflecting few. The efforts of Peter the Great of Russia—of Joseph the Second of Austria—and of the present Grand Signior of Turkey—to introduce certain improvements into their respective empires, will serve to show how difficult and dangerous it is to change popular customs, opinions and habits, even in matters of comparative indifference. Roger Bacon, Copernicus and Galileo, were duly persecuted for adventuring beyond the prescribed limits of orthodox philosophy. Wickliffe, Jerome and Huss became the victims of ecclesiastical bigotry, because they dared to think for themselves in an age when implicit faith was the only passport to honour in this world, or to salvation in the next. Hampden, Sidney, Russell, Milton, Locke, laboured and wrote and suffered in behalf of human liberty, long before the public mind was prepared to profit by their example or their lessons.

So slow is the progress of moral truth into the general mind, that numerous pioneers and martyrs in the holy cause have been required to ensure it an incipient existence, and to give it a progressive impulse; that it might, peradventure, under happier auspices, grope its way into the dark places and strongholds of error, superstition and despotism. In recurring to the history of Christendom, during the last three centuries, we shall, on the whole, descry much substantial ground of encouragement to persevere in similar exertions for the benefit of mankind. Luther and Newton triumphed where Galileo and Jerome failed. And the writings of Sidney, Milton and Locke prepared the great public, in another age and in a distant hemisphere, to *act* at the bidding of Franklin, Washington, Adams and Jefferson.

The art of printing has nearly dissipated the ignorance and prejudice which had so long and so pertinaciously resisted the progress of pure science. And the fooleries of the Alchymists and Rosicrucians are not likely to be revived. Science and philosophy have gained the victory, and are suffered to advance, without let or hinderance from any inquisitorial tribunal.

Moral truth has been less favoured. Still, she has struggled nobly, and much has she achieved. The popular mind has commenced its onward march. It has discovered—what, indeed, Sidney taught, and for which he dared to die a century and a half ago—that kings and rulers were made for the people, and not the people for them. That they are the servants of the people, and that when they cease to promote the weal of the people, they may no longer be trusted with power. The kingly and priestly doctrine of passive obedience and non-resistance has been exploded. The arrogant claims of legitimacy and orthodoxy—that is, the code and the creed of the powers that be—have been boldly challenged. The infallibility of the church, and the perfection of bench-made law, are shrewdly suspected. And the whole fabric of prescriptive despotism is daily assailed by the intrepid spirit of reformation.

The world is more indebted to the immortal Franklin for the judicious exhibition and wide diffusion of useful knowledge than to any other individual within the last hundred years. His sagacious and benevolent spirit pervaded not only the mysterious laws of nature, but the whole economy of domestic life and the policy of national governments; reached the fireside of the peasant, the throne of the monarch, the altar of the priest, and the rudimental principles of all civil institutions and political associations. He imparted a momentum to general improvement which has ever since been steadily increasing; in spite of the determined opposition of arbitrary power and the invincible obstinacy of self-sufficient ignorance.

Adam Smith elaborated into systematic expansion many of the simple truths of the Franklinian school, and thus created the beautiful science of Political Economy; which is now taught in every college, and controverted (and justly, in regard to some of its principles,) in every legislative hall.

It is of great importance to young men, and to all men, to be able to appreciate the relative value of different kinds of truth. Some things may be true, and yet be unimportant. Some may be curious and interesting, and yet be merely speculative. Some may be so profound and mysterious in their very nature, as to lie utterly beyond our intellectual grasp. To dispute and contend about any of these would be idle and uncharitable. And yet most controverted points in theology and metaphysics fall under one or another of these heads; as do nearly all those which constitute doctrinal heresy in the judgment of most ecclesiastical judicatories. Practical moral truth, on the other hand—such truth as directly or indirectly influences conduct—is important just in proportion to its moral practical influence. Every patriot, every philanthropist, every good man, therefore, will esteem it his duty and make it his daily study to ascertain the genuine character and tendency of all such truth, or of all practical principles, motives and doctrines.

Thus, for instance, every American citizen is by birthright a politician: and every man of superior talents, education and influence, ought to be an enlightened politician. It is his *duty* then to study politics—not merely the general science as taught in a few standard class-books; still less, the narrow, selfish, local, party, personal politics of our village gazettes—but the great principles of government, of legislation, of jurisprudence, of international comity, of natural and social rights, of political economy, in all their applications, general and particular, which are calculated to promote the greatest good of the whole body of the people. He should study to comprehend the remote bearings, as well as the immediate consequences of every measure. He should look to the permanent welfare of the federal Union to which he belongs, as well as to the particular commonwealth of which he is a citizen. Nor ought he ever as a politician, to countenance any system or project manifestly injurious to any section or portion of the great National Republic, in order to benefit his own State, or county, or friends, or party. He should consider the preservation of our constitutional union, by all constitutional means, as a sacred obligation—as an object ever to be aimed at, and never to be lost sight of. Personal predilections and local interests ought never to bias his judgment or bribe his integrity.

The American politician ought to be an Aristides amidst the tumultuous hostilities and convulsions of popular excitement and unprincipled ambition. He ought to be a Franklin, just, moderate, sagacious, calm, self-possessed, fruitful in resources and expedients, yielding in trifles, immovable in great principles,—whenever his country is distracted by the clamour and rage of conflicting interests or imaginary wrongs. To soothe, restrain and guide the ignorant infatuated multitude,—to anticipate, counteract and defeat the selfish schemes of false patriots and knavish demagogues—will require no ordinary wisdom, firmness and address. A host of such politicians our country now demands, and will ever demand. Shall our colleges furnish them?

To show the extent and intricacy of many a question in the ordinary routine of every day legislation, the American *tariff* might be specified. Does one man of a thousand, among either its advocates or opponents, throughout these United States, comprehend its object, its character, or its ultimate tendencies? And yet all are expected to give their suffrages according to the opinion which they have been *taught* to entertain respecting it. I say nothing of its merits—whether good or evil—right or wrong—constitutional or unconstitutional—politic or impolitic—judicious or injudicious. I merely submit this as a specimen to illustrate the necessity of impartial and thorough investigation, in order to be competent to judge for ourselves and for those over whom we may have influence. Into the arena of party politics or of party religion, you will bear me witness, I have never descended. Against the bitterness, the illiberality, the prejudice and the fury of party spirit, whether in politics or religion, I have often warned you. But the politics of no party, and the religion of no church or sect, have ever been lauded or censured by me in your hearing. And my last advice on this topic, is still the same. So far as you may be politicians, live and labour —and, if need be,—die for your country.

Since I have adverted to the subject of politics, as one of engrossing interest to my countrymen, it may not be ill-timed to caution you against that precocious and inordinate desire after public offices, which is so prevalent among our young men at the present day. Scarcely have they completed a hasty novitiate at school or college, and lounged in a law office some six months or a year, off and on, when they manifest a most confident capacity and overweening eagerness to assume the responsibilities, and to wear the honours of office. Now it strikes me, that this is somewhat premature; and that it does not savour much of talent, or modesty, or patriotism. Whether they will ever acquire skill by practice—as our self-made physicians occasionally do, after killing a dozen or two of their patients by way of experiment—I pretend not to decide.

I advise you, however, to mind your own proper business or profession, whatever it be, until you shall have secured a competency to live on before you ever suffer yourselves to become candidates for popular favour—and, at any rate, before you consent to accept of any office or subordinate appointment involving pecuniary responsibility. Human frailty is not to be trusted under the pressure of wants created by a fashionable style of living, and but inadequately supplied by the meager salary and perquisites, which usually attach to most of the petty offices within the gift of the executive or legislature of the Union or of the several States. How many respectable individuals in our country, by acts of fraud and embezzlement, to which their confidential posts afforded peculiar facilities as well as extraordinary temptations, have made shipwreck of their integrity, blasted the fairest prospects, ruined their families, disgraced their connexions—and, perhaps, in the phrensy of despair, have destroyed their own lives to avoid the shame and the risk of a public trial!

Better to labour hard and long—better to eat the bread of carefulness and obscurity many years—than thus to jeopard character under any circumstances, or for any immediate relief or temporary advantage. No man will long be virtuous who is not independent.

Whoever lives beyond his income, be it large or small, has passed the limits of strict honesty, and is already in the broad road to ruin. Resolve, then, at the outset, to be independent; and never to incur a debt which you are unable to pay. Labour also to acquire as much property as will ensure your independence in any station which you may desire to fill, or to which your country may invite you.

Public offices were created for the public benefit, and not for particular incumbents. They ought always to be conferred on those who are best qualified to serve the people, and never to provide a maintenance for needy aspirants or impudent adventurers. Whoever covets an office merely to live by, gives pretty good evidence that he is not fit for it. Whatever may be said about rotation in office—and I like the doctrine, according to its genuine republican and salutary construction—it was never intended that every man should have every office or any office in turn, or that an office should pass successively to any given number of individuals, however unqualified, but merely that any individual duly qualified should be eligible at the pleasure of the electing or appointing power.

It is the duty of every man to serve his country; but it is not the duty of every man to seek, by any means, foul or fair, to govern his country. A man may be a true patriot, and not boast of his patriotism, or be eternally preferring his patriotic claims to the people. Catiline boasted—Arnold boasted—and, no doubt, their boasting satisfied some well meaning men that they were honest patriots. Cincinnatus and Washington, however, fill a different page in the world's history.

How much of moral practical truth remains yet to be discovered, or still to be introduced to general acceptance, cannot, of course, be even conjectured. The science of Political Economy is but a branch of practical ethics; and jurisprudence is another. The whole system of legislation bears more or less directly and intensely on the moral character of the people. The legislator, the statesman, the judge, is a moralist *ex cathedra* for good or for evil.

All laws giving an arbitrary direction to the employment of capital—affecting the production, the distribution or the consumption of wealth; the tenure and transfer of real property; the rights of persons; popular education; the elective franchise;—defining or regulating pauperism, bankruptcy, oaths, appeals, rules of evidence, religious tests, trials by jury, freedom of the press, libel, taxation, judicial forms and procedures, the entire criminal code—must necessarily exert a moral influence of some kind. Thus, for example:—

An injudicious system of Banking, established by law, may open upon a community the floodgates of iniquity, and lead to all manner of swindling and profligacy. Witness the condition of several of the Western States a few years ago.

Foreign commerce may be so regulated and restricted as to render smuggling a lucrative, and even a reputable business; and thus operate to the discouragement of honest industry, and to the diminution of the very revenue which it was designed to augment.

Laws prescribing the market price or interest of money may be so arbitrary and ill-timed as to serve no other end but to tempt men to the legal crime of usury.

A militia system, requiring occasional musters of the people, may, by the manner in which they are conducted, be directly demoralizing. And it is always inequitable when it exacts as much from the poor man as from the rich—to say nothing of its utter inefficiency, as military men have pronounced it to be in most of the States.

To incarcerate an honest but unfortunate debtor, is always gratuitous and unavailing oppression. In most instances, the creditor is more culpable than the debtor. The latter is often the mere dupe of the former. In nine cases out of ten, perhaps, the creditor ought to be imprisoned rather than the debtor.

Three-fourths, it is universally admitted, I believe nine-tenths of the crime, disease, pauperism and wretchedness in our country, are fairly attributable to intemperance. That is, to the current and *temperate* use of ardent spirits by the people generally. The criminal—made so by intemperance—is duly punished. But the cause of his ruin remains untouched. The manufacturer and vender of this moral and physical poison may sit in judgment upon the victim of his avarice, and doom him to the penitentiary or the gallows.

Gambling—that is, games of hazard—may be interdicted under heavy penalties; while horse-racing and lotteries, which are themselves modes of gambling, and which are always accompanied by every other species of pernicious gambling, may be authorised and encouraged by one and the same legislature.

Oaths may be administered so frequently, and with so little solemnity, as very nearly to destroy their legal utility, and utterly to divest them, in the eyes of the people, of their religious character and sanctions. Quakers and Moravians are proverbially remarkable for their strict adherence to truth; and their simple affirmation is much less frequently questioned or suspected than the more formal oath which is customarily exacted from other Christians.

Excessive legislation, no less than vicious legislation, is an evil, and is always to be deprecated. Men will ever make a distinction, with or without reason, between things *mala in se*, things in themselves unlawful, and *mala prohibita*, things which become unlawful from being prohibited by the legislature.

But I leave to jurists to expose the immoral tendency of particular enactments, and of the whole mysterious and labyrinthian system with which they are officially and most painfully conversant. I merely present, as a universally acknowledged grievance, the delay, the uncertainty, and the expensiveness, of the system. This is an evil which all feel, and of which all complain.

The army of the law — as it has been significantly styled — comprising judges, magistrates, lawyers, marshals, sheriffs, constables, &c.—amounts to some twenty thousand men in the United States: and the annual expense of the whole system cannot be less than twelve or fifteen millions of dollars. That there is ample room for improvement therefore, in some fashion, none will deny. How the work is to be achieved, admits of much question, and assuredly demands the gravest consideration. Some experiments have been made, both in the old world and in the new, which promise lasting benefit—either from the adoption of *new codes*, or from a judicious revision and simplification of ancient, complex and ill-defined statutes and judicial decisions, and from their lucid classification and arrangement under distinct titles and intelligible principles.

The regret has been often expressed by several of our most eminent patriots and statesmen, that, when our fathers emancipated their country from the tyranny of the British Government, they did not also free it from, what they esteemed, the more galling tyranny of British jurisprudence. Whether such an opinion were too unqualified, or altogether untenable, falls not within my humble province to decide.

My object, in this passing notice, is not to suggest the remedy, but to testify against the evil—if it be an evil—that some of my wiser and more enlightened pupils, whose future lives shall be devoted to legal studies and pursuits, may keep the subject steadily in view, and be induced to give it that thorough, patient, philosophical and patriotic investigation which its immense and daily increasing importance demands.

It is difficult for the uninitiated to believe that the administration of justice must necessarily assume that formidable, tortuous and everlasting delusiveness which has hitherto distinguished it. It is difficult to believe that the law must be made a profound, intricate, and almost *unlearnable* science or mystery—requiring the life of a Methuselah to comprehend and to expound it. It is difficult to believe that laws cannot be so clearly expressed and rigidly interpreted as to be within the intellectual scope of ordinary well educated men, or that such men might not be safely entrusted with their righteous application. It is difficult to believe that puzzling technicalities or cabalistic terms and phrases contribute, in the least, to truth and equity;—however much they may avail the purses of those who are duly skilled in the adroit use of them.

I cannot think well of a system which is peculiarly onerous and vexatious to peaceable, honest, industrious, meritorious citizens; and auspicious chiefly to the quarrelsome, the idle, the mischievous, the unprincipled—to the wily knave or reckless desperado—whose case can never be made worse, but may be greatly alleviated under the operation of its complex and ticklish machinery. The former therefore dread and studiously avoid it; while the latter are eager to court its smiles and to presume on the chances of victory or acquittal. The innocent and the injured are harassed and oppressed by it: the guilty and the litigious alone look to it for favours. And, in both cases, the community is a grievous sufferer.

The every day operations of our common law courts (as I have witnessed them in other States,) exhibit proof enough of the chicanery, the charlatanry, the absurdity, the mockery and the abominable extortions to which the *high-minded* freemen of my country are often subjected in their pursuit of justice.

I have heard veteran lawyers declare—and they ought to know, and to their opinion I always most respectfully defer—that an honest unlettered farmer of good common sense, would, without the aid of any other law than that which is engraved upon the human heart, decide the petty differences which usually arise among neighbours more equitably and satisfactorily, in general, than is now *practicable* in any court whatever. Than is *now* practicable, they add; because, allowing the decision to be *right*, yet the *expense* incurred will make it a *wrong*—will convert justice into injustice. And, in forty-nine cases out of fifty, those who win in court according to law, will lose in purse, and be much the worse for their gains.

"Laws (says Mr. Jefferson) ought to be made for men of ordinary understanding, and should therefore be construed by the ordinary rules of common sense. Their meaning ought not to be sought for in metaphysical subtleties, which may make anything mean everything or nothing at pleasure." It should not be left to the sophisms of advocates whose trade it is to make the worse appear the better reason, and to clear their clients *per fas et nefas*, or to hold them in suspense until they shall be fairly fleeced of all their earthly substance, and be no longer worth the serving.

If the system which has hitherto prevailed, be, in its

very nature, perpetual and unalterable—if nothing can be done to relieve future generations from the dogmas of the present or the past—if we must continue to pin our faith upon the sleeve or the ermine of a series of courts without beginning or ending—then let us boast no more of the march of mind and the triumphs of liberty. Let us rather sit down in despair, with folded arms, under the dark shadow of the deep-rooted tree of despotism, which has been growing, and flourishing, and spreading wide its branches, ever since the age of good king Alfred, or at least since the glorious epoch of *Magna Charta*, and which seems destined to grow and flourish while an English world shall exist to feel its influence, and to acknowledge its blighting dominion.

I put all this, however, hypothetically—not dogmatically. I admire the *theory* of the common law, when it is said to be reason and the perfection of reason—or the "application of common sense, disciplined and directed by certain established principles, to the affairs of men." The most perfect civil and penal codes that human wisdom could devise, would not be literally and invariably adapted to all times, cases and contingencies. Much latitude of construction and discretionary jurisdiction would still, of necessity, attach to the judicial tribunals. In all civil cases not clearly provided for by statute, they would be compelled to assume original powers and to decide according to the spirit and analogies of the great legal system of their country, and agreeably to the universally recognized principles of reason and equity. Such is the beautiful theory which we already possess. It is the abuse and perversion of the theory—sanctioned by immemorial usage, and rendered capricious, versatile, captious and oppressive in its practical applications—that provokes censure and denunciation. The decrees and judgments of courts, instead of being subjected to the severe scrutiny and critical revision, to the controlling power and modifying process, which the theory implies and enjoins, have too often usurped the prerogatives of the theory itself, and been blindly received as the very oracles of reason and justice. Whether it is possible to recur once more to simple elementary principles—to avail ourselves of the wisdom and experience of other ages and nations—and thus to set out upon a safer plan, and to pursue a more natural, direct and obvious course, under the guidance of pure unsophisticated reason—will be seen when our future Marshalls and Kents and Livingstons shall have expended their intellectual stores and vigour upon the mighty task.

Cicero in his treatise *De Legibus*, remarks, "that law (*i.e.* general, not positive law,) is the perfection of reason, seated in nature, commanding what is right, and prohibiting what is wrong. Its beginning (he adds) is to be traced to times before any law was written, or any express form of government adopted." And wherever natural reason retains and exerts her paramount dominion and plastic influence, unchecked by absolute or arbitrary power on the one hand, and unperverted by the ignorance or passions of the people or of the people's servants on the other, no system of written or unwritten law will prove incurably and desperately vicious. It will be gradually meliorated and reformed with the improving and advancing spirit of the age. It will not be deemed sufficient to ascertain what the rules of courts are: —the policy of the rules themselves will be open to discussion; and they will be fairly and thoroughly canvassed.

I am perfectly aware that innovation is not always improvement. And that the wildest visionaries may be found among radical reformers, political Solomons, and economical *utilitarians*, as well as among religious zealots and enthusiasts. But before an enlightened, sober, reflecting, practical people, the schemes even of the visionary and the fanatic may be canvassed without danger. They will ultimately be estimated according to their value.

With us, the people are sovereign. They rule our rulers. They give the tone and impulse to the entire machinery of government. They constitute the empire of public opinion—the last tribunal, from which there lies no appeal. When they are wrong, all is wrong. Improvement of every kind must commence with them and be consummated by them. Every new principle of action—every new moral or political truth requiring a change in the popular habits—must first take root and effect among the people, before it will reach the halls of legislation or the bench of justice. The wise and the good, indeed, must first agitate, arouse, and inform the people;—but the people themselves must decide what shall eventually be law and usage. How true, and yet how lightly appreciated is the maxim of our republican sages, that, upon the broad basis of universal intelligence and virtue must rest the proud fabric of our boasted liberties and popular institutions?

Many wise men in Europe view with no friendly eye the progress of knowledge among the people. They augur no good, but much evil, from the universal spirit of improvement and revolution which is everywhere manifest. They anticipate the utter subversion of ancient and venerable institutions, and the probable prostration of all order, religion and government. They dread the influence of the schoolmaster who is abroad, and the lessons of reform which he diligently inculcates. With their apprehensions I do not sympathize. But with us, where every man already possesses the elective franchise and is himself eligible to office, there remains no alternative, but either to submit to the government of an ignorant mass, who are themselves controlled by knavish demagogues, or to give instruction to that omnipotent mass that they may be fitted to govern, or to exercise the right of choosing our governors in a judicious and independent manner.

A little learning, it has been said, is a dangerous thing: and so it is, whenever it is mistaken for a great deal. And here is the danger to which we are now exposed. Popular education is all the rage. Very well—I am an advocate of popular education. I will go as far and do as much to promote popular education as any man in the commonwealth. But let us keep in view the legitimate ends of a popular education. Is it to supersede or to nullify every other species of education? Is it to elevate every man who can read and write, to the rank and dignity of a dictator in the body politic? Is it to convert the labourer into a statesmen, and the workshop into a nursery of faction and discontent?

A vast deal of pains are taking by certain individuals in various parts of the country, to operate on the passions and prejudices of the *working people*, as they are styled, for purposes best known to themselves.—As if the said working people were subjected to any privations, hardships or disabilities, which are not common to every class, order and description of our citizens. When or where, since the foundation of our Republic, has a working man been denied a single privilege or excluded from a single office, simply because he was a working man? Have not the people always exercised the right of judgment and of suffrage unrestricted and uncontrolled? A working man stands on precisely the same footing with every other man. If the people choose to honour him with their confidence, no power on earth can hinder them. Other things being equal, the working man—the farmer—the mechanic—has the chances decidedly in his favour. And all this is just as it should be. It is in accordance with the spirit of our Constitution—with the genius of republicanism—and with the character of all our institutions.

But, then, the mere fact of being a working man does not *therefore* qualify a man for public office or entitle him to it. He may be a good blacksmith—and as a good blacksmith, be a very respectable and meritorious citizen. But, assuredly, because he is a good blacksmith, it does not follow that he should represent his district in Congress or his country at the court of St. James. If, however, in addition to his mechanical skill, or in spite of the disadvantages of his position—if by extraordinary genius and persevering application—he should acquire the requisite intellectual qualifications, then he may and doubtless will enact the honourable part of a Roger Sherman or of a Benjamin Franklin in the councils of his country or among the diplomatists of Europe. But neither Sherman nor Franklin rose from obscurity because they had been bred mechanics; but because they nobly cultivated the faculties with which they were gifted, and thus created for themselves a path to future eminence. And the same path to glory is still open to every aspiring cottager's son in our land. No patrician blood—no hereditary wealth—no family influence is necessary to ensure success to any youth who will submit to the training and discipline essential to the end at which he aims. Ought more than this to be coveted or conceded?

Now, a common school education will not do this—Lyceum lectures will not do this—no system of instruction designed for the body of the people will do this. They may be taught enough by these means to become more useful citizens, more skilful farmers and mechanics, and better judges of public men and of public measures. And with the elements of knowledge, thus acquired, many will advance to higher attainments, and finally reach, perhaps, the most exalted rank of intellectual culture or of political distinction.

To become an accomplished statesman, a profound

jurist, or an erudite scholar, must constitute the business of life—whether the apprenticeship be served at the plough, in the workshop, or in the college.

Within the whole range of moral research, RELIGION, of course, must ever occupy the first and highest rank. No reflecting person can be indifferent to it. Man is a religious animal, and he cannot, if he would, divest himself of its influence, under some form or other. Religion, like civil government, has ever been found indispensable to social existence. If religion, like civil government, were left to the option of human wisdom and discretion;—still, as there is much room for choice among the various forms of civil government and modes of administration, so would there be ample scope for the exercise of judgment in selecting from among the numerous religions in our world, that which, on the whole, is best. In this view of the subject, it is probable that no diversity of opinion would exist among ourselves, as to the particular religion that should be adopted. I imagine that, if all our wise statesmen and patriots were assembled in general congress, to choose a religion for their country, they would, without controversy or hesitation, vote for the Christian religion. I do not say, for any one of its perverted sectarian forms, but for simple unadulterated Christianity. I think they would prefer it to Judaism or Mohammedanism, or to any species of Paganism or modern Illuminism. If so, we have at least as cogent reasons in behalf of Christianity, as we have in behalf of a republican government—to the exclusion of all others. It is the best we can find. We must take *it*, or be content with a worse. For with no religion, we cannot exist. Since then a religion we must and will have—and since the Christian religion is incomparably the best ever known—who will, who *can* honestly object to it?

This simple view of the subject furnishes also no mean *a priori* argument in favour of the higher and more awful claims of Christianity to the faith of mankind. It is the best—and *therefore* most likely to be true—to be, namely, what it purports to be, a revelation from the Deity.

My object, however, at present, is not to argue this or any other matter. It is merely to guard you against that specious sophistry and sluggish incredulity which too often check or preclude all serious inquiry at the very threshold, and leave the mind forever in darkness, doubt and error. Christianity craves no aid or indulgence from human ingenuity or from human weakness. There—in the Bible—lies the unsophisticated record of her birth and character. Examine for yourselves. She has had her enemies. These have slandered and misrepresented her. Listen not to their *ex parte* testimony. She has had false friends. And these have traitorously betrayed her cause, and perverted her noblest attributes for the basest purposes. Be not deceived by their plausible glosses or dogmatical interpretations.

Distinguish between the truth and excellency of Christianity as taught by Christ and his Apostles, and the contradictory, extravagant and absurd exhibitions of it by any merely human teacher or authority whatever.

These may all be wrong; and yet Christianity may be good and true notwithstanding. Much infidelity, no doubt, has arisen from a superficial glance at Christianity, as displayed in the books, creeds, formularies, ceremonies, temper and conduct of certain Christian sects and individuals. Even the ingenious and philosophical Hume confessed that he had never perused the New Testament with attention. Probably, most living skeptics would, on inquiry, be found equally ignorant. They take no pains to separate the gold from the dross —the reality from its counterfeit. They look at the muddy and poisoned streams, but never ascend to the pure and living fountain. Whatever appears irrational, or puerile, or degrading, or monstrous in Christian tenets, rites or practice, they hastily ascribe to the Christian system; and then deliberately sit down "in the seat of the scornful"—as if the question were settled positively and forever. Be not seduced by such an example—however exalted may be their station or their talents. Their procedure is as preposterous, as it may prove ruinous and irretrievable.

The Bible, of course, is the only authentic source of information respecting Christian truth. It never can be learned, in all its extent and genuine spirit, from any human author or from any living teacher. Nor will it ever be fully discovered by those who consult the Scriptures merely or chiefly in search of argument to sustain a pre-conceived system of theology—a system in which they may have been educated—a system which they may have bound themselves, by the most solemn vows, to inculcate—a system which has been adopted, and, as it were, incorporated with their habitual thoughts, feelings and actions, previously to any study of the Bible whatever—a system, which, instead of modestly approaching the sacred oracles and humbly listening to the divine response, boldly and presumptuously brings Heaven's record to the test and to the torture of its own self-sufficient, infallible and despotic tribunal.

In our country a loud and angry clamour has been recently raised against Christian ministers, and Christian philanthropists, and Christian efforts to spread the gospel:—as if a general conspiracy had been formed to undermine our political fabric and to usurp the civil government. We hear much about priestcraft, and ecclesiastical ambition, and religious intolerance—whether with or without reason, I shall not inquire. I entertain no alarming apprehensions on this score, from any sect, church, or party, which freely gives the Bible to the people, and which urges upon them the duty of studying it, and which permits them to exercise their own judgment in its interpretation. But I do apprehend danger from the enemies of the Bible, whether avowed or secret, whether infidel or Christian in *name*. The Bible is either true or false. No honest man, believing it true, could in conscience withhold it from the people. If false, by what better or severer test can it be tried than the ordeal of public opinion? Infidels, if candid and sincere, cannot consistently dread its influence: especially as they do not impugn its moral precepts, or pretend that it is hostile to liberty and the rights of man;

and more especially as it does not come in competition with the higher claims of any other religion which they would offer as a substitute.

What then shall we say of any class or denomination of Christians, who, while they profess to reverence the Bible, as their own standard of faith and practice, do nevertheless studiously and systematically refuse it to the people, as too profound and mysterious for their comprehension? The truth is, they are actuated by selfish, sinister, sectarian motives. They are aware that their own peculiar *craft* would be endangered,—that the simple purity and verity of the gospel would be arrayed against all their hypocritical pretensions,—and that their usurpations over the consciences and understandings of the people would be uprooted and dissipated forever. Are there any such *Christians* in our country?—And do *they* prefer accusations of dishonesty, intrigue, bigotry or ambition against their fellow-Christians? Do they charge the friends and distributors of the Bible with the foul project of compassing a union of Church and State? If there be such men among us—and if they be actuated by such a spirit—we venture to lay the sin and the danger, of which they complain, at their own doors. They are precisely the lurking, insidious, jesuitical foes to Christianity and to both civil and religious liberty, whom our real patriots have most reason to dread and to guard against. Their actions and their dogmas contradict their specious declarations and ostentatious parade of zeal in the sacred cause which they affect to espouse.

Should this announcement, hypothetical as it is, be deemed invidious or uncharitable,—I beg to ask my hearers what they would think of any number of American statesmen, who should, while *professing* to be constitutional republicans, be artfully decrying the Constitution, and disparaging its merits and sanctions, or aiming to prevent its circulation among the people:—or who should declare it to be a capital crime, like treason or murder, for any man to read, or to possess a copy of, the Constitution; or who should insist on their exclusive right, at all times, to substitute their own commentary or interpretation in lieu of the instrument itself; or to issue their own proclamation as the paramount law of the land? Would it be uncharitable to doubt whether the said *professing* constitutional republicans were truly and honestly constitutional republicans at all? Thus much, on this topic, we offer in self-defence. We have ever advocated the cause of liberty and the Bible. In the present state of the world, we believe the cause to be one and indivisible. We mean to wrong no man or set of men. The case supposed may be purely fictitious—and if so, our application and deductions will be harmless and inoffensive.

Young men, and old men too, are exceedingly credulous oftentimes in listening to the tragic story of Christian enormities;—as if every abomination perpetrated under the Christian name, were chargeable to Christianity. And because a *spurious* Christianity has been for ages lording it over the world—proudly seated upon the throne of empire, and controlling the policy and the destinies of nations—they therefore infer that *genuine* Christianity must also be ever seeking after political supremacy.

True it is, religion has been and still is interwoven with the civil polity of all nations upon our globe, with only one exception. All governments, ancient and modern, Jewish, Pagan, Mohammedan, (and even Christian since the beginning of the fourth century,) had and have their religious establishments. And all religions, except the Christian, seem naturally and necessarily to enter into the very essence and structure of the governments which sustain and protect them. But here we take our stand, and peremptorily challenge the universe to produce an instance of any other religion besides the Christian, which has ever obtained a permanent existence among men, without the aid of human government—of the sceptre or the sword. No such case can be cited.

Be it known then—and let the calumniators of the gospel blush while they are constrained to admit the fact—that, when the Christian religion was first promulgated, it disclaimed and rejected all State alliances. Instead of courting the smiles and patronage of any earthly potentate, it boldly met the frowns and hostility of every government under heaven. Silent and suffering, patient and forbearing, charitable and unassuming, self-denying and unambitious, it advanced in the popular favour by its own native beauty and intrinsic excellence, by the energy of truth and love, by the faithful and benevolent labours, under God, of its own devoted and disinterested advocates. It encountered national Judaism in Palestine, and national Paganism throughout the rest of the world. For three long centuries, it sustained the unmitigated and malignant assaults of philosophy, learning, wit, pride, power and superstition. When a majority of the people had declared in its favour, the politic Constantine became its champion and protector; and artfully adopted it as the State religion, instead of heathenism, which, until then, had constituted part and parcel of the imperial code, as it had previously done of the republican and regal systems, up to the days of Numa and Romulus.

Here then, ancient usage was followed—the usage, namely, of Pagan Rome. Her emperor had been the head and hierophant of her religion and her temples; and he was not the personage to divest himself voluntarily of any of his inherited or acquired prerogatives. His courtiers too were as pliant and obsequious as courtiers, at all times, are wont to be. Had every Christian bishop in the empire denied his right to rule the church, and protested against this spiritual usurpation; still, the master of the world would have been at no loss for instruments to effect his designs. The priests of Jupiter—dignified Roman Senators—ambitious aspirants of any name or rank—would have eagerly assumed the crosier and the mitre, and discharged, with becoming gravity, the prescribed functions of their now exalted and powerful order. Princes can, at pleasure, manufacture orthodox tools out of unprincipled sycophants. And no doubt, at that period, there were enough of the right stamp, within the pale of the visible Christian church, to meet the demand.

From the reign of Constantine down to the present day, the Christian religion, in some form or other, has been incorporated with the civil government, or established by law, in every Christian land, with the solitary exception of our own Republic. History, I repeat, does not record another exception: nor can another be found in our world at this moment.* Genuine religious liberty has never been enjoyed in any other country. The very acme of modern attainment, even in enlightened Christian Europe, is only a species of ill-natured, stinted, grudging, jealous, extorted *toleration* of dissenterism. If persecuting bigotry no longer celebrates its *acts of faith*, or lights the fires of martyrdom, or fills with victims the cells of its inquisitorial dungeons, it is because it *dares not*. And pray, why not dare to do *now* what Constantine, and all his successors in Church and State, for some twelve or fifteen centuries, did not scruple to perform? It is because the people are reading the Bible, and unlearning the cruel and slavish dogmas of worldly domineering hierarchs. Wherever the Bible has had unchecked circulation, there the demon of persecution has become comparatively powerless. Let Britain and Spain, in contrast, serve for proof and comment.

Is it possible, then, that the advocates of the Bible can be plotting against the liberties of their country, while in the very act of dispensing to the people the

* France, perhaps, excepted, since the revolution of July, 1830.

New Testament, which is the most perfect charter and guarantee of human rights, ever yet contrived by man or bestowed by Heaven? Let Mr. Jefferson speak to this point. Christianity is, says he, "a religion of all others most friendly to liberty, science, and the freest expansion of the human mind—when brought to the original purity and simplicity of its benevolent institutor."

The American people, before and at the period of the Revolution, were better acquainted with the Bible, probably, than any other nation. This fact may, in part, account for their devotion to the cause of liberty and independence; whilst the neighbouring French colonies of the Canadas, among whom the Bible was comparatively unknown, adhered to the government of the mother country. And, for the same reason, I suppose, it may be announced, without breach of charity, and in strict accordance with historic verity, that, among Protestant Christians universally, juster notions of liberty are entertained and exemplied in practice, than among Roman Catholic Christians. If the fact be not so,—(not, indeed, in reference to eminently enlightened and gifted individuals, but to nations and the body of the people generally,)—I shall cheerfully reject the inference drawn from it.

But, we are told, priests covet power.—That they would all be popes if they could.—That they are as ambitious as Cæsar, and when they cannot be first in Rome, they strive to become first in a village.—That, if the most aspiring among them cannot attain their object in any existing church, or become the leaders of existing sects, they forthwith set up for themselves, become the apostles of a new doctrine, and the generals of a new army in the church militant. This charge, to a considerable extent, may be well founded, for aught I know to the contrary.

I think it may, with more truth however, be affirmed, as it has been, that "the grand pursuit of priests, as of all other bodies of men, is power; and that their peculiar object is power over the belief of men,"—which, of course, includes or ensures every other sort of power. I here distinguish between personal ambition, and the ambition of a *body* or *order* of men. Between the *spirit of corps* [*esprit de corps*] and individual interest. The individual may be perfectly honest and disinterested, so far as he is himself directly concerned, and yet be blindly and absolutely devoted to the systematic advancement and elevation of his own particular fraternity or profession. This ambitious self-aggrandizing spirit is as characteristic of lawyers, physicians, tradesmen, merchants, and other *bodies* of men, as it is of priests—though not so objectionable or dangerous in the former as in the latter. And what is remarkable, a numerous body or corporation of men will steadily and ardently pursue a system of measures to effect their favourite object, which not one of them would resort to or justify for his own special benefit. Thus it is that the religious sects in our country, with probably few exceptions, are labouring to augment their respective numbers, wealth, power and influence;—and by means too, oftentimes, which a private Christian would be ashamed, in his own case, to employ or openly to approve. It is precisely from this irresponsible spirit of professional or sectarian ambition—as distinct from personal or individual ambition—that some good men augur peril to our civil liberties, or, at least, to our domestic tranquillity; and, at any rate, to all the generous and ennobling charities of genuine Christianity.

When I witness the strifes, the controversies, the mutual jealousies and recriminations of opposing rival sects, I am constrained to ask, what might not result, should any one of these gain the ascendency, after years of angry, embittered and furious conflict? For a majority, be it remembered, *will* govern. And a majority of religionists of any name whatever, if sufficiently large and powerful, united and determined, reckless and unprincipled, or ignorant, deluded and head-strong, can do what they please—can alter the Constitution—can demolish the government—can establish Judaism, or Paganism, or Deism, or Atheism, or Romanism, or Quakerism, or Episcopacy, or Presbytery.

It is well known that the several sects are now boldly striving to organize sectarian seminaries of education, of all gradations, in every part of the country, in order (say their enemies) to exert the greatest possible influence upon the rising generation. We see them everywhere issuing sectarian newspapers and journals, which, while they profess to be exclusively religious, do not fail (say their enemies again) to exhibit their own political temper and predilections, on all convenient occasions.

And we may, (continue their accusers,) ere long, see them mingling directly in all the party political agitations of the day, and becoming important engines in our popular elections. It is an easy matter to give to every political measure a religious aspect. Not a question can be agitated in any legislative assembly but may be associated with religion. Every measure will be deemed *right*, and therefore religious, by its advocates—while the same measure will be denounced as *wrong*, and therefore anti-religious, by its opponents. The most indifferent question imaginable is capable, in this way, of being presented to the people as a religious question. Such was the actual state of the Christian world, only a few centuries ago, when every principle or question in politics, in morals, in science and philosophy, was matter of religion, and subject to ecclesiastical regulation.

No feeling, sentiment or passion is so strong and uncontrollable as religious passion; and, in the bosoms of the ignorant unreflecting multitude, it usually amounts to phrensy. Candidates for office, in such a season of religious ferment, will, of course, put themselves at the head of one or another of the dominant sects. A majority of some one sect may thus eventually prevail in the State and National Legislatures—and then the government virtually falls into their hands—and then, who shall check or restrain them, when the people themselves have become their abettors and coadjutors? Suppose a large majority of the citizens of Tennessee were zealous aspiring Jews—would not all the offices in the State be speedily filled by Jews? And if this were the case throughout the Union, would not every officer of the Federal Government be, of course, a Jew? And what should hinder them, if so disposed, from establishing by law, the Mosaic ritual and Temple worship as the religion of the nation? The name being changed, the argument is equally applicable to any Christian denomination. Nor would the prospect be in the least brightened by substituting infidelity for Christianity. All the evils now contemplated have hitherto proceeded from infidel Christianity or Christian infidelity. For, in the garb and under the guise of Christianity, infidelity has perpetrated deeds of cruelty and madness which Paganism might blush at.

Infidelity too, in its own proper character, has been equally intolerant, bigoted, persecuting and ambitious, whenever it has had a theatre for action. Infidelity may aspire to the mitre or triple crown, in one age or country—and in another, erect altars to the goddess of reason, and exterminate all who refuse to offer incense to its idols. There are, no doubt, infidels in our country, who, to gain political power, would either court a religious party, or denounce any and all religious sects, just as the popular sentiment might happen to be propitious to the one course or the other. Had Frederick the Great been as pious or superstitious as James the Second, his host of literary parasites would have been as religious in appearance, as they were infidel in heart. Unprincipled men never hesitate about names or means. Our liberties may be abridged or cloven down under a Christian or infidel pretext—by the orthodox or the heterodox—by the Puritan or the liberal—by the Catholic or the Protestant—whenever the *people* shall be prepared to rally around the standard of any desperate adventurer—*but not till then.*

Thus far I have merely traced to its natural consequences, the tendency of all religious party spirit, when acting strongly upon the popular mind. If there be danger in the case, as has been proclaimed and reiterated by a thousand pens and tongues—or if there be no danger whatever—and I leave others to judge—the argument, as addressed to the people, proves invincibly, that, in order to avert the danger, or to be assured that no danger threatens, *they* must become sufficiently enlightened and wary to be above the arts and beyond the reach of any insidious traitor or canting hypocrite.

In our country, all religions are equally favoured and protected by the Constitution and laws. Not a shadow of preference is shown to any one over the rest. The rights of conscience are secured to all men without distinction. Here there is perfect equality. The Constitution speaks not of *toleration.* Toleration is a term unknown to our codes. Dissenters and heretics we cannot have among us. Nor has any legal tribunal the authority to arraign or harass or question any mortal on account of his creed or mode of worship. All religious sects stand on precisely the same footing. They are equally orthodox and equally respectable in the eye of the law. This being the fact, what right have the several sects to abuse, asperse, and anathematize one another? What right has one sect to denounce and unchurch another sect? What right has one church, professing to reverence the Bible, to pronounce another church, equally acknowledging the Bible, as its standard, to be unchristian or heretical? Or what right has either to reprobate the other as aiming at an ecclesiastical establishment? When the *spirit* of both is the same: and the spirit would, if it could, create a despotism over both Church and State.

What right has any preacher of the gospel to inveigh against the absent and unoffending members of another sect—to assail their principles and their motives—and to render them as odious to his own people as possibly he can? Whence did he learn his lessons of charity and meekness—or acquire that moral courage which prompts him to say of his fellow-Christians publicly and collectively what he would not *dare* to utter, in a private circle, of any one of them individually and by name? Is he specially privileged to infringe the Constitution of his country and the gospel of peace—to deal out slander by the wholesale—and, with impunity, to libel his neighbours by the thousand? If the common tale-bearer, the vulgar tea-table gossip, the officious retailer of village scandal, is universally despised—if the malignant calumniator, the deliberate unprovoked slanderer, is liable to severe legal pains and penalties—what shall be said of the puny, arrogant, inflated, self-sufficient zealot, who, from the pulpit, hurls his poisoned shafts, Sunday after Sunday, against his brethren, the followers, it may be, of another shepherd, just as wise, liberal and infallible as himself? No species of persecution is so vexatious, exasperating and injurious, as that which fastens a bad name upon its victims. The law of libel and defamation ought to reach the pulpit as well as the private domicil.

A preacher, undoubtedly, has the right to promulgate whatever doctrines, or to inculcate whatever lessons he pleases, or whatever his church or party may require. But he is not the keeper of other men's consciences, nor the judge of their actions—of those, I mean, who do not appertain to his own flock or sect. Besides, he is never candid when he enters upon controversial ground. He never deals fairly with those whose tenets he oppugns. He bears false witness against his neighbour. I have seldom heard from the pulpit a just representation of any sect which it was the design of the preacher to attack or to criminate. Nor have I ever read, in any polemical treatise, a full and impartial account of the sentiments or practice of the party which it was the object of the author to confute, expose or write down.

I am willing that all sects should manage their own affairs in their own way, and within their own legitimate spheres. That they should believe what they please, and employ as much spiritual terrorism, as they deem expedient, among their own voluntary disciples and associates. I leave them where the Constitution has placed them. Let them never pass the boundaries of their own spiritual territories, nor invade another's dominion. Let them learn to treat each other with courtesy and Christian charity—with that "charity which suffereth long, and is kind; which envieth not; which vaunteth not itself, and is not puffed up.—Which seeketh not her own, is not easily provoked, thinketh no evil: rejoiceth not in iniquity, but rejoiceth in the truth;—Which beareth all things, believeth all things, hopeth all things, endureth all things."

If I believe my neighbour, or any entire sect, to be living in darkness and error—such as must, in my opinion, endanger their salvation—I may go to him or them, and endeavour kindly to enlighten, convince, reclaim and save them. But assuredly, as a minister of the gospel of reconciliation and good-will to men, I cannot presume to stigmatize them, unheard, and by me certainly never warned or instructed, as heretics, infidels or hypocrites. I cannot ridicule, traduce, insult, or affect to despise them. I cannot hate, and therefore seek to torment and destroy them, soul and body, in time and throughout eternity. I would not treat a heathen thus —even were he a Nero or a Domitian—and shall I thus act towards my Christian brother?—who, perhaps, after all, (if the scene were laid in Britain,) differs from me only in having been born on the opposite bank of the Tweed, and in having been educated in a different Protestant National Church—while both his church and mine may be recognized as orthodox, and be equally protected and cherished by the same common civil government—and both acknowledge the same sovereign as their temporal and spiritual head.

But am I individually, or is my church wantonly assaulted, misrepresented, calumniated—may I not retort with equal severity, and not merely repel the charge, but render evil for evil, slander for slander, carry the war home into the enemy's camp, and do him all the injury in my power? No, I may not. My master has taught a different lesson—"Blessed are ye when men shall revile you, and persecute you, and shall say all manner of evil against you falsely for my sake." He has left us an example of patient suffering, which we are commanded to follow:—"who, when he was reviled, reviled not again; when he suffered, he threatened not; but committed himself to him that judgeth righteously."

In my remarks upon the *legal* equality of all religious sects, and upon the charitable spirit which ought to characterize their mutual intercourse, I have not intended to intimate that there is no reasonable ground of choice or preference among them—nor that they are all equally right or equally wrong—nor that it is immaterial which should prevail—nor to designate which it would be wisest and safest to encourage. These are matters which I would not presume to decide for any man. Were I asked for an opinion in the case, I would refer the inquirer to the Bible, as the only sure guide to enable him to judge of the temper and claims of any sect whatever. He could not greatly err in associating with any Christian church, which practises Christian charity, and which arrogates no powers inconsistent with Christian liberty, and which acknowledges no standard of ultimate appeal but the Christian Scriptures. I have already said that I fear no serious evil from any sect (except the *sectarian spirit*, upon which I have animadverted,) which freely permits, or rather directs every individual to "search the Scriptures." I give my hand cordially to any man, bearing the Christian name and exhibiting the Christian temper and character, who is willing and anxious to put into the hands of all the people the WRITTEN CONSTITUTION of the great Christian Republic. About minor points I will not contend. And while I claim the liberty to understand and interpret the Scriptures as best I can, I cheerfully concede the same liberty to all others.

The people, if capable of reading and understanding, will soon learn from the Bible to distinguish between the ambitious zealot or spiritual demagogue, and the honest minister of truth and righteousness. They will learn that the religion of HIM "whose kingdom is not of this world," needs not the strong arm of any civil government to enforce its claims. That all intolerance, superstition, bigotry and persecution are forbidden by its very letter and by its universal spirit. That no human tribunal has a right to control the thoughts and the opinions of men, or to coerce and regulate the conscience. That pharisaism, sectarism, *churchism*, is a very different affair from genuine Christianity. That to "contend earnestly for the faith once delivered to the saints," does not mean to fight, torture, hang or burn men for the orthodoxy of any human church, or of any ecclesiastical dictator, or of any adventurous reformer.

They will learn, that the most noxious heresy is uncharitableness; and that the worst enemy to pure Christianity is sectarian ambition.

They will learn, that not one of the creeds of any existing church is formally and explicitly prescribed in the gospel, and therefore cannot claim either to supersede the gospel, or to constrain any mortal to believe, or assent to, what *he* cannot find in the gospel.

They will discover, that no precise forms of worship or of ecclesiastical government are enjoined by the great Master himself—and therefore that none of them can have exclusive preference or dominion, any further than as voluntary associations may have adopted them. That great diversity in matters of indifference or of mere expediency—in externals, in forms, rites and usages—may accord with the spirit of liberty and charity which the gospel uniformly inculcates. And therefore ought never to be made the ground of schism, or of mutual hostility and excommunication.

They will learn, that *practice* is the only sure test of orthodoxy or of personal religion. That the tree may always be known by its fruits. That man can judge of his fellow-men only by their lives—by their daily habitual temper and conduct, walk and conversation. And whenever this grand fundamental truth in Christian ethics shall universally prevail,—there will be an end of short-sighted, illiberal, persecuting, ambitious, inquisitorial sectarism and priestcraft.

Let the Bible, then, go to the people, without note or comment. And we shall no longer dread the influence of missionaries and preachers, whether male or female, Christian or heathen, native or foreign—nor the machinations of priests or infidels, of alarmists or fanatics, of any sect, name or party.

If I have wearied my audience with this lengthened

discussion of a theme not strictly classical, and perhaps, to most persons, not very interesting, I must find my apology, not merely in the intrinsic importance of the subject itself, but chiefly in the extraordinary excitement of the public mind generally in regard to some of its features and bearings.

Religion pure and undefiled, and its abuse and perversion, are totally different matters; and yet they are too often and too easily confounded, both by the crafty and the ignorant—and by none more fearlessly than by vivacious youth. To draw the line of distinction clearly, and to remove this *prima facie* and most insidious objection to Christianity, I supposed would be rendering a valuable service to my worthy pupils, at the moment of their entrance upon the wide theatre of action and of danger, which now awaits them, and which will soon command all their talents and all their energies.

I have freely admitted and exposed the prominent evils, incident to human frailty in the management of religious affairs; and I have pointed out, what appears to me, the only certain and permanent remedy. The odious usurpations of priestcraft, I have not spared. Nor have I been indulgent to the obliquities and the sinister policy of the *sectarian spirit* wherever it obtains. To this spirit I have shown no favour; while I have carefully abstained from all censure, either of particular sects or of particular individuals. And candour compels me here to add my testimony to the general integrity and benevolence of the great body of our clergy, of all denominations, who adhere to the Bible. A more faithful and devoted ministry of the gospel, I verily believe cannot be found in any country. Of their disposition to effect a union of Church and State, I solemnly aver that I know nothing. In the course of my life, I have not heard a syllable from any clergyman, in private or in public, from the pulpit or the press, which could be construed or tortured as indicative of any such purpose. And if there be one such disguised enemy of liberty and the gospel; I doubt if he has dared to utter his sentiments, even in a whisper, to his dearest friend. He would not be tolerated in any company, or by any party, which professes to respect the Bible, and which is willing to be judged by the Bible. From my earliest youth to this day, I have heard from clergymen but one opinion on this subject—and that is, a decided reprobation of all religious establishments. And were any political or unchristian party to attempt to bring about a union of Church and State; or, in other words, to usurp dominion over the conscience—I feel assured that the clergy would be the first to rise in arms against such a project.

Still, notwithstanding this explicit declaration, I retract nothing that I have advanced. And all history, and the known character of human nature, warrant the justice of my animadversions and inferences. The blind, obstinate, overbearing, supercilious, aspiring *spirit* of sectarism is ever to be feared, and must be closely and vigilantly watched, to prevent the consequences to which it naturally tends. This must be done with good sense, judgment, discretion, mildness, and thorough knowledge and discrimination—lest religion itself be overwhelmed in the ruins which the madness of jealousy and alarm might occasion. Intelligence and the Bible, universally diffused among the people, alone will preserve us from both extremes.

The signs of the times, assuredly, are not propitious either to dispassionate inquiry or to political integrity. Nor is it strange that the cause of true religion should be involved in the rude assaults made upon its outworks, or endangered by the indiscriminate abuse heaped upon its imprudent or false-hearted supporters. Still, we are free—and our unparalleled Constitution is still worth defending. We are religious still—and the Bible of eternal truth will forever command the veneration and the faith of all conscientious reflecting men. The whirlwinds of party fury and religious fanaticism will subside. The true patriot, the enlightened politician, the common sense moralist, the guileless Christian advocate, will yet be heard with respect by the people. I do not despair of the Republic. Nor do I despair of the gospel of charity and salvation.

The Republic and the gospel demand your vows of eternal allegiance and fidelity to their sacred cause. Live and die for your country, and for that holy religion, whose author is God, and whose aim is universal peace, liberty and happiness.

Our aged and venerable sires—all who now direct the affairs of Church and State—must soon pass away from this busy scene, and give place to another generation. You, my young friends, in common with your contemporaries, will occupy their stations, and control the destinies of your country.

That you may live long, honoured and beloved, useful and happy—that, when full of years and mature in piety, you may behold the youth of another age more enlightened, patriotic and virtuous than their fathers—that so you may depart in peace and holy triumph, and enter the blissful mansions of the celestial paradise, there to unite in the hallelujahs of the Redeemed forever—is, and will be, the fervent prayer of him, who now bids you an affectionate and a last FAREWELL!

BACCALAUREATE ADDRESS.

[CUMBERLAND COLLEGE, OCTOBER 3, 1832.]

BACCALAUREATE ADDRESS,

AT CUMBERLAND COLLEGE, 1832.

HITHERTO, the graduates of our American colleges have sustained a character altogether worthy of the high privileges with which their juvenile novitiate had been distinguished, and eminently creditable to their respective seminaries. Proudly, indeed, might the guardian Genius of our prosperous Republic contemplate the noble band of patriotic youths, who, from year to year, have issued from our Academic Halls, and exclaim, with the exulting mother of the Gracchi, "these are my jewels!" Through all the perils of revolution, of war, of party strife, they have proved the faithful and intrepid champions of national independence, of civil and religious liberty, of popular rights, of constitutional government, and of human happiness. There may have been among them honest differences of opinion, but in regard to radical principles there has occurred but little to disturb the harmony and peace of the great political confederacy. They have cheerfully and zealously co-operated in the one grand work of achieving the greatest happiness of the greatest number of citizen freemen. That there may not have been some selfish, ambitious, reckless, and even traitorous spirits among the number, it would be presuming too much on human virtue to affirm. But a solitary *Judas* will not entail dishonour upon the whole body of the faithful.

Happy—thrice happy my country—glorious beyond all previous example would be her destiny—could it be assumed that all her enlightened and liberally educated sons will ever be found true to her cause and devoted to her welfare! May we reasonably indulge in hopes and anticipations so grateful and auspicious? Are there no ominous symptoms of yielding integrity, of spurious treasonable ambition, of factious parricidal enterprise, of desperate fraternal discord, already visible? Have not some, at least, of our wise and learned and honourable men begun to calculate the value of our National Union, and even to threaten its dissolution? Is then the fair fame of our infant Republic to be tarnished, and the hopes of mankind to be blasted, by the very class of citizens who should have died to prevent a catastrophe so humiliating and disastrous? Whence is it that such men should thus be induced to jeopard national blessings and national glory, actually possessed or certainly within our reach, which have never yet been paralleled in our world? I am willing to believe that there is more delusion than knavery in the case—that it is a momentary phrensy which will soon pass away; and that the gathering cloud will disappear long before the tempest shall burst upon our still peaceful habitations.

But the existing crisis, whatever may be the issue, is full of warning and instruction. Ten years ago—and who would have hazarded the prediction that the value of the Union was likely to become, within any assignable period of time, a subject of grave calculation or even of speculative discussion? And yet, already, it is the common theme of every newspaper and of every party. The importance and stability of the Union, the advantages and disadvantages of the Union, are freely and universally canvassed. Its destruction therefore is among *possible* events. And this is itself a fact of most portentous bearing. It speaks a language which cannot be misunderstood: and it necessarily creates doubt, misgiving and apprehension in regard to the future. We may take for granted, as we confidently do, that the measures of the *present* agitators and *nullifiers* will be triumphantly defeated; but still the melancholy conviction fastens on the mind, that the union of these States may hereafter, and perhaps at no very distant day, be destroyed forever! "One and indivisible" is no longer the sacred motto of every American. In evil hour the subtle enemy has invaded our delightful paradise—has cast the apple of discord into our once united and therefore invincible host—is eagerly prompting brother to imbrue his hands in the blood of brother:—and yet who, of all our honest industrious millions, has descried his approach or suspected his insidious purpose? Are *they* about to surrender their understandings, with their lives and liberties, as a sacrifice to the very demon of avarice and ambition—blindly—unconsciously—without motive—nay in direct contravention to every principle and consideration which ought to influence rational and responsible agents?

It has been often remarked, that where superior learning is restricted to a few, it is likely to be perverted and abused to the injury of the many. And all history affords ample evidence of the fact. Every species of tyranny and high-handed injustice, practised on the people by government, has found advocates and abettors among the learned. They surrounded the throne and crouched at the feet of Augustus and Nero, of Charlemagne and Haroun, of Alfred and Henry VIII., of Saladin and Tamerlane, of Elizabeth and the Stuarts, of the Popes and the Bourbons. Nor is there any lack of them, at this day, in St. Petersburg, Rome, Madrid, Lisbon, Cairo or Constantinople,—so far as the mere instruments of despotism or superstition may be required. Their talents, science and skill are essential to the schemes and political machinery of their masters. Thus too, in the all-grasping aristocracies of ancient Rome and modern Venice, learning, as well as wealth and power, centred chiefly in the patrician order, and was therefore generally its ally and apologist. And thus it has ever been when monopolized by a small number. It is its diffusion among the people which causes iniquity in high places to tremble—and either drags the despot from his throne or converts the tiger into a lamb. What are now the prerogatives of an English monarch compared with those exercised by the Stuarts, the Tudors, and the Plantagenets? Had the people of England remained stationary in their primitive darkness and ignorance, like those of Spain and Portugal, neither English nor American liberty had ever been the theme of history or of song.

But, unhappily, it is even yet possible for the people, both of England and America, to be misled by the crafty and ambitious, when aided by learning and intelligence. A Gracchus may play the demagogue as well as a Marius or Catiline. Ignorant people may be deluded by a Wentworth or a Wilkes, by a Lord Gordon or a Mr. Cobbett: and men have been everywhere eager to avail themselves of popular excitement to gratify a vaulting ambition. Our country, it is feared, has at length reached the period of relaxing selfish prosperity, when a few of her gifted sons are preparing to raise the whirlwind and the storm of popular fury, in order to mount to that dazzling pinnacle of distinction which they despair of attaining by more legitimate means. Such men can operate only on the ignorant and credulous. In no State of this Union are the people so corrupt, venal, or barbarous as deliberately to sanction any system of measures manifestly unjust or iniquitous. They are not, like the beggarly rabble of degenerate Rome, ready to sell their suffrages or services to the highest bidder. Nor do they resemble the degraded populace of a modern European Metropolis, that may be roused by the flattering blandishments of a cunning reformer or military adventurer. Our people are still free and honest citizens. They will espouse the cause of truth and liberty and justice, whenever they clearly comprehend it. The demagogue therefore, who would mould them to his purpose, must first make them believe that his object is righteous.—That the cause in which he would enlist their zeal is absolutely and unequivocally just. No man in this nation is sufficiently talented, eloquent, and popular to seduce a large body of the people, in any section of the country, to his standard, unless they become thoroughly persuaded that his aim is honourable and patriotic. They could not be hired or flattered to abet injustice, or to elevate personal lawless ambition.

But in regard to measures of policy and legislation which they do not understand, it is easy, by incessant misrepresentation and artful appeals, effectually to blind and mislead them, until they fancy themselves egregiously wronged; and that they are called on, by every consideration of duty and interest, to seek by force that relief or redress which is denied them by government. While under the spell of this delusion, a fictitious grievance is the same to them as a real one. They will contend for what they believe to be right, as sturdily as they would do were they assured of the fact by a divine revelation.

Now precisely such is the present aspect of our national affairs. Questions are in agitation before the public, which but few of our ordinary citizens are capable of fully investigating and appreciating for themselves. The Bank—the Tariff—Internal Improvements—how many even of our most enlightened sages are masters of these perplexing themes of universal discussion and concernment? They have a length and a breadth, a height and a depth—they involve so many apparently dissimilar and conflicting interests—they reach so far into the future, and affect so many rights, so many branches of industry, so many local privileges or prejudices—they bear so directly on doubtful unsettled constitutional doctrines or constructions—are alarming or harmless, beneficial or noxious, according to opinions already formed relative to the powers reserved by the several States or conceded to the General Government—that the wisest statesmen need not blush to acknowledge the difficulty of an equitable adjustment, and of arriving at clear, definite, unqualified opinions which may be fearlessly inculcated at all times and in all places.

Are these vexed questions, then, within the competency of every village editor and of every village declaimer summarily to pronounce upon? Are the people—the mass of the people anywhere—adequate to this high duty? Of course not. And hence the wily demagogue has ample scope for the exercise of his peculiar gifts. He may dogmatize in learned phrase and pompous diction, without fear of rebuke or exposure, until his auditors feel the conviction that all is right or that all is wrong—as the case may be. For both these opposite effects are produced by the same means in different places at the same time. And in each case the people are equally innocent and equally imposed on. They receive as oracular, the statements and illustrations of their leaders—to whom they habitually look for information upon such intricate matters

They are flattered too, at the same time that they are cheated. Not that their immediate instructors are always wilful deceivers. They may be more fool than knave. They may themselves be the mere unconscious instruments of some great magician, who moves the wires unseen behind the curtain; and whose mandate is law throughout all his dependent and affiliated ranks.

I have such entire confidence in the unsophisticated native integrity and good sense of the great body of our people, as to affirm without hesitation, that not a single State or county could be found which would advocate injustice, knowing it to be injustice. The people of Massachusetts, for example, would not vote, if they could do it with impunity and with the certainty of success, to levy a direct tax on the citizens of South Carolina for their own particular benefit. Nor would they sustain the tariff a single day if they knew it to be oppressive to one portion of the Union, and beneficial only to another. They are taught, and they believe, that it is equally advantageous to all. They support it therefore as a great national blessing. If they err, it is because they have been badly instructed. Send them to college, and perhaps they will be able to form a better judgment. This would be wiser and cheaper, more humane and more logical, more republican and more Christian, than to attempt their conversion at the point of the bayonet.

In like manner, the good people of the South oppose and eschew the tariff, not because it is in their view a fair and equitable system of taxation. They are willing to bear their due proportion of the public burdens. Nor do they denounce it because it promotes their own industry in common with that of the whole Republic. But because they are instructed that it is a Yankee project to render them tributary to the avaricious North. That it is virtually a direct and almost prohibitory tax upon their agricultural staples, and therefore ruinous in its character and tendencies. They are further made to believe that it is the settled policy —the inflexible determination of the despotic, arbitrary, covetous North, to maintain this odious tariff, at all hazards, henceforth and forever. And that the only possible remedy is *nullification:* which may lead—but no matter—to civil war and to the dismemberment of our glorious Union!

Here, then, is a two-fold delusion. First, as to the fact; and second, as to the remedy. The South is made to believe that the North is deliberately unjust and oppressive. Whereas, among the plain people of the North, there exists no such design or desire. The people, as such, would not do injustice to the Hottentots —much less to their own brethren. The tariff may be as partial and mischievous as the South represents it; but the North does not perceive or believe it to be so. There is some difference between an injury inflicted ignorantly and unconsciously, and another committed with malice prepense and aforethought. And the very *gist* of the matter lies in the *quo animo*—the purpose—the intention. I do not believe that a majority of any one thousand American citizens, including manufacturers themselves, could be found in any vicinage of New England, New York, or Pennsylvania, who would insist on a continuance of the tariff, if they believed it to be as onerous on the South as the Southerners themselves proclaim it to be. Nor would the Southerners be thus madly exasperated, if they fully understood the sentiments of their well intentioned brethren at the North. Nor would they, if left to themselves, ever dream of nullification as a remedy for their grievances—admitting them to be as gross and monstrous and unbearable, as they are currently portrayed in many of their leading journals and by not a few of their most prominent statesmen. The remedy would be infinitely worse than the disease, and could never secure the object professedly aimed at, nor compensate for a thousandth part of the miseries which it might entail upon themselves and upon the whole Republic. I leave out of the account political chieftains on both sides. They have their own game to play. And it is precisely to expose this foul play that I have glanced at a topic so unclassical, and apparently so uncongenial with the spirit of a literary festival.

What then is the proper and only remedy for all such evils? Undoubtedly, it is simply this: The people must be more thoroughly instructed. If a dozen or twenty knowing individuals can thus misguide and deceive the multitude, either at the North or at the South, they must be met and encountered by other knowing ones of equal ability, if not of better principles. When the number of intelligent men in any place is comparatively large, it will not be in the power of one or a few to impose on the whole community. In no State, city or county, could even a Pericles or a Tully long control the popular mind, if opposed by a Franklin or a Henry. It would be vain to eulogize the tariff in Philadelphia, if the people could discern and estimate its [reputed, I do not say, acknowledged] injustice. And equally vain to preach up nullification in Charleston, were the whole subject thoroughly comprehended by the citizens generally.

Since then we cannot prevent the existence and constant growth of learned men of some sort and to some extent, let us have as many as possible. If they are rogues all—why, then, set a rogue to catch a rogue. If fifty league together to do harm, let us have a thousand, and then union will be impracticable: and fifty thousand will be still less dangerous. The more the better. And if the whole sovereign people would get knowledge, like Franklin in the workshop, or like Jefferson in the college, or like Washington on the farm and in the camp, or like Whitney everywhere, they would probably be none the worse either as private citizens or public benefactors.

And here I take occasion to remark, for the special benefit of my youthful charge, that if they would become qualified to command respect in the world by their talents, their virtues, or their attainments, they have yet a great work to perform. We have heard and read much of self-made and self-taught men.

The truth is, that every eminent man—especially among the literary, the scientific, the professional—has been a self-made man. Bacon and Locke, Milton and Newton, Burke and Mansfield were as truly self-made and self-taught men, as were Johnson and Franklin, Furguson and Rittenhouse, Herschel and Fulton. The first enjoyed the advantages of a college directly, the latter indirectly: and all attained distinction by the same intellectual process. They severally availed themselves of all the instruments and sources of knowledge within their reach: and persevering industry, as a law of their existence, ensured them victory and honour. Rumford, Hutton, Davy, Sherman, Pope, Wythe were as much debtors to the college as were Barrow, Edwards, Dwight, Fox, Scott or Canning. The books, the science, the literary taste, the universal consideration attendant on superior mental endowments, which colleges had created, multiplied, diffused, and everywhere exhibited, led Franklin, as they have led thousands, to imitate, to master, to emulate, to rival the excellence thus presented to their view and to their ambition. Had there been no colleges or seminaries of liberal learning—no literary or scientific enterprise or spirit abroad—Franklin might have been a Confucius or a Numa among barbarians, but he would never have been the first of philosophers and statesmen among the most enlightened nations of the earth.

The great men of Greece were all nurtured in her colleges, in one or other of the modes just specified—

as had been those of Egypt and Babylon and Phœnicia, centuries before. Her statesmen and her generals were thoroughly educated and literary men. Among her distinguished warriors were Pericles, Themistocles, Aristides, Socrates, Æschylus, Sophocles, Thucydides, Xenophon—the brightest names also in the catalogue of her literature, eloquence and philosophy. Nor did the Roman hero and politician disdain the arts and accomplishments of conquered Greece—as the Gracchi, the Scipios, the Bruti, the Catos, the Luculli, the Cæsars, the Ciceros may testify. But when the learned colleges of Athens, of Rome, of Alexandria were extinguished by barbarian conquest, and all western Christendom had become the prey of ignorance and despotism, letters and refinement still lingered within the proud walls of Bagdad, of Cordova and of Constantinople. At length, in the 13th and 14th centuries, the university again resumed its proper office, and began to scatter light amidst the surrounding darkness—especially in Italy, France, Germany, Holland and Britain. The ancient classics were disinterred from beneath the rubbish of ages—were studied, edited and admired. The art of printing was seasonably invented. The capture of Constantinople by the Turkish Moslems, in the 15th century, dispersed a host of veteran Grecians among the schools of western Europe. Colleges were everywhere established, enlarged and improved. And the first grand result was the glorious Reformation. Here was the dawn of modern liberty, and of that vast process of amelioration which has been advancing and extending far and wide ever since. The influence of enlightening literature has been felt, not only in Protestant Christendom, but throughout Roman Catholic Europe; and is penetrating the strongholds even of Mohammedan and Pagan priestcraft and degradation. All this marvellous improvement has been effected by the university and the schoolmaster. Let no man deem lightly of the instrument which has elevated himself and millions of his kindred to so lofty a height in the scale of being.—Which secures to him liberty of conscience, the rights of humanity, the fruits of his industry, and all the blessings and immunities of free institutions and of self-government.

Wherever the university has been suffered to flourish and expand, and to send forth its salutary streams among the people, there have been growing up both the capacity and the determination to resist all gross oppression. And *there* too a decided progress has been made in all the arts of peace, and especially in the science of government. In Spain, Portugal and Russia, a fool or a ruffian may be tolerated on the throne, because the university has been kept in bondage and the people in ignorance. But were a Nero seated on the throne of England to-morrow, he would not dare to violate a single law of the realm. He could no more enact the part of a Richard or a Henry, than the meanest subject could commit murder with impunity.

But in our country, though we may not dread the cruelties of a Nero, or the proscriptions of a Sylla, or the usurpations of a Cæsar, yet we may dread the arts of a popular favourite acting upon an ignorant and excited people. We have no refuge or security from popular insanity but in the virtue and intelligence of the people themselves. This is our only bulwark against the inroads of ambition and the wiles of selfish profligacy. Every sensible man among us knows this to be the fact. Our Washingtons and Franklins and Jeffersons have long since announced it: and though dead, their warning voice is still heard and respected by every enlightened patriot. Base and reckless and suicidal is the policy which seeks to prostrate the college and university under the specious pretext of giving to the people a common school education.

I care as little about names as any man. If the *name* of college or university be unsavoury in the ears of the people or of the people's guardians and conscience keepers, let it be cashiered. Let our colleges and universities be called academies, lyceums, gymnasia, common schools, or popular intellectual workshops—or by any other republican appellation, if any more acceptable or less invidious can be invented. It is the thing—the substance—the knowledge—the mental enlargement and energy and power—that I would give to the people in as ample measure as possible. That they may be sovereign in fact as well as in name. That they may be capable of knowing and guarding and asserting their own rights and liberties, without the second sight of any political juggler or officious bankrupt Solomon.

I would create here in Nashville, or in Knoxville, or in Memphis, or in each, a university or great common school—with accommodations for a thousand pupils—with able instructors, libraries, apparatus, and all manner of useful fixtures and appurtenances—at the expense of the Commonwealth. Every poor youth, properly qualified, should be admitted to its privileges *gratis*. The rich might pay for their sons. But none should be excluded for want of means. If more than a thousand pupils should offer—enlarge the establishment, or erect others upon the same plan. This would be a species of internal improvement worthy of the Republic, and which would elevate Tennessee to a rank never yet attained by any people. And the Legislature which shall boldly lay the corner stone of such a magnificent temple of popular instruction, will deserve and will gain a glorious immortality, whatever may be the verdict of their constituents or of their contemporaries. Their magnanimous and enlightened patriotism will be celebrated a thousand lustrums after the petty interests and conflicts of this selfish generation shall be forgotten.

I have asserted that colleges have done good, or that learning has been useful. That, like wealth and power, when possessed only by a few, it has been often abused to the injury of others. That our college graduates have generally been the faithful sentinels and advocates of popular rights. That if any appear to be swerving from the straight path of rectitude, it is because they have discovered an ignorant mass on which to operate. That the only remedy for the evil—the only preventive of its recurrence and of its rapid increase—is the immediate education of a much larger proportion of the people. Not the giving them what is called a common school education—the most of them have this already—and it does not suffice. The man who can merely read and write is no match for the thorough-bred political gladiator. He cannot dispel the sophistry even of the village attorney or of the village gazette. He is just the man to be led astray by the newspaper essayist. And the newspaper is the very engine employed to gull the people who can read, but who are too ignorant to discriminate, to reason and to judge.

None but enemies of the people will ever gravely maintain that a common school education, in the ordinary meaning of the phrase, is all they need.* This would be virtually telling them to be hewers of wood and drawers of water under political task-masters forever. Why is it that our lawyers rule the nation, and fill all our lucrative offices, from the Presidency downwards? Simply and solely because they can do something more than read and write. If our mechanics and farmers would enter the lists with our lawyers, they must acquire the same degree of intellectual power and address. Nor would this prove a very difficult achievement. Take the common run of our lawyers—and like

---

* That I am hostile or indifferent to *common schools* will not be suspected by any person in the least acquainted with my views on the subject. I have been their public and zealous advocate on all suitable occasions. Among others, I may refer to a series of essays, which appeared in the Nashville Republican, during the winter and spring of 1831, under the caption of "Public Schools."

our parsons—they are *no great things.* The mechanics and farmers might easily beat them at their own game and with their own weapons. If they did but understand their interests, they would unite with the schoolmaster, make common cause with him, and assert their natural rights and influence in society. Let them take this matter of schools and colleges into their own hands. Let them rally around our most respectable and meritorious, though poor, persecuted and much reviled university. Let them contribute the trifle of a hundred thousand dollars or so, to its funds, and send to it a few hundred of their clever youths to acquire the art of lawyer-fighting—and we shall soon see them at the head of affairs, as they ought to be. This is the best advice that I can give them. If they prefer ignorance, and are determined to keep their sons in ignorance—then, farewell to all their greatness, and to all the dignity which their position might justly command. They may frown upon colleges—they may abuse them—they may starve them—they may scatter them to the winds—but they only sink themselves the lower in the general scale of humanity. Instead of training their own sons to illustrate their names and to adorn the Commonwealth, they will become the spoil and the scorn of every European or Eastern adventurer who may choose to settle among them. For they cannot interdict the ingress of as much talent and learning from abroad as will suffice to discharge those public and professional functions to which they would themselves be totally inadequate.

I have been pleading the cause of farmers and mechanics for some ten or a dozen years past. Because upon them, as enlightened, judicious, independent, patriotic citizens, depend the destinies of this Republic. The question is, shall they lead or be led? Shall they arrest and put down the factious spirit of unprincipled ambition, or shall they tamely lend themselves as the instruments and the victims of its desperate and treasonable purposes? The crisis has arrived when the people must speak and act wisely and resolutely, or their ability to speak and to act, with decisive efficiency, will be lost forever.

The lawyers are now our sole political guides and instructors. They engross the learning of the country; I mean all that learning which is brought to bear on government, legislation and public policy—for the physicians rarely intermeddle in these affairs; and the clergy ought forever to be excluded by law, if not by a high sense of duty. Our farmers and mechanics therefore, who constitute the great body of the people, are governed by the lawyers. Now it is not in human nature, that in such a country as ours, there should not grow up a sort of professional aristocracy, which in time may become irresistible. Wherever there is a privileged order, no matter how constituted—whether like the *patrician* of ancient, or the *ecclesiastic* of modern Rome—it will, if not duly checked and counterbalanced, in the long run, become overbearing and tyrannical. I look to the college for a seasonable supply of countervailing agents. I look to a well educated independent yeomanry as the sheet anchor of the Republic. I look forward to the period when it will not be deemed anti-republican for the college graduate to follow the plough; nor a seven days' wonder for the labourer to be intellectual and to comprehend the Constitution of his country.

I am not unfriendly to lawyers. I could say much in their praise, were I in the humour of pronouncing encomiums. In their proper sphere, they are useful and necessary. But that they should engross the legislative, judicial and executive functions of the government, is neither republican, nor safe, nor, upon any ground, defensible. There would be reason in the thing, if, like the farmers, they composed a large numerical majority of the population. But that a few thousand of any particular profession, class or order should rule over millions is as anomalous, and as inconsistent with the genius of our popular institutions, as would be an hereditary aristocracy possessing the same exclusive privilege. The farmers have no alternative but to yield their necks to the yoke, or to open up for their sons a great highway to the scientific halls of the university. Belonging, as I do, to their respectable fraternity by birth, by early association and by all the ties of kindred—the son of a labouring farmer, the brother of labouring farmers, and the father, it may be, of labouring farmers and mechanics—I cannot be indifferent to their welfare even upon the most selfish considerations. But I feel conscious of a higher motive. I seek to elevate my country, by imparting to all her sons the noblest attributes of humanity. That we may be forever a nation of enlightened, generous, high-minded, self-governing freemen. The envy and the admiration of the world.

I have availed myself of every suitable occasion to impress on the minds of my pupils the sacred duty which they owe their country, of endeavouring through life to promote the cause of popular education. To do their utmost to enlighten the public mind, and to establish a system calculated to diffuse useful knowledge among the labouring classes of the community. Let them be the persevering, intrepid, uncompromising advocates of the good old orthodox doctrines of our revolutionary heroes and sages. Countenanced by such a veteran phalanx of wisdom and philanthropy, and animated by the noble purpose of perpetuating the liberty and happiness of their country, they may well disregard the undeserved and groundless hostility which lofty virtue seldom fails to provoke.

I shall not stop to inquire what Tennessee has attempted or effected for the instruction of her half million of freemen. One thing I have heard however, which, though too monstrous to be credited, I feel constrained just to glance at. It is this—that some former legislatures, so far from having directly and munificently aided the paramount cause of education amongst us, have actually withheld from the schools and colleges funds which had been solemnly appropriated to their use by the National Congress. This I presume to be mere gratuitous slander. For, if true, it would be enough to impart fresh lustre to the everlasting fame even of the Goth and Vandal! History, however, will detail the facts: and impartial posterity will sit in judgment. I trust the present or a future legislature will correct the error, if any have been committed by their predecessors, so that the faithful historian may be enabled to record the satisfaction to justice, law, and honour, upon the same page which shall transmit the story of the people's wrongs.

There is magic in a sound—in a name—in country. Who does not love his country—one's own native country—the hallowed home of his infancy, of his kindred, of his fathers' sepulchres? How does it strike the ear and thrill the bosom of the pilgrim in a foreign land? What citizen of this vast Republic, when abroad in distant climes, has not felt the glow of patriotic enthusiasm and exultation mantle his cheek when the proud name *American* has greeted his ears from the voice of approving strangers—or burned with indignation if mentioned in terms of disrespect or measured praise? And are we about to forfeit our inherited title to this glorious appellation? Are we to be known hereafter as Tennesseans, or Carolinians, or Georgians, or Kentuckians, or New-Yorkers—and not as AMERICANS? We are the only people on this immense continent who have acquired and appropriated, by universal consent, the distinctive national epithet of *Americans.* The rest are Canadians, or Mexicans, or Peruvians, or Columbians, or Bolivians, or Brazilians. We, and we only, are Americans. And who so base as tamely to suffer this illustrious name to be merged in a dozen or twenty little party provincial by-words—to be scoffed at by all the world?

Every individual of a great, magnanimous and honoured nation, is himself a sharer of his country's glory. Her reputation is reflected upon himself. He becomes thereby more respectable in his own eyes, more chivalrous in his sentiments, and more sternly patriotic in all his purposes. His country's name, like a coronet of nobility, is a passport to honour and distinction whereever he goes. Thus it was in the better days of the Roman Commonwealth. *Roman* was a more august and commanding title than that of satrap, prince, or king. I am no blind admirer of Roman policy or of Roman virtue. But I do admire that personal self-devotion which could yield everything to country; and, as it were, identify individual existence with the prosperity and glory of the Republic. The patriotism of the old Roman was large and generous, though utterly regardless of every principle of international justice and morality. To Rome, as his supreme divinity, he consecrated his energies and his undivided homage. For her, he laboured and fought and conquered and died. His worst crimes were national, and were perpetrated to advance the grandeur of Rome. He never dreamed of elevating himself at the expense of his country. Of all such mean, stupid, selfish, infamous ambition, he was innocent and unsuspected. There was sublimity in his single-hearted devotion to country—however lamentably defective may have been the standard by which his martial achievements were estimated.

Happily for us, American patriotism and ambition may be gratified in a more legitimate sphere. Not in conquering other nations—not in extending the territorial limits of the Republic—not in enriching our Metropolis with the spoils and ruins of a thousand cities—not in blotting from the map of the world any rival Carthage or splendid Corinth—not in triumphs and ovations and gladiatorial butcheries to amuse an idle, besotted, rapacious rabble. We have no such objects of national ambition. War is not our congenial element. We covet no enlargement of territory. It is as vast already as even Roman ambition could desire. We have only to preserve it undivided and undiminished as a rich legacy to posterity. Upon this grand point our patriotic efforts must be concentrated. The union of the States must be maintained at every hazard and sacrifice. This is the first grand maxim of our political creed. It should be inculcated in every school and by every patriot. It should be instilled into the heart of every child, as a sacred principle, by every parent. THE UNION OF THE STATES should be the motto and the watchword of every American, and be engraven upon the arms and the banners of every party, sect, and institution of the land. It should be heresy, treason, infamy, to compass its destruction or to impair its foundations.

The Union safe—we have other noble national objects to achieve. The arts of peace—science, literature, religion—whatever embellishes, whatever elevates, whatever purifies the character, and contributes to the happiness of mankind—these it will be our study and our ambition to promote. We have a national literature to create. Englishmen have affected to despise us as a degenerate and vulgar race. We have taught them some seasonable lessons at the cannon's mouth, both on the land and upon the ocean. This species of bloody rivalry, we trust, is at an end. We must now contend for the prize of intellectual supremacy. For though English literature is as much our inheritance as the English language and English jurisprudence, yet since we are refused the boon and are daily stigmatized on account of our literary poverty and meagre scholarship, let us have a literature strictly American—such as Americans may be proud of, and such as British criticism may no longer ridicule or annihilate. Let every department of useful learning, of profound science, of elegant letters, of manly authorship, be boldly essayed and perseveringly prosecuted.

Providence has placed us on a lofty and conspicuous eminence. The eyes of the world are upon us. We have a glorious part assigned us: and deep and damning will be our infamy if we fail to perform it. To us has been intrusted the experiment, never yet fully tried, whether a people can govern themselves without kings or nobility or standing armies. To us is allotted the enviable distinction of demonstrating, on the largest scale, that any number of millions of free and equal citizens may dwell together in peace, and exercise all the prerogative of self-government without tumult, anarchy or domestic warfare. We are to exhibit the phenomenon of a well educated, intelligent, virtuous nation—free without licentiousness—religious without a religious establishment—obedient to laws administered by citizen magistrates, without the show of official lictors or fasces, and without the aid of mercenary legions or janizaries. We have it in commission to instruct the world in the science and in the art of government. Should we march onward in the career of peaceful philanthropy which Heaven seems to have destined and marked out for us—what an invaluable inheritance shall we not bequeath to the latest generations, in the honoured—universally honoured—hallowed name of AMERICAN?

In conclusion, I adopt the language and the sentiments of an eminent living statesman: and sure I am that every American, to whom the unsullied splendour of his country's glory is dearer than life, will respond a hearty Amen.

"While the Union lasts, we have high, exciting, gratifying prospects spread out before us, for us and our children. Beyond that, I seek not to penetrate the veil. God grant that, in my day, at least, that curtain may not rise. God grant that on my vision never may be opened what lies behind. When my eyes shall be turned to behold, for the last time, the sun in Heaven, may I not see him shining on the broken and dishonoured fragments of a once glorious Union; on States dissevered, discordant, belligerent; on a land rent with civil feuds, or drenched, it may be, in fraternal blood! Let their last feeble and lingering glance rather behold the gorgeous Ensign of the Republic, now known and honoured throughout the earth, still full high advanced, its arms and trophies streaming in their original lustre, not a stripe erased or polluted, nor a single star obscured —bearing for its motto no such miserable interrogatory as, *What is all this worth?* Nor those other words of delusion and folly, *Liberty first, and Union afterwards*— but everywhere, spread all over in characters of living light, blazing on all its ample folds, as they float over the sea and over the land, and in every wind under the whole Heavens, that other sentiment, dear to every true American heart—Liberty *and* Union, now and forever, one and inseparable."*

Young Gentlemen: We now part, perhaps to meet no more on earth. Soon, very soon, we must all meet at the bar of the eternal Judge of quick and dead, to hear the last solemn award which shall fix our destiny for weal or woe forever! How trivial are all terrestrial concerns—the honours of literature, the renown of heroism, the achievements of the patriot, the reputation of the statesman, the delights of popularity, the rewards of painful industry, or even the glory of country—when compared with the awful and resplendent realities of a future world, the blessings of immortality, the felicity of Heaven, the holy friendship of angelic spirits, the unspeakable love and approving smile of the King of kings and the Lord of lords!

To follow the meek and lowly example of HIM who

* The Candidates were then admitted to their Degrees with the customary formalities, and the following remarks were addressed to them.

went about doing good—to imitate the unobtrusive virtues of HIM, who, when on earth, had not where to lay his head—to secure a refuge in the mercy and righteousness and atoning sacrifice of HIM whose kingdom is not of this world—to suffer contumely, reproach, scorn, contempt, poverty, persecution and death for HIM who endured them all, without a murmur, for our sake—will, in the great day of universal reckoning and retribution, be accounted infinitely more glorious and honourable than to have conquered armies or governed empires, or than to have founded or saved republics. The humblest disciple of the despised and crucified babe of Bethlehem will then eclipse, in celestial splendour, the proudest genius that ever astonished or delighted mankind. The martyr's crown will then have acquired a value and a radiance, even in royal eyes, which a thousand worlds could not purchase.

Therefore, set not your hearts upon this transitory and delusive scene. With all your getting, get understanding. Covet chiefly that pure, enlightening, saving wisdom which is from above. Seek first and above all things the kingdom of God and his righteousness, and you will be armed against every foe and be sure of the divine favour and protection. Be Christians, that you may be happy in time—happy in death—and happy forever!

BACCALAUREATE ADDRESS.

[UNIVERSITY OF NASHVILLE, OCTOBER 1, 1834.]

BACCALAUREATE ADDRESS

AT THE UNIVERSITY OF NASHVILLE, 1834.

YOUNG GENTLEMEN:

Ten years have now elapsed since the attempt was made to resuscitate and reorganize the institution which this day enrolls your names among her *Alumni;* and which you are henceforth to cherish and to honour as your Alma Mater.

During this brief space, many extraordinary events have occurred both to adorn and to disgrace the page of our world's history. And even among ourselves, the current of affairs has not flowed onward in unruffled smoothness, or without giving rise to incidents calculated sometimes to cheer, and more frequently to dishearten the friends of learning and education.

Death, too, has removed from the scene of action one and another of our veteran advocates and coadjutors. Nor has he spared the vigorous manly youth, who was just beginning to consecrate his talents and energies to the noblest cause within the scope of enlightened philanthropy. The Trustees, the Faculty, and the Alumni, have all been visited, at successive periods, by the fell destroyer: and several from each of these bodies have been summoned to their everlasting home. We have paid the last melancholy tribute of respect to the remains and to the memory of the venerable father, the talented professor, and the juvenile companion of our studies and of our affectionate counsels.

We, however, have been graciously spared to witness the celebration of the ninth joyous anniversary *commencement* of our beloved University, under circumstances singularly calculated to elicit the sentiment and the expression of unfeigned gratitude to our Almighty and most beneficent Preserver. While the exterminating pestilence* has been sweeping over the land, carrying death and desolation into thousands of happy families, our little community has been guarded and defended by the good providence of Israel's God and the Christian's Saviour. And shall we—can we—forget the hand which has thus protected and shielded us in the dark hour of peril and terror and dismay? No, my young friends, we have been taught a lesson in the school of mourning and anguish which can never be effaced from the heart of sympathizing humanity. And our future lives will be too short to evince the sense of that profound obligation which binds us forever to the cause of truth and virtue, of country and mankind, of religion and of God.

Under the auspices of my distinguished and revered predecessor†—the devoted pioneer of science in this then almost savage wilderness, and the nursing father of our still infant and still unendowed seminary—

---

* The Cholera.

† James Priestly, LL.D.

nineteen young gentlemen were admitted to the usual academic degrees. And these *first fruits* of Cumberland College, the *University of Nashville* will ever be proud to acknowledge, and to hold up as illustrious examples to all her future Alumni. Five of these, we regret to learn, have been cut down in the morning of life and hope, of high promise and lofty aspiring: and they survive only in the hearts of the few who knew and loved them as sons, as brothers, and as friends.

One hundred and ten names have since been added to the catalogue of our college graduates [exclusive of honorary members.] And of these we mourn the premature decease of four gifted youths, whose generous sympathy and support, whose moral and intellectual worth, whose private and public character, can now be estimated only by the glowing picture which hallowed friendship was fain to portray.*

---

* Alas! who can tell what a day may bring forth? Since the above paragraph was penned, and since the last setting sun, another of our worthiest and most eloquent sons has been added to this melancholy catalogue. And again we mingle our tears and our sympathy with a twice stricken, bereaved and disconsolate circle of endeared relatives and friends. Whose loss, in this world, is indeed irreparable, and above all human power to estimate or to alleviate. Let them—let us—bow submissive to High Heaven's most righteous decree: and endeavour to be ourselves also ready, at any moment, for our departure to

"That undiscovered country, from whose bourn
No traveller returns."

Oct. 2d 1834. This day, another of the Alumni, Alphonso Gibbs, Esq., of the class of 1832, died at the house of his father, Gen. Gibbs, in this vicinity. Greatly beloved and lamented by all who knew him.

The total number of living Graduates is now therefore only one hundred and nineteen.

Our University then may be presumed to number, among the living, one hundred and twenty individuals, [the precise number, so far as can be ascertained, is 120,] (exclusive of honorary members,) who have been decorated with her laurel, and who are recognized as her sons and graduates. To these may be added about three hundred and fifty others, who have been educated, to a greater or less extent, within her walls; but who did not find it convenient to remain long enough her inmates to entitle them to the first degree in the Arts. How many of the latter description may have been thus partially trained under the former faculty, I have not the means of ascertaining. Probably not less than a hundred. Altogether then, five or six hundred young men have enjoyed the privilege of studying at this institution, and of acquiring more or less of the elements of a liberal education. If these have done, are doing, and are likely to do, their duty, in the various relations, pursuits, professions, and offices of life, it will not be denied that the University has rendered the State some service. The tree is ever known by its fruits: and by these it will be judged. Deeply as we are personally interested in the fair fame and prosperity of your Alma Mater, we cheerfully submit her reputation and her destiny to this just and honourable test. We ask no stinted indulgence, no condescending favour, no constructive charity, no flattering meed of common place applause, no conventional unmeaning compliments which in courtly phrase come gently to the ear but roughly to the heart,—no, nothing in this fashion do we covet.

We say—or rather, let the University proudly say—there are our sons. We send them forth into the world. And by the world's spontaneous verdict upon their training and their bearing will we abide. We calmly and confidently await the world's decision: and we feel assured of no mortifying disappointment. Our faith is strong, unwavering, invincible. And our purpose to persevere in the good work, which has thus far been signally prospered in the midst of every species of hinderance and discouragement, cannot be shaken. The tongue which now speaks our high resolve, and bids defiance to scrutiny, to prejudice, to jealousy, to cowardice, to calumny, to malevolence, may be silent in the tomb long ere the glorious victory shall be achieved. But, WE, the UNIVERSITY, live forever! And generations yet unborn shall rejoice in our triumphs, and pronounce the eulogium which our labours will have nobly won.

It is true, we boast of no rich governmental inheritance or endowments—no splendid domain in the unappropriated lands within our own territorial limits, or within those of the Nation which stretch westward over half the continent still unsubdued and unexplored. Such a fair landed domain we once did dream of—but, "like the baseless fabric of a vision," it has evanished "into thin air," under the potent spell of the political magician: or, if you please, under the wise policy and equitable legislation of Tennessee's much honoured and most honourable statesmen. From the liberal grant of Congress, then, we anticipate no benefit whatever: at least, not until our own representatives in that august body shall cordially advocate our claims, and boldly present our appeal to the justice, honour, and magnanimity of the Nation.*

We count not on the State's treasury, nor upon legislative indemnification. We rely not upon ecclesiastical patronage, or sectarian zeal, or individual munificence: nor, indeed, upon any of the usual sources of pecuniary revenue which have reared and sustained so many flourishing institutions in other sections of our happy Republic.

We belong to no sect or party in Church or State. We open our portals wide, and proffer our instructions freely to enterprising moral youth of every political and religious creed in the land. Literature and science, language and philosophy, morals and virtue, unalloyed and unclouded by the dogmas of any sect or school, we inculcate and exemplify as best we can. And we appeal to the common sense and equity of mankind for the wisdom of our system and the honesty of our proceedings.

We are the staunch uncompromising advocate of genuine religion—of pure unadulterated Christianity—but in all matters which distinguish one class or sect or church from another, we leave our pupils to parental

* We mean not, however, to moralize or to complain. The story of our wrongs we leave to the honest pen of the future historian. Our title deeds we commit to the archives of the world's high court of chancery, and bequeath them as a black-letter legacy to the antiquarian Cokes and Seldens of posterity, to illustrate the theory of our plastic jurisprudence, and the practical omnipotence of our popular parliaments.

guidance and discretion; and to the ministerial cares of the clergy in our city to whom they severally yield a voluntary preference. Every religious denomination in Tennessee has its church or place of worship in Nashville; and to these our youth have free access at all times. And they are required to attend the public preaching of the gospel precisely as parents direct. With their religious faith or peculiar theological creed we never intermeddle in the slightest degree. That we have been perfectly catholic and perfectly impartial in this momentous and delicate concern—about which the most extraordinary solicitude and jealousy are wont to be manifested—we dare venture to affirm. And we know that we stand this day before the great public altogether above suspicion. True, we have been and still are denounced by the little bigots, and sapient gossips, and *would be popes* of all sects and parties. But their petty jealousy, and insidious misrepresentations and unappeasable malignancy, we heed not. Our course is fair, and honourable, and direct, and ever onward.

That we are making a doubtful experiment, in the estimation of most men, we are fully apprised. That an institution, thus unbefriended, unendowed, unsupported by any sect or party, without funds or patronage, should ultimately succeed, is scarcely to be anticipated in the ordinary course of events. And its failure has been often predicted, even by those whose liberal views and sentiments would lead them most heartily to rejoice in the discovery that they were no prophets.

Where then is the ground of our hope and of our encouragement? It is in the growing strength and moral influence of our own enlightened, loyal, and patriotic sons—who issue, year after year, from our classic halls, imbued with the chivalrous spirit and republican virtue of the brightest age of Greek and Roman glory; and animated by the celestial principles of Christian magnanimity and benevolence—and whose voice shall yet be heard by a generous and honest, though hitherto much abused and misguided people. It is in these, under the propitious smiles, and overruling providence of the Most High, that we place our confidence and garner up our soul's fondest aspirations. They will never prove recreant or traitorous. The claims of Alma Mater upon their affections, their zeal, their labours, their influence, their talents and their wealth, will ever be acknowledged as of paramount and everlasting obligation.

Such, my young friends, are a few of the last words which the University may be supposed to address to you at this interesting moment, when she pronounces her farewell benediction upon your heads, and offers up to Heaven her fervent prayers for your earthly prosperity and final salvation.

In the name of my respected colleagues, I congratulate you cordially upon the happy termination of your college novitiate; and upon the fair prospect of professional eminence and usefulness which now lies before you.

On leaving college, however, you will have escaped

from no irksome restraints, because none have ever been imposed by us, which the moral sense and mature reason of all good citizens would not voluntarily impose on themselves. As moral agents—as the subjects of moral discipline—you will continue through life under the same great moral code of rules and laws which the University and the world alike recognize as of universal and perpetual obligation. Do not imagine, therefore, that you are about to enjoy more liberty, or a greater license, either for the neglect of duty or the infraction of any positive statute or institution, whether human or divine.

You have not been governed—we have never sought to govern you—by mere arbitrary or magisterial authority. We have laboured to inculcate the one grand essential doctrine of self-government; and to inspire you with those just sentiments of honour, truth and virtue, which ought ever to influence and to regulate your conduct. In a word, we have taught you to govern yourselves; and to respect yourselves. We have never regarded or treated you as schoolboys. We have encouraged you to feel, to think, to speak, to act—as men, as freemen, as gentlemen—but with the modesty, gentleness and deferential docility which always characterize and adorn the well-bred, ingenuous and high-minded youth. We have lived together as friends and equals. Our mutual intercourse has been maintained by a mutual interchange of the kindly courtesies which our several duties, ages and circumstances naturally and obviously prompted and enjoined.

If any of you have ever, from youthful inadvertency

or indiscretion, passed the boundary of strict decorum—the error is already forgotten. If we have received evil at your hands, or if you have slighted our counsels or instructions, we have returned good for evil,—as the literary awards, this day dispensed, will abundantly testify. Henceforth we remember only your virtues. Upon these we shall delight to dwell and to expatiate: and these only shall we speak of and proclaim. For, of our pupils, the world never hears aught from us but good. In all their future conduct we take a deep and lively interest. Our influence and exertions in their behalf will never be expected in vain. In their fair fame and prosperity we shall rejoice. And every blessing bestowed on them will be reflected on ourselves, and constitute the principal ingredient of our earthly felicity.

As we have aimed to render you masters of the art of self-government, so likewise have we endeavoured to manage the difficult process of instruction in such manner as to make the work your own—a pleasure and not a task. We have taught you how to study—how to cultivate your own minds—how to advance, by daily, and easy, and certain progress in every scientific and literary department which you may be inclined to explore. And we now dismiss you, under the full persuasion, that you have learned how to educate yourselves; that you possess the faculty and the desire of intellectual improvement which will never permit you to be idle, or to rest satisfied with any actual attainments, while you retain the power to enlarge their value or amount.

The habit of self-government—of self-instruction—of industrious persevering application, of thorough inquiry, of profound investigation, of manly independent thinking and reflection, of legitimate reasoning, of logical induction, of rigorous demonstration, of discriminating unprejudiced judgment, of resolutely embracing and maintaining the *truth* and the *right* whenever and wherever discovered—this habit, already partially acquired, will, if duly confirmed by future exertions, insure you an honourable, enlightened and commanding influence in society.

That you may realize all the bright visions which youthful fancy may lawfully indulge—that you may be truly great and truly good—as eminently happy, honoured and useful, as talents, learning and piety can render you—is the fervent prayer of your academical instructors and associates.

Go hence in charity and peace. Fear God, and keep his commandments. Seek daily supplies of wisdom and instruction in the holy oracles of inspiration. Let the Bible be your friend and counsellor. Avoid wicked companions, seductive pleasures, corrupting honours, degrading avarice, and all the blandishments of a reckless ambition. Preserve a conscience void of offence towards God and towards men. In prosperity be meek and humble; and with gratitude acknowledge your heavenly Benefactor: and in adversity you will not be utterly forsaken, nor overwhelmed in the blackness of despair. The Sun of righteousness will illumine the darkest path, and shed a cheering radiance upon the ruins and desolations of all human grandeur. The fairy illusions of fervid youth must soon give place to the sober realities of manhood and old age. The brilliancy of genius, the hoarded treasures of knowledge, the splendour of wealth and power and rank and office, will avail nothing in the last great conflict with the king of terrors. The whole world will then appear too mean a price to offer for the humblest Christian believer's hope.

May the Christian's hope, and the Christian's faith, and the Christian's charity, and the Christian's joys, and the Christian's heaven—all be yours!

The blessing of the Father, and the Son, and the Holy Ghost—the one living and true God—be upon you, and abide with you, forever and ever. Amen!

SPEECH IN BEHALF

OF THE

UNIVERSITY OF NASHVILLE.

ANNIVERSARY COMMENCEMENT,

AT THE UNIVERSITY OF NASHVILLE, 1837.

I HAVE made several speeches heretofore, on divers occasions, in behalf of the University. I am going to trouble you again with some remarks upon the same very unpopular and very hackneyed theme. I mean *now* to make the appeal *direct* to the good citizens of Nashville; and to them chiefly, if not exclusively. In the first place, I will glance at a few objections which are currently urged or insiduously whispered against the University. And, in the second place, I shall endeavour to present a score or two of the many thousand considerations which ought to induce you to sustain it.

I. 1. The first class of objections, which we notice, may be styled *personal*. These refer to, and implicate more or less, the personal character and qualifications of the trustees, president, professors, and other officers of the institution. Of the trustees, I shall say nothing. The Board consists of ex-presidents, governors, senators, members of Congress and of the State Legislature, magistrates, lawyers, physicians and farmers: of men who have filled, or who now fill, the highest and most respectable offices in the nation: whom the people of the Union and of this Commonwealth have delighted to honour, and to whose wisdom and integrity they have confided the dearest interests of their country. If such men cannot be safely trusted to manage the concerns of a university, to whom shall we look for a superior or better superintendence? Probably no other Board of Trustees in the United States can exhibit an array of names so well known, or so eminently distinguished, or so universally popular. And if you are not satisfied with these, you must be hard to please indeed.

I shall pass the Faculty, also, without defence or eulogy. Let each member stand or fall according to his deserts. Let him be judged by his acts and by his peers. A president or professor may be incompetent, physically, morally, intellectually—or he may be culpably negligent and inefficient. But then, he is removable at the pleasure of the Board: and, at the worst, he cannot live always. He will soon be off the stage and out of the way. His incapacity therefore, whether great or small, real or pretended, ought never to be paraded before an intelligent public, as jeoparding the existence or permanent prosperity of the University itself. He, I repeat, may, at any moment, be got rid of: and at most, he is but an accident, a circumstance—while the University lives forever. You would not denounce your country or your country's Constitution and republican form of government, because you might not happen to approve the existing administration. The latter you may assail and oppose with all your faculties of reason and argument and ridicule; while yet you will stand by your country and the Constitution and the republican system, though a world were to rise up in arms against you. So, in like manner, stand by the University, whatever may be the character of its temporary governors and teachers. If the University be in itself a good thing, or capable of being made good: do not desert or renounce it, merely because some of its non-essential appendages may not be particularly acceptable to your critical judgment or keener sagacity.

2. The second class of objections assume a *party* complexion. Party men, whether political or religious, are apt to regard everything with partial eyes which belongs to their own party; and to frown upon whatever is either neutral or lukewarm or dissentient or adverse. They would have a party college—a political or sectarian college.—A hot-bed for the rearing of political partisans or religious zealots and sectarian bigots. A college which disclaims party attachments is very likely to be repudiated by all parties. Our University occupies a position somewhat peculiar. Its trustees are composed of very decided political leaders and champions of both the great parties which divide our country at the present crisis. Of the precise political creed or bias of the Faculty, the speaker is entirely ignorant. He knows not the politics of any of his colleagues. He has never conversed with them on the subject: and he has never heard an avowal of principles or predilections from one of them. He cares not what their politics are, or for whom they vote. Thus it is also in regard to religious

opinions. Both trustees and faculty belong to different sects and denominations. And the students are left to their own free choice, or to parental guidance, in both religion and politics. Their liberty has never been infringed or interfered with in either respect. No attempt has ever been made to proselyte a single youth to any faith, political or religious. We all profess to be Christians and republicans: and we fain would have our pupils to be honest Christians and consistent republicans. This is the utmost of our aim, in all our labours, instructions and exhortations—so far as politics and religion are in question. They may be Methodists, Presbyterians, Baptists, Episcopalians, Roman Catholics, Quakers — Whigs, Democrats, Federalists, Conservatives — we care not—so that they are Christians and patriots. We go for the Constitution of our country and for the religion of Christendom: and we stop not to notice or to inculcate the dogmas of any school, sect or party. Such was the system avowed at the commencement of our connexion with the University and with this community. We gave to the public a solemn pledge to this effect at the outset. Have we ever departed from our system or failed to redeem our pledge? We challenge the severest scrutiny: and we defy contradiction. Our University has never enlisted under the banners of any sect or party, and we trust she never will. The youth of all parties and of all sects are equally favoured, protected and respected within her walls. And when they cease to be so, it will be time enough to complain and to sound the tocsin of alarm.

3. A third objection arises from the locality of the institution. Nashville is a gay, dissipated, fashionable place—quite unfit for boys—dangerous to their morals and to their purses. Is it so? Then, whose is the fault? Is Nashville too wicked—too grossly wicked—to be intrusted with a University? Dare you utter such a plea, or pronounce so harsh a verdict upon your own civic character? Will the citizens of Nashville gravely affirm that they are so immoral, licentious and profligate, that the juvenile stranger may not venture to reside or sojourn among them without peril to his virtue? or will they permit others thus to asperse and to slander them? That some of our respectable and intelligent citizens have asserted and do believe that this little city is too wicked for a college to prosper among them, is true: for I have heard this opinion and belief expressed with all the seriousness and regret of deep-rooted conviction. It is obvious that the prevalence of such a notion among ourselves and its publicity abroad, must exert a sinister influence upon the prospects and fortunes of an institution just struggling for bare existence, and prove extremely discouraging to the zeal and efforts of its friends. In the abstract, or speaking absolutely, the objection may be well founded. But comparatively, or in reference to other places, it is groundless and impertinent.

Nashville is bad enough, no doubt. But it is not worse than other cities, towns and villages—whether large or small—throughout the Union. You will search in vain for a purer moral atmosphere either within the limits of our own Commonwealth, or in the adjacent States, or even beyond the mountains. If Nashville, then, be too wicked for a college, it follows, by parity of reasoning, that a college ought not and cannot be sustained in any city or town in the United States—or in the world. For vice abounds everywhere: and to an extent frequently, which would cause even Nashville to blush at the thought of a comparison. And yet colleges do flourish, and have flourished for ages, in hundreds of these graceless cities and dissolute country villages. This argument or objection then is inapplicable and nugatory. It is urged, probably, by those who know little or nothing about the real character and condition of other places. Whatever is evil and pernicious within the range of our daily observation, we notice, and reflect upon, and magnify, and talk about: while of distant towns, we hear nothing but the good and the fair and the favourable. And "distance always lends enchantment to the view."

Again, if Nashville be really too wicked for a college; it is too wicked for schools of any description; it is too wicked even for a family residence. No parent ought to live here. His children will be obnoxious to all sorts of malign influences from their birth onward, through every stage of domestic discipline; and in spite of all his vigilance and solicitude. You ought instantly to depart from a place which you pronounce so abominably depraved, and so imminently hazardous to the welfare of your offspring. But here you are, and here are your sons and daughters, and here you and they are likely to abide. Some of you, perhaps, may calculate to evade both the argument and the dangers, by resolving to educate your sons at distant seminaries—where they will learn better morals and acquire more correct habits. Very well—by and by—after three or four years of *renowning* abroad—they will return home. What now are their moral principles and habits? Are they superior in these or any other respects, to the home-bred natives of the West? Are they *now*, after all this foreign training and lavish expenditure, the immaculate paragons of virtue and intellectual refinement, which your fond hopes had anticipated or your dreaming fancies had pictured? Are they proof against all temptation and example and solicitation? Do they walk erect amidst the moral darkness and desolations which surround them? Let past experience answer these and all similar interrogatories. The truth of the matter is, the streams never rise higher than the fountain whence they flow. HOME, after all, is the source and the standard of all morality to children. In reference to this most important concern, the poet has philosophically declared that,

> "Just as the twig is bent, the tree's inclined."

It matters little where our youth learn language and science—at schools however celebrated for sound learning and rigid discipline—they will seldom appear ambitious to attain a degree of moral excellence above their fellow-citizens and every day associates. They will naturally resume the tone and bearing, the manners and customs, the sentiments and prejudices of their native city. Its fashionable follies and amusements and vices will be eagerly pursued and practised. Even the dread of being accounted singular or austere or proud or unaccommodating, will often prompt them to compliances and excesses which they otherwise might have resisted or avoided.

The standard of morals has never been elevated by such a process in any community. The reformation must commence at home, and be consummated at home. If you would train up moral children, you must make yourselves moral. And if you become moral yourselves, I take it your city will be moral. You complain that your city is immoral—do you? Pray, who have rendered your city immoral, and who keep it immoral? Is it not your own work? Do not parents govern the city? Do not parents create, countenance and sustain every nuisance, and every species of noxious dissipation and degrading amusement which abound in our midst? What do you mean by complaining, and lamenting, and whining, and mourning, and fretting, and preaching, and praying, and denouncing? Why do you not arise, in all the majesty of your resistless and united strength, and resolve forthwith to purify your own premises; and to put down every stalking monster of iniquity and abomination which is rioting upon the heart's blood of your unprotected offspring? Will *you* get drunk, and expect your children to be sober? Will you profane the name of your Maker, and expect your children to hallow it? Will you desecrate the Christian Sabbath, and expect your children to keep it holy? Will you frequent the theatre, the race-course, or the gaming table; and expect your children to shun and to abhor them?

Ah, no—you will reply—we perpetrate none of these enormities ourselves. We set a very good example, and we do not withhold seasonable counsel and reproof and admonition. But what can we do? The whole world is against us. Our city is full of grog-shops and groceries and other villanous establishments—duly licensed and authorized by law to sell whisky and to create drunkards, and to ruin our children and servants—and all this to support government, and to enable a few honest fellows to get a comfortable living. And this is your plea—is it? It shall not avail you. If your rulers misgovern you or abuse your confidence, turn them out, and elect better men. I defy any mortal to offer the semblance of a reason for the existence of a single grog-shop in our land; or for permitting any man to retail inebriating liquors to minors or servants, or to others to be drunk at his own bar or upon his own premises. This is one of the most deplorable evils of vicious and perverted legislation with which our country is afflicted. It is precisely *the evil* which has hitherto proved, and which is, at this moment, the most pernicious to the well-being of all our colleges without exception. It has been proclaimed a thousand times: and legislatures have been everywhere appealed to and entreated in vain to abate it. The late Governor of South Carolina, in his last message to the legislature, animadverted, in the most indignant and eloquent language, upon the mischievous influence of the wine and whisky shops of Columbia upon the morals and discipline of the State's University in that metropolis. The public complain of the dissipation of colleges and of the riotous conduct of the students, and none more loudly than our politicians, our judges and statesmen, and yet they very deliberately legalize and sanction and uphold the means and instruments which effect all the mischief. Verily, they are wise, sagacious, consistent, magnanimous gentlemen!

It would be useless therefore to seek for a college or school, in all the length and breadth of this mighty Republic, where intoxicating liquors cannot be procured; or where the students may not indulge in their use, or get drunk, if so inclined. If we would educate our sons where rum and grog-shops cannot be found, we must send them to Robinson Crusoe's Island or to the Penitentiary. Here, by the way, I may just remark, that the Penitentiary is the only University which the government of Tennessee has condescended to build up and to patronize. This is our grand State University: and the work of education is said to be going bravely on within its walls. It is already the people's favourite: and its accomplished graduates will, no doubt, in due time, occupy a prominent position in our most respectable and enlightened community.

Nashville, I have said, is bad enough: and I have said also, that it is not worse than other places. I will add moreover, for your especial edification and encouragement, that I do not esteem it quite so bad as many other towns with which I am acquainted. I know something of Eastern colleges and cities, and of the conduct and habits of their pupils and other youth; and I deliberately assert that our own students are at least as orderly, temperate, decorous and gentlemanly in their general deportment, and as decidedly moral in their habits, as were those of any Eastern institution whatever a dozen years ago. I then arrived at the conclusion, after much observation and experience, that our Southern and Western youth might be more safely educated at home than abroad: and I have seen no reasons since to change my opinion, but very many to confirm it. This declaration, however, is not intended as a salvo or apology for anything wrong, defective, or vicious in our own political or social organization. We have much to deplore and very much to reform. I maintain that Nashville ought not to be content with being as good as her neighbours. She ought to aspire to the highest degree of attainable moral excellence. Suppose now, that Nashville could be made, and should become, confessedly, the most moral, peaceful, temperate, tranquil, polished, intelligent, virtuous town upon this continent; and that her schools of every order and description should be inferior to none in the land: what would not be the inevitable and immediate result? Why, to be sure, every good man would wish to reside here; and every wise parent would, at almost any sacrifice, endeavour to educate his children here. And no man can estimate the increase which would thence accrue to the wealth and population of the city.

I presume that such a revolution in our moral condition would alone do more towards enriching us than all other causes and means put together.

4. A fourth objection is grounded upon the supposed or assumed inutility or inefficiency of a college education. Your college-bred youth, after all, we are told, are not superior to other youth. What do they learn at college which may not be learned elsewhere? How many drones and idlers and blockheads do not currently issue from our colleges? What are they good for? They are neither qualified for the learned professions, nor for any active business or manual labour. True, many lads go to college, and remain years at college, to very little purpose. I will tell you why and wherefore. In the first place: Multitudes enter college too young. This is a radical error. College discipline is not adapted to very young persons. They cannot be made to feel and act as men, while they are children. The college is not designed for such. In the second place: They enter college frequently, also, without the requisite literary qualifications. They are destitute of the necessary amount of elementary knowledge. They have not learned how to study—by themselves—in their rooms—without the presence and constant aid of their teachers. And, of course, they waste their time in frivolous sports or mischievous pranks or desultory reading. They seldom conquer these first difficulties. They do not know how to avail themselves of the means and facilities of instruction which a college furnishes—such as lectures, books, specimens, apparatus, experiments.

In the third place: Not a few have been spoiled at home. Their habits are irregular and vicious. They will not be governed. They resist or spurn all authority and control. They affect to be independent of college rules and restraints. They fancy themselves young gentlemen—far above the servile condition of the orderly schoolboy—no longer amenable to the law or the birch of the pedagogue—and yet incapable of appreciating any generous appeal addressed to their sense of honour and shame, to their interests or ambition. They occupy an anomalous or transitional position—a sort of *betweenity*, to use one of Mr. Jefferson's expressive *neologisms*. They can neither be chastised with the rod, nor subdued by reason or argument or admonition or reproof. They are utterly impracticable: and the sooner they run off to the army or the navy, the better for them and the college. I advise all parents who cannot or do not govern their sons at home, never to send them to college with the delusive expectation that they will be governed there. Or if their habits are vicious, let them not suppose that the college will reform them. Such a miracle will never be realized. On the contrary, it has been to me a source of animating consolation, amidst many discouragements, and of profound gratitude to Heaven, that, to the best of my knowledge and belief, not an individual youth, who had been judiciously trained at home and well taught at school, and possessed of correct principles and habits, has been hitherto rendered worse by a connexion with our university.

In the fourth place: One of the most frequent and

prolific causes of disappointment, is the practice of sending boys to college to learn a part only of the prescribed course of study. Or, in other words, to become *irregular* students—as they are technically and very significantly styled. This is a great evil—particularly in our Western institutions. Youth, thus indulged, are left very much at their own discretion. They study what they please and when they please. They are not candidates for degrees. And they care very little about their standing as scholars, or their proficiency in any department of literature or science. When they have lounged away a few sessions or months, they return to their parents and friends, profess to have completed their studies at the University; and pass as living specimens and evidences of the absolute nothingness of the University system. I do not mean to intimate that every person who enters a college should be required to study the whole course usually prescribed for graduation; or that none can derive advantage from the study of a part of said course. Many young men, of sufficient age and stability of character, may doubtless be intrusted with a discretionary power in this respect, which would be dangerous to others. Some, from the want of pecuniary resources, or from defects in their early education which they think themselves too old to remedy, or from being destined to a particular vocation which renders the knowledge of certain sciences or languages desirable or indispensable, or for other obvious and satisfactory reasons, ought to be indulged to the extent of their wishes or necessities.

Such cases, however, could be easily provided for, as they ever have been, without detriment to the institution, and much to the benefit of the parties thus accommodated. I take pleasure, on this occasion, in bearing testimony to the good conduct and persevering diligence of many of our own *irregulars* while at college, and to their successful and honourable career, as citizens, ever since. But where no specialties exist to justify a relaxation or departure from the established order, parents act unadvisedly and injudiciously in allowing their sons any license or option in the case. They are sure to abuse it. The Faculty are always the best judges in these matters, or they are not fit for their station and are unworthy to be trusted at all.

And here I am led to notice a *fifth* source of failure or of parental disappointment and mortification. It is the prevalent custom or practice of assuming to be wiser than the children's instructors. The latter, at best, have but a sorry and most unthankful office to discharge. Every father and mother, uncle and aunt, brother, sister and cousin—every big man and every little man in the village—every newspaper scribbler and every youthful orator—and everybody else—is a judge and a critic and a reformer and a very Solomon upon the subject and mystery of education. Upon this theme they can all dogmatize, in the most confident and supercilious strain of dictatorial superiority. Every little master and every little miss, long before they reach their *teens*, have learned to enact the spy and the censor upon the discipline and the code and the system and the manners of the laborious veteran schoolmaster of half a century's experience. It is a misfortune that every human creature understands the art and the science of education so much better than do our teachers themselves. We all cheerfully concede a measure at least of professional superiority to our lawyer and physician, to our tailor and barber, to our cook and coachman; and we repose some degree of confidence in their skill and judgment. But alas, for the hard worked and hard working pedagogue! He can expect neither sympathy nor justice nor candour from any quarter. Unless, indeed, he will himself set up for a radical reformer—adopt the innovating spirit of the age—denounce all existing schools and systems—declare himself the people's devoted servant, and withal, the greatest genius and most modest personage in the world—profess to teach all sciences, arts and languages, without pain or effort on the part of his pupils, and in almost no time—then, verily, he will be puffed and lauded and courted and caressed and rewarded,—to the utter amazement and mortal discomfiture of every honest, plodding, orthodox old Busby and Parr and Wyttenbach in the land. Quackery and empiricism and pretension and experimenting and mystification are the order of the day among the people's honoured schoolmasters, as well as among their favourite lawyers and doctors and parsons and vagabond *oculists* and political conjurers.

Again, sixthly: Parents ruin their sons by allowing them too much money. Upon this point, much might be said. The fact is admitted and deplored at every college in the world. The remedy or rather preventive is with the parents. If they will not withhold the means of licentious indulgence, they must bear the blame and share the disgrace.

But with all these drawbacks and obstacles and concessions and allowances, without stopping to specify any more, the University has educated, and is educating, a sufficient number of meritorious talented youth to confront the most skeptical and cavilling objector. We can muster as noble a band of accomplished *alumni*, as, from the age and circumstances of the Institution, ought reasonably to be demanded at our hands. You may view them and scan them and mark them in the legislative halls of the nation and of several of the States—in all the liberal professions—in public life and in private—as magistrates, statesmen, editors, lawyers, physicians, merchants, farmers, teachers, ministers and soldiers. Their ALMA MATER is not ashamed of them. Nor does she fear any comparison which may be instituted between them and the graduates of any college or university at the East or the West. By these she is willing to be judged: and by these let the people judge for themselves. Here the appeal lies to palpable facts, to results, to fruits—which cannot deceive, and which cannot be mistaken.

5. A fifth *ad captandum* objection, which is upon the lips of every demagogue and every aspiring sycophant of the sovereign people, runs in this wise. The university is designed exclusively for the rich—for the aristocracy—and not for the poor, the democracy,

the great mass of our labouring productive classes. This species of sophistry can rarely be refuted, because it is never believed by the canting knaves who employ it, and because those upon whose ignorance and credulity it is designed to operate, are seldom accessible, at least, on occasions when truth and intellect usually assert their claims. I will, however, briefly advert to two or three items or heads of argument in reply.

1st. The man who affects to espouse the cause of the poor—who seeks to arouse among them a spirit of discontentment, and of jealousy and hostility towards the rich—who is perpetually haranguing and blustering and clamouring about their rights and their wrongs—with a view to his own political advancement—may always be noted as a selfish, heartless, intriguing, unprincipled office hunter. He cares nothing about the poor. And when successful, he will be the first to turn his back upon them in scorn and to trample them in the dust. Such has ever been the course pursued by the popular demagogue. For a season, and just so long as it may suit his purposes, he is the bold, zealous, unflinching, furious champion of the suffering, oppressed, plundered, priest-ridden, bank-ridden, university-ridden, aristocracy-ridden poor. They believe him, trust him, vote for him, fight for him, huzza for him, toast him, worship him, bear him onward and upward, until they behold him safe in the palace and upon the throne: and then again they shout hosannas, and long live, my lord, the Protector of the Commonwealth and the Defender of the poor! But the tragedy or the comedy well over, and the delirium passed away, and they are astounded to find themselves as far beneath the footstool of their once familiar Cromwell or Robespierre as they had ever been beneath the regal pomp of the hated Stuart or Bourbon. Now, how shall the poor be disabused of this folly? how shall they be disenchanted, disinthralled, emancipated, and enabled to act for themselves? Send them to the University; where the Hampdens and Sidneys and Pyms and Fletchers and Lockes and Miltons and La Fayettes were duly qualified to comprehend the rights of man—and of all classes of men, without distinction or exception.

But, 2dly. If it be true that none but the rich can avail themselves of the privileges of a college; why should they be obstructed or opposed in this particular use of their wealth? If the rich choose to erect and endow and sustain colleges for their own special benefit: may they not do so without let or hinderance? May they not indulge their fancy or caprice or vanity or ostentation, if you please, in this matter of colleges as well as in a thousand other modes quite as aristocratic—to say the least? May they not live in palaces, ride in coaches, glitter in gold and diamonds, and fare sumptuously every day? Will you envy them or deny them every distinction and every indulgence which the poor cannot command? Now, it appears to me that, of all the ways of expending wealth, the least harmful and obtrusive is precisely this of building colleges. Suppose the rich men of Tennessee should unite in contributing the trifling sum of a million of dollars forthwith to construct and equip a decent little university, where their own sons might be taught to be modest and useful citizens: would the poor be injured by such an appropriation? Would a dollar be extracted from their empty purse? No, not the fraction of a dollar. Pray then, let the rich throw away their money upon colleges, if they happen to be so minded. Possibly, they might do worse with their money—worse for themselves, their children, their country—and worse for you. Besides, you would get all the working jobs which such an enterprise must necessarily create. And, if I do not mistake your craft altogether, you would not fail to make a profitable acquaintance with the Mammon of unrighteousness and filthy lucre during the operation.

3dly. It is a fact, not to be contradicted, that nearly all the best educated and most learned men in our country and in the world, are either comparatively poor or have been poor. If they ever attain to wealth and power and rank and office, they owe it all to their talents and learning and diligence. And thus have they been enabled to rise above their primitive lowly condition and to assume their proper station, in spite of the artificial, arbitrary, conventional barriers which wealth and fashion and pride usually oppose—and, happily, sometimes oppose in vain, to superior genius and superior science. Still, very few studious literary men are found among the wealthy classes even in our own country—where every man is the architect of his own fortune—and where every man, fool or knave, may get rich, if he will. They are either content with a moderate competency, or their organ of *acquisitiveness* is not sufficiently developed, or the people have not sagacity enough to employ them, or justice enough to remunerate them for their invaluable services.

And therefore it is that the rich themselves frequently ridicule and denounce the university and the scholar and all liberal learning;—precisely because these are associated in their minds with poverty and unthriftiness and indifference to the main chance. They cannot estimate even moral and intellectual excellence except by the *dollar standard*. It is really diverting to see, with what superlative hauteur and contempt, they can look down upon the poor student, the poor author, the poor teacher, the poor anything, however ennobled and exalted and refined by mental cultivation, and by the possession of Heaven's rarest gifts and attributes. Your unlettered, pompous, mushroom, purse-proud nabobs are, in general, not only the most inveterate foes of colleges, but the most absurd, egotistical, overweening. self-sufficient, iron-bound, leaden-headed, *braying* animals in the whole world. They live only to hoard money: and they expend it only for display. It requires a most thorough education to know how to use a fortune *genteelly*—not to say liberally and munificently. And of all the caricatures of our common humanity, save from the pencil of a Hogarth, the vulgar rich man who apes the manners and polish and etiquette and fashionable *bienseances*—the airs, graces and *persiflage*—of the high-bred gentleman! Why, such a lumpish millionaire *parvenu* cannot eat a good dinner—as a good dinner was ordained to be eaten by all Christian men. He eats as if he were running a race for a wager, or as if a customer were still waiting at his counter to give him a bargain. It is tantalizing, beyond the endurance of all Greek and of all Roman philosophy, to be seated at a dinner table, furnished and appointed in all respects, *comme il faut*, merely to see the whole array of good things evanish in the twinkling of an eye, and the momentous affair concluded, determined and summarily despatched, before the genuine classical epicure could be well prepared for a quiet and dignified discussion of the first course.

Here then, we have a sort of two-edged objection against colleges. The poor would fain cashier them, because they are the pets of the rich. And the rich are indifferent, because they do not help their sons to coin money. Both are equally wrong: and both equally mistake their own true interests. Both may be—both have been—greatly elevated, and rendered better, wiser, happier and more useful by this very instrumentality—which the ruder and more illiberal portions of each seem so eager to destroy.

4thly. But, in the fourth place, the university has ever been pre-eminently the poor man's friend. Most of the older modern European universities were originally charitable foundations—designed especially for the gratuitous instruction of poor youth: and they have retained much of this character and continued to perform much of this work to the present day. It has created the entire republic of letters, almost exclusively out of the plebeian and indigent and humbler classes of society. It has constrained monarchs and nobles, wealth and power, to do homage to enlightened and cultivated intellect. Wherever it has flourished, untrammeled and unrebuked by royal or popular arrogance, it has mitigated or removed the evils of superstition and despotism, of immemorial usage and prescription. It has ever been the zealous advocate of genuine liberty and righteous government; notwithstanding the reproaches and calumnies of the demagogue and the cynic. But I will not dwell upon these topics, nor further enlarge upon the *objections* which constitute the first division of my subject.

These objections and a thousand others may be well founded. In some instances, they may be literally true. The university, no doubt, has been perverted and abused. And so have liberty and religion and science and reason, and every human blessing and faculty. The university has never been perfect; neither has any work or attribute or institution of mortal man ever been perfect. The university has been made the engine of error and tyranny and priest-craft and all manner of high-handed iniquity, in some age or country: so have the church and the civil government, divine revelation and human philosophy. Indeed, every *name*, capable of abuse, and of being rendered subservient to the purposes of avarice or ambition or selfish aggrandizement in any form, has been thus employed and dishonoured. If colleges are imperfect and sometimes pernicious, so are common schools and the domestic nursery. And yet, I suppose, we shall not attempt to abolish either families or common schools. Though, it must be confessed, the spirit of *abolitionism* is abroad in our land: and while Eastern *perfectionists* are preaching up the doctrine of the immediate and universal abolition of slavery at the South and the West, and while certain benevolent politicians proclaim the necessity of abolishing the whole banking and commercial machinery of the country, there are also sundry *fair* knights errant boldly enlisted in behalf of the rights of woman, who seem resolved to abolish all family monopolies, and to create a new social arrangement altogether independent of man's lordly and usurped supremacy. Indeed, abolitionism, and radicalism, and agrarianism, and ultraism, and amalgamationism, and Loco-Focoism, and Lynchism, and Fanny-Wrightism, are all the rage: and whether any existing law or usage or institution shall survive the ferment and the struggle, is beyond our prophetic ken to decide or to conjecture. But as our motto is "never to despair of the Republic," we shall proceed with our thesis, upon the presumption that the University, at least, is to endure and to triumph. And thus we arrive at the second grand division of our augument or rather of our homily upon colleges.

II. We promised to suggest some reasons in favour of colleges, and of our own University in particular. Here I may remind you that, in rebutting certain attacks and objections, I have already incidentally glanced at many of the positive benefits which result from colleges. I may further remark, that whatever consideration can be urged in favour of education or of learning generally or of any degree of it, is available and pertinent to the cause in question. If a little learning be good and desirable, a great deal is better and more desirable. If a limited and imperfect education be worth something, a superior and really excellent education must be worth still more. And any argument which sustains the former, will *a fortiori* apply to the latter.

Please, moreover, to remember my former concessions. I am not contending for shadows or for names. Universities, like common schools, may be and frequently are very puny and pitiful affairs. In pleading for the University, I plead for the University as it ought to be —not as it actually is, either here or elsewhere. It is the grand paramount cause of education and learning, in the highest and noblest acceptation of the terms, which I advocate. *University* is the word, used by common consent, throughout the world, to designate the species of institution where the largest amount and extent of liberal and useful knowledge may be acquired, under the most auspicious circumstances, and with the surest guaranty to the public against imposition and charlatanry.

Now the University of Nashville, compared with my own *beau ideal* of such an establishment, is but an element—a mere atom—a foundation—a nucleus—a corner stone—a first essay towards the glorious consummation and perfection of my own cherished hopes and anticipations. And I could say little more of any other university in our country. I regard them all as being still in their infancy; or, at most, in their early youth: and that their *right* to the title of *university* is yet to be proved and confirmed by their future growth to vigorous manhood and generous maturity.

The course of study provided for undergraduates, is much the same in nearly all our colleges; and but few of them have ventured further. To this extent, we claim to be on an equal footing with our neighbours and sisters. Our undergraduate course is *professedly* as extensive and diversified as usually obtains anywhere in our country: and as high an order of intellectual attainments is expected and required of our candidates for degrees.

Several of our universities have the Faculties of Law, or Medicine, or Theology, or all three, in addition to the ordinary Faculty of Arts and Letters, or Philosophy. These, of course, approximate nearer to the proper character of a university than do the others. The English universities of Oxford and Cambridge are similary constituted, and have served as the models of our own. In theory, at least—and in reference to the government, discipline, systems and modes of study and instruction, terms and periods of college residence, board in commons, monastic seclusion, forms, habits, statutes, qualifications for graduation, and other details—the undergraduates of the English and American universities would seem to occupy the same relative position. And so far as the undergraduates are directly and exclusively concerned, the number of professors, whether larger or smaller, may not be very material—provided always, there be enough to teach all the pupils whatever they are capable of learning within the allotted seasons of study. Neither are very large libraries important to this class of students. They cannot read or consult many volumes besides their text-books, during this brief period. And were the university designed for no other or higher end, it might be content with some dozen or twenty professors or tutors for each hundred or two hundred students; together with a few score thousand volumes in its library; suitable apparatus for scientific experiments and illustrations; museums of Natural History; mineralogical cabinets; and whatever specimens, preparations, instruments and fixtures might be available either to professor or student.

But all this and vastly more would not reach our idea of a complete or adequately furnished university. Neither an English nor an American youth has *finished* his studies, when he becomes entitled to the degree of Bachelor of Arts. He is then but barely qualified to enter upon that wider and more interesting field of investigation to which the great University invites or ought to invite him. He is yet to prepare himself for public and professional life. English and American *graduates* are seldom, on leaving college, further advanced in years and learning, than are the young men on the continent of Europe when they commence their studies at the university. Hence the university system of the latter differs essentially from the former. The two ancient English Universities can boast the most splendid college edifices in the world; and libraries among the largest and most valuable in existence. And their resident graduates may prosecute any course of solitary and unaided study and reading which they deem profitable or agreeable. Endowed fellowships also support a certain number of the most accomplished and promising poor scholars: who frequently remain for years in the assiduous pursuit of knowledge, and in the tranquil enjoyment of the extraordinary advantages afforded by a highly cultivated literary society and daily access to the accumulated wisdom and erudition of the illustrious dead. These are privileges which can never be lightly estimated. But they fall far short of the German and other continental universities. The English have comparatively few living teachers—scarcely none for the liberal professions—while the German are abundantly supplied. The English aim at great excellence in the Greek and Latin classics and pure mathematics; and to these they chiefly restrict their public examinations for University honours and degrees. And while the German aim at and attain still higher excellence in the classics and mathematics, they are ambitious also to teach, or to possess the means of teaching, every art, science, language and literature, ancient and modern, speculative, practical, experimental and professional.

The German universities consist of four distinct faculties: Theology, Medicine, Law and Philosophy. Not such meagre faculties as bear these names in England and America. Instead of one, two, three, or half a dozen individuals for Law or Medicine as with us, they frequently exhibit an array of a dozen or twenty or forty names, of the most learned, gifted and laborious men upon earth. Their office is no sinecure. They are working men. Thus, in Berlin, the Law Faculty consists of fourteen members, and the Medical of thirty-two. This University was founded in 1810. And it already ranks among the first in the world; and in some branches of science the very first. In 1830, it had upwards of 100 professors and about 1800 students: among the latter were 400 or 500 foreigners. The German universities are in fact *professional* schools, and are resorted to only by young men, who are preparing for the active duties of life, and never by boys, as is the case in our colleges. Their Gymnasia, in which preparation is made for the universities, correspond in many respects with our colleges. In the faculties of Law, Medicine and Theology, is taught, of course, whatever pertains to those professions. The faculty of Philosophy comprises everything not embraced by the other three. And no adequate idea of what this *everything* really imports, can be formed except by a perusal of the *programme* of lectures usually delivered at a German University, during a single term, by the professors in this Faculty. They may be said, almost without hyperbole, to treat in their course of prelections, public and private, *de omni scibili et quibusdam aliis*. They are working men, as I have said: but, then, they do not labour for naught and find themselves. They are amply remunerated both in honour and by solid *Louis or Frederic d'ors*. They frequently attain to the highest political distinctions and civil offices. They are created barons and counts—are employed as State counsellors and ministers, and ambassadors to foreign courts; and their society is eagerly sought by nobles and princes and monarchs.

It is not my purpose, however, to attempt elaborate descriptions and statistical details. Whoever has studied the history, genius, character, government, modes of instruction, endowments, revenues, and all the concentrated ways and means and facilities of communicating knowledge, which distinguish the most celebrated European universities, will be able to comprehend our meaning when we speak of them as an order or species of institution altogether unknown in the United States. We have nothing like them or approaching them. If Harvard and Yale resemble old Cambridge and Oxford, it is only the likeness of the infant to a giant, or of the Indian tumulus to an Egyptian pyramid. If the new Universities of Virginia and of the City of New York exhibit features similar to those of Edinburgh and Glasgow or the recently established London University; still, they are but miniatures, and humble imitations—a mere flotilla of gun-boats arrayed against Britain's proud navy of gallant seventy-fours. But of the German, French, Italian, Swedish, Dutch, Danish and Russian Universities, we have no specimen or example in all our vast Republic. Whether we ought to essay the creation of precisely such institutions among us—or whether, if established, they would be duly patronized and sustained by our busy, restless, speculating, money-making people—are questions open for discussion, and which we shall not argue or decide on the present occasion.

For the ordinary purposes of educating boys, generally between the ages of fifteen and twenty-one, we have no hesitation in giving the preference to such colleges as we already possess: provided always, that they be made in *fact* what they assume and profess to be in *name*. Such institutions, scattered over the land, at convenient distances from each other, are better adapted to the habits, wants and circumstances of our widely dispersed and comparatively poor population. They correspond to the individual colleges, which collectively constitute the great universities at Oxford and Cambridge: and which, in the opinion of Milton, would have proved more generally useful and less objectionable on the score of immoral influences, had they been erected seperately at some thirty or forty different points in the kingdom. They resemble also the Gymnasia of Germany and the colleges [so called] of France. A more rigid, effective and salutary discipline and government can be maintained in seminaries of this class over boys of a tender age, and where the number would seldom exceed one or two hundred, than could be exercised over the same description of youth in a large university where a thousand or more might be congregated. For it must be borne in mind, that the students in the German, Scottish and most other European universities, are governed as men and subjects, not by the Academical Faculty, but by the laws of the land and the city police—and, when necessary, by the strong arm of the military legion.

But I would not stop here. While I would duly encourage and improve the common college, as we should the common school, there ought to be in every State, at least in each of the larger States, one institution of the highest order and most comprehensive and commanding character. If we cannot achieve this object in five or twenty years, it may be done perhaps in fifty or five hundred years. If we cannot hope in our day, to rival Berlin, Munich, Gottingen, Leipsic, Copenhagen, Vienna, Halle, Leyden, Paris, Moscow or St. Petersburg; we may commence the enterprise, and leave posterity to carry it onward towards completion. For *complete,* in the nature of things, it never can be. It must be growing, advancing, enlarging, accumulating, till the end of time. No university in Europe is complete—not even in any one department. With libraries, for instance, of from 100,000 to 700,000 volumes, they are still adding to the number, and must do so while a book or manuscript, not already procured, can be found; or so long as new books shall be written and published. Now there is not, in the United States, a single library which can be styled large or respectable.—Not one, containing more than 30,000 or 40,000 volumes —corresponding in numbers and rank to the tenth or twelfth rate of European libraries. So it is with all other collections, whether of the products of nature or of art. No limit can be assigned to their increase. And while America has scarcely begun this work, and while Europe is obviously a century or two in advance of us, it may yet be affirmed that neither Europe nor America will ever have *completed* either the whole or any one of its thousand divisions.

If our National Government had appropriated the surplus revenue, (while such a thing existed,) say, some fifty millions of dollars — to the construction and endowment of a national university — as I think should have been done — a very substantial and well-proportioned foundation at least might have been laid — far superior indeed to the present actual condition of most European universities. Still, this would have been only a foundation—a mere beginning after all—bold and colossal in its features and dimensions, it is true; and worthy of the Republic and the age which *dared*—or rather dared *not*—to hazard the glorious undertaking. Such a foundation, with an annual allowance of a few millions, might, in the course of a thousand years, become a world's wonder—a something to be proud of and to talk about.

A National or State University ought to possess, or to aim at possessing, the means of teaching all the sciences, and everything, indeed, which it is desirable for any man to know. Thus, in its libraries should be found one or more copies of every valuable book extant in any language, ancient or modern. Not that any mortal could be expected to read even the title pages of a tithe of them: But that persons of every variety of taste and pursuit, might be able to gratify their curiosity, and to acquire the specific information needful for any purpose or vocation.

In like manner, and for similar uses, specimens, living or preserved, of every vegetable and animal and mineral, peculiar to the earth, the air and the waters of our planet, (or in their stead, the finest engravings and lithographs,) ought to be sought for with diligence, and procured at whatever cost of time or money.—Together with botanic gardens, astronomical observatories, anatomical and physiological preparations, models of all sorts of machines and useful inventions, and the works of the noblest artists or well executed copies of them.—Such varied and opulent collections (still imperfect, indeed,) as already adorn many of the cities and universities of Europe.—Where may be seen and studied every department, and almost every known product of nature and of art; arranged, too, in the most convenient and scientific and tasteful order, and imparting gratuitous pleasure and instruction to all visitors and amateurs, whether natives or foreigners. *There* are museums of antiques, of coins, of gems, of busts, of statues, of pictures, of manuscripts, of engravings, of medals, of monuments, of machines, of models, of casts in gypsum, of fossils; of natural history, in each and all its branches and provinces; of Egyptian, Etruscan, Grecian, Roman and other remains of ancient art and genius, still speaking in behalf of the mighty dead, and of ages and nations long since passed away.

I might accompany you, for examples *ad rem,* to Florence, and Rome, and Turin, and Milan, and Naples, and Berlin, and Dresden, and Munich, and Vienna, and St. Petersburg, and London, and a score of other places, not unknown to scientific fame. But let us pause a moment in Paris, and glance at two or three of its marvellous creations, creditable alike to the liberality of the government and the scientific taste of the nation. Behold the *Jardin des Plantes:* with its numerous and diversified establishments, of some half a mile in length; with its groups of plants from almost every region of the globe; with its green and hot houses of more than 600 feet in length; with its vast menagerie of wild beasts of every climate and latitude, distributed and secured in ample and comfortable enclosures; with its aviary, embracing every bird known in France and many from foreign countries; with its splendid museum of natural history, also more than 600 feet long; with its unrivalled zoological and fossil departments; with its curious specimens of the animal remains of the antediluvian world, not elsewhere to be seen; with its extensive library and invaluable cabinet of comparative anatomy; with its unequalled agricultural and botanical gardens; with its noble amphitheatre, in which public lectures are delivered on all the physical sciences and their application to the arts, and where Jussieu, Buffon, Hauy and Cuvier have recorded their names for immortality. We pass the *Pantheon,* with its choice selections in natural history, antiquities and paintings: The *Conservatory of Arts and Manufactures,* with its infinitude of machines and models: The *Musee d'Artillerie,* the repository of every warlike weapon, instrument and engine: The *Royal Library*, with its 700,000 volumes and its 80,000 precious manuscripts; and other public libraries, containing a grand total of 2,000,000 books. And we arrive at the *Louvre*, with its proud halls of sculpture; and its magnificent gallery of paintings, 1400 feet in length; overwhelming alike all the powers of human reason and imagination. But here we *must* stop. And yet, we are but at the threshold of this mighty world of miracle and enchantment!

We have spoken of collections and fixtures. Our University must have the requisite *teaching force* also. Professors of every language, dead and living; of every science, in all its branches and subdivisions, in all its bearings and applications. To be more particular: There should be professors or teachers,

Of Ancient classical languages and literature:

Of Oriental languages and literature:

Of Modern European languages and literature:

Of Mathematics, Natural Philosophy, Astronomy:

Of Chemistry, Geology, Mineralogy, Comparative Anatomy:

Of Archæology, in reference to ancient nations, governments, jurisprudence, geography, mythology, arts, science, and still existing monuments:

Of Philology, Eloquence, Poetry, History:

Of Physiology, vegetable, animal and comparative:

Of Ethics, Politics, Logic, Metaphysics:

Of Constitutional and International Law:

Of Political Economy, National Statistics:

Of Architecture, Sculpture, Painting, Drawing, Engraving, Music:

Of Engineering, civil, military, and naval

Of Mechanics, principles and practice:

Of Agriculture, Commerce, Manufactures:

Of Fencing, riding, swimming, and other manly and healthful gymnastics:

Of Natural History, in every department:

Of all the Liberal Professions:

Of Biblical Literature: And of Religion, in such forms and modes as may be satisfactory to the judicious and reflecting portion of the community.

[The above is not given either as a complete enumeration or proper grouping of the subjects for professorships, but rather as a brief summary or outline of the more obvious and important.]

There should be schools, in short, for all the sciences, arts, languages and professions. So that no youth need ever cross the ocean to study and learn what ought to be taught much more safely and advantageously at home.

Now, whatever other nations have achieved in behalf of science, learning and education, we could accomplish, sooner or later, by the aid of our national treasury. As nothing, however, may be expected from the General Government, and very little from the State Governments, until the spirits of Washington, Franklin, Jefferson and Clinton shall preside in our councils, it follows, either that our contemplated University must remain a *castle in the air*, or it must be built up by the people—

by rich people too—or, at least, by those who possess some property. It must be effected by private munificence, effort and enterprise.

If the Legislature of Tennessee will not create and endow a university suited to this Commonwealth, the people must do the work, or it will never be done. Were I a member of that body, and free from all collegiate and clerical connexions, I might possibly attempt an argument or a speech upon this unpopular theme. And I might say some *plain* things about justice and honour and integrity—of imdemnification for wrongs inflicted and rights withheld—of legislative, as well as individual, obligations to fulfil contracts, to redeem pledges, to pay debts, and to discharge, with a scrupulous and rigid fidelity, all the duties of a responsible and voluntarily assumed trust and guardianship. But as I am not entitled to the floor, I will not address the House at present. If the Legislature, however, will elect me their representative to the Senate of the United States, I will exert my humble faculties to the very uttermost to induce the Government to make a new grant of a few hundred thousand acres of wild land to our hitherto neglected and poverty-stricken colleges and academies; and to absolve the State from all her past iniquities and existing liabilities on this score. I hope the HONOURABLE GENTLEMEN will maturely deliberate upon this singularly disinterested and modest proposition of mine, before they proceed to a final choice. They will find me, moreover, a most orthodox, independent, decided, old-fashioned, constitutional politician; who will listen respectfully to all their instructions, and then act just as he pleases.—Always "taking the responsibility," and hazarding the consequences.

Let us now consider what we *can* do, and ought forthwith to undertake. Though we might despair of ever attaining to the regal grandeur of Berlin or Paris or Oxford, we may assuredly venture to follow the example of the little republican Swiss Cantons of Zurich, Berne, Basle and Geneva. Of Geneva especially: the population of which, including both city and country, scarcely amounts to 50,000—not much exceeding that of Davidson county. The University, or Academy, as it is commonly styled, of Geneva, has flourished during a period of more than 450 years.* "The Genevese are as much distinguished by their devotion to science as by their public spirit. And it excites admiration to see how much they have done, and are still doing, with their limited means, for the interests of learning and the advancement of society. This patriotic spirit extends even to the labouring classes, who, to give an instance, in 1815, when Decandolle wished for a Botanic garden,

* It has a public library of about 70,000 volumes; an observatory; a museum of natural history, comprising Saussure's collections of minerals, petrifactions, volcanic productions, insects and birds, together with his choice assortment of philosophical instruments and chemical apparatus; Dr. Jurine's cabinets of ornithology and entomology, and the fossils of St. Gothard; the mineral collections also of Pictet, Tollot, Tengry, De Boissy, and De Luc; Haller's herbarium; Pictet's philosophical apparatus; cabinets of optical and mathematical instruments; anatomical preparations and antiquities; models in gypsum of ancient statues, groups, busts, and bass-reliefs; and some fine paintings

offered voluntarily to build, without remuneration, a hot house with all suitable appurtenances, and to furnish the necessary glass at their own expense."

"The system of education which prevails at Geneva, is perhaps not surpassed by that of any other city in Europe. It relates to the studies of childhood, to those of adolescence, and to those of the learned professions of divinity, law and physic. The first or lowest of these departments resembles Eton and Westminster schools in England. It is conducted by eleven masters, called *regens*, under the superintendence of a rector, a principal, and the academy of professors. Children from the age of five to fifteen or sixteen are successively taught reading, writing, orthography, arithmetic, geography, Greek, Latin and Mathematics. The college (as this department is designated) is divided into nine classes, each having a separate and commodious class room. The scholars generally continue a year in each class, and no one is permitted to leave his form, till he is fit for being promoted to a higher one. An account of the degrees of good and bad conduct of every boy is regularly and faithfully kept, which is summed up at the end of the week. Twice every year prizes are distributed for good conduct, and for progress in study; and once in the year, generally in June, exercises are proposed to each class, and prizes are adjudged to the best. These prizes are distributed on the day called the day of promotion—the day before that on which the properly qualified students are promoted to a higher class. A grand solemnity is on this occasion celebrated in the cathedral church, and is attended by all the public bodies in their robes, and by crowds of citizens of every class. On the celebration of this *fete*, in June 1814, eighty-eight silver medals were distributed." Such is the PREPARATORY SCHOOL of the University of Geneva.

"The second department (college proper of our country) of the system of education at Geneva, is intrusted to the professors, who occupy the highest station in the Academy. It is subdivided into classes, called *auditoires*. Four years' attendance is necessary to complete the studies of this department. The first two are devoted to the Belles Lettres, and the last two to the different branches of philosophy. When the student has completed this course, which he generally does at the age of 18 or 20, he may proceed to the study of divinity, law or physic." Lectures are delivered upon the most important subjects, scientific, literary and professional, by some twenty or thirty learned professors. This excellent establishment, in which are usually educated more than 1000 pupils of all ages, is supported exclusively by a population of about 30,000. The professors are held in the highest estimation: and, when the pecuniary circumstances of the party will permit, the *honour* of teaching is considered a sufficient compensation for its labour. Even the inferior teachers, or *regens* of the lowest department, are sometimes chosen members of the Representative Assembly. "There is certainly no place in the world to which a father may send his children with fewer anxieties than to Geneva." So eminently distinguished is this beautiful and favoured city for the intelligence, simplicity, refinement, moral purity, courtesy, and literary spirit of its inhabitants. I would recommend Geneva as a model and exemplar for Nashville. What Geneva is, and long has been, Nashville may become; if she will direct her attention to moral and intellectual improvement, rather than to the frivolities, absurdities and extravagance of fashionable luxury and parade.

Again, there is no college or university in our own country, which is above our ability to equal or even to surpass. Expensive edifices may be dispensed with. Neither the Scottish nor the German universities are noticeable on this account. With a few exceptions, their college buildings are cheap and plain—designed chiefly for lecture rooms, libraries and other collections. While the students generally board at private lodgings. A few additional professors would render our undergraduate department, or *college proper*, equal to the very best, and superior to most, of our already popular and flourishing institutions. Let us examine two or three of our ancient and most celebrated colleges in reference to this point. The Faculty of Arts, in nearly all of them, it may be remarked, consists of from two to six professors. At venerable Harvard, the oldest of them all, we find an array of twenty-two professors, lecturers and instructors,—besides the president, who is not a teacher, and the tutors, whose office is temporary and their number variable. Of these, two are *Law* professors, six are *Medical*, and reside in Boston, and three are *Theological:* so that only eleven permanent instructors remain for the undergraduates. And four of these belong to the department of Modern languages and literature: leaving after all only seven to do the work which five perform at our college. Compared then with Harvard, and excluding the three learned professions, our present deficiency exists chiefly in the department of Modern languages. At Yale college there are five or six professors, besides those of the Law, Medical and Theological schools or faculties. Both Harvard and Yale usually employ each six or eight tutors, according to the actual number of students—averaging commonly between two and three hundred. These perform all the drudgery of elementary drilling, and attend the daily routine of recitations in the class room. While the professors read lectures, and maintain the dignity of science and of the *Senatus Academicus*. Harvard possesses a library of 40,000 volumes—Yale about 8,000. Our three college libraries contain upwards of 5,000 volumes. In scientific collections and apparatus, we are not far behind either of them.

Next to Geneva, *New Haven* might serve as a pattern for Nashville. It is celebrated, not only for its university, but for its superior boarding schools and smaller seminaries for the young of both sexes. The average number of persons who are here from abroad for the purpose of education is supposed to be rarely below a thousand.

In the University of Virginia there are nine "Schools," as they are styled; or, in simple English phrase, nine Professors; each the sole teacher of one school. These schools or professorships are denominated as follows: 1. Ancient Languages. 2. Modern Languages. 3. Mathematics. 4. Natural Philosophy. 5. Chemistry and Materia Medica. 6. Anatomy and Surgery. 7. Medicine. 8. Moral Philosophy. 9. Law. Two and a half or three of these professors teach the Medical students, and are in fact the Medical Faculty. One occupies the chair of Law. Leaving five or five and a half, including the professor of modern languages, to perform the duties assigned to the Faculty of Arts in our colleges. Here it is obvious to remark, that several of these "schools" must be radically defective. One man, for instance, can scarcely ever be found competent to teach more than one living tongue; that is, if correct pronunciation and purity of idiom and accent be required. Yet, in the school of modern languages at this University, are taught by its single unassisted professor, "the French, Spanish, Italian, German and Anglo-Saxon: and if desired, will be taught also by the same individual, the Danish, Swedish, Hollandish, and Portuguese languages. Lectures on the literature of each of the nations whose languages are taught, are delivered twice a week, by the professor; and also lectures on modern history, and the political relations of the different civilized nations of the present day." If all this be *well* done by the *existing* professor, I venture to affirm that the like has never been performed heretofore or elsewhere, and to predict that the like will never be successfully accomplished again. This custom of appointing a professor of half a dozen or more modern languages, which obtains so generally in our colleges, must be discontinued.

In the School of Ancient Languages, "are taught the Latin and Greek Languages, the Greek and Roman History, Geography and Literature, and the Hebrew Language." The instruction given by prelections and examinations, comprises a list of subjects, which occupies more than a large closely printed octavo page, in the bare enumeration—as published in the Catalogue of the University for the past year. From the same authority it appears that the number of students attending this school or professor, during the last session, (ending July 4th,) was 78. Comment upon such a programma of *promises* would be superfluous before any adequate judges of classical and philological tuition. In most European schools, half a score of teachers, at the least, would be required for the same amount of labour; and nowhere else, in our own country, has any similar feat been attempted. But I will not pursue a criticism and comparison which might be deemed invidious and uncandid. My object is not to disparage other colleges, but to show how easy it is to reach their standard, and to transcend it if we please.

The following professorships are already established in the University of the City of New York. 1. Civil Engineering and Architecture: 2. The Literature of the Arts of design: 3. Intellectual and Moral Philosophy and Belles Lettres: 4. Greek Language and Literature: 5. Latin Language and Literature: 6. French Language and Literature: 7. Italian Language and Literature:

8. Spanish Language and Literature: 9. Associate professorship of do.: 10. German Language and Literature: 11. Hebrew: 12. Mathematics: 13. Natural Philosophy and Astronomy: 14. Chemistry and Botany: 15. Law: 16. Geology and Mineralogy: 17. Arabic, Syriac, Persian and Ethiopic: 18. The Evidences of Revealed Religion. Here are five professors for four modern languages; and three for the Latin, Greek and Hebrew. Eight altogether for the usual undergraduate course, exclusive of modern languages. This University, according to its original plan, embraces four Faculties, namely: 1. A Faculty of Letters and the Fine Arts. 2. A Faculty of Science and the Arts. 3. A Faculty of Law. 4. A Faculty of Medicine. There are two General Departments in the University. The first embraces the usual collegiate course of instruction which has obtained in our country: and the second is designed to embrace instruction in the higher branches of literature and science, and in professional studies. The latter Department will probably resemble the European universities more closely than any other in our country. The beginning augurs well for the liberality of the great commercial metropolis of the Western hemisphere.

Our first effort, here in Nashville, should doubtless be to elevate the only department which we have hitherto attempted to establish; that is, the college for undergraduates, or the Faculty of Arts, Science and Literature. It is desirable to have professors of German, French, Italian, Spanish—perhaps of some other modern languages—though a knowledge of none of them has been made indispensable to graduation in any college. Still, provision for their study is important. A professor of Civil Engineering is loudly called for by the special exigencies of our country; though even such a professor is hardly yet to be met with at any of our older institutions. There is ample scope also for new professorships, by dividing and subdividing those already established. And it will be easily perceived from my previous statements, that distinct professorships may be multiplied without limit—provided the pecuniary means for the purpose can be obtained.

Whether a Preparatory Department should be connected with our University, has been doubted. If it should be resolved on, I have no hesitation in giving a decided preference to the system of Geneva, already adverted to.*

How soon it may be practicable to add the Faculties

* For various weighty reasons, I have hitherto objected to any such connexion. Of course, in comparison with other Western colleges, our catalogue of students may frequently appear diminutive. In all of them, the preparatory department, or college grammar school, furnishes a large proportion of the names which are periodically published in their catalogues of students. The four or five excellent classical seminaries in the town of Nashville, with many others throughout the State, constitute in fact the preparatory department of the University: which is organized, in all respects, agreeably to the plan which long experience at the East has sanctioned as the most eligible. With this explanation, our number of students, attached as they all are to the four college classes, will be found superior to that of the same order in most Western institutions. This number, for several years past, has generally averaged from 100 to 125—not merely on our books, but actually present.

of Law and Medicine; and what shall be their character; are questions more easily asked than answered. Such faculties might be organized immediately, were we content to be on a par with Harvard, Yale, and Virginia. But one or two professors of Law, and three or four of Medicine, would not meet our views. There is, in fact, no Medical School in America or Great Britain at all comparable with many on the continent of Europe, or equal to the wants of the profession. Thus, in Paris, for example, the Medical Faculty consists of twenty-three professors, eleven honorary professors, and twenty-four associates—in all, fifty-eight. "In order to obtain a Medical Diploma, the candidate must previously have received the degrees of Bachelor of Letters and Bachelor of Science, which imply an intimate acquaintance with the Greek and Latin languages, History, Geography, Moral and Intellectual Philosophy, Mathematics, Natural Philosophy, Chemistry, Botany, Mineralogy, Zoology, &c. &c. He must then assiduously devote himself to the study of Medicine for four entire years, and attend all the regular lectures. He is then admitted to an examination, (held principally in the Latin Language,) and if this be passed creditably, to his degree." Not a few Americans, after being graduated at our medical schools, resort to Paris to complete or rather to extend their elementary studies.

As to Theology—probably, the least said or done, the better. Still, if the various religious denominations would consent to the measure, each might attach a Theological School or Faculty to the University, for the sole benefit of its own adherents, and to prepare ministers for its own churches. The requisite funds would be raised, managed and controlled by the party creating such school, and be subject to withdrawal at its pleasure. In like manner, the professors would be nominated and removed by the church or sect supporting them. Thus, there might be a Faculty, composed of Episcopal clergymen, nominated by the Bishop or the Convention of the Diocese; others of Methodists, Presbyterians, Baptists, &c. subject to their respective ecclesiastical judicatories. I could point out many advantages as likely to result from half a dozen or more learned Theological Faculties of divers sects, together with their pupils, all residing at the same grand literary Head Quarters, and freely associating, studying, conversing and disputing with each other. I do not suppose that they would ever agree to think alike; or that proselytes would be gained by any one from the rest. They might, however, acquire a more tolerant, indulgent, catholic spirit; and agree to differ, with sentiments of mutual respect, good-will and Christian charity. They might learn that the worst heresy is uncharitableness; and that a holy life is the best, if not the only, evidence of orthodox principles.

We are now endeavouring to make such additions to our buildings and such improvements upon our college grounds as will furnish the necessary accommodations, and render the whole establishment more classical and tasteful in appearance than it has hitherto been. For the completion of this enterprise, already in progress, we have been compelled to appeal to the liberality of our citizens. We think the appeal will not be made in vain. We ask for only fifty thousand dollars at present.

The "Alumni Society" of the University stand pledged to endow a professorship of one or more modern languages. They will doubtless succeed.

Our library may be increased indefinitely and rapidly by individual contributions of such books as are not needed by their owners or which can be very conveniently spared.

Let each citizen also add to our collections whatever specimens of natural history or of art he may happen to possess, or be able to procure. Thus, we shall soon have large libraries, cabinets and museums.

I will now briefly advert to certain local habits or conventional usages, which confer on the Northern colleges peculiar importance, and which elevate them greatly in the public estimation.

In the first place: Throughout New England, New York and New Jersey, the office of a trustee is regarded as a most honourable distinction: and it is eagerly coveted by the learned, the wealthy, and the most eminent citizens. No man, in those States, can be so exalted as to feel or fancy himself above or indifferent to this academical trust: and, in general, it is very punctually and faithfully discharged.

In the second place: The office of president and professor is universally looked up to as the highest and most respectable which can be attained by the aspiring candidates for honourable rank in society. No political or professional station takes precedence of these. Nor would the head of any distinguished or opulent family be ambitious of a more creditable vocation or post of honour for a favourite and talented son, than that of a college professorship. Hence it not unfrequently happens that a wealthy individual will spare no pains or expense in educating a son expressly for this service. And should no vacant chair seasonably offer, he will perhaps himself endow a professorship in some college on purpose for his son's accommodation. Thus, the present Professor of Greek in Yale College, occupies a chair endowed exclusively by his father—lately a respectable merchant in the city of New York. On all public solemnities and celebrations also, the principals of universities and colleges appear in the first or highest rank. Thus, the people are taught to respect and reverence the literary character, and the literary institution, and the literary professor, and the whole teaching *corps* of the Commonwealth.* We have little of this spirit among us at the South and West. The vocation of the teacher is not respected: and hence not many respectable men will seek it as the business of life. Indeed, such is the preju-

---

* In Europe, as we have seen, the university chair is often illustrated by knights, and baronets, and barons, and counts, and marquises—who have as fairly earned and won the title as any successful military or naval officer, as any fortunate statesman or accomplished jurist: as witness, Count Berzelius, Sir John Playfair, Sir Humphrey Davy, Sir David Brewster, Sir John Leslie, Count Lagrange, Baron Cuvier, Sir Daniel H. Sandford, Baron Humboldt, Count Berthollet, Baron Dubois, Marquis de La Place, Baron de Sacy, &c.

dice, such the ignorance, and such the absurd injustice and impolicy which prevail on this subject, that a man of letters and science is hardly deemed fit for public office of any kind. If he can write a book or deliver learned lectures *ex cathedra*, it is taken for granted that he is good for nothing else. At the East, not only the most accomplished divines, physicians and lawyers, but the most eminent statesmen and judges also, have been *elevated* to university professorships and presidencies. Of the latter class, may be named, among others still living, Duer, Quincy, Butler, Kent, Story, Everett, Adams. During the revolutionary war, the president and a professor of the College of New Jersey were members of Congress—and the first, a signer of the Declaration of Independence. The present Governor of Massachusetts will, no doubt, reach the uttermost goal of his ambition, when he shall be privileged to finish his brilliant career in the University where he first acquired that reputation which attracted the popular notice and demand for his political services. Here, I may remark by the way, that Massachusetts is perhaps the only State which continues to bestow spontaneous honours and unsought offices upon superior talent, learning and integrity. And this is precisely the best educated and most thoroughly democratic Commonwealth in the world. Here, too, have been, from the commencement of its colonial existence, and still are, more and better colleges, academies and common schools than in any other province or State of this continent.

In the third place: The great men of the East attend

the anniversary commencements of their respective universities. The trustees, of course, are present—the clergy of all sects—teachers of every description—the lawyers and the physicians—the Alumni from every quarter—the governor and suite—the judges and the legislature—the mayor and corporation—the wealth and fashion and beauty of the vicinity—all the world are there. It is a high day—the most joyous and interesting day in the calendar—the grand literary festival of the State. Legislatures and courts, if in session, adjourn to participate in the intellectual banquet and to contribute to its pomp and brilliancy. They will not merely make a *show*, of attendance—march into the church and march out again—but will remain, without moving or fidgeting, to the end of the exercises, or of the exhibition. They will sit it out—nay, sometimes, *stand* it out. I have seen gentlemen, old gentlemen too, literally stand for five successive hours, and listen attentively and respectfully to all the juvenile performances of the occasion. Neither their *dinner bell*, nor a *horse-race*, nor a *cock-fight*, would divert them from the proper duties and proprieties of the day. We, too, may hope for something good and great, when we shall learn to manifest a like sympathy and interest and zeal; and to act a similar part in the periodical celebrations of our literary institutions.

But I have too long lost sight of the main scope of the second division of my discourse.

The consideration which should induce us to sustain a first-rate university at Nashville, may be divided into *special* and *general*. The *first* relate to advantages accruing chiefly to Nashville from its location. The *second* to those which it will afford alike to the whole community.

Under the first head, we remark,

1. That a flourishing university will add greatly to the wealth and prosperity of Nashville. This is an argument which all can comprehend and appreciate. If no other or higher motive should prevail, this would be sufficient with any people, sagacious enough to discern and to pursue their own interests. Such a university would enable us to educate our sons at home; and thus prevent the sending of many thousands of dollars out of our city and State, to be expended abroad and for the benefit of strangers. It would invite multitudes of youth from all parts of the country and from the neighbouring States, to study here and to spend their money here: and thus would thousands of dollars flow into the place, which otherwise would not come hither at all. It is well ascertained that Southern students at our Northern colleges, spend, on an average, a thousand dollars each per annum. A hundred such youth therefore, while resident at the North, consume at least a hundred thousand dollars annually of Southern capital, without yielding the slightest pecuniary return. And, in like proportion for any number, more or less. This is an enormous tax upon the natives, and ought not to be tolerated. The education of one hundred Tennessee youth in Connecticut for instance, during only the college term of four years, would withdraw from Tennessee

the round sum of four hundred thousand dollars. And yet, the judicious expenditure of half this amount at our own doors, and for the benefit of our own mechanics, would provide a better institution of learning than any which Connecticut can boast. Other schools, too, of every gradation, would grow up around us and in the midst of us, as preparatory and auxiliary to the University. So that, in a few years, a thousand boys (to say nothing of the girls) might be in training here from the States south of us: and how much money they would bring along with them, I leave you to calculate.

But this is not all. Numerous families would select this as their temporary or permanent residence, with a view mainly to the education of their children. Thus enhancing the value of all your property, and of all your trades and avocations. Every house and lot in your town, and every pleasant country seat or site within a compass of five miles around you—would be in demand. I could not name a more lucrative speculation or investment for any portion of your funds. The dividends, or pecuniary benefits would be shared equitably and *pro rata* by all: and none could possibly be a loser. Your cotton crops may fail—your banks may fail—your trade and commerce may decline—your merchants and manufacturers may run away—but the University will never fail you, if true to yourselves, while there are children in the land to be educated.

2. The University will confer upon our good city a reputation and a celebrity, otherwise unattainable, and in all respects the most desirable.

3. The University will gradually create and collect a literary society among us. Such a society exists in every city and village in our country, where the university has been fairly domesticated, and nowhere else. We have not what may be called a literary society in Tennessee. Nothing like it. The phrase, even, is scarcely understood. Our social parties and intercourse manifest its total absence. We meet together to eat, drink, sing, play and dance; and never to converse as intellectual and intelligent men and women.* Now I am no particular admirer of pedants or *blue-stockings.* But I do entertain the fancy that *rational* beings might occasionally assemble at the social fireside for a rational purpose: and where neither the *Grecian* nor the *savant* would be voted a *bore* or a *bear.* I doubt whether it be wise or expedient or creditable to ape the extravagancies and ostentation of a London or Paris, of a New York or Philadelphia. We cannot afford it. We are too poor. Why, I have heard *poverty* pleaded by not a few of our reputed wealthy citizens, as an excuse for not giving a paper dollar, when I have called on them in my official character as BEGGAR GENERAL for the University; and urged, too, with that peculiarly grave and lugubrious expression of countenance which never fails

* I have not said, nor do I mean to insinuate, that there are no literary *individuals* in Tennessee. There may be as large a proportion of literary men and women in Tennessee and in Nashville as can be found anywhere, or as any native may choose to claim; still, all that is assumed in the text may be strictly true. There may be no such thing as a literary *society,* or as social intellectual intercourse.

to awaken my tenderest sympathies. And I do intend, by and by, to get up something or other—it may be a musical concert, or a subscription ball, or a benevolent association, or a ladies' fair—for their especial relief and benefit. Alas, the tyranny of fashion is too hard upon them, and upon us all. We sport our dashing carriages and expensive equipments of all sorts, at the hazard, sometimes, of our honesty, and frequently at the sacrifice of all manly independence and domestic comfort and generous hospitality. We give sumptuous entertainments, and squeeze and jam and stuff and *wine* our friends to death or under the table; in order to be envied, or laughed at and ridiculed for our pains. In a word, we imitate the *aristocratic* excesses of the great cities: while we overlook and disregard altogether what in them is most worthy of our emulation and fully within our reach—and withal, vastly more simple and *democratic*. Their literary taste and superior intelligence and refinement, we might aspire to, and successfully aim at, and profitably cultivate. A Parisian or Genevese or Italian *coterie*, or *soiree*, or *conversazione*—where the scholar, the artist, the author, the wit, the ethereal spirits of both sexes, the *beaux esprits* of every *clique* and profession, partake of the "feast of reason and the flow of soul," free from the restraints and pains and penalties of conventional formalities and courtly etiquette—never costs much to the host, and generally proves exhilarating and delightful to the guest. Could we introduce somewhat of the latter custom or fashion into our social arrangements, I think we should be the gainers both in our purses and in our enjoyments. The University will effect the revolution, and infuse the proper spirit, and raise up the requisite elements for the purpose—all in due time. I might expatiate much more largely upon this topic—especially in reference to our children, and to the general welfare of the community—but I forbear.

4. The University will present facilities for the higher education to the people here, which they could not otherwise command. So that hundreds of parents might send their sons to college, while they can board and clothe them at home, who could never send them to a distant seminary, where board and all other charges must be paid for in cash and at high prices. Indeed, every industrious, prudent, temperate man, however humble his circumstances, living within a mile or two of the college, might give his sons a liberal education; and thus fit them for any station, rank or profession, within the scope of their talents and ambition. This would be no common privilege. And experience, in other places thus favoured, shows that the poor are not backward in availing themselves of it; much to their credit, and to the future advancement and prosperity of their children. Of all men in the world, therefore, the poor assuredly, are the very last who should object to the establishment of a university, calculated so directly to improve and elevate their own condition, and to secure to themselves advantages not otherwise attainable,—but which the wealthy could purchase elsewhere and at any expense.

I now proceed to a hasty review of the *general* benefits

which the university proffers and insures to all classes of the people wherever it exists and prospers.

I use the term *university*, I repeat, as equivalent to the best possible system of education, and in reference to the highest order and degree of intellectual and moral cultivation. Wherever, and by whatever process, the human mind is most effectually imbued and enriched with the purest treasures of science and knowledge, and where the whole man is duly trained and qualified for the greatest usefulness, *there* is *my* university. Let this definition be kept in view. I will not dispute about words.

I affirm then, that the UNIVERSITY, as just explained, ever has been, is now, and ever will be, the grand *conservative* principle of civilization, of truth, virtue, learning, liberty, religion, and good government among mankind. To the university are we indebted for all the useful arts, laws, morals, enjoyments, comforts, conveniences and blessings of civilized society. There has never been a nation or community, highly enlightened and civilized, where the university did not dispense its kindly influences, or where it did not occupy a commanding position. The universities of Egypt, Chaldæa, Phœnicia, Assyria, were the sources and depositories. not only of the science, literature and arts which so preeminently distinguished those ancient States during a dozen or more centuries; but they were the schools at which the Grecian sages,. Thales, Pythagoras, Plato, and others, studied for many a long year; and whence they transferred to a European soil the fruits of their laborious researches; and which, finally, the Roman and other Western universities contributed to cherish and to preserve, and to transmit to successive generations.

Had I time for the task, I should like to trace the history of civilization from the garden of Eden, where was planted the first university, with the Deity at its head, and with the gifted father of mankind as his immediate representative and vice-chancellor; thence onward to the universal deluge; from Noah's ark, along the banks of the Tigris and the Euphrates and the Nile, over the plains of Shinar and upon the eastern and southern shores of the Mediterranean; lingering awhile at old Nineveh and Babylon and Tyre and Sidon and Thebes and Memphis; until we arrive at the golden age of Grecian beauty and perfection; thence to republican and imperial Rome in her most literate and palmy estate; with an occasional glance at the Grecian cities and colonies in Asia, Egypt, Sicily; and note the condition and character of the university at each and every step of our progress. Here would be instructive matter for volumes, exceedingly appropriate to our argument; which we must pass, however, without remark. But the paramount influence of the university or of the higher learning, during all these varying epochs, as a preservative of civilization, will be apparent to every competent and candid observer.

The nations of antiquity degenerated, or sunk into barbarism, just as the university was neglected or became extinct among them. During the Middle or Dark Ages, the university throughout Christian Europe, was as a light hidden under a bushel; ready, indeed, to shine forth in all its pristine splendours, as soon as the *Vandalism* of the exterior and surrounding world could be abated, and rendered docile and practicable. Still, even, while the Christian university had, as it were, retreated within the walls of the cloister and the monastery, and seemed resolved to leave the rude and vulgar millions to their fate, it was gloriously exalted and honoured among the Saracenic Moslems. If Athens and Rome had been deserted by the muses and the philosopher, it was only to find a more congenial home at Cordova and Bagdad. If the doors of the university were, for a time, hermetically sealed to the inquisitive and aspiring youth of Christendom, they were thrown wide open in every city of the Arabian Prophet's vast empire—from the Indus to the Pillars of Hercules. Thus the CRESCENT, at length, protected and fostered the science which the CROSS affected to despise. But at no period of our world's history, has the university been utterly prostrated, in all countries, at one and the same time. Civilization and the university have stood or fallen together. They have never been divorced. They were created together; and amidst all the changes and revolutions of human governments and religions, they have dwelt together in peace and harmony. The university has never been found among savages or barbarians: and all the nations and tribes upon our globe are barbarians or savages at this day, where the university is not, or where its cheering and illuminating beams have not penetrated.

If to this broad statement, it be objected, that science, literature and refinement abound in regions where no university has been established; I answer, that the beneficial effects of the university are oftentimes experienced at great distances from its actual location. The universities of Egypt extended their salutary and redeeming spirit even to barbarous Greece. Those of Europe are felt in America. And those of Massachusetts and Virginia may operate in Tennessee and Texas. In the present condition of the commercial and missionary world, the influence of the university is visible in almost every quarter—in New Holland and the South Sea Islands—on the banks of the Ganges and the Congo and the Amazon—and wherever European or American civilization has acquired even a partial or temporary resting place.

If again, we be directed to self-taught and self-made men, as a triumphant negative to our whole theory; I tell you that self-taught men (as they are styled,) such as Franklin, Ferguson, Shakspeare, Watt, Arkwright, Henry, Fulton, Davie, are or were just as much indebted to the university, as were Bacon, Selden, Newton, Burke, Jefferson, Jay, Madison or Whitney. The latter drank at the Fountain; the former at the streams which issue from it. Had Franklin been born and bred among savages, he might have become the first among the prophets or chiefs of his tribe, but he would never have been enrolled among the greatest philosophers and statesmen of the civilized world. Washington, too, might have been the Tecumseh or Black Hawk of the wilderness, but not the Saviour, the Founder, the Father of a mighty Republic of enlightened and happy freemen. He had studied in the school of Locke and Milton, of Sidney and Hampden, of Tell and Phocion; and like them, was *liberally* educated. He was not a *scholar*, in the strict technical meaning of the term; though his scholarship was respectable, and far superior to that of many a college graduate. But a man may be a scholar without being liberally educated or liberally minded, as he may be liberally educated without being a scholar. Mere professional men, whose studies and practice are restricted to their professions, as lawyers, physicians, theologians, linguists, mathematicians, seldom possess those enlarged, catholic, comprehensive views and sentiments which constitute genuine *liberality;* and which are essential to the character of the philosopher, the publicist, the statesman, the philanthropist. They may be admirable and exceedingly useful in their respective and appropriate spheres, and worthy of all praise, while they are content to act well the part which they have learned and understand. Thanks again to the university for both the larger and the lesser stars; but let them move and shine in their own proper orbits.

But after all, we may be told that we need only a small supply of university scholars; and that it is not worth while to be at the expense of such an institution for so trivial an object. Conceding, for a moment, what I do not admit, that only a limited number of thoroughly educated men are actually required, or are, on any account, desirable in such a community as ours, let us see how many are wanted, and whence they are to be procured. It has generally been assumed that lawyers, physicians, clergymen, judges, jurists, cabinet ministers, ambassadors to foreign courts, and teachers of the liberable sciences, ought to be learned and accomplished men. I suppose it would not be amiss also, if our legislators and politicians, our editors of public journals, our civil engineers, our bankers and financiers, our conductors of all great private or corporate establishments, were well educated. If so, the number must be large—several thousand at the least. These must be suitably educated here at home; or a sufficient number of our youth must be sent abroad for the purpose; or we must import them, ready made, from Europe or the other States, that is, we must intrust to foreigners or strangers our most important interests, offices and professions; or we must get along without them, in other words, employ incompetent men. The latter alternative, I know, will prevail; and, I know also, that it is popular. We do employ incompetent men—sometimes from necessity—oftener from choice, when we might get better. And this arises from our general ignorance. I do not believe that any man would employ an ignorant lawyer or doctor, if he knew the fact, or were capable of judging of the qualifications of the one or the other. Nor would our people elect to any office a candidate whom they believed too ignorant to serve them faithfully and efficiently. But a very little *show* of knowledge and ability, with a good deal of cunning and impudence, will easily impose on honest unsuspecting credulity. Here then, the university will remedy two defects at once. It will furnish learned men of every station where learning is needful: and it will gradually enlighten and elevate the *general mind* so as to be able to discriminate between the sciolist and the scholar, between obtrusive overweening self-sufficiency and modest sterling merit.

If we could compute in *dollars*, by any species of arithmetic, the loss of property and life, of health and comfort, and the injury to morals and religion, occasioned, during a single year, by ignorant blundering, specious, dogmatical, illiterate lawyers, doctors and preachers, by vicious or excessive legislation, by judicial injustice, by unskilful or fraudulent banking, by venal, lying, superficial newspaper editors, by bullying grog-shop politicians, by stupid drivelling schoolmasters, by reckless, drunken, untaught steamboat and railroad masters and engineers, by avaricious irresponsible stage-coach proprietors and agents, by travelling mountebanks and impostors, by all sorts of rogues and asses in high places,—we should sum up an amount sufficient to purchase, in fee simple, a dozen German principalities, universities and all; or enough to create a fund, the interest of which would support our State government and institutions forever.

Ignorance never did any good, and never will or can do any good. Ignorant men are good for nothing, except so far as they are governed and directed by intelligent superiors. Hence it is the order of Providence that, in every well regulated community, children and all grossly ignorant persons are held in subjection to age and wisdom and experience. No species or portion even of the humblest manual or mechanical labour can be performed until the party be taught how to do it. The least that can be required of any man is, that he be qualified for the office or vocation which he aspires to occupy or pursue. Invincible ignorance alone is excusable. But even this will not justify his ambition or desire to transcend his proper sphere, or his bungling attempts to do what he knows not and cannot do.—As, for example, to construct a telescope or chronometer, when he has learned only to head a nail or point a pin; or to amputate a limb and heal the sick, when he has been trained to ply the axe or drive a dray; or to dabble in the law, because his speaking organs have caught the *perpetual motion;* or to guide a train of railway cars, after having duly served a six years' apprenticeship to the barber's craft and mystery, as was lately done in Virginia to the destruction of a score of lives and the fracture of a hundred limbs; or to preach the gospel, in utter defiance of the well-known canon, "ne sutor ultra crepidam," "let the shoemaker stick to his last and the tailor to his goose." Now the barber may be a very useful citizen and a very worthy gentleman—as *gentlemen* are ye all, in this country, except us poor schoolmasters—but if he has learned nothing more than to shave the lieges and to rig out new upper stories for ladies of a certain age, then may I be spared the pleasure of a railroad jaunt when next he enacts the ambitious Phaeton or daring engineer!

I do not mean to insinuate that a mechanic or ploughman may not become an accomplished lawyer, artist, statesman, or college professor. But, then, he must study and learn whatever his new profession implies or demands. His skill in the shop or the field will not avail him here. Franklin was an excellent printer: but his *trade* did not make him a philosopher or diplomatist. Roger Sherman was a very good shoemaker; but he studied law and politics before he commanded the ear and the reverence of Congress. James Ferguson was bred a poor shepherd's boy: but his reputation as a writer and lecturer upon Astronomy and Mechanics, was won by his mastery of Newton's astonishing discoveries and revelations. And the most learned Orientalist in England, and a Professor in one of her imperial universities, was once an illiterate labouring carpenter. But the *saw* and the *plane* did not unlock for him the temple doors of science or raise him to a peerless throne among its votaries.

I honour every mechanic, and every farmer, and every working man, who diligently and honestly pursues the noiseless tenor of his way, without ever seeking a different or higher calling. But if he would fain become a ruler or office-bearer in the land, I must examine his credentials and be certified of his knowledge and qualifications. If these prove satisfactory, I will cheerfully accord to him my suffrage and confidence, and the respect to which his extraordinary merit may be justly entitled. I would rather be a good blacksmith, than to be a sorry, empty-headed, pettifogging lawyer. The blacksmith, for his particular vocation, is the better educated, and the better principled, and the more deserving citizen of the two. I suppose there are some five hundred "attorneys at law" in Tennessee, who might be converted into tolerably decent blacksmiths, much to their own and the public's benefit, could they be induced to submit to a reasonable discipline and schooling in our Legislature's favourite university; which is, at once, the cheapest and most efficient, manual labour establishment in all the land. Its value and importance, too, will be more apparent every year; and just in proportion to the lack or failure of other institutions, and to the increase of ignorance, idleness and quackery among us.

As the periodical press and the pulpit are calculated to exert a more powerful influence upon society, for weal or wo, than any other instrumentalities whatever, it follows, that, of all men living, ministers of the gospel and newspaper editors ought to be the most talented, and the most profoundly and extensively conversant with every species of human learning. The editors of our daily, weekly, monthly, quarterly journals, furnish a large proportion of the *reading* of our people. They wield an engine therefore of the most tremendous, potent and responsible character. And if the university be needed for any one class of public instructors or functionaries rather than another, it is to furnish accomplished and erudite and trustworthy editors. Such as Franklin became: and such as the illustrious and classic authors of the Federalist might have been, had they chosen to be editors, instead of being anonymous contributors and correspondents.

As to preaching the gospel, I am aware that some men fancy that human learning is quite superfluous. And that just in proportion to its absence, will be the evidence of the preacher's inspiration and paramount claims to the implicit faith and respect of the people. All Scripture, history, reason and experience, however, teach a very different doctrine. The university is indispensable to the minister of the gospel. A large amount and variety of intellectual furniture must be acquired by the preacher, whether settled or itinerant, whether pastor or missionary, or he will never be eminently useful—probably altogether useless—or, most likely, injurious to the sacred cause which he professionally and ostensibly labours to advance. If knowledge sometimes puffeth up, and renders its possessor vain and arrogant, does it therefore follow that knowledge is an evil, and at war with virtue and charity? Who are more assuming, intolerant, dogmatical, overbearing, opinionated, exclusive, self-sufficient, bigoted or ostentatious, than your ignorant, superficial, boisterous, declamatory preachers? It is notorious also, that the unlearned habitually make a greater display of learning, parade more Greek and Hebrew without understanding a word of either, sport more scholastic technicalities, and talk more about books and authorities and incomprehensible mysteries, than any genuine scholar would ever adventure upon in the pulpit or out of it. They thus expose themselves, and too frequently their *cloth* and the cause of Christianity itself, to the contempt and derision of the intelligent and discerning—who know little or nothing of the Bible, and who judge of religion chiefly from the conduct and exhibitions of this class of preachers.

If it be said that the Deity has no need of human learning to propagate his religion, it may be replied, that, neither has he any need of human ignorance. He could, if he chose, dispense with human agency altogether. But we have yet to learn that Infinite Wisdom has ever selected an insufficient or inadequate agency for any purpose whatever. In the days of prophecy and miracle, from Moses to Paul, he never employed *human ignorance* in the work of religious instruction. If they were not all educated in the universities of Egypt as was Moses, or of Judea as was Isaiah, or of Babylon as was Daniel, or at the feet of Gamaliel as was Paul, they were well trained somewhere and by competent masters, as were the fishermen of Galilee by Christ himself, besides being endowed with the gift of tongues and extraordinary communications for every emergency. Witness the prophets and apostles, and the primitive fathers and martyrs of the church. And since that period, witness the reformers and missionaries and all the bright luminaries of Christendom. If they did not all study at the university, as did Wickliffe, and Huss, and Jerome, and Luther, and Melanchthon, and Zuinglius, and Calvin, and Knox, and Cranmer, and Latimer, and Whitefield, and Wesley, and Eliot, and Brainerd, and Edwards, and Horsley, and Martyn and Swartz, yet they learned from those who had been graduated at the university, or from books which the university had created and multiplied.—As was the case with Richard

Baxter, Andrew Fuller, William Carey, Robert Morrison, Adam Clarke, Thomas Scott, Cornelius Winter, William Jay, Joshua Marshman, William Ward, and a host of similar spirits. None of whom ever despised or neglected human science, or affected to be above the wisdom of the university. If any of them commenced their ministerial labours, imperfectly prepared, as, no doubt, many did, they soon discovered their own deficiencies; and, like honest men, as they were, put themselves to school again and became humble persevering learners. And thus, by extra effort and diligence, kept in advance of their own pupils and hearers; and, in process of time, rose to distinguished eminence among the most profound theologians and erudite scholars of their day. Thus it has ever been, and ever will be, with all truly conscientious ministers of the gospel. However ill-instructed or poorly qualified at the outset, they will, like John Bunyan or John Newton, read and study, and meditate and reflect, as best they can, whether immured in a prison or sailing upon the ocean. Nor can I conceive of a more pitiable object than a public teacher of the Christian religion who is not always seeking and thirsting after knowledge as for hidden treasures, or who denounces learning, and is content to lead a life of idleness and ignorance.

The Bible is a book, or rather a collection of books, composed by divers authors, in dialects long since obsolete, during a period of some fifteen hundred years, and treating of the most difficult, momentous and dissimilar topics. And there is not a single science or branch of literature, within the whole range of human research, which may not be profitably consecrated to its exposition and illustration. Nor has there yet lived the man, who found himself encumbered with too much learning for this sacred work, or who could not bring his every attainment and his every faculty to bear upon it and to contribute to its better accomplishment. Such men as Selden and Grotius and Locke and Newton and Jones and Kennicott have amply testified that, to grapple with the Bible, was no child's play. The astronomer, the historian, the chronologer, the critic, the antiquary, the traveller, the chemist, the geologist, have all and each in turn, made discoveries which they fancied must tell against Moses and his successors. And theologians, in their ignorance and zeal, have hastily condemned and repudiated their *science*, as well as their gratuitous and false application of it. But a more thorough study of Moses by the scientific, and a deeper acquaintance with science by the theologian, have undeceived and reconciled both parties. So that the two great volumes of Nature and Revelation, equally the product of the same unchanging Divinity, are now acknowledged to harmonize and to speak the same language. Not a principle or fact has been established or brought to light, by the brilliant labours of a Hutton, a Playfair, a Kepler, a Herschel, a La Place, a Cuvier, a Hauy, a Champollion, a De la Beche, a Buckland, a Lyell or an Ehrenberg, which does not accord with the Mosaic history and philosophy, when rightly interpreted; as the ablest living divines cheerfully concede. Hume and Gibbon and

Halley and Voltaire and D'Alembert and Buffon and Condorcet and Volney have yielded to a more enlightened school; as have the persecutors of Roger Bacon, Galileo and Copernicus given place to a more tolerant, charitable and scriptural theology.

But again, in a country like ours, where the people govern, the university is greatly needed to furnish a class of men sufficiently numerous and qualified to enlighten the mass of the people upon general politics—upon the Constitution, government, laws, jurisprudence, and institutions of the Republic. If every individual cannot become familiar with these subjects by his own reading and reflection, it is desirable at least that an adequate instructor and guide should be at hand on whose information and judgment he may safely rely. Now the people are called on, at every election, to decide upon some of the most intricate, complex and difficult questions of State policy—involving their own and the interests of posterity to an indefinite extent. And how shall they vote upon measures which they do not understand? What do *they* know, or what do our comparatively wise men know, for example, about the just principles of taxation, or tariff, or finance, or banking, or usury laws—of our foreign relations, of our Indian policy, of internal improvements, or of any constitutional doctrine or controversy—or indeed, of the very elements of political economy or jurisprudence or legislation? And yet, they are expected annually to pronounce *ay* or *no*, without hesitation, on a dozen or more untried projects, which it might puzzle even a Solomon fully to appreciate, in all their bearings, after the most intense study and mature deliberation. Our political candidates for office and our newspaper editors are the exclusive monopolists of this entire department of popular instruction. I have two objections to this monopoly. (1.) Forty-nine out of fifty of the said politicians and editors are themselves too ignorant for the service. And (2.) were they ever so well informed, they cannot be trusted. It is their interest and their vocation to mislead, deceive, *humbug* and mystify the whole body of the sovereign people.

The university has ever been the friend and the nursery of common schools — when left to its own natural freedom of action. In modern times, where-ever the university has flourished untrammeled and unrestricted by jealous, arbitrary authority, *there* the common school has taken root and prospered also. This fact is notorious, indisputable and undisputed. In no country, at this day, do we behold the slightest approach to a good common school system, except where the university is honoured and liberally sustained. Scotland, Prussia, Germany, Holland, New England and New York may serve as proof and comment. I hold the attempt to create and foster common schools, without the aid of the university, to be utterly vain and nugatory. It cannot be done. But establish an efficient, free-working university anywhere—whether among the Turks, the Tartars or the Hottentots—and the common schools will spontaneously grow up around it and beneath its influence.—As certainly as light and heat flow from the sun in the firmament. It is in fact the great Luminary of the intellectual firmament. The common school is the child and not the parent—the effect and not the cause—of the university. The university will furnish the teachers and the learning which are indispensable to the inferior schools and seminaries: and it will awaken the desire and the ambition among all classes to acquire knowledge and to support schools.

It would be impossible, at this moment, to find in Tennessee a hundredth part of the duly qualified instructors necessary to put into immediate operation any general school system whatever. No man can teach what he does not thoroughly understand. Whatever art or science he professes to teach others, he must first learn himself. If you would have competent teachers of reading, writing, arithmetic, grammar, history, geography, the Constitution and laws of the land, and whatever else our youth ought to learn at school in order to become useful citizens, you must first provide for their proper training. That is, you must send them to the higher schools and colleges and universities of your own or some other State. A thousand young men ought now to be thus in training, or in a course of preparation for the business of school-keeping. Send them to the University, at the State's expense, and they will not fail to become qualified for the service in due time. Or, enable the University, by suitable endowments, to open her doors to all comers, and to educate every poor talented youth without charge; and you will soon be supplied with indigent but accomplished scholars, who will be glad to teach for a livelihood. They will themselves become piogeers and missionaries in the cause of education. They will search out and expose the wants and destitution of the people, and will plant schools in every village and in every neighbourhood where children can be found. Tennessee, with her present ample resources, might organize and endow a university which could impart gratuitous instruction to all her studious and deserving youth; and thus eventually elevate the standard of education, and insure its advantages to every portion and order of its rapidly increasing population. If Nashville should not be deemed the most eligible site for such an establishment, let the Legislature select a better.*

The university, again, is the steadfast ally and the consistent advocate of liberty and the rights of man. It ever has been so, except when checked and enslaved by political or ecclesiastical despotism. The light of truth and freedom has occasionally gleamed from the

---

* Having on various occasions heretofore, discoursed at large on the subject of common schools—having reviewed the systems which obtain in all our States and in several countries in Europe—having expressed my opinion freely upon each, and also upon the expediency of providing schools for the education of teachers, &c. it was not my purpose, in the above remarks, to do more than barely to point out the dependence of common schools upon the University. Our *poor* college graduates will, after all, prove our best common schoolmasters, even though they may not be *ambitious* to teach for life. Well educated and clever Americans will not be content to work like Prussians, in comparative obscurity and poverty. The planter's overseer or negro-driver is better paid for his *learned* labours, than any common school teacher in all the valley of the Mississippi.

portals of the university, even when most enslaved, and when more than *Cimmerian* darkness prevailed around it—as in the ages and persons of Roger Bacon and John Wickliffe. While, at each successive struggle for human liberty, from Luther to Hampden and Wilberforce and Brougham, its most efficient champions and defenders have issued from the university.

It was the university which awakened or rather created the desire of civil and religious liberty in France. And all the incipient measures and movements of her grand, but disastrous revolution, were suggested and directed by the wisest and most intelligent of her educated sons. And had the people been sufficiently enlightened to submit to the counsels and guidance of Lafayette and his illustrious coadjutors, the result had been widely different, and as glorious as the cause was just and honourable. She failed, because the university had not been suffered to operate upon the popular mind.

Greece, too, at the instance of her young men, who had studied at the universities of France and Germany, and at those of her own Bucharest and beautiful Scio, shook off the Moslem yoke, which she had tamely worn for centuries. And if her present institutions and forms of government are not as liberal and generous as they were in the days of Pericles and Miltiades, of Plato and Socrates, it is because the university has not yet illuminated and elevated the ignorant and besotted mass of her degenerate population.

The university is, moreover, the dread and terror of

every legitimate despotism in modern Europe. In spite of all the vigilant jealousy with which it is guarded in order to repress the spirit of free inquiry among its professors and students, it is well known that they are secretly imbibing principles which will one day reach, if they have not already reached, the cottage and the palace, the army and the church; and cause tyranny, under every guise, to relax its iron grasp, or to fall beneath the universal conviction of its injustice and imbecility. In fact, already throughout Germany, and several other countries, the condition of the people has been greatly meliorated and improved, in consequence of the diffusion of knowledge by the university; so that the arbitrary or capricious exertion of despotic power is seldom felt or witnessed. In this respect, they are incomparably better governed than Spain, Portugal, Italy or Russia, where the university has been still more effectually controlled and fettered by the monarch and the priest. I repeat then, that wherever the university is itself free, it will, sooner or later, make the people free—even while living under a nominal monarchy or despotism. And it will as certainly qualify them for self-government.

Spanish America has become independent—but the people are not free. While, throughout British America, whether colonial or independent, the people are and ever have been free. The university was transported to this new world in the gallant "May Flower," which landed upon Plymouth rock the first little colony of Anglo-American republicans. And it was forthwith set up, in good style, in the town of Cambridge, where it has ever since been the nursery of common schools and the guardian genius of constitutional liberty. In the university were bred the noble and gifted patriots, who dared to assert and maintain, at every hazard and sacrifice, their own and their countrymen's indefeasible birthrights—as free born Englishmen—against every insidious or violent effort to subject them to arbitrary illegal domination. By these choice spirits was our independence achieved: and to these are we indebted for our national existence, and for all our free republican privileges and institutions. Our college graduates and our college students were the first to speak, the first to act, and the first to fight, in the cause of their country. They were all Whigs then: and they will be Whigs forever.

It is worthy of special remark, that the principal men—the leading influential characters—the master spirits of all the primitive English colonies, from Massachusetts to Georgia, were individuals of the highest order of talent, morality, education and respectability at home. They came hither, not for wealth or power, but in search of that political and religious freedom and tranquillity, which the peculiar circumstances of the fatherland seemed likely to deny them. They left behind them the monarchy, the aristocracy and the hierarchy. They brought with them the learning, the virtue, the piety, the enterprise, the indomitable love of liberty, which distinguished England's noblest sons, and whatever was strictly republican in her institutions. With such excellent materials, and under the most favourable auspices, they commenced the experiment of governing themselves in the far off wilderness, agreeably to their own interpretation of the English constitution, and with such modifications as were adapted to their singular position. From the beginning they were free: And it is the glory of every true-hearted American, that his ancestors have never been slaves; and that they would never submit for a moment to oppression in any form. They would not be taxed even a farthing, without their own consent. And they boldly drew their swords to maintain, and to transmit to their children, the grand fundamental doctrine of political rights, that taxation and representation go together, and cannot be disjoined, while *Magna Charta* remains the bulwark and the boast of English liberty.

Had our fathers been the degraded, sottish, ignorant, pitiable and despised outcasts of British bridewells and dungeons—as malice and envy have often proclaimed—our destiny had been humble and wretched indeed. Then we might have been slaves—hopeless and helpless—from the prison-ship of our Adam and Eve—grovelling and writhing beneath the tyrant's scourge, and weeping tears of bitterness and anguish, through ages of despair, to this dark and cheerless moment. But Heaven had otherwise ordained. And the University, not Newgate, freighted the vessels which bore to this then savage hemisphere, the founders of the freest and greatest Republic that the Sun has ever shone upon. Shall we continue free and great? Shall we—

will our posterity—always prove worthy of our and their illustrious parentage? Yes—while we cherish, and honour, and generously sustain the university—and not a day longer.

There is no opinion or doctrine more universally recognized—none more frequently or earnestly inculcated by the advocates of liberty everywhere—than that a purely republican form of government cannot be maintained except by a highly intelligent and virtuous people. To the very existence of our Republic therefore, the university must ever be indispensable. Intelligence there may be without virtue. But there can be no virtue without intelligence. Every exercise of virtue, or every virtuous act, implies some degree of knowledge. The principles of virtue or of ethics and religion must be studied—just as geometry is studied. No man can practise or perform what he does not understand, or has not learned how to perform. Intelligent virtue or virtuous intelligence, if I may be allowed such forms of expression, constitutes, just in proportion to its degree and extent, the true dignity of man. As citizens and as Christians—as the subjects of a human and a divine government—as responsible to society and to posterity and to High Heaven for all our conduct, for all the good we neglect to do as well as for all the evil we commit—we cannot be too diligent or anxious in studying and learning how to discharge the various and important duties incumbent on us; or in ascertaining in what way or by what means we may accomplish the greatest amount of good.

And hence I am led to my concluding remarks upon the general subject.

Intellectual pursuits are always salutary to body and mind and heart.—The best preservative of good morals.—The surest preventive of criminal and ruinous indulgences and practices.—The never failing source of the purest enjoyments. Study contributes to health and peace of mind. Studious men live the longest: and they are generally the happiest men in the world. They are harmless and inoffensive members of society. They seldom annoy anybody, or meddle with other people's affairs. They never engage in mobs or riots or popular tumults of any kind. [I do not here allude to college boys—who are not studious—and who are often turbulent and disorderly for that very reason.] I speak of men, devoted to science and literature. They are peaceful and tranquil in their habits. And even when they seem to do no good, they cannot be said to do any positive mischief. Very rarely, indeed, have they been charged with flagitious enormities or condemned for capital crimes. Not an individual of their number can, at this day, be found in any prison or penitentiary in our own country—perhaps, in no country. In England, the names of Eugene Aram and William Dodd, stand forth solitary and prominent exceptions to a general rule. And the fact, that their fate has created a sensation not yet allayed or forgotten, proves how unexpected and startling were their guilt and ruin. Educated and learned men have often been the victims of tyranny and despotism. They have suffered every species of cruelty in person and estate—under barbarous and sanguinary codes of law—administered by mercenary courts and packed juries—by bills of pains and penalties, and *ex post facto* statutes, enacted for the occasion—and by that most convenient instrument of legal ingenuity and refinement, *constructive treason*, which could consign to the scaffold or the gibbet the most innocent and meritorious objects of a tyrant's jealousy or hatred. They ever have been, as they ever will be, foremost to suffer and die, martyrs to the sacred cause of truth and liberty. For *State crimes* and for *religious heresies*, they have been often unrighteously murdered, like Socrates and Tully and Sir Thomas More, according to forms of law, or without law, or in defiance of all law. But the world has long since reversed the sentence of their condemnation. For real crime however—for the commission of the *mala in se*—very few have hitherto, in any age or country, been condemned to death or to infamous penalties. Of traitors, our own protracted revolutionary war produced but *one;* and he, assuredly, was not a literary or college-bred General. And if a single individual since, of a liberal education and cultivated mind, has been justly or unjustly chargeable with treasonable designs; let his lonely name be recorded as the only instance of the kind which has occurred during the half century of our national existence. And let it serve as a beacon and a warning against all inordinate, unhallowed and desperate ambition! No university catalogue in all our land, during a period of more than two hundred years, has ever been disgraced by the name of a single graduate, *convicted* of an infamous crime, or doomed to an infamous or capital punishment. And it is yet the glorious and unparalled distinction of our own favoured Republic, that not a drop of blood has ever been judicially shed upon her virgin soil for a *State* offence.

Finally: Reason or understanding ought to be assiduously cultivated and improved, because God has conferred it on man for this very purpose. Intelligence is an attribute of the Deity; and a part therefore of that divine image in which man was created. If, then, he would be like his Maker or seek to regain his image, he must daily grow in knowledge as well as in holiness; or rather in knowledge in order to holiness. We are nowhere commanded in Scripture to get money or to hoard up riches. But we are everywhere commanded to seek after knowledge, to get wisdom and understanding—to advance in every virtue, grace and moral excellence, even to the most exalted standard of perfection—to become holy as God is holy. Now, to be useful or virtuous or holy *one degree*, implies *one degree* at least of knowledge. And so on, proportionably, to any extent whatever. But we are bound to become as useful, virtuous and holy as possible—to do all the good in our power. And consequently, it is our duty to study and labour, with unremitting ardour and zeal, to acquire every species of information which can qualify or aid us to do good. And I have not yet heard of any science, taught in the university or elsewhere, which may not enable its possessor to be more useful; and which therefore ought not to be learned when practicable. No man can be "growing in grace" or becoming better, in the scriptural sense or in any sense, who is not constantly advancing in knowledge and wisdom. Nor will any man evince extraordinary judgment, candour or modesty, by boldly denouncing the study of any science or language with which he is himself unacquainted.

The universal passion for wealth, which everybody cherishes and encourages, is condemned in Scripture and by sound philosophy also, as avarice, covetousness, idolatry. We are exhorted to seek after "the true" and more enduring riches—such as will accompany us to another and a better world. It certainly does seem preposterous and puerile for a man to labour incessantly, during his whole life, to amass wealth, without enjoying it himself or sharing it with others, without helping the needy or advancing any great interest of society, deriving pleasure only from its acquisition and rapid accumulation; and yet to be conscious, all the while, that death, in a few brief years, will rob him forever of his uttermost farthing. It will not descend with him into the grave. He cannot carry it with him either to heaven or hell. It has absorbed his every faculty while living—closed up all the avenues of knowledge and sympathy and benevolence and charity—rendered him selfish, hard-hearted, proud, overbearing and oppresive,—and yet left him to perish, at last, the veriest slave of the meanest and most relentless tyrant. But the intellectual treasures of the inquisitive and persevering virtuous student will never be lost or forfeited. Of these, no earthly power can despoil him. These belong to the soul—to the immortal spirit. And, if rightly employed, and honestly consecrated to their legitimate uses, they will constitute a large measure of his heavenly inheritance and felicity. And he will be still adding to his intellectual possessions, and be approximating to the glorious likeness of his omniscient Creator by new and continually increasing attainments, while infinity remains to be explored and exhausted, and throughout the illimitable ages of an ever beginning, but never ending ETERNITY.

A LECTURE

ON

POPULAR EDUCATION.

LECTURE

ON

POPULAR EDUCATION.

If there be any one truth, principle, maxim or doctrine more universally recognized among our countrymen, at the present day, than another, it is this, namely: That a free, republican, representative government can be permanently sustained only by an enlightened and virtuous people. Without an adequate knowledge of their rights and duties, the people cannot maintain the one nor discharge the other. And without moral integrity, they will soon become indifferent to both. An ignorant and vicious community will ever be the victim or instrument or sport of the ambitious, the crafty, the venal, the factious, and the desperate. Neither the intelligence, nor the wisdom, nor the virtue, nor the patriotism, nor the self-devotion, nor the unwearied efforts of the few—supposing a few such to exist—can check or control or counteract the capricious, furious, and ever downward torrent of popular ignorance and corruption. In such circumstances, the people themselves will eagerly assist in forging the chains which are to bind them to the triumphal car of their own favourite chieftain—whether political demagogue or military conqueror—nor will they dream of danger until their liberties shall have been destroyed and their destiny sealed forever.

We have been so long accustomed to hear these positions proclaimed and reiterated, that we are ready to conclude not only that they are everywhere perfectly understood, but that they are practically illustrated throughout the length and breadth of the Republic. That we are the freest, most enlightened, most virtuous, prosperous and happy nation in the world, is always assumed as a matter of fact—about which there can be no question—and whereof we may reasonably glory and boast on all occasions, and in style and phrase the most hyperbolical and overweening. If all sorts of travelling and book-making foreigners do not praise us to our heart's content, we at least make ample amends by praising ourselves. Self-knowledge however—agreeably to the ancient adage, "know thyself"—has ever been justly esteemed the most important kind of knowledge, and, indeed, the first step towards the attainment of all other useful knowledge, so far as individuals are concerned. And I see no reason why the same rule and test should not be as applicable to nations as it confessedly is to individuals. If, as a nation, we have defects, and wants, and faults and vices, we ought to know them, in order to ascertain the proper remedy. Are there not then symptoms sufficiently portentous, and daily occurrences sufficiently alarming, to awaken the suspicion that our great national fabric is not constructed altogether of the soundest, purest and most enduring materials? Are the excellent constitutions of the Union and the States everywhere duly revered, and most sacredly guarded and obeyed? Is the supremacy of the laws universally affirmed and maintained? What mean the popular riots and mobs and tumults which are currently witnessed in every corner and section of our country? Do these betoken no inherent malady, and no danger to our institutions? Are our office-bearers and office-seekers. like their predecessors of the good old Washington school, the fairest specimens of genuine patriotism, of political integrity, of magnanimous bearing, and intrepid moral courage, that the sun has ever shone upon? I leave these and a hundred similar inquiries, to the sober judgment and truth-speaking conscience of my hearers. I feel assured that, in relation to this whole subject, they will not charge me with rhetorical exaggeration, nor set me down as an idle and fanatical alarmist.

That we have reached a crisis which demands extraordinary attention, and which threatens disastrous results, will hardly be denied. Still, I do not despair of the Republic. We may experience all the horrors of the storm and tempest, of the hurricane and tornado, of the earthquake and volcano; and yet be preserved from utter ruin. While there is life, there is hope. The body politic may be diseased and convulsed, and yet may revive and flourish with renewed vigour, under the judicious treatment of the skilful patriotic physician.

In many respects, our country has hitherto been the theatre of novel and untried experiments. Our whole system, indeed, has been from its commencement, regarded by the old world as a mere experiment. And not a few of our radical innovations have been denounced as rash and hazardous in the extreme. In every stage of our progress, we have been narrowly watched, and jealously scrutinized, and invidiously depreciated, and often malignantly misrepresented. Obstacles too, neither few nor small, have been purposely thrown in our way; and every species of unkindly and insidious foreign influence has been exerted to thwart and impede our onward march towards national vigour and maturity. At the close of the great revolutionary struggle for national independence, we were comparatively a homogeneous people—brave, intelligent, uncorrupt. The sturdy and well trained descendants of the pious pilgrims at the North, and of the chivalrous companions of the gallant Raleigh, Smith and Oglethorpe at the South, were amply and equally qualified for the arduous task of self-government. But they did not foresee the immense territorial expansion of the Republic which a few short years were to realize; nor the unparalled enlargement of the population both from natural increase and from the sudden importation of hundreds of thousands of degraded, dissolute, turbulent European paupers. They could not anticipate the changes, the dangers, the corruptions, which might thence speedily ensue. And, of course, they did not provide the necessary preventive or remedy. They were not insensible to the benefits of education, both intellectual and moral.—For they had shared them liberally. And they wisely laboured to secure the same advantages for their children. We do not find, in all the writings and official documents of the sages of that glorious and heroic period, one heretical or discordant sentiment upon this vital subject. They inculcated the importance—they urged the necessity of universal education as their only ground of hope for the preservation of the liberties and privileges which they had periled life and fortune and sacred honour to achieve. But they did not dream that the men of that generation—the citizens of the original Atlantic States—were in duty bound to provide also for the education of half a continent besides. Let us not therefore lightly arraign or rashly censure our noble sires, because they did not forthwith devise the ways and means to plant schools and colleges and churches throughout the wild forests and luxuriant prairies of the mighty west; nor commence the work of training the thousands of teachers about to be required to instruct the then unborn millions by whom the transmontaine wilderness was presently to be subdued and cultivated.

But however we may dispose of such preliminary speculations, the simple fact is, that our population from two and a half millions, has, within some fifty years, been augmented to at least fifteen millions. The means of education have not been furnished in a proportionate ratio. Far from it. The deficiency is great in several even of the oldest States, and much greater in all the new ones. True, the public mind is beginning to be alive to this enormous deficiency. The actual condition of the people is gradually becoming known. It is already proclaimed in our public journals: "That there are a million and a half of children at least who have no teacher; that thirty thousand schoolmasters are needed at this moment, and that an additional annual supply of four thousand will be needed for the regular increase of our population." If this statement be even an approximation towards the truth, it is enough to appal the heart of the boldest and most sanguine philanthrophist.

I do not repose implicit faith in the statistics of ignorance, or intemperance, or profligacy, or irreligion, which have been of late so officiously paraded before the public, in anniversary speeches and reports, in pamphlets and periodicals, for the benevolent purpose of awakening the sympathy and commanding the purses of the rich. Still, it must be admitted, there is a vast amount of deplorable ignorance and reckless depravity among our people. Of this fact, every man must be convinced, who will trust to the evidence of his own senses within the range of his daily observation,—however limited that may be. Let him investigate the moral character and condition of his own county, city, town, village or neighbourhood; and he will be no longer incredulous on this score. He need hardly read over the delectable catalogue of absurdities and fooleries and quackery and frauds and abominations inflicted and perpetrated by *Mormonism* and *Shakerism* and *Owenism* and *Agrarianism* and *Thompsonism* and *Partyism* and *Lynchism* and *Abolitionism* and *Perfectionism* and *Fanaticism* and all sorts of political and religious *ultraism*;—which everywhere find ample scope and encouragement, and oftentimes reap most golden harvests from the hopes or fears or excited passions of a besotted and uninstructed people. These and other similar extravagances and monstrosities prove indeed the existence of much shrewdness and cunning and misdirected intelligence on the one hand, as they do of a vastly larger amount of gross ignorance and invincible stolidity on the other. The first constituting the essential attributes of the accomplished knave and successful impostor, and the latter supplying in abundance the necessary dupes and victims to be operated upon and mystified at pleasure by the former. But an observer may leave out of view or pass over all this, if he please, and yet witness enough to be satisfied that the land is teeming with a wild luxuriant growth of untamed, untutored, and licentious mobocracy.

All this is so obvious and palpable, that I feel conscious of having uttered the merest truisms in the hearing of every reflecting person present. Be it so: then are we prepared to grapple with the real difficulties of the case. *A perfectly equitable republican government—such as our own claims to be—can be maintained only by an intelligent and virtuous people.* Granted by you all. A republican government may be as unjust, as arbitrary, as oppressive and despotic as any absolute monarchy upon the earth. Everything depends on the character of the sovereign in either case. And as in a republic the people are sovereign, we must rely exclusively upon the wisdom and honesty of the people for good laws and faithful magistrates. Multitudes of our people are neither intelligent nor virtuous:—granted. This fact bodes evil to the Republic—granted again. The only prospective remedy or curative process, is the suitable education of the young and rising generation, and of each future generation:—granted, once more. How are all the children of the Republic to be educated?—By the establishment of good common schools all over the land, say our statesmen and politicians: and the people respond, amen! Very good. This then is the all-sufficient and acknowledged *panacea*. I shall not stop now to analyze or to controvert its claims to our confidence. I concede, for the sake of argument, the perfect adequateness of the system recommended. I assume that the universal diffusion of knowledge, by the agency of COMMON SCHOOLS, will effect the desired reformation, and insure peace and prosperity to the Republic forever.

The question recurs: How are such schools to be established and maintained in sufficient numbers to meet the demand? or is there no other possible mode of reaching the same end? As to the first inquiry, we have the example and experience of a few of our own States and of several European kingdoms, which may aid and guide us in our researches and speculations. New York, New England, Virginia, have tried the common school system under divers forms and regulations, and with various success. It will suffice, for our present purpose, to notice briefly three of the systems referred to; and which indeed, with slight modifications, comprise the whole which have been thoroughly tested in our own country. These may be distinguished and described as the systems, 1st. of Connecticut, 2d. of Massachusetts, and 3d. of New York.

In these several States, there is in one respect, a coincidence of plan: That is, the Legislature has declared that all youth *shall* be educated—the children of the poor as well as of the rich. The difference lies in the collection and distribution of the funds. In these States, legislative aid is generally afforded only in providing teachers. Books are furnished by parents. The schoolhouse is erected by tax, imposed at a legal meeting of the district; and all other incidental expenses are defrayed either by a direct tax or by voluntary subscription.

The means of paying teachers are derived in Connecticut from a fund: in Massachusetts from taxation: and in New York, from taxation and a fund united.

1. Connecticut has a productive school-fund of about two millions of dollars. The dividends annually made to the schools, average about one dollar to each child between the ages of four and sixteen. And the acknowledged result of the experiment is, that the children of Connecticut are not so well educated now as they were previously to 1795—when the present system went into operation. The public schools in Connecticut are notoriously failures. And wherever a good school in that State can be found, it is altogether supported by private associations. The Connecticut system has scarcely an intelligent advocate at home, and none elsewhere. It aims at too much, and therefore accomplishes little or

nothing. It cannot afford a reasonable compensation for the services of half the number of *competent* instructors demanded by the population. And hence, either not more than half the requisite number can be employed, or, what is worse, thc schools must be committed to the most illiterate, indolent and worthless of the whole tribe of pedagogues: who are content to doze away their life for ten dollars per month rather than labour in the field or shop for twenty. Besides, while the people depend absolutely and exclusively on the *great State fund* for the adequate support of their schools, they very naturally become indifferent to the whole concern. They feel no motive or stimulus for individual effort and enterprise. They blindly and heedlessly, and yet confidently, look to the government for the schooling of their children—as they do to Providence for air and water—while they rarely reflect on the importance of the one or the other. Men seldom value what costs them nothing. A public fund for the instruction of youth in common schools, is of no comparative worth, merely as a means of relieving want. Whether it can be made to subserve a nobler end, we shall inquire hereafter. The good people of Connecticut, as we learn from published official documents, actually expended about an equal sum before their school-fund existed,—and upon half the present amount of population. And yet they never murmured at this expenditure as burdensome or excessive.

Tennessee does not possess, and cannot hope soon to accumulate such a fund: and if she could, the Connecticut system ought not to be thought of by her judicious and patriotic sages.

2. In Massachusetts, *taxation* is the sole reliance of common schools. What may be feasible and safe for her, might be hazardous for other States, where the people have not *inherited* the system of taxation, and where public sentiment attaches less value to education. It obtains however in New Hampshire, Vermont and Maine. In all these States it works well: and appears to answer every desirable end contemplated by the most zealous friends of common schools. The *mode* of raising the pecuniary means is of little consequence, provided the *people* approve it. That the plan succeeds, and that the people are satisfied, in the States just mentioned, cannot be doubted.

The late Governor Bell of New Hampshire, says: "The effect of this system has been very salutary. Scarcely a native citizen under forty years of age, of either sex, can be found who has not been taught to read and write their native language. It has elevated the character of our population, in point of intelligence and correct moral habits."

A distinguished individual in Vermont thus writes: "However defective our laws on this subject may appear to those who are abroad, the beneficial effects that have resulted cannot be questioned. Very few men or women can be found in this State, natives of the State, who cannot read and write, and employ figures for common purposes."

Gov. Lincoln of Massachusetts says: "The practical

operation of the laws has been to secure in *every district* and *village of the Commonwealth*, the means of regular instruction to children in the elementary branches of learning, and where there was wealth and population to justify the occasion, the establishment and support of schools of competent character to prepare youth for admission to college, or to enter upon the active business of life. Certain it is, that there has never been any want of interest manifested here, either in raising a sufficient amount of money, or in attending to its most useful application."

The late Governor Paris, of Maine, observes: "The sum required by law to be raised in each town, is equal to forty cents for each inhabitant the town contains. The penalty for neglect is a fine of not less than twice, nor more than four times the amount of the failure or deficiency. There is not an individual in any town within the limits of the State, who may not give his children a good English education. In this mode the school-fund is annually collected from the pockets of the citizens; and is paid with more cheerfulness than any other tax to which they are liable. The effect of this system, is an intelligent and enlightened population, not confined merely to the large towns, or their vicinity, but spread throughout the State."

While I take it for granted that the good people of Tennessee will not submit to *taxation* for the purpose of educating their children; I must be permitted to add, that, if ever a tax should be levied on the whole property of a community for the benefit of all the citizens;

the most reasonable, the most equitable, and the most useful, both in its immediate and ultimate results, would be a tax for this specific object. No other object, indeed, aimed at by any species of taxation, is, by many degrees, comparable in importance to this. Cannot the poor man be made to discern and to appreciate the boon which he would receive from the rich, when they should provide the means of tuition for his children? Cannot the rich comprehend the advantages which would redound to themselves, as well as to the whole population, if they would consent to contribute their mite towards the common education of all our youth, instead of being reduced to the necessity of paying ten-fold more to support thousands of idle paupers, vagabonds and criminals—by poor rates—in poor houses—or in jails and penitentiaries? From the latter burden, which is daily augmenting, they can never be relieved, except by the thorough instruction and discipline of the young and rising generation. A little skill in vulgar arithmetic—in the rule of Loss and Gain—to say nothing of ethics or political economy—will enable them to *calculate* to which alternative their own pecuniary interest should incline them. Moreover, the existing system of supporting the poor, and of punishing or reforming the criminal, is not only the most expensive that can well be devised: it is utterly nugatory in its operation and effects: it is a positive encouragement to pauperism and profligacy. The philanthropists and statesmen of England, where this preposterous and suicidal system has had ample scope for some three centuries past, pronounce it absurd, inefficient, and ruinous alike to both rich and poor. Let experience teach us wisdom. Let the axe be laid at the root of the evil. Let ignorant children be duly instructed; and we shall be rid of ignorant thieves and beggars. The schoolhouse and the schoolmaster will be found cheaper than the prison, the sheriff, and the judge.

Again, if the poor would examine their own relative position in society, and the proportion of the public burdens which they actually sustain, they might possibly discover some ground of complaint: and also that they are in fact *taxed* already to an amount which, if wisely appropriated to the object, would be amply sufficient to educate their own children. As *militia men*, they are taxed equally with the rich. Whether they regard this as a privilege or an imposition, I have never inquired. The law however commands every poor man, between the ages of 18 and 45, to attend militia musters four days in the year. That is, virtually, to pay four dollars *cash*, as a direct tax towards this one object of common defence. His incidental expenses cannot be less than four dollars more. Here then are eight dollars, positive tax, demanded from every poor man of a certain age, annually. Nor is this all. If we take into the account the time wasted at military elections—the money expended by officers and men in sundry ways which it is needless to specify—the average annual expenditure per man, rich and poor, officer and private, may be fairly computed at ten dollars. I do not know the number of our militia: But set them down at only

50,000; and here is a sum of $500,000, cheerfully paid by our tax-loathing people every year:—a sum which, if judiciously expended, would make every cottage smile with intelligence, peace, comfort and independence. Will the poor—will the rich—passively endure all this without a murmur? and yet refuse to tax themselves for precisely the noblest end at which even the most selfish parental ambition ought to aspire?

The militia system in general vogue after all is confessedly a nuisance to the community. It does no good. It has no tendency to form soldiers. Such is the opinion of every real military officer in the Union. Several of the States have already abolished the whole system: and others are in a fair way to follow their example. It is admitted that neither military tactics, nor military principles or habits are ever learned or acquired on the militia parade ground. But if we must pay for a whistle—though at the rate of half a million per year—let us also be willing to pay something to insure to posterity an enlightened, virtuous, free, and happy Commonwealth.

3. In New York, a mixed system obtains. She has combined both the plans already described. And the happy effects of her system, directed, as it is, by an able and laborious Superintendent of Common Schools, are fully illustrated in the annual Reports made to the Legislature on the subject.

The State possesses a productive general school-fund of nearly two millions of dollars—besides lands held for the same purpose—and also local funds in several of the counties.

The interest of the general fund, (about $100,000) is annually distributed among the School Districts simply as an incentive to self-taxation and voluntary contribution. It does not amount, at the utmost, to more than one-sixth of the sum annually paid to teachers alone: and to not more than one-tenth of the whole sum actually expended by the people in support of their schools. The statesmen of New York have wisely adapted their school-policy to the known selfishness of human nature. They hold out a motive to self-exertion and liberality which is rarely resisted. They say to a school district: we will give you from the State fund so much—say $100,—upon the condition that you raise by tax on your property an equal sum towards paying your teacher: and that you provide a school-house and defray all other contingent charges by voluntary contribution. It is not known that a single district has forfeited its right to participate in the public bounty by a failure to comply with the conditions prescribed.

The peculiar features and pre-eminent advantages of the New York system are so well understood and so universally acknowledged, that I deem it unnecessary to enter into further details. These have been presented to the public, from time to time, in nearly all our periodical journals and newspapers; and of course, must be familiar to my hearers.

"Schwartz, one of the most eminent writers on education in Germany, observes, in his History of Education, that the State of New York has the greatest number of children in its schools in proportion to the whole population, of any country he has found." Whether, in this respect or in any other, New York excels Massachusetts, I have not the means of accurately determining.

But supposing a school-fund to be provided or contemplated, there can be no question about the decided superiority of the New York system of disbursement over every other which has been subjected to the test of experience in any part of our country. If Tennessee therefore were already in possession of such a fund, or should she ever be so fortunate as to procure one, either from her own resources or from the public lands of the national government, she will not hesitate, it is presumed, to follow the salutary and successful example of New York.

Still, *rebus extantibus*, what is to be done? We will not tax ourselves: and a school-fund we have not. It would require the saving of years to accumulate one sufficiently large to be of any avail, even for distribution upon the New York plan, in the shape of rewards and premiums to self-taxation. In the mean time, several hundred thousands of our children may grow up in ignorance. Until a new generation shall arise so utterly ignorant and barbarous as to despise learning, and be ready to vote all schools a nuisance, and the growing school-fund good prize money to be shared among themselves or their loving representatives.

Must we then wait: or must we despair? Neither the one nor the other. I doubt the utility—(always excepting the New York system) certainly the necessity—of any school-fund whatever. Common education, as we have seen, was on a better footing in Connecticut fifty or a hundred years ago than at this moment. In the Southern States, every project of the kind has failed. Mr. Jefferson declared in 1822, that the plan of *primary schools* in Virginia had proved completely abortive, and must be shortly abandoned: "after costing us (he adds) to this day [1822] one hundred and eighty thousand dollars, and yet to cost us forty-five thousand dollars a year more until it shall be discontinued: and if a single boy has received the elements of common education, it must be in some part of the country not known to me. Experience has but too fully confirmed the early predictions of its fate."

New York has been fortunate in accumulating an ample fund wherewith to incite the people to help themselves. Her policy in regard to common schools, academies, colleges, and other scientific and professional institutions—in regard to roads, canals, penitentiaries, and houses of refuge for juvenile delinquents—is worthy of all praise and of general imitation. In all these respects, she has gone far ahead of most of her sister republics.

But the question recurs: What can *we* do? I answer: Present a *motive* sufficiently strong to induce the people to educate themselves, or their children, by their own industry. I mean not now to designate the precise motive which ought to be thus addressed to the people. I will merely suggest two or three as illustrative of the general principle—which may however be practically applied in a great variety of ways. It is evident that some individuals, both rich and poor, do educate their children, without any aid or impulse from the government. They, of course, have a motive of some kind which urges them to this duty. Well-educated parents, for example, be their circumstances what they may, seldom fail to educate their children. They can appreciate the value and importance of an education: and with them, this is a sufficient motive. This is, in fact, the operating principle and mainspring of the excellent Massachusetts system. Were all our people thus enlightened, no other motive would be wanting to insure the universal education of their children. But until this shall be our happy lot, some motive must be sought which will come home to the interests and feelings and ambition of the great mass even of an illiterate community. Such a motive is *money.* New York has sagaciously addressed this motive to her population; and her object is achieved. She hires her citizens, or tempts them by a trifling gratuity, to do for their children what they could just as easily accomplish without it. For one dollar in ten is too paltry a sum to be thought of as relief or assistance. Whether this is the *best* motive that could have been proposed, is of no consequence to inquire. As we, however, cannot at present hold out this *golden* motive, it is worth while to ascertain whether some other will not answer quite as well.

In Austria—for even there the schoolmaster is abroad, and his magic influence will ere long be acknowledged by the proudest despotism in Europe—no person is allowed to marry who cannot read, write, and cipher. Suppose we had such a law in Tennessee. In less than a year, every marriageable bachelor and maiden in the State would be able to read and write, at least. And all the children in the country, of twelve years old and upwards, would be striving to acquire the requisite qualifications for matrimony—for every boy and girl means to be married. Thus then, without the expenditure of a cent of public money, or the imposition of any tax whatever, or the delay of another year, we might behold the entire rising generation stimulated to exertion and enterprise, which would insure them all the advantages of a common school education—be the amount of it whatever the Legislature should be pleased to enjoin. How the people could command the means and facilities for self-instruction, will be explained hereafter. My object now is to submit motives to induce the desire and the effort. That the one just named would prove effectual, I have no doubt. And that it would promote the grand cause of matrimony itself, (a consideration by no means to be disregarded in a new country,) may be assumed; since this would be viewed as the ultimate aim and reward of every lad and spinster in seeking an education. Nor would the end ever be lost sight of till it should be secured. The whole race of old bachelors would speedily evanish from our smiling and happy land: and our fair daughters would no longer be doomed to the pains and penalties of "single blessedness." Every American statesman ought, in spite of Malthus and the Pope, to be the champion of matrimony—while a quarter section of our virgin soil remains uncultivated. Education and matrimony would thus go hand in hand: they would mutually act and re-act upon each other: and all the benefits that *might* result from so wise and opportune a measure, would doubtless far transcend the calculations of the most sanguine *utilitarian* dogmatists of either hemisphere. On this subject, "the American figure of Anticipation," as the English critics invidiously style it, might have free scope, without danger of running into hyperbole.

To this sage scheme, I see no very cogent objection; provided it be within the constitutional limits of legislation. If not, the remedy is with the people. They, like the British Parliament, are omnipotent. They can create or demolish, alter or amend, constitutions at pleasure. They can mend a bad, as well as spoil a good one. And if they do not elect to foster popular education in this *Austrian* fashion, they may authorize some other mode of reaching the same end.

For example—and I am merely giving examples or specimens of what is practicable; leaving, as becomes a loyal subject, the final choice to the wisdom of the common sovereign:—let it be ordained by law or by the next amended Constitution, that, after a certain specified day, no man shall be eligible to office or have the privilege of voting at elections, who cannot read and write. This, too, would be a sufficient motive. And, in a few years, scarcely a man of twenty-one years old and upwards, could be found in the State incapable of reading and writing. Such a rule would be no hardship. Qualifications for office and for the elective franchise, of some kind, are universally required by law. Thus, a certain age has always been prescribed as a qualification. This is purely arbitrary—as many an individual could vote with more discretion at the age of fifteen, than others at the age of thirty. And yet it is necessary that there should be a known invariable rule on the subject. Property qualifications are always invidious, unequal, and utterly inapplicable as a test of judgment, honesty, or patriotism. But the ability to read and write, is a qualification directly to the point. It is indispensable to the attainment of any correct information in regard to our government, Constitution, jurisprudence, public measures, and public men. Without it, voters are but mere machines, to be impelled by extraneous force—by the arts, intrigue, flattery and misrepresentations of demagogues. They are, in general, no better qualified to give their suffrages at an election than so many infants. I say, *in general,* because there have been shrewd well-informed men who could not even read. *Some* such there doubtless are now, and ever will be. They are exceptions however to a great law of civilized human nature.

It is absurd to talk of their *rights* to a people who cannot comprehend them. Savages and slaves are always ignorant: for none but grossly ignorant men will remain in the savage state or submit to slavery. And ignorant men are of necessity slaves in the worst sense. They are the dupes and passive instruments of the more crafty and knowing.

All this may seem harsh and anti-republican. It is nevertheless the doctrine of our Franklins and Washingtons and Jeffersons and Jays and Marshalls, and of every honest enlightened republican in the world. They all declare that there can be no civil liberty—no religious liberty—no approach to self-government—except where the *people* are thoroughly instructed: so as to be capable of judging correctly and independently of public men and of political measures. They all point to popular ignorance as the chief, indeed the only, source of their apprehension and despondency in regard to the stability of our admirable institutions, and the future destinies of this glorious Republic. Examine their solemn, deliberate, recorded opinions—their last legacies of patriotic affection—full of counsel and warning upon this very subject—exhorting and entreating their countrymen, as they value liberty, and would transmit it unimpaired to posterity, to seek after knowledge above all things, and to diffuse its celestial light over every dark corner of the land. Listen to the voice of the living veteran, who has survived the wars and struggles and perils to which his country has been exposed since the morning of her independence, and you hear the same counsel and the same warning.

Desperate diseases demand desperate remedies. But, in this case, there is nothing harsh or desperate. It is proposed to elevate all our citizens to the rank of freemen.—To induce them, for their own good, to qualify themselves to be in *fact*, what they claim to be in *name*. —To emancipate their minds from the thraldom of ignorance, and to render them fit to share the sovereignty of the people with the people. Will they demur at such a measure? What *wise* father, if he foresaw that he should leave his children penniless, friendless, and destitute of instruction, would not rejoice on his death-bed in the assurance that his country had furnished a motive to the acquisition of knowledge, which could not fail to insure its ultimate attainment? Why should stature, or age, or colour, entitle the human animal to privileges or functions which he can neither appreciate nor fulfil? Would the condition of a child be improved, or his happiness be promoted, by freeing him from parental control and permitting him to exercise all the rights of a citizen? Is the untaught white man any better, any wiser, any more noble or trustworthy, than the untaught African or Indian? Wherever important rights are vested or responsible trust confided, *there* ought to be found correspondent qualifications—adequate intelligence, integrity, and judgment.

Do I expect then, that Tennessee will ever sanction the principle, that the elective franchise should be associated with intellectual cultivation, or be exercised by those only who have been, or who shall be, educated to a certain specified extent? Assuredly not. I cherish no such visionary fancy. I believe it, indeed, the very best measure that can be suggested in order to secure the great object of universal education—and *therefore* I despair of its adoption. The people will be told that it is anti-republican. And yet, by the new Constitution of Republican Colombia it is ordained that, after 1840, no person shall enjoy the rights of citizenship who is unable to read and write. But, if the example of our younger sister be deemed unworthy of notice; or if we disdain to imitate where we imagine our superior age entitles us to take the lead; or if her doctrine be condemned as heretical; I have a home precedent to cite, directly relevant to the question.

By our own State Constitution—both old and new—*clergymen* are ineligible to office: or in other words, they are virtually disfranchised. I suppose, because they are regarded as either too ignorant and opinionated, or too wily and slippery, to be trusted: that is, because they are knaves or blockheads. This is, no doubt, a most salutary, judicious, and strictly republican provision. And I laud the framers of the said constitution for their sagacity and independence. They might however, it appears to me, have ventured somewhat further, and extended their excluding or disqualifying clause to all other knaves and blockheads: and, if it had so pleased them, to all who thenceforward should be unable to read and write. There is nothing therefore in the *principle* which can be pronounced by the sovereign people objectionable; since they have already sanctioned it to a much greater extent than is now proposed: in reference, namely, to one entire class and profession of the community.

And here I take leave to recommend that, in our next

reformed Constitution, the article excluding from office be made to comprehend all persons except FARMERS. So that none but actual farmers shall be eligible to office. This would be perfectly equitable, because the farmers constitute the great body of the people, and therefore ought to govern. It would prove singularly beneficial to the Commonwealth, inasmuch as it would keep in their proper places, all pragmatical, self-sufficient, beardless, pettifogging lawyers—all impudent, blustering, *cure-all,* high-pressure-steaming, quack-doctors—all meddling, graceless, noisy, dogmatical, bigoted, ambitious parsons—and all idle, dapper, brainless exquisites and loungers of every name and degree, who have neither purse, character nor occupation. While it would hold out the greatest possible encouragement to agriculture, and the strongest incentives to a generous ambition among all classes and professions. Thus, the lawyer, the physician, the schoolmaster, the merchant, the mechanic, and even the newspaper editor, who should aspire to political distinction, would of course strive to acquire by honest industry, the means of purchasing a farm and retiring seasonably from professional pursuits and engagements. Thus the business of farming would be honoured, as it ought to be. And the public would ever have before them experienced, intelligent, upright, independent and responsible candidates for every office. This, too, would excite a spirit of laudable emulation among the young men brought up as farmers. They would be eager to enter the lists with the accomplished lawyers and all others, expected presently to settle as farmers in their vicinity, and to canvass among them for the honours of the Republic.

The only exception to be provided for, would be large towns and cities—where agriculture cannot be the occupation of any portion of the people—and where offices must be filled, and representatives be elected, without any connexion with the adjacent country.

As a political economist—for I disclaim all desire and intention of intermeddling with personal or party or local politics—I might, in this connexion, add a remark or two upon the expediency of taxing landed property upon any plan or principle whatever. In a State, like ours, where land is the most abundant article in the market—where it is a mere drug—where millions of acres are still unappropriated or unsubdued—it would seem good policy, by all equitable and judicious means, to encourage the ownership and cultivation of the soil to the greatest possible extent. If so, then land ought to be exempt from all onerous and discouraging impositions.

1. Because it is the common parent of the whole people—the source and fountain of their necessary subsistence—the sole efficient basis and nursery of all other pursuits and avocations, and of the well-being and prosperity of the entire population, whether considered collectively or individually.

2. Because capital vested in land is usually far less productive than almost any other species of investment. Farmers generally throughout the State cannot, with the same pecuniary outlay and with the most unwearied industry and rigid frugality, reap as large profits as the

merchant, mechanic, or manufacturer. For years to come, even under the most auspicious circumstances, much of their land also must remain utterly unproductive—an idle or dead capital upon their hands.

3. Because, in order to secure a permanent, useful, thrifty, contented, attached body of citizens, they ought to be induced to own visible, tangible, immovable property. Land is such a property. And land-holders or farmers are universally regarded as the bone and sinew and main reliance of a free State. Land therefore ought to be precisely the kind of property which every man should most covet and most earnestly labour to possess. This will never be the case where land is more heavily taxed in proportion to its net yield or profit than other modes of employing capital. Every shrewd, calculating, enterprising capitalist will contrive to own as little ostensible taxable property as possible. He will devise a thousand ways to keep it out of sight and yet most gainfully employed. He will send it abroad—to the North or to the South—wherever he can find a lucrative market or an object of speculation:—or he will exact usurious interest from his less fortunate or less wary fellow citizens.

4. Because we are surrounded by half a score of young Republics, where land may be had almost without price—and where it may be improved without dread of sheriff or tax gatherer. Emigrants will not come hither, if they can do better elsewhere. Our own farmers will run away to Arkansas, Mississippi, Texas, or Oregon, when they shall feel the pressure of an unequal system

of taxation, and find their pockets growing empty in spite of their honest efforts to fill them.

5. Because, with a territory of 40,000 square miles just emerging from its primitive forest state, the most ample facilities and urgent motives for its rapid melioration and solid improvement should be held out to the people.

What is it that enriches, adorns and beautifies any country? and renders it lovely and delightful to the eye, and desirable to live in? Is it not well cultivated fields and gardens and meadows—substantial farm-houses, mills, factories, barns, granaries, fences, hedges, orchards, vineyards, flocks and herds—good roads, turnpikes, railways, canals, bridges, and every possible facility for safe and speedy travelling and transportation—with a due sprinkling of flourishing hamlets, villages, towns and cities; abounding with well-built-churches, school-houses, colleges, markets, and other public edifices? And what should we deem of a system destined or purposely devised to discountenance and to prevent all such improvements? Tax them—or tax the land in a ratio commensurate with all such useful and ornamental fixtures—and the system is adopted by yourselves. Tax land agreeably to its augmented value under the creative hand and skilful management of the most deserving portion of the people: and you paralyse the arm of domestic industry. The farmer will hold on to his log cabin and worm fences and horse-mill; and never dream of erecting a comfortable mansion of brick or stone, or durable structures of any sort, which would add thousands to the value of his estate and to the general wealth of the community—because, for these additional unproductive thousands, he must be taxed! And taxed as highly as if the said thousands were yielding a revenue of ten per cent in the shape of Bank stock, or of twenty or fifty per cent in the capacity of *shaving* loans—which last, by the way, would escape taxation altogether, as they have heretofore done, in spite of legislative ingenuity and legal terrors. I need not ask, what would be the blighted, cheerless, poverty-stricken aspect of our hitherto prosperous Commonwealth under the operation of a system thus partial and ill-devised. It requires not the gift of prophecy to predict its inevitable doom.

The policy can never be safe or sound, which tempts to concealment or evasion or subterfuge or trickery or falsehood or dishonesty. No man ought to be deterred from any useful pursuit or vocation, nor be afraid or ashamed to acknowledge and to enjoy his possessions openly before the world. No vexatious domiciliary intrusions or visitations by the legal assessor or collector ought to be dreaded by any freeman. Nor ought laws ever to be enacted which shall have the slightest tendency to place him in such an awkward predicament.

Again, if land must be taxed, it should be taxed according to its actual yearly product—and not according to its gross valuation, arbitrarily determined, whether productive or unproductive. Or the land might be distributed into classes (as first, second, third rate, &c.) according to the quality of the soil; and the tax be apportioned aggreeably to such a fixed and well understood system of classification. The last would probably be found the least objectionable mode.

6. But in the sixth place: In such a Commonwealth as this—encompassed as we are by an illimitable wilderness of fertile soil—land, farmers' land, I mean, (for I say nothing of town lots,) ought not to be taxed at all. Let the land go free—free as the water of our springs and rivers—free as the pure atmosphere of heaven—and then all our people will aspire to a landed competency and independence. We shall be a community of intelligent and happy farmers. The poorest mechanic and day labourer will instantly realize the benefits of such an exemption—as they would be the first to experience the evils of a contrary policy. Land cannot be taxed, without taxing every individual and every occupation and every commodity in the State. The very milk and bread and meat which the poor man eats, will be taxed; because they are the product of a taxed soil. He must either labour for less, or pay more for each and all the necessaries of life.

Should we expunge or alter one short section of our new or amended constitution, and then boldly resolve, that, henceforth, the fair lands of Tennessee shall be free from taxation—free forever, or for a definite period, sufficiently long for a satisfactory experiment—say for fifty or one hundred years—the great body of my fellow citizens might live to see this become *one* of the most flourishing, if not absolutely *the* most flourishing Commonwealth upon the globe.

7. Taxation is always an evil, and should therefore be rendered as light as possible. Men should be taxed, not according to the gross value of their property, nor according to their annual income or net profits—nor according to what they own or produce or lay up as clear gain—but according to their actual consumption or expenditure. Tax not what they earn, but what they spend. This is the only fair and uniformly equitable *principle* of taxation. Tax consumption (always excepting the necessaries of life) and you allow the people an option whether to pay or not, and also, to what amount. This is the system adopted by the General Government. Certain imported articles are taxed: but no man is compelled to eat, drink, wear, use or possess any foreign commodity whatever. He can produce or procure all the mere necessaries of subsistence at home, or of home production. He may purchase the taxed or dutiable foreign goods or forbear at pleasure. He uses little or much, as he chooses; and pays according to the quantity or value actually consumed. Now although this precise mode of taxation cannot be resorted to by any particular State, yet the *principle* of taxing consumption may be made the basis of any revenue code, and be applied in a different fashion.

Objection 1. All this will be met with the triumphant assertion, that, the entire State tax will be so very small that none can feel it. I answer, that, it is the *principle*, not the amount of the present burden, which deserves attention and should awaken solicitude. Our fathers fought seven long years for a *principle,* and not for the paltry tax of three pence upon the pound of tea.

Objection 2. But the new Constitution has settled the whole affair, and the land *must* be taxed *ad valorem.* I answer, let the article upon taxation be repealed or amended by the people, agreeably to the mode prescribed by the Constitution: and the sooner the better.

That the farmers of Tennessee should have consented to the introduction into the *great charter* of their rights, an article requiring the perpetual infliction upon themselves of the most annoying and oppressive species of taxation ever yet devised by impolicy or injustice, is passing strange. They have sanctioned an instrument, and delegated a power, which can scarcely be so construed or exerted as not to prove detrimental, and which *may* be used with tremendous effect. Assuredly, our farmers have not yet studied their own interests, or learned how to govern themselves in the cheapest mode. After all, the pecuniary burden is a trifle, compared with the moral evils which the novel experiment seems likely to occasion. These have been hinted at already: and if a tithe of them shall be realized, then, farewell to our character as well as to our prosperity.

Now, in all these remarks and suggestions, I profess to aim directly at the welfare of the poor. I believe myself to be their honest friend, and the uncompromising advocate of every measure truly designed to better their condition. I am equally sure that the interests of both rich and poor are perfectly identical, under any code of free and equal laws, impartially administered. The chief object contemplated, and supposed to have been effectually asserted by our revolutionary sages, was precisely to secure to every man the fruits of his own industry, talents and enterprise. In other words, to enable the poor to become independent and wealthy. Were our people wisely governed, faithfully instructed, and duly trained to habits of virtue, industry and economy, there would be no abject or hopeless poor in all the land. To bring about such a grand moral revolution, is or ought to be the principal business of the Legislature. When this object shall be attained, the governing and law-making powers will have very little to do. Their work will have been accomplished: and they may thenceforth rest from their labours.

But, to return from a rather long and perhaps not very pertinent digression.

The people must be taught and induced to help themselves. This is the only effectual remedy for ignorance, poverty, and all sorts of misery. To relieve a beggar for the moment is a trifle. But to put him in the way to earn an honest and competent livelihood for the rest of his life, is commendable and substantial charity. I have shown that it is possible for a wise and paternal Legislature, when duly authorized, if not already authorized by the Constitution, to put into practical operation a system of common school education, by simply rendering such an education essential to the possession or exercise of certain civil functions and franchises. As I intimated, nothing more was intended than to illustrate the *principle* of stimulating the people to self-exertion by some commanding and paramount *motive*. What *that* motive ought to be, I leave others to determine.

The people need be no longer dazzled or blinded by the splendor of a magnificent school-fund—which they will never live to see—however much they may hear of it from those, who, for their suffrages, are ready enough to make golden promises, and to excite extravagant expectations, while they care not a rush for them or their children. I have no great confidence in the legislative management of large funds of any description or for any purpose. Past experience, in nearly all the States, affords ample ground for this general distrust. And the history of Tennessee legislation has no tendency to diminish it. The College and Academy fund of this State—originally the gift of Congress—might have proved, under other auspices, adequate to the noble purposes for which it was designed. I will not ask how or wherefore that fund has been scattered to the winds and nearly annihilated. But I do not hesitate to say, that it has proved a curse rather than a blessing to this Commonwealth.

In the first place, the people relied with implicit confidence on the sufficiency of this large fund for the establishment and support of colleges and academies: and therefore never felt the obligation of attempting any thing in behalf of those institutions, either through the instrumentality of the State treasury, or by individual munificence and voluntary contributions. The consequence is, that, to this day, almost nothing has been achieved.

In the second place, this same fund has been, from the first, a bone of contention, on all possible occasions and in every variety of form. And when the controversies and enmities which it has excited and fomented, will be allayed or extinguished, it is impossible to predict. Better had it been—infinitely better for the interests of science—if no such benefaction had ever been bestowed or accepted. But let us forgive and forget the past—while we submit to be taught a seasonable and useful lesson from experience.

We should not *blindly* follow even the good example of other States. Had we, at this moment, a school-fund as ample as that of New York, and were we to copy her entire school code *verbatim*, I have not the most distant idea that the practical operation and effects of the system *here* would be equally salutary or at all similar. Everything depends on the judicious and efficient administration of the system—on the skill, fidelity, wisdom, zeal, perseverance, and strict accountability of all the agents employed—and very much, I may add, on certain moral, local and conventional peculiarities, to which we are, and ever must be strangers. The scattered population of the South and South-West—even other things being equal—will never admit of a school arrangement similar to that which obtains in the Eastern villages. Mr. Jefferson distinctly perceived and pointed out this difficulty in Virginia. And Louisiana, after expending many thousands upon the experiment, has since made the same discovery. I am aware that the sparseness of a *planting* population presents a difficulty formidable to every plan of public schools, designed for all classes of the people—a difficulty which must be fairly met by the advocates of any system whatever.

I would not have it inferred, however, from these remarks, that I object to any feasible project for the immediate or eventual accumulation of a school-fund. But the grand heresy on the subject, which infects the brain of not a few of our popular sages, is this eternal *projecting* of some splendid visionary scheme for posterity—while the existing thousands are neglected. The people are continually directed to the future—to their children's children—to the third and fourth generations—when all ignorance is to be suddenly dispelled—when the long wished for millennium is to dawn—and universal intelligence, order, virtue, peace and prosperity to prevail! This dilatory, procrastinating, delusive policy in regard to popular education, appears to be signally characteristic of no small number of these States—whatever may be said of our own.

The best preventive of future evils, is the speedy eradication of existing evils. If we would render succeeding generations intelligent, virtuous and happy, we must commence with the present. Delays are always dangerous; and on no subject more so, than in regard to the suitable discipline and training of our children. Is there a reflecting parent among us who will be satisfied with the mere indefinite promise or prospect that provision may be made hereafter for the education of his remote posterity, while his sons and daughters are growing up around him like the wild natives of the forest?

My creed on the subject may be propounded in few words: Instruct the present generation; and the whole work is achieved at once, effectually, and forever. When the impulse is fairly given to the intellectual mass, the march of improvement will be progressive: and no ordinary obstacles will ever arrest it. There will then be no lack of adequate motive to exertion and enterprise in this behalf. Each enlightened and cultivated generation will take good care of the succeeding. And thus will the light of knowledge be transmitted from father to son, without interruption, to the end of time—or, at least, until, by some terrible convulsion, our whole political aud social fabric shall be buried in the ruins of expiring liberty and civilization.

Will it be pretended that the wealth of the State is not sufficient to educate the children of the State? Were a law enacted to-morrow, no matter upon what ostensible plea, requiring, under adequate penalties, every parent to teach, or cause to be taught, his children to read and write: would it be objected that many of the people are too poor, by any efforts or sacrifices, to do this? I answer fearlessly, the fact is not so. There exists not in Tennessee, (nor in this Union,) a poor man, healthy, industrious, sober and economical, who could not do it with perfect ease. And if such a law should tend to make poor men temperate, industrious and frugal: would not this be a great blessing to themselves, to their families, and to the public? How much of time and money does every poor man squander annually in modes and upon objects which are needless or injurious? I might read a lecture upon this subject to our thriftless poor, from the pages of Franklin, Adam Smith, Say and Jefferson, which, if it should be listened to, could hardly fail to convince them, that self-denial, persevering industry and rigid economy would soon render them as completely independent, and as capable of duly instructing their children, as the wealthiest nabobs of the land. But such a lecture, though enforced by the grave authority of all the political and domestic economists from Solomon inclusive to the present day, would probably be no more regarded than an orthodox sermon against fashionable amusements. Ay, the fashion!— This is the tyrant that grinds the poor and befools the rich. Our people pay, as I have said once before, half a million of dollars every year to support a useless, oppressive and absurd militia system—because it is the fashion! They pay another half million to be well governed; and to be duly entitled, through the agency of their obliging attorneys, to the contingencies and tender mercies of their most wise and equitable laws. They cheerfully pay two millions annually to the whisky cause. They participate in all the excesses of the race-course, (the worst species of *gambling*, by the way, ever yet contrived by human depravity,) and a thousand other extravagant follies. They build prisons and penitentiaries for the comfortable accommodation of petty rogues, who have not wit or money enough to escape detection or conviction; while your dashing swindlers and gentlemanly assassins walk at large, and laugh to scorn your whole array of legal terrors and penalties. All this and more they endure and pay for—because it is the fashion. And yet, forsooth, they cannot teach their children to read and write!

Suppose now, in order to insure the immediate instruction of all the children in Tennessee, it be assumed that a system of common schools similar to that of New York or Massachusetts is indispensable: is it practicable, without a fund, to put so expensive a machinery into operation forthwith? Undoubtedly it is; so far as the mere matter of expense is in question. It is just as easy, for example, to build schoolhouses and acadamies as it is to build jails and courthouses. And when the former shall be erected, they will probably be less burdensome than the latter in the keeping. In Maine—and the common school system is said to be nowhere more flourishing and effective—the average annual cost to every inhabitant for its maintenance, is, as we have seen, only forty cents. If the same system would answer equally well here, and if it could be sustained at the same rate: would it be impossible—would it be grievously burdensome—to demand forty cents a year from every white or free individual in the State, for this confessedly most urgent and most important object? Or would it be impracticable to levy the amount equitably upon the *productive* property of the Commonwealth? I put all this hypothetically—and I really think that a deficiency of pecuniary resources cannot be even speciously pleaded in bar of any such scheme. Whether, on other accounts, it be expedient or politic, to tax industry in support of idleness, or to tax virtue in favour of profligacy—is quite a different affair. Whether the rich—that is, whether those who have acquired wealth by honest labour and skilful management—should be taxed in order to educate the children of the poor, that is, of the indolent or the abandoned, any more than they should be taxed to feed and clothe them—is well worthy of grave consideration.

But again: If the people will do nothing for themselves, nor submit to any species of taxation; and if the State treasury admit of an immediate appropriation of ten, twenty, thirty, or forty thousand dollars to this object—would it not be expedient for the Legislature so to dispose of this sum as to secure the thorough instruction of a definite portion of the people's children, rather than to fritter it away in unavailing gratuities to every section of the State at once? Why not provide effectually for one, two, or more counties at a time, according to the means at command? I am perfectly aware of the objection to any such measure. It would be denounced as partial and unjust. The simple reply is, that it is better to do a little well, than to attempt a great deal and accomplish nothing. But how, or upon what principle, shall the selection be made? Shall Wilson or Bedford be favoured, while Davidson and Rutherford are neglected? If no satisfactory rule could be established;—let the choice be determined by lot. I am a friend to equal rights, and to an equal distribution of a common fund. But here the question would be, whether a given sum of money should be expended for a valuable purpose, or be thrown away. In the latter case, no mortal could be benefited—in the former some might. And a lottery would silence even the most invidious and unreasonable objector. This is but another hypothesis. Constitutional objections may be obviated, as in other cases, by amendment.

Instead however of the latter mode, superior as it certainly is to the one generally prevalent, (to that, namely, of doling out a small fund, by the dollar, over a wide surface upon which it could produce no sensible effect,) I would recommend a different course altogether. I would appropriate such a fund exclusively either to the erection of one great central school or university for the gratuitous instruction of whatever youth might choose to attend it; or to the education of a certain number of schoolmasters in some well-conducted existing seminary. The best and speediest mode of enlightening a community, is to provide accomplished teachers for the children and youth of such a community. One brilliant blazing SUN in the firmament, will shed around and beneath infinitely more light and heat than a thousand twinkling stars. Plant a noble university in our midst: and from its portals will issue streams of cheering light upon every dark corner of the land. Whereas, if you are content to get up a few scores of old-field schools, that is, of mere farthing candles or feeble rush-lights at various distant points in the wilderness, you will but render the darkness more visible and repulsive. No country was ever enlightened or elevated by such a process. Show us a thoroughly intelligent population anywhere upon earth—and you shall trace that intelligence to the higher and the highest seats of learning—and never to the inferior or lowest. Where are to be found the best common schools in Europe and America? Precisely where the college and university are most honoured and cherished. I defy the most captious to furnish a solitary exception. Light flows only from the Sun. The moon and stars do but reflect and diffuse the lustre derived from this original fountain. The University has created, and still nourishes and upholds, all the common schools in the world. Demolish the university—and you not only blot out the SUN of science forever, but you extinguish all the humbler and dependent luminaries. Establish a University in New Holland or Caffraria, and give it full scope and fair play; and the common school shall grow up spontaneously around it. I speak the words of truth and soberness—because I speak the language and proclaim the results of experience.

The universities of Chaldea, Assyria, Phœnicia, Egypt, Greece, Rome, were the fountains whence all the rivulets of knowledge flowed among the people. Adam (or his wife) was the first teacher of an elementary or infant or common school. He was also the first founder, as he was the first President, of a great and opulent and most learned university. And he had been educated and qualified for his high destinies in the UNIVERSITY OF HEAVEN.

Let Tennessee enable the University of Nashville to train up a hundred young men annually for the sole business of school-keeping, if she please—either by a generous endowment at once, or by an annual appropriation for the purpose. Or let the Legislature resolve to educate, under their own special supervision, one hundred poor youth, more or less, at this or some better institution, upon the express condition that they shall serve the State as schoolmasters, or refund the money thus advanced together with interest—and we shall soon witness the rise of common schools in abundance, and of a character vastly superior to those currently known under this denomination. Give us men competent to teach, and desirous to teach for a living: and they will work their way to public favour and patronage. The universal complaint, even in the older States, is, that the teachers of common schools are, in nine cases out of ten, utterly unfit for their vocation; and bad teachers are worse than none. To commit children to bungling, lazy, intemperate, swaggering vagabonds, knaves, and smatterers, is very like perpetrating intellectual and moral treason or assassination with malice prepense. If there be one object under the whole heaven which parents should be eager to purchase at any price or sacrifice—which is indeed above all price—it is the proper education of their children. If there be one good object, which pre-eminently demands the profoundest attention of the Legislature—it is this. When they, or the people, shall succeed in obeying the divine command: "Train up a child in the way he should go,"—the promise annexed will as certainly be fulfilled: "and when he is old, he will not depart from it."

In regard to those States where common schools are allowed to be on the best footing; it is worthy of inquiry, whether they have proved reasonably and satisfactorily efficient in promoting virtue and good morals. Here, truth constrains me to answer, that, from public official documents, it appears that crimes have fearfully increased in Connecticut and New York during the last eight or ten years. Whatever may be urged therefore in behalf of the intellectual discipline adopted in their schools—there must be a lamentable deficiency of moral and religious instruction. This is a radical defect—acknowledged and deplored by their own best citizens. It adds another to the thousand melancholy proofs already before the world, that no species of mental cultivation can ever be truly beneficial, where the pupils do not, at the same time, acquire moral and religious principles and habits. Every teacher, in every school, from the infant nursery up to the university, ought to be deeply imbued with the purest spirit of Christian morality, and to labour assiduously in moulding the hearts and lives of his youthful charge agreeably to the only standard of virtue and integrity which is recognised among Christian men. To educate Christian youth as heathens or atheists, is at once absurd and monstrous. To expect such youth to become good, moral, peaceful, orderly, religious men, is to expect a miracle. In this all-essential attribute, the New York system is little superior to that of Connecticut: and both have proved egregious failures.

I will never advocate or countenance a system which does not tend directly to form good as well as intelligent citizens. And it is perfectly fair and equitable to judge of any system by its effects—as it is to judge of a tree by its fruits.

In New England, with the exception of Connecticut and Rhode Island, the school system is represented as eminently successful in its moral and religious agency. Her citizens are reputed to be the most intelligent, the most enterprising, and the most virtuous in the world. Such, at least, is their own estimate of themselves: and they ought to know. If the fact be so, we may cheerfully accord to their system the pre-eminence which it has hitherto challenged in the opinion of mankind. Should a Southerner or Backwoodsman happen to express any doubt about the fact, in consequence of certain unlucky specimens of the Yankee character, which may have fallen under his own eye, in the shape of tin-pedlers, book-agents, school-hunters, college-builders, venders of wooden clocks, horn flints and such like *notions*, and especially of reverend money beggars for all sorts of *pseudo* literary and benevolent projects—if, I say, he should be thus led to question the *piety*, though he might concede the full measure of shrewdness and intelligence claimed, he will be told that such is the unparalleled purity of the moral atmosphere throughout New England, that rogues cannot breathe it—that they will not be tolerated at home—and that, therefore, to escape the frowns and contempt of their countrymen, and to be at a safe distance from the penitentiary and tread-mill, they invariably emigrate or run off to the South and West—*there* to live by their wits, that is, by cheating the natives. It is thus, we are assured, that the term *Yankee* has acquired a notoriety and a meaning so equivocal and unsavory. We are invited to study the Yankee at his own fireside, and among his granite hills and beautiful villages; and we are boldly defied to point out his equal upon the globe. All this is right. A people should be studied at home, and be estimated according to their *home* character. If it be true then, in Massachusetts for instance, that public opinion is so sound and so potent as to render it unsafe, undesirable or impracticable for the profligate or dishonest to remain within her limits—that they must either remove, or certainly be hanged or imprisoned—we must admit the general excellence of the system under which, as children and youth, they have all been trained. What would have been the result of the experiment, if she had not been favoured with a thousand safety valves to let off superfluous steam and noxious gases—or if she had not been situated upon the borders of an interminable wilderness, ready to receive and to welcome all the idlers and knaves which she could possibly furnish—it is bootless to inquire.

There are certain rather ominous indications however just now, which may cause a momentary suspension of our faith in the New England creed. Sundry Quixotes in that region have been, for several years past, engaged in a crusade against all manner of error, wickedness and oppression, and in endeavouring to *right* all the *wrongs* in the world. In their search after new fields of benevolent labour, they have at length descried, and they appear to have taken a special fancy to, the *coloured* population of the South and West. Under the goodly and significant appellations of *Anti-Slavery Societies, Abolitionists, Amalgamationists, Immediatists,* &c., they have manifested a *calculating* zeal and *prudent* courage worthy of all admiration: while, with perfect safety to their own persons, they have been busily digging the mine and laying the train to blow *sky high* both the negro and the white man throughout one-half of the Republic. How New England is to be eventually discharged of this rapidly increasing host of fanatics and agitators—is the question. She cannot creditably retain them unchecked and unrebuked in her own bosom. Will her neighbours receive them? Will she eject them by force? Will she restrain their liberty of speech or action? Will public opinion expel them, as it has heretofore expelled multitudes of rogues, enthusiasts and impostors? One thing is certain: they will not, as their predecessors have been hitherto wont to do, venture to seek their fortune or risk their necks south of the Potomac or Ohio—so long as the right worshipful Judge *Lynch* and the most redoubtable Captain *Slick* shall hold office and be duly honoured amongst us.*

* The author having alluded to certain practices in a way that might possibly be misunderstood, begs to state that he holds in utter abhorrence every assumption of power and every infliction of punishment by any mob or portion of the people whatever, unauthorized by the laws of the land. Abolitionists have the right to publish their opinions whenever and wherever they please, if not prohibited by law: and to the law only, and to tribunals established by law, are they amenable.

Upon the whole then, I conclude that the New England school system—though very good, perhaps the best in the world—is not absolutely perfect: inasmuch as *all* her sons are not trained up in the way they should go; otherwise, when old, they would not become either strolling sharpers or meddling *emancipationists.*

I have thus submitted to the consideration of my indulgent hearers, sundry plans of common school education which have been tried, or which are now in operation in the several States—together with my own comments upon them, which may go for what they are worth. I have also thrown out a variety of suggestions upon the subject generally, and in reference to other possible modes of meeting the actual exigencies of the country. And all this with a view chiefly to provoke or to induce reflection and examination, and an interchange of opinion among the people, upon this topic of deep and universal concernment: That *something* may, at length, be done towards the removal of the stigma which has hitherto fastened upon the character of this land of heroes, in the eyes of our sister Republics. Will Tennessee—proud, gallant, chivalrous Tennessee—consent to become the Bœotia of the Western World?

I shall next consider the subject under a different aspect.

A population, consisting chiefly of planters, or farmers and labourers, where land is cheap and abundant, must necessarily be thinly scattered over a large surface. Such is the fact in regard to the great body of the people in this State. In the Eastern and Middle States, the people reside in villages, or in clusters upon small farms adjacent to each other. It is comparatively easy, in the latter, so to arrange the school districts as to accommodate all the inhabitants. Such a convenient distribution or location of schools cannot be made among us. I leave out of view, at present, our towns and compactly settled neighborhoods;—because in them any description of schools, that the people choose, may be maintained. But how is the country at large to be supplied? Where only a few families occupy a space of several square miles, it is obvious that a *central* school would not suffice; because it would be too remote from the homes of most of the children: and it is equally obvious that a school could not be provided for each family, or for each half dozen families, thus circumstanced. Some other mode of meeting the demand, besides the ordinary school, must be devised. This is one of the local difficulties to be surmounted, at which I formerly hinted. This difficulty may prove less formidable than I have supposed. I presume it to exist, however, to a considerable extent. And in endeavouring to provide for such an exigency, I hope to suggest some considerations which may not be irrelevant to the condition and wants even of those who are, in this respect, more fortunately situated.

The first and most important acquisition which a child ever makes, next to that of articulate speech, is the art of reading. The second, in importance, is writing: and the third, is the knowledge of figures or common arithmetic. It is certainly desirable that all our youth of both sexes should be instructed in these three useful arts at the least. But, in no case, ought a child to be suffered to grow up amongst us without being taught to read. Can this be done without public schools? I believe it may: and I will tell you how. If, in any family, there be one individual who can read, that individual could, without serious interruption or detriment to any ordinary occupation, teach all the other members of said family, old and young, to read also. If, in every settlement or vicinage, consisting of a dozen or twenty individuals or families, there be one who could read, that one could teach all the others in like manner to read. Let voluntary associations or classes, of from six to twenty persons, (the members, for instance, of one family or of several contiguous families,) be formed; and let them agree to meet twice or thrice a week, for one or two hours, as their numbers or convenience may suggest,—to learn to read. And not many weeks or months will elapse before all shall be readers.

In order to learn to read, it is by no means indispensable that the tedious everlasting method of the schools for children should be adopted. The process may be rendered extremely simple and easy. It is not necessary to commence even with the alphabet, or to go through a course of spelling in Dilworth or Webster. Adults have been recently taught to read in penitentiaries and elsewhere, in a very short period—even within one or two weeks, in some cases—who previously did not know a letter. The chaplain or teacher opens his Bible—directs the eye of his pupil to the first verse of the first chapter—reads it distinctly—points out each *word* to the learner, and makes him repeat it—and so on to the end of the verse. In a few minutes the pupil can read the verse backwards or forwards. He now knows the *words* by their *phasis* or *appearance* in the book. Here, perhaps, the teacher stops awhile, and analyzes a word, naming each letter according to its proper sound—and presently the pupil will distinguish and name the letters also. They then proceed to another verse, and to another: and, by and by, the division of words into syllables is explained—or the syllabic analysis may precede the alphabetical—and thus the whole mystery of learning to read is dispelled; and it becomes an affair of a few days or hours. If convicts in a penitentiary, who are compelled to labour from morning to night, and to be shut up in solitary cells from sundown till daylight, can find time to acquire, from the lips of charity, so invaluable an art: will it be pretended that our free and happy labourers could not spare time for the same purpose? And will none among themselves be willing to officiate as guides?

That all this, and more, is practicable, is perfectly known from well-authenticated facts officially before the public—from the testimony of scores of our contemporaries and countrymen, grounded upon their own observation and experience. Many children have also been taught to read in this manner by individuals who have never heard of *M. Jacotot*—and long before he was born. By him, indeed, the method, with certain modifications, has been announced to the world as a grand discovery; and it constitutes the first stage in the process of his ingenious and greatly admired system of instruction. Let every teacher, however, do the best he can. Let him adapt his mode of instruction to the circumstances of his pupils. He will succeed, upon any plan, within some three or six months, in teaching his class or company to read. Were such a system to be put immediately and universally into operation in Tennessee, there would not be an individual, between the ages of six and fourscore, incapable of reading, at the end of a year, throughout the State. Not a dollar is wanted for the purpose. Any books will answer. Any place will do. Any hour of any day or evening will suffice. Now, if there be but one intelligent, patriotic, benevolent individual in each district, town or county, who will undertake to enlighten the people on this subject, and persuade them to co-operate in this good work of self-instruction, it will be speedily accomplished. Sunday schools judiciously conducted, in all parts of the country, would certainly and easily effect the same object.

Writing and arithmetic may be taught in the same way. And in general, whatever the teacher knows, he can communicate. Or, in other words, whatever is known by any member of a class or association may be possessed by all. But as I wish to avoid minute or prolix details, I shall proceed no further in the development of this voluntary, mutual, self-teaching system: being confident that wherever it is attempted merely in reference to reading, it will be amplified and extended, as occasion may require. Our city and village Lyceums are, in fact, but a higher order or degree of the same species of liberal, gratuitous, mutual instruction.

To distinguish this from the common school system, I have heretofore, on divers occasions, denominated it the *Social* or *Domestic* system of education. And while it seems singularly adapted to the wants and condition of the great mass of the poor and ignorant, the wealthier and more cultivated classes may avail themselves of its benefits also. Might not the *domestic* system, in its strictest sense, be made to supersede the *public* common school system altogether? Why should a little child ever be sent to school, who has a mother at home capable of teaching? A mother who *can* teach, and who possesses the genuine spirit of maternity, is always the best possible instructress for her children, until they reach the age of eight or ten or twelve. She can teach them all that is expected from a common school infinitely better than any schoolmaster. This she might do without interfering with the business or comforts of a well ordered domestic establishment. Children ought never to be closely confined at an age when they cannot study. Do young children *study* while constrained to sit, book in hand, through fear of the birch, during six long hours, upon the bench (and such a *bench!*) at school? They have not yet learned *how* to study: and, of course, must either go to sleep, or passively submit to the daily irksome and stupifying penance of doing nothing. At home and under the eye of their mother, they can play or work or receive instruction, as she directs, and as best suits their years, capacity and disposition. How much misery and vice and mischief and vexation of all sorts might not thus be happily escaped? What a generous ardent love of knowledge might not thus too be excited and cherished? instead of that dogged indifference or unconquerable aversion to letters so frequently evinced by boys, after a brief trial of the ordinary school discipline? And who so fit as a pious mother to instil into the heart of her child the purest principles of virtue and religion?

By far the larger proportion of schools for boys under twelve years of age, with which I have been acquainted in the course of my life, I would not hesitate to denounce as nuisances and impositions. I have seen them in every part of our country from Maine to Tennessee: and I feel confident that most parents might, if they would, form a *domestic school* at home, a thousand fold preferable to ninety-nine out of a hundred, on an average, of the whole number of *common schools* in the United States at this moment. Such has been my honest, deliberate and avowed opinion for many years past. And that this project of domestic education is not an idle day-dream or visionary speculation, may be learned from the following statement, made by Doctor Henderson respecting Iceland, which he had then recently visited, and whose work has been for several years past before the public, and is well known.

"On inquiring (says he) into the state of mental cultivation in Iceland, we are struck with the universal diffusion of the general principles of knowledge among its inhabitants. Though there be only one school in Iceland, and that solitary school is exclusively designed for the education of such as are afterwards to fill offices in church or state; yet, it is exceedingly rare to meet with a boy or girl, who has attained the age of nine or ten years, that cannot read and write with ease. Domestic education is most rigidly attended to; and I scarcely ever recollect entering a hut, where I did not find some individual or another, capable of entering into conversation with me on topics which would be reckoned altogether above the understandings of people in the same rank of society in other countries of Europe." Here it is worthy of special remark, that the only public school in Iceland is the University! The great mass of the children are taught by parents at home: and common or primary schools are unknown among them.

In further proof that my general estimate of common schools is not unsupported by high authority, I cite the following passage from the late Governor Clinton's Message to the Legislature of New York in 1826. "In the first place, there is no provision made for the education of competent instructors: of the eight thousand now employed in this State, too many are destitute of the requisite qualifications, and perhaps no considerable number are able to teach beyond rudimental instruction. Ten years of a child's life, from five to fifteen, may be spent in a common school: and ought this immense portion of time to be absorbed in learning what can be acquired in a shorter period? Perhaps one-fourth of our population is annually instructed in our common schools; and ought the minds and morals of the rising generations to be intrusted to the guardianship of incompetence? The scale of instruction must be elevated: the standard of education ought to be raised: and a central school on the monitorial plan ought to be established in each county for the education of teachers, and as exemplars for other momentous purposes, connected with the improvement of the human mind."

Should the *social* and *domestic* system be adopted in Tennessee, so far as to enable all persons to read, and many to write and keep accounts, then a large proportion of our people would be educated to as great an extent as is now practicable in most common schools: and none would be destitute of the means of indefinite intellectual improvement. Teach all to read, and multitudes, with this humble outfit, would find or create a path to the richest stores of knowledge. But we ought not to stop here; nor rest satisfied with what may be acquired at home, or from the voluntary aid of friends and neighbors. A little learning is better than none, and is never dangerous except when mistaken for a great deal: or when perverted and applied to unworthy purposes. But, with a *little*, we are not to be content, if it be possible to enlarge it. We must still have public schools. If children, however, when they begin to go to school, can read, and, in many instances, write and cypher also; it is obvious that it will be necessary to establish a totally different species of common schools from those which now exist among us. As many would be content with the instructions of the social or domestic school, fewer public schools would then suffice: and these comparatively few might be made of a very superior order. In them might be taught all the useful and ornamental branches of an English education, which are now restricted to the High School or College.

In most of the States where a legal provision is made for the support of common schools, the privilege of attendance is limited to pupils between the ages of four or five and sixteen. Now, will any mortal pretend that it is necessary to be at school ten or a dozen years to learn what is usually taught in our common schools? The whole might, by a judicious and skilful teacher, be taught in one year—or, at most, in two or three. In our ordinary academies too, seven precious years are wasted in picking up a wretched smattering of Greek and Latin, wherewith to enact the pedant, and thereby expose to scorn and ridicule the very name of classic literature; or in imbibing towards it a spirit of relentless and embittered hostility. Whereas, all that a youth needs from a teacher, and a hundredfold more than he commonly gets, might be acquired in less than half the time—together with a taste for classical studies which would be cherished and cultivated to the end of life.

Great and successful efforts are now making, in various parts of our country, to elevate the character of common English schools, as well as of all the higher seminaries. This is an object well worthy the serious attention of the patriot and philanthropist.

The intelligent public are aware that much has been done also towards improving the methods of instruction, in all its stages, and in every department of every species of school or college. Education itself has become a *science:* and it deserves the most profound study of all who wish to be esteemed skilful and thorough *educators.* It is well known that Edgeworth, Bell, Lancaster, Pestalozzi, Fellenberg, Jardine, Pillans, Dufief, Lasteyrie, Degerando, Wilderspin, Hamilton, Harnisch, Jacotot, Brougham, and others, have, in our times, been zealously labouring to benefit the world by their experiments and publications on this subject.

Education, indeed, is a topic about which everybody feels competent to speculate and to dogmatize—while few comprehend the nature or philosophy of the process. Men who have had much experience in the business of instruction, might, in general, be presumed to know rather more about it than those who have never made the attempt. At this particular time, the cause of education seems to attract universal attention: and almost every tyro fancies that he can enlighten the world upon this commonplace and yet all-absorbing theme.

Whether the Greeks and Romans were novices in this art, will be best ascertained by recurring to the pages of their own historians, and to the monuments of classic genius and literature which still command the admiration of mankind. Whether we can hope to train, by any novel machinery, greater and wiser men and women than grace the annals of our English ancestry or our own revolutionary epoch, may be shrewdly questioned. I am, however, the advocate of improvement in every thing. I do not subscribe to the doctrine: 'let well enough alone;' provided the said *well enough* can be made better. But innovation is not always improvement. In every revolutionary period, novelty is liable to be mistaken for amelioration. This is the revolutionary crisis of education. Men's heads are teeming with Utopian projects and fantasies of reform: and the present speaker may possibly be numbered among the vain schemers of the times, by those who are religiously wedded to the good old ways of their venerated grandsires.

I have not been able, however, to discover in any of the authors already named, much that is really useful, which had not been previously and forcibly exhibited in the pages of Montaigne, Comenius, Cowley, Carew, Ascham, Bacon, Locke, Milton, Fenelon, Dumarsais, Tanaquil Faber, Bossuet, Lowe, Clarke, J. T. Philipps, D'Alembert, Condillac, and others of a preceding generation. And whether these have added much to the science or art of education, as unfolded by a still more ancient school—by the Quinctilians and Ciceros and Xenophons and Aristotles and Solomons of Rome and Greece and Judea—may also admit of question. I am not sure that even our modern Bacons and Lockes and Miltons are entitled to higher praise than that of modestly following in the orbit of the great luminaries just cited.

But however wise men may speculate about systems or modes of education or about modern improvements in the art, in one most essential point they all agree. And this one point involves the whole mystery or philosophy of education under every rational system. *No man can teach what he does not himself understand.*—Every man can teach, *if he will*, what he does perfectly understand. The teacher then must be able and willing, or apt to teach. He must possess the requisite intellectual furniture, and also moral principle—or he cannot be trustworthy. He must be able to do the work, and he must also love the work.

Thus, for instance, no man can teach Greek, who knows nothing of Greek. Here is the real secret, by the way, of the general antipathy manifested by our Western youth towards Greek. They hear it denounced and ridiculed—and they ridicule and denounce it—as useless or unlearnable or both,—because they have never been *taught* it. Now Greek is just as easily taught, and may be just as easily learned, as any other language—provided the master understands his business. If our classical schools had thorough first rate Greek scholars at their head, no such complaint would ever be uttered. Boys would learn Greek as readily and as cheerfully as they learn English. Our country is filled to overflowing with adventurous *Greeklings*. But where are our Grecians? They do not come to us from the *far East*—nor can they be found there. Not one in a hundred of our American Greek professors or linguists would dare to encounter the shades of a Busby, a Bentley, a Porson, a Parr, a Burney, a Gesner, a Heyne, a Wolfius, a Hemsterhusius, a Wyttenbach, or of any one of the mighty phalanx of European literary giants, who have been the delight and the terror of their day and generation. Happy, thrice happy would it be for the Commonwealth, if a legislative *veto* could be imposed on this species of most villanous charlatanry—by which our pockets are picked, our understandings insulted, and the admission of our children to the classic groves of Academus effectually precluded.

Supposing the teacher to be duly qualified—and of course both judicious and sagacious—he will adapt his instructions to the age, capacity and actual attainments of his pupils. He will act towards them as a skilful physician does towards his patients. One uniform prescription will not answer for every age and habit and constitution. The systems and methods of others he will not despise. He will not servilely tread in the footsteps of his predecessors;—nor strike out a new path merely for the sake of novelty or from an affectation of singularity. His aim will be to communicate instruction in the most expeditious and effectual manner. He will borrow light and information from every quarter—will combine the good properties, as far as practicable, of all the known systems—and yet will teach in a manner peculiar to himself. He will constrain his pupils to love their studies. He will make it their delight to advance in knowledge and wisdom. And (as Milton has it) will insensibly lead them up the hill-side of science, usually indeed laborious and difficult at the first ascent, but under his kindly guidance, will appear so smooth, so green, so full of goodly prospect and melodious sounds on every side, that the harp of Orpheus could not be more charming.

To furnish an adequate supply of gifted teachers—

to induce men of the highest order of genius and talent to become teachers—should be the policy of every wise paternal government. The profession ought to be among the most honourable—and in order to this, among the most lucrative—in the land. Our statesmen, judges, governors—our lawyers, physicians, divines—are all formed by the school and university. And if we expect the former to be enlightened and faithful, we must make the latter as nearly perfect as possible.—The principal officer or commander-in-chief of every great literary institution or seminary for juvenile instruction, ought to possess a large measure of the wisdom of Solomon, the learning of Selden, and the patience of Job. But no man of superior intellect and lofty aspiring will ever look forward to the occupation of the *schoolmaster* as a *profession* to live by—while greater consideration and better pecuniary recompense await him as a politician or lawyer. The fault is in the very structure of our society. The thorough education of our children is a matter of secondary or trivial moment—and we grudge every dollar that it costs us. Were a good education universally esteemed the most desirable object of human ambition, as it ought to be—the people would be willing to pay for it. And accomplished teachers would be instantly forthcoming. Create a demand, and a supply will follow. Talent, like the diamond, will seek the best market.

Socrates, Plato, Aristotle, were the master spirits and the master pedagogues of Greece—and their illustrious disciples did honour to their schooling. Give us such a constellation of glorious intellect—refined and purified by Christian ethics—elevated and expanded by Christian hope and Christian charity—and the Republic shall live forever.

Suppose each county in the State to be divided into a convenient number of school districts, and a good common school to be duly organized and maintained in each district: suppose each county to contain one or more well-conducted classical schools or academies: suppose the State to be provided with a first-rate university or with several excellent colleges: Then let the poor children, boys and girls, be *all* taught gratuitously in the common schools whatever can be learned in such schools: let a certain fixed number of the best behaved, most talented and studious boys be selected from each of the common schools, by competent judges appointed for the purpose, and sent to the academy at the public expense: In due time, again, select from these, in like manner, a certain proportion to be educated at the college or university. Such a system would directly benefit the entire population, and especially the whole poor of the State; and would ensure a liberal education to the most gifted and meritorious of our poor youth. This is another obvious and practicable mode of diffusing the benefits of every species and degree of education among the most indigent and neglected classes of the community. Why should it not find favour with the legal guardians and professed champions of the poor? Why denounce the higher seminaries as unfriendly to the poor, while no effort is made to render them the greatest possible blessings to the poor? Nearly all the great men in this nation and in the world have risen from the humblest ranks; and chiefly through the agency of the college, directly or indirectly. But such a result is seldom or never realized, except where especial provision is made for poor scholars. The poor youth of Tennessee can never hope for such facilities and advantages from the colleges of other States.

A distinguished German divine, towards the close of the 16th century, thus quaintly expressed himself, in a sermon directed against those who said that high schools were of no use: "Such thoughts come from the suggestion of Satan himself, who is an enemy to schools. If there were no high schools, the stronger would put the weaker in a sack, and there would be no end of this till people ate one another up. Head-law, and not fist-law, must govern the world; but then men of learning do not grow on the trees, so that one has only to shake them down, and, with reverence be it spoken, put a pair of boots below for them to fall into."

I have so frequently advocated the cause of education, in reference to every class and description of my fellow-citizens, that I cannot hope, on this occasion, to command attention by the mere novelty of argument or illustration. I rely solely on the importance and truth of my positions, and upon the universal application, for even a patient hearing. I have often pointed out the evils resulting, or likely to result, from an illiberal hostility to colleges and professional seminaries: and I have demonstrated that the people at large must ever be wronged and oppressed by such a policy. If we have no great literary institutions of our own, still some of our opulent youth will find their way to distant institutions; or educated individuals will come to us from other States or from foreign lands; and thus we shall have among us a sufficient number of comparatively intelligent persons, at least to monopolize the profits and emoluments of professional and official stations, and to control the popular sentiment for their own special benefit. I need hardly stop to expose the dangerous tendency of such a monopoly. It is virtually vesting all power in the hands of a few, and accords much better with the genius of despotism than of democracy. The Grand Turk and the Russian Czar have long since adopted this very system. They choose to have about them some eminently learned and accomplished ministers to do their bidding—to aid in sustaining their dignity and in executing their arbitrary measures. Without them indeed, their crowns and thrones would speedily pass into other hands. They know full well that knowledge is power: and that mere brute force can never be skilfully directed or successfully employed without it.

It is evident that the common schools will not suffice to educate the *governing mind* of any civilized empire, kingdom, or republic. These will but prepare the people to be the more easily managed and imposed on by the specious sophistry and selfish cunning of the more intelligent and ambitious few. The question with us is not, how much or what kind of learning will qualify a man to be a decent farmer or merchant or mechanic?

But what will enable the farmer and mechanic to become the most useful and influential citizens—to constitute in fact the governing mind of the Commonwealth? Clearly, if they aspire to the government of the State, they must become the most enlightened body in the State. Even upon the hypothesis that much learning is dangerous or pernicious—that it is apt to render men proud, arrogant, overbearing, knavish or aristocratic—still, so long as its possessors will contrive, by means foul or fair, to usurp or engross all the prerogatives of sovereignty—the farmer and mechanic must learn to wield this very dangerous but most potent engine, or tamely yield the sovereignty to their wily superiors. They, too, must go to college.

I have been pleading the cause of our farmers and mechanics for some dozen years past. Because, upon them, as enlightened, judicious, independent, patriotic citizens, depend the destinies of this Republic. The question, I again repeat, is, shall they lead or be led? Shall they arrest and put down the factious spirit of unprincipled ambition which is rife and running riot in the land, or shall they blindly lend themselves as the instruments and the victims of its desperate and treasonable purposes? The crisis has arrived when the people must speak and act wisely and resolutely, or their ability to speak and to act with decisive efficiency, will be lost forever.

I care not where or how they acquire the requisite amount of intellectual furniture, so that it be acquired. If they can and will create and uphold institutions, suited to their purpose, superior to the university and the college—so much the better. But let them not be deluded by the fancy that common schools will ever insure to them or their children, the rank and influence and power which their numerical strength might fairly claim. They will be priest-ridden, and lawyer-ridden, and doctor-ridden, and demagogue-ridden, to the end of the chapter of human perversity and chicanery, if they continue to pin their faith upon the popular scheme of elementary schools to the neglect of all superior institutions. Let me not be misunderstood. I am the staunch advocate of every species of *good* common schools, and of every practicable plan for the diffusion of useful knowledge among the people—whether in larger or smaller measures—whether by the State government or by individual effort and munificence. But no system of popular education can be complete or efficient or permanently successful, which does not embrace within its liberal scope the college and the higher sciences as well as the common school and the spelling book. I would not exclude the farmers' sons from any intellectual cultivation which the wisdom and the wealth of the State could place within their reach. I would bid them welcome to the privileges and instructions of the noblest university in the land. Or rather, I would create a university for this very purpose, which should be second to none in the world.

In population and political influence, Tennessee already ranks among the most important members of the great Federal Union. And hitherto, she has done precisely nothing for the education of her children, either rich or poor—except upon paper. About thirty years ago, Congress granted one hundred thousand acres of land for the endowment of two colleges within her limits, and appointed her legislature their trustee to locate said land in a body, and to sell it at not less than two dollars per acre; and thus to provide a fund of at least two hundred thousand dollars for the support of the two colleges. Had the legislature fulfilled the condition of this sacred trust, in good faith, the original donation, at the *minimum* price for which the land was to be sold, would, in twenty-five years, at six per cent. *simple interest,* have amounted to five hundred thousand dollars. To this day, the colleges have received little or nothing from the avails of said land. They have still therefore a legal right to the whole sum last mentioned. The legislature is bound by every principle of honour and law and equity, to indemnify the colleges to the full extent of the injury inflicted. The very best thing that the legislature can now do in behalf of popular education is, forthwith, to perform an act of simple justice. To resolve, namely, to pay to each of the colleges *two hundred and fifty thousand* dollars, or an annuity of fifteen thousand dollars to each forever. Virginia, after expending half a million of dollars upon the edifices, libraries, and apparatus of her University, has heretofore appropriated, and has agreed to appropriate in future, the sum of fifteen thousand dollars per annum for its maintenance. South Carolina has been equally liberal; and yet neither was ever assisted by Congress. Several of the States have done much more, and all have done something for their colleges. Tennessee is the solitary exception. In this respect, she stands alone and unrivalled among her peers. She is the only civilized community upon the globe, which occupies so enviable a position—which can boast the singular distinction of not only neglecting and frowning upon her colleges, and of never having bestowed a dollar upon one of them—but of having positively withheld from them the charity of strangers! True, the legislature is but the creature and servant of the people, and must do their pleasure. And the sovereign people, I suppose, like other arbitrary and absolute sovereigns, can do no wrong; or, like the Pope, must be deemed infallible. So much for the colleges. The academies, with an equal grant of land from Congress, have been dealt with after the same equitable, royal, popish, summary fashion.

But it will be triumphantly urged, as a redeeming set-off to the above, that much has been done and is doing for common schools. [Which, by the way, be it remembered, are designed to teach nothing more than every mother is or ought to be qualified to teach much better at home.] Yes, truly, a vast deal of legislation has been expended upon common schools, and large sums of money have disappeared from the public treasury upon this service: but I defy any mortal to designate the school or the child which has received the slightest benefit from the one or the other. Upon this theme, however, it is useless to descant. Every popular folly must live its day out. A mammoth school fund will be raised. The people have decreed it. Their lands and limbs, their bread and labour, will be taxed to procure it. And when procured, it will regularly pass into the hands of honest *dis*interested school-agents or commissioners, who will take good care of it—or it will get into the vaults of some favourite State Bank to be kindly nursed and increased for the benefit of posterity—or it will be distributed in convenient loans to certain trustworthy citizens who live only to serve the public—and finally it will puzzle the lawyers, after receiving their fees from every party concerned, to discover the *whereabout* of its actual existence, or to point out the course of its flight beyond the reach of legislative control.

Am I then opposed to the common school fund system which is so universally approved throughout the country? I answer again: I am opposed to no system which will insure good schools or valuable instruction to the people or to any portion of the people. I am opposed to the system of doing nothing. I am opposed to the system of robbing the people of their money under the ludicrous pretext of providing for the education of their great-grandchildren's children. While no living man's son or daughter will ever be taught a letter of the alphabet or the difference between good and evil, right and wrong, by the agency of any school fund *in esse* or *in posse*. Reasoning from the past and the present, I can discern nothing in the signs of the times or in the tone of popular morals to warrant the anticipation of a more auspicious result for the future. Greatly should I rejoice, however, at any evidence or indication which might justify a different and more cheering train of reflections; or which might be calculated to inspire the brightest visions of hope in regard to the existing and each successive generation of my countrymen.

But, another hypothesis, and I have done. If the people or their rulers were really desirous to educate the poor children of the State—why not do it instantly and effectually? If none of the modes already suggested should be acceptable, yet certainly the work could be done, for example, in the same manner as paupers are fed and clothed at the public expense. Let each county be required to provide for the adequate instruction of its own poor children, just as it provides for the comfortable subsistence of its poor citizens. There is no more difficulty in the one case than in the other. Nor would the burden be very grievous. I doubt whether ten poor children can be found in each county, upon an average, whose parents or relatives could not afford them a *common school* education. I will undertake to teach, at my own cost, all the *poor* children of Tennessee not fairly included in the number and description just specified.

I had intended to say something of the school systems which obtain in Scotland, Sweden, Holland, Switzerland, Prussia, and the smaller German States—but I forbear. Republican America may however learn much, even from European monarchies, upon this vital subject. And it would be quite as reputable, to say the least, to follow their example in the judicious education of our children, as to imitate them in their fashionable vices, amusements and absurdities.

Of our own humble University, it is not my purpose to speak. It may not be worth your notice. I shall certainly not pronounce its eulogium, nor recommend it to your special patronage or consideration. It has *existed* during the brief space of eleven [now thirteen] years. Its history, if fairly told, would be curious, and not altogether devoid of instructive incident. But it is enough, on the present occasion, to be able to announce, that, under the good providence of God, it has survived the hopes and fears and wishes and predictions of both friends and foes. And that it continues to exist, in spite of untoward circumstances and events—in spite of local nuisances and unsightly accommodations—in spite of poverty and injustice—in spite of ecclesiastical and political indifference and neglect and hostility—in spite of all sorts of misrepresentation and abuse and opposition from all sorts of people—in spite of the lawyers, and clergy, and physicians, and merchants, and farmers, and mechanics, and schoolmasters, and office-hunters of every name and degree—in spite of religious sectarian jealousy, fanaticism and intolerance—in spite of infidel self-sufficiency and mawkish sentimentality—in spite of innovating perfectionists and fault-finding purists—in spite of whigs and tories, democrats and federalists, nullifiers and consolidationists—in spite of Nashville and all its wicked inhabitants—in spite of Tennessee and all its great men and little men—in spite of the Legislature and the Trustees, the President and the Faculty—in spite of the Presbyterians, high church and low, old school and new—in spite of all the reverend bigots and dogmatists and *would-be* popes, of every denomination, in the Commonwealth:—yes, the hitherto unbefriended University still exists. And, if her *Alumni* choose to inscribe, in adamantine capitals, upon her walls of granite or marble *yet* to be erected,

ESTO PERPETUA!

It shall exist and flourish a thousand ages after *we* shall be forgotten, and *our* names be obliterated from the records of this world's glory and insignificance.

BACCALAUREATE ADDRESS.

[UNIVERSITY OF NASHVILLE, OCTOBER 3. 1838.]

BACCALAUREATE ADDRESS

AT THE UNIVERSITY OF NASHVILLE, OCTOBER 3, 1838.

HAVING completed the course of study prescribed by the laws of this Institution, we congratulate you, Young Gentlemen, upon the arrival of this auspicious, and by you long wished for day, which sunders forever your college ties and associations. About to enter upon a new scene of study and of action, you, doubtless, with the elastic temperament peculiar to youth, anticipate much, very much, from the fair world which lies before you. This is natural: and we cordially mingle our sympathetic hopes and aspirations with yours, while we fervently pray that you may never be disappointed.

Would you learn how to live, so as certainly to escape disappointment? This is an inquiry unspeakably momentous to youth, however circumstanced; and especially to those who may be destined to exert a more than ordinary influence in their day and generation:— or to feel themselves more acutely than others the mortification and the anguish of blighted hopes, and the failure of well concerted plans and persevering labours.

But the protracted exercises of this Anniversary have already preferred so large a demand upon the indulgence of our respected auditory, that, I shall be readily excused for not venturing into any elaborate details or formal discussions on this or any other topic. Nor is it necessary that I should. For all the lessons and counsels, moral, religious, economical, literary or philosophical, which it would be in my power to impart, have been communicated and reiterated, from time to time, in the familiar style of the lecture room, while, together, we have examined the theories and speculations of the wise and good of different ages and schools, or scanned the motives, principles and ends of human conduct, as developed by reason, experience and revelation. You have been directed also to the ablest and purest sources of information; as well as taught to investigate, to reflect and to judge for yourselves. I shall, therefore, trespass but a few minutes further on the patience of my hearers.

When I contemplate any one of the little bands of youth which annually issue from our colleges into every section of this extensive Republic, it is impossible for me not to follow them in imagination into the busy world and to trace with prophetic pen the various parts which they seem likely to act on the great stage of public life.

One, on whom rests the meek, gentle, dovelike spirit of heavenly wisdom, bids fair to become an eminent herald of the cross—a joyful messenger of peace to a distracted world—a patient, laborious, faithful minister of reconciliation to the guilty, the wretched and the perishing.

Another promises to adorn religion in the more retired walks of private life:—Where, by his holy example, by his active, unobtrusive benevolence, to shed a lustre on the Christian name, and to inspire peace and joy into many an aching bosom, while he kindly fosters every institution and patronises every plan which is calculated to meliorate the condition of suffering humanity, and to promote the glory of his Master's name.

Many are looking forward to the bar, to the healing art, to the army, to the navy, or to merchandise as their future fields of enterprise and emolument:—but, with what views and motives they will commence and prosecute their several schemes and labours, the Searcher of hearts alone can know. Paternal affection bids them all, God speed—but with a fearful anxiety, lest some of them at least should venture to go forth without the divine blessing and protection.

One, and another seems likely to take a distinguished part in the government of his country, perhaps to become a leader in the legislative councils,—a Senator—a Judge—or even the Chief Magistrate of the nation—for who shall set bounds to the ambitious aspirings of America's talented and privileged sons?—With what trembling solicitude does the tenderness of friendship watch his every footstep, and mark his progress towards the goal of his wishes! Will he be the stern, uncompromising friend of virtue, of truth, of righteousness? Will he rule in the fear of God? Will he prove a benefactor or a scourge, a blessing or a curse, to the people who shall honour him with their confidence?

But I behold another,—not, I trust, among the beloved pupils here before me, but merely in mental vision,—

perhaps a young man of native genius and high promise —on whom parental fondness dotes—whose departure from sacred home to the venerable temple of science was the occasion of many a fervent prayer to Heaven for his welfare—who received a kind father's parting benediction and a weeping mother's sad farewell embrace, with a heart melted to tenderness, and resolved to gratify their every wish. I behold him now, after an absence of a few months or years, associating with the licentious and the profane—neglecting study for the haunts of vice and folly—sacrificing his precious time and the principles of virtue with which parental piety had imbued his once susceptible mind, at the shrine of forbidden pleasure —at the festive board of intemperance—at the infernal table of the gambler—and subsiding by degrees into a state of habitual sensuality and confirmed skepticism! Is this a spectacle which any man, whose heart is not made of adamant, can contemplate with indifference?

A young man, the pride and the hope of his family, standing, as it were, on the threshold of life, and just going to enter upon the world's wide theatre—with libertine principles and habits—with a hardihood in vice which has steeled the mind and seared the conscience against every good impression—into how deep a gulf of perdition is he sinking? With what awful forebodings do I follow him in that downward career which he seems determined to pursue! Of how much misery and crime may he not yet become the author? How much moral devastation may he spread around him in society? What ruinous and abominable principles may he one day disseminate? How many innocent persons may his seductive example and insinuating manners lead astray from the high road of virtue and peace—till they become as hardened as himself—and with him, sit down in the seat of the scornful there, with united efforts and augmented wiles, strive to extend their dominion over others still—and to spread wide the tempting and decoying net to catch and to hold fast the unwary and unstable wherever they can be found?

Will he become the apostle of infidelity—the bold, active, determined enemy of revelation—a Voltaire, or a Paine? Or will he be the subtle, systematic, refined, philosophising freethinker—a Hobbes, a Tindal, a Bolingbroke, a Hume or a Gibbon? Or will he be content, in a lower sphere, to indulge in all the vanity of sensuality and riot—to be what Rochester and Gardiner were, before the grace of the Highest had awakened them from their delirium of profligacy, and reclaimed them, when on the verge of perdition—to live, at once, a warning to the rake, and an encouragement to the returning prodigal?

Can he be destined for any great offices in public life? Yes—even this is possible. For the world has seen the infidel, the scoffer and the libertine elevated to posts of honour and power—and hailed with the loudest acclamations of an infatuated multitude.

But whatever may be his lot in life, however exalted, or however humble—he must have influence of some kind. The veriest vagabond on earth is scarcely so degraded as to be unable to find a companion who may not be made worse by his agency and example. He has relations and friends and associates—and among these he may appear even respectable. He may form connections, and become the head and the guide of a family, which will look to him with affection and confidence for counsel and direction.

Where, in the Universe, is the benevolent being who would not be constrained to say—better were it for this young man, better for his friends, better for society, better for future generations, that he had never been born, than thus to live, a curse to all within the sphere of his contaminating principles and example!

God grant, that these remarks may never apply to a single youth who has heard them pronounced—much less to any of those whom I directly address.

Do you wish to be respected, useful and happy in any profession or calling in life, whether public or private, in the Church or in the State? Youth is the golden season to prepare for it. Lay broad and deep the foundation now. Let religion—the Christian religion, pure and undefiled — be the corner-stone on which the whole edifice shall rest. Aspire with a noble daring, to the loftiest eminence. But let religion guide you in every stage of your progress, and influence every act of your lives, and consecrate to God the object at which you aim. This is the only kind of ambition which will conduct you to true, substantial and ever enduring greatness: and preserve you from those cruel disappointments which drive to despair so many of the unsuccessful candidates for worldly honours and distinction. For if your views be limited exclusively or chiefly to this world, you will assuredly be disappointed, even if you gain the objects which you covet, and after which you strive and labour with the most invincible ardour, resolution and perseverance. Like Solomon, in the midst of all his wealth, and luxury, and splendour, and power, and grandeur, and glory, you will, with an aching heart, inscribe "vanity of vanities" on all your honours and possessions. Or like Alexander, after gathering the laurels of a hundred victories, sigh for other worlds to conquer. Or like Grotius, after ranging over the rich and varied fields of science and literature in search of fame, or of the philosopher's chief good, be constrained to confess that you have wasted life in laborious trifling. "Heu vitam perdidi operose nihil agendo."

Disappointment will meet you, sooner or later, take what course you may. The dearest objects of your affections may be torn from your embrace, or converted into instruments of unceasing torture. Your idols may be dashed in pieces before your eyes—and the fragments lie scattered around you,—the ever present and upbraiding mementos of your disloyalty to heaven's righteous King, and of the folly of every earthly pursuit which does not subserve the great end of your probationary existence. Sorrow and pain and anguish and bitterness of spirit will be yours, in spite of all your prudence, sagacity, talents, courage and integrity. To the wicked there is no peace. To the enemy of God there can be no permanent prosperity. To the votary of this world, in any of its ten thousand alluring forms, there is ordained inevitable disappointment. Every sublunary good will fail, and leave you comfortless. The evil days will come, and the years draw nigh, when you shall say, with the sigh of anguish and despair, we have no pleasure in them.

But in the Bible you will find an antidote and a remedy—a preventive and a solace—a sure guide and an infallible physician. Here you will be taught to *expect*, what the world styles, misfortune, calamity, tribulation, adversity—perhaps persecution, poverty, disgrace: yes, even character, which is dearer than life to every upright man, may be tarnished and prostrated, for a season, by the insidious machinations of envy and jealousy and malice—or blasted by the foul breath of infamy itself—or you may be wounded in the house of your friends—(Zech. xiii. 6,)—for "the disciple is not above his master, nor the servant above his lord." Still, if your trust be in God, you will not be overwhelmed by any disaster: you may have reason to say with an eminent Apostle—"We are troubled on every side, yet not distressed: we are perplexed, but not in despair; persecuted, but not forsaken; cast down, but not destroyed."—2 Cor. iv. 8, 9. Or with holy Job, be enabled to exclaim, when stripped of all things—"Though he slay me, yet will I trust in him."—Job, xiii. 15. Or in the language of heavenly resignation—"Father, not my will, but thine, be done."—Luke, xxii. 42.

Let the Bible, then, be a lamp to your feet, and a light to your path—the man of your counsel and the hope of your soul. (As this was my first—and has been my constant—so let it be remembered as my last advice to you, on this solemn and interesting occasion.)

I am aware that it has long been, and still continues to be fashionable, among well educated men, to disregard and neglect the Bible, as beneath or unworthy their notice. They often affect to disbelieve it and to despise it—and why? Because they know little or nothing about it. Such persons are frequently met with—men distinguished for wit and learning—lawyers—physicians—statesmen—politicians—philosophers—accomplished authors—who are nearly as ignorant of the characteristic features and distinctive principles of the Christian religion as heathens;—and yet they are as dogmatical in their opinions about it as if they were the only competent and legitimate judges of its claims.

Now, as you will, probably, soon rank among some of these classes, I counsel you to be a little more modest, and candid, and equitable—and carefully to read the Bible through, before you undertake to assert what it does or does not inculcate. If you can find, anywhere else, a system of morals or of faith, so well calculated to render men good and happy in this world, and to furnish them support, and peace and hope and confidence and joy and triumph in death—or if you can account for the fact, that, all mankind have been, and still are, polytheists and idolators, except Jews, Christians and Mohammedans, who confessedly are indebted exclusively to the Bible for their knowledge of the apparently simple, obvious and natural truth, "that there is but one living and true God"—then you will have discovered two reasons (as yet unknown) for the rejection of the Bible. And until you can attain satisfaction upon these two points, it will be hardly worth your while to travel far abroad in search of other objections and difficulties which necessarily attach to infidelity. For as to the boasted and boasting and all-sufficient theism of the modern school, it may be passed with the remark, that it has never been heard of except where the light of divine revelation has shown forth from the pages of the Bible —even upon those who fain would extinguish it forever.

Again—and for the last time, probably, while I live—I charge you, in the dread name of the eternal Jehovah, to study this sacred volume thoroughly and honestly, prayerfully and habitually. No man ever did this, and remained a skeptic or an infidel—or became a bigot or fanatic, an enthusiast or hypocrite, a churl or an anchorite. Let not the authority of great names bias your judgment or command your assent. Spare no pains or efforts in the search of truth—and when found, dare to acknowledge and embrace it. Ignorance, among learned men, is the parent of skepticism—as it is of superstition among the great mass of the unlettered.

Christianity, in several respects, may be regarded as a science—and it must be studied as carefully, diligently and thoroughly as any science, in order to be understood. It involves too the most deeply interesting—the most profound—the sublimest philosophy:—the philosophy of human nature or of the human heart —of man as a rational accountable moral agent—of man, in all his diversified and complex relations with his fellow-men and with his Maker—during every stage of his existence in time and throughout eternity. Your progress in this truly divine philosophy will be marked by practical results which cannot be mistaken. It will be apparent in your temper and conduct. It will be manifested by effects which no other philosophy has ever produced—and which may be summed up in two words, utterly unknown to every other system, and which the world to this day can scarcely appreciate—Humility and Charity.

Be the friends and advocates of genuine religion, as taught and illustrated by living example in the Bible: and you will also be the steady, efficient and successful friends of humanity, in every possible mode—the advocates of every good principle, cause, enterprise, plan and institution which the most enlightened wisdom and benevolence shall be capable of devising and executing. Take the Bible for your guide—and I have no fear of the result. Your *Alma Mater* and your country will never be ashamed of you—but will cherish you as their favourite and favoured sons. Patriotism and philanthropy will claim you as their own. The ignorance, the illiberality, the persecuting bigotry, the exterminating intolerance of proud, supercilious infidelity, with all its ostentatious hypocritical pretensions to kindness and candour and charity—will blush in your presence—and shrink away abashed, like the friend of darkness from the face of angelic purity and majesty.

Your country has need of learned and Christian lawyers, physicians, clergymen, statesmen—as it has of Christian and learned mechanics, merchants and farmers. The cause of religion, of education, of patriotism, of humanity—is one and indivisible. Dare you, before God, this day, pledge yourselves to support and to advance it?

A patriot without religion—like a gentleman without honour—is a contradiction, virtually and in fact, if not in terms.

Where, in all the annals of the ancient world—*mankind*—whether Jewish or Pagan—classical or barbarian—did you ever read of a true patriot who was not also a religious man—or who at least, was not a friend to the religion of his country? Look over the catalogue of Greek and Roman worthies—and then answer the interrogatory. And where on the page of history have you found—or where upon this earth can you find—men ashamed of religion—except—in Christendom? And is Christianity, let me ask, the only religion ever yet promulgated in our world of which man or woman has reason to be ashamed? (Shall woman too be ashamed of the Christian religion?) I have told you that if you seek this world only, you will be disappointed:—either by not reaching the object aimed at, or by discovering its utter insufficiency to yield you solid comfort and enjoyment when possessed.

I have told you also, that if you set out in life with the fear of God before your eyes, and with his love in your hearts, you *may* meet with much and various tribulation—but that this will not make you wretched or drive you to despair. On the contrary, if you absolutely commit your ways to the Lord, you may pass, not only unhurt, but triumphant, through the hottest fiery furnace that human or diabolical malignity has ever prepared for the destruction of the faithful. Or if you be summoned to the horrors of martyrdom with James, and Paul and Peter—your bosoms may still be calm, and full of heavenly peace and hope and gladness—and your fame, like theirs, will not be eclipsed by the persecuting and murderous Herods and Neros who may doom you to the stake or the scaffold.

The usual course of Providence however is in this wise—The votaries of the world flourish and prosper for a season—and then come disaster, defeat, misery, chagrin, ruin—or at the best, disgust with the present, remorse for the past, and horrible misgivings and apprehensions for the future.

While, on the other hand, good men are frequently proved at first by many severe and painful trials—for, strange as it may appear to this world's wisdom, "whom the Lord loveth he chasteneth, and scourgeth every son whom he receiveth."—Heb. xii. 6.

But, by and by, the dark clouds which, for a period, lowered so portentously over their apparently devoted heads—begin to disperse. The sun of prosperity begins to shine—and shines brighter and brighter upon their advancing years. Their old age is tranquil and happy. They die universally respected, beloved and lamented. Thus it was with Moses, and Job, and Joseph and Daniel—and, many others, whose lives are recorded by the pen of inspiration for our encouragement and instruction.—"For them that honour me (saith the Lord) I will honour, and they that despise me shall be lightly esteemed."—1 Sam. ii. 30.

But there is another world to prepare for, and "godliness is profitable unto all things, having promise of the life that now is, and of that which is to come."—1 Tim. iv. 8. Therefore "seek ye first the kingdom of God, and his righteousness; and all these things shall be added unto you."—Matt. vi. 33.

"Trust in the Lord with all thine heart, and lean not unto thine own understanding. In all thy ways acknowledge him, and he shall direct thy paths. Be not wise in thine own eyes: fear the Lord, and depart from evil."—Prov. iii. 5, 6, 7.

With this word of counsel, I commend you to the grace of God, and bid you adieu. May the blessing of the great Father of mercies be upon you and attend you through a long, a useful, a prosperous and a happy life:—May his Spirit sustain you in the last struggles of dissolving nature—and may the joys and the glories of the heavenly Paradise be yours forever and ever! And again, I bid you a long, a last, an affectionate FAREWELL!

SPEECH ABOUT COLLEGES.

SPEECH ABOUT COLLEGES.

AT NASHVILLE, COMMENCEMENT DAY, OCTOBER 4, 1848.

It is often remarked of college graduates, that they rarely excel those who have been far less favored on the score of education; and that, in fact, but few of them ever attain to great eminence. This remark is made either, 1, as an objection to the whole system of college discipline—as being calculated rather to depress than to encourage the aspirations of genius and the development of intellect: Or, 2, as a direct censure upon the facility with which academic degrèes are usually awarded; namely, that they are frequently, if not generally, conferred upon unworthy candidates.

1. As to the first objection, it may suffice to remind all cavillers, that eminent distinction is rarely attained by individuals of any class or profession or description of men, under any circumstances whatever. But few, exceedingly few, of the vast multitude of lawyers, physicians, clergymen, artists, teachers, poets, orators, authors, warriors, ever rise above mediocrity; or acquire that kind of relative or acknowledged superiority which will insure a permanent reputation, or an honorable niche in the grand temple of fame. The *nomina clara*, the brilliant

luminaries, the master spirits, of any age, must ever be few in number, in any given sphere of active or studious enterprise. Of the many thousands of astute politicians or political adventurers, of office holders and office seekers, at the present day, in our own and in other countries, how many, think you, will ever be known to posterity as eminent statesmen, legislators, jurists, patriots, or philanthropists? Brief, indeed, is the catalogue of names which really adorn and dignify the page of our world's history, during the three thousand years of which authentic records have been preserved.

I do not make this statement with a view to disparage or undervalue moderate or unobtrusive merit; or to intimate that the million, who live and die undistinguished among their contemporaries, are therefore not useful in their day and generation. Far from it. They may act well their part according to their several abilities and opportunities; and thus will have discharged their duty, and satisfied every reasonable expectation. I have adverted to an established law of humanity, to a universal order of Providence, as applicable to colleges as to other associations or communities; and not more stringently applicable to them than to all others. Let any man, who has a fancy for the task, run over the vocabulary of human greatness—whether Oriental, Greek, Roman, Mediæval or Modern,—and he will probably discover that a fair proportion of the whole had been regularly trained in the colleges or high schools of their respective countries. So much for the objection under this particular aspect. The university will never be found in arrears, when compared with the dominant spirit of the age and country. Political or religious despotism may impress upon it a character in Spain and Italy widely different from that which it assumes in Britain or America.

But if we regard the useful, the good, the laborious, the faithful—in all the vocations where superior intelligence is essential or available—we shall be able to form a much juster estimate of the obligations which the world owes to the university system; whatever may have been its vices or imperfections. Let us be thankful for the benefits, and strive to remedy or remove the evils and defects.

2. Colleges confer degrees upon unworthy candidates.—I admit the fact. I wish it were otherwise. Of honorary doctorates, perhaps the least said the better. Happily, with one exception, they do but little harm, even if they do no good. I think that colleges, in this great model Republic, might, with manifest propriety, cease to grant the doctorate altogether. I see no reason why American preachers, and schoolmasters, and authors of spelling books and grammars, should not assume the D.D. or LL.D. at pleasure, according to their taste or self-appreciation; just as our whig and democratic loafers and politicians contrive, by some process or other, to become entitled or accustomed to the prefix or suffix of Colonel, General, Esquire, Honorable, or His Excellency. Why not? The exception just alluded to, is the doctorate of medicine. This, whether conferred *causa honoris* or *in course* upon ignorant or unprincipled persons, is a grievous injury to the public.—Because an M.D. is a passport

to popular confidence and practice. Here the people cannot judge for themselves. They rely on the testimonials thus dishonestly furnished by learned and responsible corporations. And hence irreparable wrongs may be inflicted and endured before the *Doctor's* utter incompetency can be detected and exposed. That a reform is needed here and everywhere, in the Medical Schools and in reference to medical practice, I believe, is the opinion of the enlightened profession generally, on both sides of the Atlantic.

But the objection relates chiefly, I suppose, to the first degree—the degree, namely, of Bachelor of Arts. Very true: this degree is conferred by all the colleges in the Union every year upon some unqualified—perhaps, in the aggregate, upon many unqualified and very unworthy individuals. This arises from several causes. 1. From the fact, that a portion of the youth who enter our colleges are deficient in intellect. They do not possess minds capable of high and liberal cultivation. Here the native or raw material is wanting. "Non ex quovis ligno Mercurius fit." No college professors can work miracles, or convert a blockhead into a Solomon.— "Though the ass may make a pilgrimage to Mecca, yet an ass he will come back." 2. From idle habits—from lack of industry and application. No brilliancy of talent will master any science or language without labour. While persevering labour will ultimately triumph over all difficulties, and insure success to even comparatively humble genius. 3. From a defective school education —the want of the requisite qualifications for a college life—or from the extreme youth of the party when admitted.

In two words: Our lads enter college too young, and without due preparation. They ought seldom, if ever, to graduate under twenty years of age; and consequently, should not enter the Freshman or lowest class younger than sixteen. Up to this period, ample work might be provided for them in the primary and classical school or by the parental fireside. Let them be thoroughly drilled in Greek and Latin—in Arithmetic, Algebra, Geometry, Geography—in one or more modern languages, when practicable—at all events, in the English, so as to be able to speak and write their own vernacular with grammatical accuracy and idiomatic propriety.

At school, boys may readily learn the accidence—namely, the inflections, the orthography, the etymology, the signification of words—together with the mechanical structure, the syntax and prosody of the ancient languages. And thus be prepared, in due season, to attend the lectures and illustrations of the accomplished classical professor. In reading Greek and Latin books, the first object usually is, to acquire verbal knowledge—a kind of knowledge which children acquire with eagerness and facility under judicious instructors. The second and final object is, to become acquainted with the mind of the writer or with the argument of his book. Thus, at school, boys often read portions of the most celebrated authors—as Virgil, Ovid, Tacitus, Livy, Horace, Juvenal, Cicero, Xenophon, Homer, Thucydides, Herodotus, Aristotle, Demosthenes, Euripides, and others, more or less —but then, as a general fact, they achieve little more than a mere mastery of words and phrases. They do not yet perceive, or comprehend, or relish the various recondite beauties and peculiar excellencies, for which the ancient classics have been studied and admired by the ripest scholars of every enlightened age and nation. They must be carefully grounded in the rudiments; and gradually advanced, step by step, until their faculties—strengthened, expanded, matured, and wisely disciplined —become capable of holding "high converse" with the mighty dead: with the sages, the poets, the orators, the historians, the heroes, the statesmen, the patriots, of glorious old Greece and Rome.

Now it so happens, that a large portion of our college students [Western as well as Eastern] are, at the period of matriculation, but smatterers in the whole grammar school course.—Not always from any fault of their own, it may be, but of their teachers. Some of them can hardly decline a noun or conjugate a verb, or distinguish a square from a triangle. Nevertheless, they must be admitted, and into a high class too. Their fathers urge and insist on a trial.—The boys are such fine fellows, so clever and diligent, they will soon make up all deficiencies: just give them a chance among the *juniors* for a few weeks; and if they cannot go ahead, why then put them back or down into their proper place—that is, into a lower class. To be sure, such ill-furnished or rather unfurnished youth are about as fit for the Junior class as for the Freshman. And they might as well be graduated forthwith, as after a two years' *rubbing* and *shamming*, and making much ado about nothing. By the way, as to going back: whenever a novice is permitted to study on probation with any class, and is found unable to proceed or to keep up with such class, he invariably complains of injustice if removed from it; and loudly blames the Faculty for the very indulgence which he and his papa were so earnest in soliciting at the outset. Very hard to please, are some boys and some fathers!

Here I take occasion to state, that the classification of applicants for admission into our college, is left exclusively to the professors. They examine all candidates, and put them into such classes as they think proper. Each of them is sovereign in his own department, and exercises the *veto* power at discretion. He may prevent the advancement of a student into a higher class, or exclude him at last from the privilege of graduation, by declaring him deficient in the studies of his own particular professorship. Thus the whole affair of scholarship and academic rank is committed to the sound judgment and wisdom of those who are constantly engaged in the business of teaching.

Again, most of the studies pursued at college require maturity of intellect and judgment, as well as large stores of elementary knowledge. For example: Of what use are lectures upon standard English classics, involving all the principles and properties of style and sentiment and taste and criticism, to persons who have never read a page of one of them?—Or upon history, political economy, ethics, logic, jurisprudence, international or constitutional law, philology, metaphysics?—Or upon any grand division of philosophy or of elegant literature? The fact is, college prelections and discipline are designed for well educated youths, on the verge of manhood. And these only can adequately profit by them.

"Smart boys" are apt to be discouraged when they cannot keep up or advance equally with their class-mates: and they frequently relinquish the attempt in despair. They would rather be expelled than be turned back, or *degraded*, as they unwisely term and esteem it. Hence, they are ready for fun and riot and mischief and all sorts of "renowning," which the *genius loci* may suggest, countenance, or abet. Here, especially, they are prone to display their *Spartan* craft and prowess in dissecting and analyzing, according to the newest imported fashion, with jack-knife or hatchet, sometimes with broad-axe and sledgehammer, the architectural beauties of our magnificent and unparalleled temple of science and the muses! —Upon yonder "hill side, so smooth, so green, so full of goodly prospects, and melodious sounds!!!"—*

[Milton was a capital schoolmaster.]

To be sure, in all this matter, parents judge erroneously and act injudiciously. Instead of approving and sustaining the college authorities in directing the

* A mere trifle, compared with the feats of Vandalism often perpetrated in Eastern colleges. Our Western *green-horns* have much to learn before they can approximate the sublime daring of the brotherhood in some of the old States. *Here* no college buildings have ever been burnt or blown up: here no professors have ever been killed, or wounded, or assaulted, or threatened, or insulted—by students.

studies of their sons, they complain whenever their own favourite views and plans are not successfully carried out.—That is, whenever their sons do not accomplish impossibilities.

Thus again, when a college censure or penalty is inflicted upon a student—no matter how notoriously idle, disorderly or licentious he may have been—his parents and relatives are sure to be offended, perhaps irritated, or greatly exasperated. They become his advocates, apologists, defenders. They criminate, abuse, denounce the poor Faculty, without stint or measure. The son is a high-minded, honourable, brave, generous, good-hearted young gentleman; who scorns all subterfuge and meanness; and who would not *lie* for the universe! Not he. In this particular at least, he is above suspicion; and, like the Pope, infallible. While the Faculty are a parcel of paltry pedants, pedagogues, bigots, charlatans—without feeling, spirit, kindness, honesty, or common sense. I am so accustomed to this result, that I never look for or anticipate a different. I never expect any official statement of ours to weigh a feather against that of the darling boy.—We are all blind to our own faults and to those of our children; while the eyes of the whole world around us are wide open to both. While, therefore, one parent complains loudly of injustice, in cases of college discipline, a dozen of his neighbours are ready, from their own knowledge and observation, to pronounce the complaint, in that particular instance at least, unreasonable and groundless.

No gentleman, or gentleman's son, will lie. Of course,

not. I therefore never question the veracity of a student under any circumstances whatever. Nor do I ever insinuate the charge of mendacity or falsehood under any ambiguous guise or less offensive phrase. I never imply an accusation by word or look, or cherish unkindly suspicions. I assume that every person is truthful, honest and just, until he is proved to be otherwise: and I treat him accordingly. I hold up truth everywhere as too sacred to be tampered with; and that a man should die at the stake, rather than forfeit his word or trifle with his conscience.

In this connection—and to account for certain rather startling *esoteric* phenomena in college life—I take leave to specify one remarkably liberal and convenient feature of the ethical code, which obtains throughout the venerable institutions of the far East, namely, that, "to lie to the Faculty, is no lie at all." The STUDENT-CRAFT indeed, in all ages and countries, rise above vulgar prejudices, and give a loose rein to adventurous genius. They make it a point of honour to protect one another at every *verbal* hazard or sacrifice, in all their wild feats of mischief and jollification. They will not lie; assuredly not; they do not call it lying; they merely invent marvellous fictions like Homer, or tell merry tales like Shakspeare; just to mystify credulous tutors, or to tranquillize the minds and lighten the purses of the good old folks at home. They were off at a Fancy Ball, perhaps, some twenty miles distant. The learned professor is made to believe that they were at their places in the recitation room all the while—but that he was so absorbed by his subject or spell-bound by the magic of his own glowing eloquence, that he did not see them! In short, their object would seem to be: 1. To do as they please, and to play off as many tricks as possible upon all sorts of officials. And, 2. To come off with flying colours at last—and with Latin diplomas which they cannot construe; and which testify to as many untruths as currently grace an ordinary newspaper editorial. Whether this oriental improvement in morals has found its way into our *backwoods'* apologies for Yankee universities, I leave the curious to inquire.

College students, you see, reason and act like all other well assorted bodies or fraternities of great and wise men. Like politicians, who never dream of lying, when they utter falsehoods, that is, tell tough stories, about their political opponents or in their own behalf. Because, with them, "all is fair in politics." Or like the clerical leaders of religious sects, who, believing themselves always in the right and all others in the wrong, never hesitate to declare and publish whatever may be likely to advance their own cause or to damage their adversaries. Because, in their creed, "the end justifies the means." These honourable and reverend gentlemen have adopted the principle of the aforesaid college code, namely, that to lie to or about certain other antagonist parties, is no lie at all. Thus the college, at last, is about at par with the rest of the world. Not worse even in this respect—but rather better.

Perhaps it would not be prudent to make any further revelations in regard to university mysteries, or I might add, that I have known some dashing lads, at our time-honoured colleges, who, on the joyous day of commencing Bachelors of Arts, were as innocent of Greek, Mathematics, Chemistry, and all the *onomies* and *ologies* as any of your graduated city belles—and not half their equals in English syntax and orthography—who have nevertheless astonished the natives by their subsequent performances.* Upon the *stump*, in the legislative hall, at the bar, in the metropolitan pulpit, at the camp-meeting, they have fairly distanced competition, and borne off the palm from the whole bookish tribe of rival aspirants. These, to be sure, are rather strange abnormal cases; and, according to the orthodox philosophy of cause and effect, ought never to have occurred. Now whether this brilliant success be ascribable to genius, to good fortune, to post-collegiate development and diligence, or to the extreme facility with which the people yield up head and heart to the charm of musical delivery, ready utterance, rhetorical flourish, bold assertion, dogmatical assurance, indomitable self-possession, commanding presence, or brazen impudence—is still a mooted point among transcendental casuists; and must be left, like the authorship of Junius or the quadrature of the circle or the

* Such perplexing, inopportune, eccentric phenomena, though vastly encouraging to American go-ahead intrepidity, have proved the very *cruces criticorum* to the plodding *genus* pedagogue, and overcast with desponding gloom the anxious visage of many a laborious candidate for the dearly-bought and well-earned honours of a legitimate ambition.—Whose place, at last, will be found, it is feared in the galaxy of some popular heroic Dunciad.

political faith of presidential candidates, to the decision of posterity.

Whether any such prodigies have arisen in our own Great West; or whether any species or specimen of eloquence, inferior to that of Demosthenes or Tully, would be tolerated by our enlightened, poetical, chivalrous population; may be answered by those who best know, or who claim the right of pronouncing judgment in the premises.

The morality of a college is always regulated by that of the community in which it exists. It can seldom be elevated above the prevailing standard: it will rarely fall below it. Boys cannot be persuaded that anything is wrong, much less criminal or disreputable, which they daily witness at home and in the families with which their honoured parents associate. This is so obvious a truism, that I might well pass it in silence, were it not so generally overlooked by our dreamy "perfectionists" in the theory of education. They expect that idle, vicious, disobedient, reckless, profligate boys, who cannot be controlled by father or schoolmaster, will be forthwith reclaimed, thoroughly reformed, and converted into diligent, dutiful, ingenuous, exemplary, accomplished college students. Parents are often most urgent to guard their sons, while at college, against the very practices and indulgences which were never prohibited or rebuked under their own roof.* Students at college will always

* A lady once requested me to cure her son (as she expressed it) of the bad habit of profane swearing. At the same time, adding, that his father was unfortunately addicted to the same practice at home among his children.

exhibit or reflect the moral and religious character of their domestic training. The code and conduct approved at home, will be approved and exemplified in college. I do not mean to affirm that parents are always culpable or responsible for the faults or crimes of their children. I judge no man or set of men. But this is certain: that parents need never look to a college for any miraculous moral regeneration or transformation of character.

Parents are not always sagacious in their selection of schools. They seem not to be aware, that a man who does not govern and bring up his own children judiciously, is not competent to exert a salutary moral influence over those of other people. Whenever the sons of a teacher are ill-bred, ill-mannered, disorderly, riotous, profane, intemperate, lazy, vulgar, quarrelsome, unprincipled—you have standing palpable evidence before your eyes of his utter incapacity. His discipline is either nugatory or vicious.

I repudiate the doctrine that popularity is the only proof, or any proof, of sterling merit. Or that a college is to be estimated by the number of its students. A large number is not desirable under any circumstances:* and these should be duly qualified in all respects. I wish none to apply for admission into our college except such as are desirous to learn—who know how to study—who have acquired correct moral principles and habits—who are capable of taking care of themselves, without the constant oversight of tutor or superior—who are cor-

* Such was the opinion of Milton. See his Tractate on Education.

dially disposed to comply with the rules of the institution—and who will cheerfully study with any class or division of a class, which the Faculty may designate as best suited to their actual attainments, and most conducive to their future progress.

Of the little company already educated at our institution, the discriminating public can fairly judge for themselves: and by their verdict we cheerfully abide.* They have been, or may now be seen in both houses of Congress, in several of the State legislatures, in the presidential cabinet, at foreign courts, in many other important official stations, in the editorial chair, in all the liberal professions, in the various respectable walks and vocations of private life, in many of our best schools and colleges as educators—and upon every battle-field from the lagoons of Florida to the shores of the Pacific.† And when or where has one of them failed in duty or been recreant to his trust? Our university furnished more officers and men to the army, during the late Mexican war, than any other literary institution in the land. Has a coward, think you, ever issued from her portals, crowned with her laurel, or honoured with her credentials? Who, among them, has disgraced the proud banner of his country? or shunned the post of

* The number of regular graduates is 398. About 1500 have pursued their studies at the University for longer or shorter periods, without graduation.

† Not a few of them served as volunteers in the Florida campaign of 1836,—and a much larger number in the late war.

danger? or refused to lead the forlorn hope, or to die in the arms of victory?

Thus it was during the revolutionary struggle: thus it has been ever since. The college has proved, at all times and in all countries, the genial nursery of patriotism and chivalry.

When this college was revived and reorganized at the close of 1824, there were no similar institutions, in actual operation, within two hundred miles of Nashville. There were none in Alabama, Mississippi, Louisiana, Arkansas, Texas, Middle or West Tennessee—and none in Kentucky, nearer than Lexington. There are now some thirty or more within that distance [of 200 miles;] and *nine* within fifty miles of our city.* These all claim to be our superiors; and to be equal at least to old Harvard and Yale. Of course, we cannot expect much "custom," or to command a large range, of what is miscalled, patronage. With so many formidable rivals and opponents at our very doors—eager to welcome pupils of all ages, and of every and no degree of literary qualification—with capacious preparatory departments for A, B, C—*darians* and Hic, Hæc, Hoc-*ers*—promising to work cheap; and to *finish off* and graduate, in double quick time, and in the most approved style, all who may come

* I have a list, now before me, of twenty-five colleges or universities in Tennessee alone.—Several of these belong exclusively to individuals; and are bought and sold in open market, like any other species of private property. They are invested with the usual corporate powers, and may confer all university degrees at pleasure. This is probably a *new* thing under the sun: but Solomon's geography did not extend to America.

to them—it is wonderful that the regular classes of our humble "concern" should be maintained in a state of even *quasi* vitality. Or that a frugal, sagacious, dollar-loving public should condescend to remember us at all.

Besides, the several religious denominations have colleges of their own. And it is right, natural and proper, that they should sustain them. As we belong to no sect or party, we have no sect or party to stand by and befriend us; to praise, puff, glorify, and fight for us. This is, perhaps, the worst possible position. To be neutral—of no side, of no party, of no creed—why neither politician nor pedagogue, church or school, would be regarded or trusted by any class. The *juste milieu* is a paradox—an anomaly—not to be tolerated in this fair land of religious freedom and equal rights.

Nearly all the preachers, teachers, editors, demagogues, and other friends of the people, are hostile to us and to Nashville. They give us a bad name. Our goodly city they represent as a very dangerous place for youth.* And even some of our own grave citizens, occasionally, admit the charge and confirm the imputation. I offer no defence or apology, and make no complaint. Let time do its appropriate office: and the millennium will arrive at last—in spite of colleges and croakers.

---

* Should a stray copy of this very learned and grave discourse happen to fall into the hands of a distant reader, it may be proper to remind him, upon the highest authority, that: "The citizens of Nashville are distinguished for intelligence, refinement, courtesy, hospitality, morality and religion." Young men of good habits may live here as cheaply and safely as in any town in the Union. Young men of bad habits cannot live safely or cheaply anywhere.

> "Per varios casus, per tot discrimina rerum,
> Tendimus in Latium."—

We should despair, indeed, but for one cheering consideration. We have, or ought to have, and eventually must have, all the ladies on our side. Their interest, their wisdom and their affections will enlist them in our cause. How can they help it? Do not they see that the much envied, and therefore calumniated, University furnishes the best husbands in the world? Here I may safely rest.—*Causa dicta est.* The ladies govern. And all good young men will come hither to learn how to win them.

The University has received, from the highest source, one gracious complimentary notice, which I cannot forbear, in this rather auspicious connection, just to glance at; and which I am pleased to recognize as appropriate and well-merited. In substance, it is this: Our graduates generally, on leaving college, appear to wear their academic honors meekly. They assume no haughty or silly airs of superiority.—Betray no arrogance, pride or vanity.—Affect nothing of the "Odi profanum vulgus, et arceo," which is so often and so offensively characteristic of the cloistered pedant, and of the *lions* of the village school and country college. They seem to think their education only just begun—not completed. Whatever may have been their previous views or habits, they are evidently anxious now to learn—to improve—to acquire more and larger stores of knowledge. They are desirous to attend the most distinguished colleges and professional seminaries; or to sit at the feet of any eminent Gamaliel who can instruct or counsel them. They do not think more highly of themselves than they ought to think.

To bring youth to this point—to this modest correct self-appreciation—is a great achievement; and worth more than any abstract amount whatever of mere linguistic or philosophical lore. This is the crowning glory of a university education. Indeed, this is its very essence—its refining, elevating, life-giving spirit. Now it is worthy of remark, that this happy result, this invaluable consummation, is often secured or attained amidst the contact and collision of mind with mind of the youth among themselves, in their common pursuits, discussions, debates, and other trials of intellectual strength—and under the gentle *mesmeric* influence of the daily lectures of sensible and respected professors—by many who master but little of the "hard studies" of the prescribed curriculum.

But with this priceless acquisition—this enlightened feeling, if I may so express it—this deep conviction that they must labour all the more for time and opportunities wasted or neglected—they go forth, true men, to do or die. They often reach the highest honours: and they always attract esteem as high-minded and right-minded gentlemen.

In fact, I think that this is, chiefly and pre-eminently, what is meant by a LIBERAL EDUCATION.

[The concluding monitory and religious portion of the discourse, designed more especially for the graduating class, is omitted.]

NAME OF OUR REPUBLIC.

NAME OF OUR REPUBLIC.

"UNITED STATES OF AMERICA."—"AMERICANS."—SHALL WE ADOPT A NEW NAME?

[BEING PART OF AN ADDRESS DELIVERED IN NASHVILLE ON COMMENCEMENT DAY, OCTOBER 3, 1849.]

AT successive periods, since the achievement of our national independence, various propositions have been made to change the name of our Republic, on the ground, first, that we have no right to our present appellation; and, second, that it is neither distinctive nor appropriate. Individuals of high character [as Noah Webster, Washington Irving, etc.] and respectable literary associations [as the New York Historical Society—See Report of Committee, March 31, 1845,] have argued the case with all commendable zeal and ability in favour of a change; and they have gravely recommended other names as more pertinent and expressive, as well as less anomalous, ostentatious, and exclusive. I shall not repeat the arguments or reasons, *poetical* or *political*, specious and imposing though they be, which have been thus ingeniously advanced. I take a different view of the subject.

I maintain that we have the best possible *right* to the style and name of "United States of America" and

"Americans;" and that no others could be substituted equally legitimate, significant or proper.

We assumed the name when there was not a single independent State or nation of European origin upon the whole western continent. A name theretofore unknown and unappropriated. A name to which no other people on the globe could then prefer a shadow of claim.

This name has been recognized by all nations without question or hesitation.

It has been used in all our public acts, documents, constitutions and treaties—from its consecration in the Declaration of Independence to this good day.

Our citizens have always, and everywhere, been called Americans by friend and foe. They have never been known by any other name. It was spontaneously conferred or rather adopted by all Europe, at the very outset of our national existence. Even our kind-hearted mother England did not hesitate, though in scornful derision, to denounce us as American rebels, or rebel Americans—at all events, as Americans. And the treaty of Paris finally settled the question, even in her mind, never again to be mooted or debated.

The mere fact that other independent States have since been established upon this continent, neither deprives us of our right to our own original name, nor furnishes to any of them, either ground of complaint, or the slightest title to the same appellation.

Mexico, Peru, Bolivia, Brazil, Chili, Colombia, and the rest, must be content with such names as they have acquired or may choose hereafter to adopt. They, too, all concur in styling *us* Americans. If any of these had been constituted simultaneously with our own government, there might have been reason for an amicable convention upon the subject, had a difficulty of the kind arisen.

Ours, then, is *the* American Republic—The United States of America—and we are Americans. A name sufficiently euphonious, specific, definite, comprehensive—and fairly won. Who would exchange it for Freedonia or Alleghania or Apalachia, or any other hitherto suggested or hereafter to be invented? Is it not pleasant to the eye, grateful to the ear, dear to the heart, and precious to the faith, of every honest Whig and Democrat amongst us?—nay of every hopeful friend of freedom and humanity throughout the world?

Ought we not to rejoice in it? resolve to preserve it unsullied? strive to elevate its true dignity? enlarge its influence? increase its brilliancy?—until it shall acquire a moral power and grandeur more effective, and a lustre more resplendent, than any other which has ever graced the page of history or inspired the muse of poetic genius?

Washington, in his Farewell Address, speaks thus: "The name of *American*, which belongs to you in your national capacity, must always exalt the just pride of patriotism, more than any appellation derived from local discriminations. With slight shades of difference, you have the same religion, manners, habits, and political principles:—you have in a common cause fought and triumphed together: the independence and liberty you possess, are the work of joint counsels, and joint efforts, of common dangers, sufferings, and successes."

Our goodly name, it is true, has not been uniformly and universally treated with as much respect as we are prone to arrogate as its just due. We are rather sensitive, fastidious and irritable under the lash of criticism and rebuke. Yet gross slander, unmitigated abuse, deliberate misrepresentations—circulated not merely in the daily metropolitan gazettes by mercenary jobbers, but stereotyped in the sumptuous octavoes of the national classic historian,* would seem to afford matter of grave indignation, if not of charitable retaliation. Forbearance may cease to be a virtue. But time heals disputes as well as diseases—works miracles and exorcises evil spirits and wicked demons. A brighter day is dawning. For although *American* has been, for more than half a century, a term of reproach and derision in certain quarters, yet even *there* a revolution appears to be in progress and not unlikely to succeed. At least, present symptoms are promising. Even the *ultra* tory British press, though rather ungraciously, and as if by constraint, abates much of its accustomed rancour and virulence when discoursing about our strange country; and, now and then, puts forth an utterance which almost savours of laudation. These faint indications of returning rationality and justice, bespeak more of envy, jealousy or fear, perhaps, than of frank generous good-will and hearty encourage-

* See Alison, vol. i. p. 153.

ment. Still, the bare semblance of righteousness is somewhat more grateful than indifference or contempt. They cannot any longer even affect to despise us. That day has gone by—we are no longer a mere mass of vulgarity and pretension—the refuse of European outcasts and outlaws—the grovelling worshippers of Mammon—an illiterate unwashed herd of democratic dolts and blustering demagogues—of semi-savage, barbarous, cowardly, swaggering, insolent, braggadocios—of beastly inebriates, duellists, cutthroats, lynchers, gamblers, knaves, fools, manstealers, scoffers, atheists—and whatever else of choice epithet their own classic Billingsgate might supply at command. Verily, we are at length *somebody*—a positive quantity—a real substantive entity—and no mistake! We are now recognized as a great nation, a gigantic empire, a commanding and most potent republic—fearless, intrepid, invincible—where difficulties exist only to be overcome—and in whose vocabulary the word *impossible* never occurs.

Truly, this is a marvellous and very opportune discovery!

We have survived all manner of trials and disasters—have passed through many perilous scenes of domestic strife and bitterness and exasperation—have triumphed over nullification and bankruptcy and repudiation—have been to school, and learned how to make a book or two for Edinburgh Reviewers to *read* and perchance to patronize, and a few others for English Barristers and Benchers to study, and to cite as authorities in the highest courts of the kingdom—have achieved a trifle in sculpture and painting, as well as in practical mechanics and scientific researches—have extended the steamer, the canal, the railway, the electro-magnetic telegraph, all over the land and the waters—have supported religion, the church and the clergy, by the voluntary action of the people—have cherished the common school as an indispensable element of republican health, vigour and prosperity—have shipped millions of cotton to Europe, which ought to have been manufactured at home—have welcomed to our shores and broad lands hundreds of thousands who could find neither food nor shelter in the old world—have cheered the hearts and saved the lives of Ireland's famished and perishing hosts, by our gratuitous and bountiful supplies, during the most critical and expensive period of hostilities with a border republic—have governed ourselves to the entire contentment of the Whigs and the Democrats, as either happened to be in the ascendant, without standing armies or onerous taxation, and without dread of insurrections, tumults, treasons or rebellions—have never hanged a man for political crimes, nor abridged the rights of conscience, or the freedom of speech, or the press—have occasionally, too, exhibited a martial spirit and prowess, which few among the great potentates of the earth would care to challenge or provoke—and we shall outlive all present impending signs and tokens of calamity and disunion, from provisoes and compromises, wise or foolish, from *pro* slavery ultraism or abolition fanaticism, and from all sorts of political agitation, insanity, ambition, or empiricism. "Our Union, it must be preserved!" *It shall be preserved*—is the loud, determined, fervent response of the universal American heart. The very name is a bond of union—and we will never yield or forfeit the one or the other.

Here I must stop at the threshold of a tempting and prolific theme—opening largely to self-gratulation for the past and of glorious promise for the future.

We have been accused of ambition—of egregious territorial enlargement propensities—because we have annexed to our Union other States by fair purchase or by the free consent and desire of their inhabitants—or because we whipped the Mexicans with infinite odds against us; and then paid them for a portion of their savage useless deserts [the gold regions were not then dreamt of,] a larger sum than they would probably have demanded for the same, with Texas included, prior to the conquest. This was at least magnanimous on our part—if not customary, wise or politic. And yet we have never held a single province, however acquired, as a mere tributary dependency; to be governed and oppressed at pleasure by avaricious viceroys or licentious pro-consuls. Every addition becomes, in due time, and by a single constitutional provision, an integral part of the Republic—a new State, with the same privileges, laws and immunities as the immortal old thirteen. Such has been the good fortune of Louisiana, Florida and Texas.—And such will be the speedy lot of California, Oregon and the rest of the conquered and purchased territory, wherever situated or however circumstanced. Now, who is benefited by this American system of annexation? Not the general government at Washington

—not Massachusetts, nor Ohio, nor Georgia, nor any individual State—but simply and exclusively, the citizen, native and immigrant, of the annexed provinces. I do not suppose that Tennessee derives any direct pecuniary profit or advantage from Texas—but the good people of Texas are immense gainers by the transfer—as any able economist may calculate, who will apply his arithmetic to the task. That such additions of free-trading communities greatly enlarge the sphere of commercial enterprise, of friendly intercourse, and of successful speculation, will not be questioned. But these are benefits common to all our citizens of every State. Hence all controversy about a division of the spoils of a conquered people, between different sections of the Union, is frivolous and nugatory. There are no spoils or plunder to be distributed. Not a Mexican has been robbed or deprived of his property. And no American can get a dollar's worth of it, or a foot of land, without paying for it.

History does not furnish, according to my poor reading, many illustrations of a similar spirit or conduct. Neither ancient Rome, nor modern Britain or France or Russia ever conquered in this fashion. The civilized, intellectual, refined, benevolent, chivalrous, Christian England, queen of the seas, and the avowed champion of universal negro emancipation, holds, at this moment, in absolute serfdom or colonial subjection, more territory in Asia, Africa, Australia, America, and the Islands of the Ocean, than would equal in extent a dozen of our moderate and modest republics.

In this sense, and in the European style, we have not

been, and never can become, without a radical change in the genius of our people and institutions, a conquering or ambitious nation. We are ready enough to fight in a just cause, and when the crisis arrives, we shall repel the invader—come whence he may. We will submit to neither injury nor insult. But we have no disposition to become aggressive—to create a war merely for the sake of conquest. Such is not our vocation. Should our neighbours, however, either at the North or South-west, think proper to attack us, we shall beat them of course — subdue them — and, if we please, annex their country to the Union. What then? We shall merely create a convenient number of sovereign independent States like our own, and make all their people fellow citizens and orthodox republicans. Such is the expansive character of our confederated democracy, that it admits of indefinite extension—while it leaves all domestic, local, municipal jurisdiction and control in the hands of the people at home. I take it for granted, that our Republic will, in reasonable time, embrace the whole of North America. I think the inhabitants of the adjacent countries will ask for annexation. It will come peaceably and as a matter of course—if we 'bide our time.

Here again I forbear. We have grown up into a Republic,—such as the world had never witnessed before. I do not mean in magnitude or power, but in *kind*. It stands in no historical category. Its model or similitude can be traced in no human record nor in any locality upon the globe. Our ancestors were a peculiar people—were nurtured and trained under peculiar circumstances—and were eventually fitted to enact a peculiar part—to construct a peculiar system of self-government, exactly adapted to their then extraordinary position, and to their subsequent growth and development—however rapid, or however stupendous. Let us cherish a grateful filial reverence towards our noble ancestors—whether Puritan, Quaker, Catholic or Cavalier. They were all men—good and true. The fatherland could have furnished no better. They were always freemen. They came hither to live and die freemen. They were often annoyed, harassed, worried, vexed, during a long colonial novitiate, by an unwise, illiberal, jealous administration at home.—But they never surrendered a single attribute of the freeborn Englishman. They endured much, remonstrated with dignity, and resisted manfully every attempted encroachment. The trial at arms came at length. The first effort to coerce obedience to unconstitutional demands, was met, as none but the free and the brave can meet the mercenary veteran legions of imperious despotism.

The story of our singular colonial apprenticeship—of the revolutionary war, [which was conservative not destructive, undertaken to assert, maintain and perpetuate our inalienable English rights, not to try novel experiments or to demolish existing establishments,]—of the causes and embarrassments which led to the adoption of the Federal Constitution—of the origin, conduct and consequences of the war of 1812—and of various extraordinary political and other phenomena down to the present day—is, in some respects, familiar to everybody;

though few, perhaps, are conversant either with the undisguised facts, or with the real motives, good and bad, of the prominent actors. No master pen or pencil has yet portrayed—pictured to the eye—engraven upon the heart—the heroic and classic age of our American history—the age of Washington. But the main facts and results are patent to the whole world.

We are now universally known and honoured as Americans. Honoured as are none besides. From Archangel to the Cape of Good Hope—from Dublin to Canton—no national epithet will pass as currently or command as high respect, as that of American. Abroad, our citizens are all Americans:—not Tennesseans or Carolinians or Vermonters—not Whigs or Democrats or Federalists. They are proud of their country, of their name, of their government, of their sages, heroes and statesmen.

All local, political or other domestic party distinctions are lost, forgotten, disregarded—merged or absorbed—in the one august name which reaches over and includes the entire Republic.—One and indivisible forever!

We have a name gloriously illustrated and illustrious. Our sacred duty is to maintain it untarnished. Every educated youth especially, is a depositary and champion of his country's good name. By his conduct and bearing, at home and abroad, in private and in public, he can do much to deepen, enlarge, exalt, and perpetuate the favourable prepossession with which the *American* citizen is everywhere received and welcomed.

Let every American, who travels or sojourns in a

foreign land, remember that he is, for the time, upon his good behaviour, as the accredited official guardian of his country's honour. As an American citizen, he has no superior in rank or title. He is by birth, and may be by his intelligence and deportment, the peer of transatlantic nobility and royalty.

To be a *Roman citizen*, was once a distinction, coveted by the proudest natives of every province and kingdom conquered or protected by the Roman arms. It was not only a passport, honorary and credential, the wide world over, but a talisman of defence and security against all arbitrary provincial tyrants, great and small, even under the most corrupt and despotic forms of consular and imperial fanaticism.

"Civis Romanus sum,"—"I am a Roman citizen,"—was the eloquent and effective plea, which caused the unrighteous judge to tremble, which opened prison doors, which arrested the executioner's arm, and which procured for the doomed and otherwise helpless victim, a fair hearing and impartial trial, according to the laws of Rome, and before her most august tribunals.

"I am an American citizen,"—shall, may we not hope, prove not less potent or availing, when uttered by the humblest of our countrymen, in the wildest and remotest regions of the globe?

But there is yet a name, which, when adequately appreciated, rises, in its vast comprehension of the present and the future, infinitely above all Roman, all Greek, all American, lustre, fame, and grandeur. That name is Christian. He who possesses all that the name implies, is a citizen of the Almighty's universal and everlasting empire. He is advanced forever above and beyond the reach of pain, disaster, sorrow and death. Ingratitude, detraction, slander, falsehood, envy, jealousy, ambition, revenge, malignity, persecution, and the ten thousand other evil passions and devices of wicked men, may assail him, or even adorn his brow with the crown of martyrdom,—but still he is safe—for he is a citizen of Heaven! Who would not be a Christian? as well as an American? Why should not the two be inseparably united? Why should not *American Christian* become the characteristic distinctive appellation of our people? so that we might justly be esteemed as the noblest, holiest, happiest, freest, most disinterested and charitable portion of the human family? Then would the philanthropist, the patriot, the republican, the Christian, be all combined and blended in the one great name, American. And he would be joyfully hailed as the missionary of liberty and light, of religion and peace, of mercy and salvation, to an oppressed, benighted, and perishing world.

LIFE AND CHARACTER

OF

PROFESSOR GERARD TROOST.

THE LIFE AND CHARACTER

OF

PROF. GERARD TROOST, M.D.

A DISCOURSE DELIVERED IN NASHVILLE ON COMMENCEMENT DAY, OCTOBER 2, 1850.

OUR University has sustained numerous painful bereavements within the last quarter of a century. Between seventy and eighty of her ingenuous and gifted Alumni have thus early been numbered with the dead. We have wept over their apparently premature departure, and deeply sympathized with the sorrows of surviving relatives and friends. Could we spread open before you our brief college catalogue, and glance at the names to which is prefixed the usual token of mortality, we should revive reminiscences and associations most thrilling to the heart of the speaker, and not less so to that of many a hearer. We could tell of genius, talent and industry—of rich and varied attainments—of rare intellect, ripe scholarship, pure morals and gentle manners—of modest worth, generous ambition and noble philanthropy—in a word, of the thousand juvenile indications of future eminence and usefulness; all to be suddenly crushed and withered in the very buddings of anticipation;—but we may not linger upon this melancholy, though grateful theme. The memory of their virtues and high promise is engraven upon the hearts of those who knew and loved them best.

But, our fathers: where are they? The honourable and respected Board of Trustees have been visited, too, by the inexorable king of terrors. Alas, how many endeared and distinguished names have been stricken from the roll, and their remains consigned to the silent tomb! Nineteen regular members of the Board—besides three Governors, CANNON, CARROLL and POLK, who were members *ex-officio*—have deceased during the period of my connection with the University, [26 years.] Of those who were members on my first arrival at Nashville, only seven continue to hold that relation at the present time. Thus speedily have passed away from this mortal scene, the good, the great, the wise, the brave—the soldier, the statesman, the jurist, the physician, the divine, the diplomatist, the Governor, the President—men of power and renown—destined, some of them, to live in the hearts of their countrymen, and to illustrate the page of the world's history throughout all future generations.* I may add, that every member of the first or original Board, whose names are recorded in the charter of 1806, has deceased.

Of the Faculty, seven Professors and three Tutors, my colleagues and associates, at different periods, have been removed by death.—Only three of them, however, while in the actual service of the University; namely, Pro-

* Among the number were two Presidents of the United States, ANDREW JACKSON and JAMES K. POLK.

fessors Bowen, Hamilton and Troost. The first (Prof. Bowen,) died, after two and a half years' labour among us, and after giving ample evidence of superior qualifications for the chair of Chemistry—esteemed and lamented by his acquaintance and by the votaries of science throughout the land. He had been a favourite pupil of Professors Silliman and Hare, at New Haven and Philadelphia. Probably, no young man of that day had in prospect a more brilliant career in the judgment of the most accomplished of his scientific contemporaries.*

Professor Hamilton was better known. He was with us many years; and so recently, that few of our citizens could have been strangers to his person or to his worth. A more exemplary, conscientious, modest, consistent, unobtrusive Christian gentleman has rarely been met with anywhere: and a more faithful, patient, judicious, persevering and successful teacher could not be desired in any school or college. A thorough enthusiast in his professional studies and pursuits, it was his chief delight to acquire knowledge, and to impart it to his pupils. Amiable, gentle, respectful—never abrupt, harsh or repulsive—always accessible and cheerfully communicative—meek, humble, sincere—abounding in works of charity and goodness—he calmly fell asleep, in the full assurance of a happy resurrection and a glorious immor-

---

* George T. Bowen was born March 19, 1803, at Providence in Rhode Island; and was graduated at Yale College in 1822. He was here elected Professor of Chemistry in the autumn of 1825. He entered upon the duties of his office March 6, 1826. He died October 25, 1828, in the 26th year of his age.

tality, through faith in the merits and atoning sacrifice of the Son of God, in whose name he had been baptized in infancy, and to whose service his life had been devoutly consecrated.*

But a still more recent and most afflictive bereavement must be the subject of our present discourse and sorrowful meditations. A few weeks ago, the University and the citizens of Nashville were summoned to pay the last sad tribute of respect to the remains of the venerable Professor Troost. No similar event has, probably, ever created a greater sensation in this community, or called forth a more general or generous expression of feeling, sympathy and regret. We all felt and acknowledged that our loss was irreparable; and that we should never look upon his like again.

In speaking here of such a man, I feel both the delicacy of my position, and my inability to meet the demands of the occasion. Could I have foreseen that this melancholy duty would so soon, or even ever, have devolved upon me, I would have eagerly embraced the many opportunities which a daily intercourse afforded, of learning from the lips of my venerated friend, the most remarkable incidents of his somewhat eventful life and varied fortunes. I would have inquired more

---

* James Hamilton was a native of Princeton, N. J., and was graduated at the college there in 1814. He was highly distinguished as a classical and mathematical teacher in Trenton and Burlington, N. J. He was Professor of Mathematics and Natural Philosophy in the University of Nashville sixteen years, at three several periods. He died of cholera, June 21, 1849.

minutely about the course and progress of his studies; the character and number of his publications; and whatever else might contribute to a fair biographical notice or decent obituary. Though for a year past, it was obvious that his physical strength was gradually diminishing under the weight of years and of a painful chronic disease; yet so calm, so cheerful, so uncomplaining, was his habit, that I did not, could not realize that his days were already numbered and his work accomplished. I beheld him speechless and dying before I dreamed of any immediate danger—much less of so sudden a dissolution.

The few facts and circumstances which I have since collected from other sources, may be soon told. The information expected from his brother in Missouri, and which, it was hoped, would be ample and satisfactory, has not yet been received.*

Dr. Gerard Troost was born at Bois-Le-Duc, in Holland, March 15, 1776. He died August 14, 1850, aged 74 years and five months. He was educated in the schools and universities of his native country—chiefly at Leyden and Amsterdam. He appears, at an early period, to have manifested a zealous devotion to Chemistry and Natural History; and more especially to the then infant sciences of Geology and Mineralogy.

In 1801, the College of Amsterdam (Collegium quod Civium Amstelodamensium saluti prospicit,) conferred upon him, after a strict examination, the degree of

* Dr. Benoit Troost, Kansas, Missouri.

"Master in Pharmacy," (in arte Pharmaceutica Magistrum,—as his diploma has it.) * * * "Accuraté cum in Latina lingua, Plantis, cæterisque simplicibus, et varia ex his componendi modo, ut et in Theoria Chemico-Pharmaceutica examinavimus; et quæ ex lege requiruntur ab eo composita Galenica, et Chemica medicamenta confici vidimus. In quibus omnibus cum peritiam suam et dexteritatem sufficienter probasset, quem petebat, in arte Pharmaceutica Magistri titulum lubentes concessimus," etc.—[Copied from his Diploma.]

Thus declaring him duly qualified and authorized to practise as a *pharmacist* [or pharmaceutist.] We must not confound this profession with that of the ordinary druggist or apothecary in our own country.

Pharmacy [or pharmaceutics] is the art of preserving, preparing, compounding, and combining substances for medical purposes. As these substances may be mineral, vegetable or animal, theoretical pharmacy requires a knowledge of botany, zoology and mineralogy; and as it is necessary to determine their properties, and the laws of their composition and decomposition, a thorough mastery of practical or experimental chemistry is equally indispensable. The preparation of medicines was anciently performed by the physicians themselves, who also administered them to their patients. It became a distinct branch of medical science at Alexandria in Egypt, some 300 years before the Christian era. And in most enlightened countries since, it has been regarded as worthy of special governmental regulation and encouragement. Pharmacy too, like its parent or sister art of medicine, has followed the fortunes of science and the general diffusion of knowledge among the people.

The medical reforms of Paracelsus, in the sixteenth century, introduced important changes into pharmacy. Many chemical preparations were adopted; and the use of mineral specifics, as, for example, antimony and mercury, became more common. Still, the operations were conducted without reference to scientific principles: but, since the middle of the seventeenth century, the natural sciences have continued to make steady progress; and pharmacy, as well as medicine, has experienced the effects of the improvement. So that the practice of pharmacy is regarded in several European States, not only as a learned and liberal profession, but as a highly responsible trust or office. The degree, therefore, of Master of Pharmacy, or Doctor in that art, as our colleges would express it, implied no ordinary scientific attainments and moral qualifications. It would be well for this and every other country, were the vocation placed by law and usage upon an equally elevated basis with that of the regular physician.

Dr. Troost, it is understood, practised, as a pharmacist, both at Amsterdam and at the Hague—though for a brief period. As we find him soon after *at home* in Paris; and familiar with its language, and its immense repositories of nature and art. He was, for several years, a pupil and companion of the celebrated Abbé René Just Hawy,—the author of a new system of Crystallography —in fact, the founder of the modern or present school of mineralogy. For this distinguished and most excellent man, he ever cherished a filial, grateful and affectionate respect. He here translated into the Dutch language, one of the earlier works ["The Aspects of Nature,"] of Alexander Humboldt, [a copy of which he has since presented to our college library.] For this service he received the cordial thanks of the author: with whom he maintained a friendly correspondence to the last.

About 1809, he was appointed by the King of Holland one of a scientific *corps* to accompany a naval expedition to Java. The English effectually prevented the sailing of the Dutch fleet: and it became necessary either to relinquish the scientific enterprise or to devise some other mode of conveyance. In order to escape capture by the British during the long sea-voyage, he embarked for New York or Philadelphia in an American vessel, to seek a passage thence to the East Indies under the protection of our then neutral flag. Soon after his arrival here, Louis Napoleon abdicated or resigned the crown of Holland, [July 1, 1810;] and that kingdom was by the imperial decree of July 10, 1810, incorporated with the French empire. Java too, in the following year [1811,] surrendered to the British arms, and ceased to be a part of the Dutch colonial possessions, until the general restoration of 1814.

In these circumstances, Dr. Troost resolved to remain in this country, and to become an American citizen. He first settled in Philadelphia—where he assisted in forming the American Academy of Natural Sciences in 1812; and of which he was several years the President.

Here he was occupied in scientific investigations, or in the direct application of science to practical purposes. Near the close of the late war with England, he engaged with others in the manufacture of alum near Annapolis in Maryland—the first of the kind ever attempted in the United States. In this connection, owing to the failure of the proprietors, he was a great sufferer in a pecuniary point of view.

He then returned to Philadelphia; where he was appointed Professor of Mineralogy in the Philadelphia Museum, 1821. He there delivered public lectures upon that science, and also upon chemistry at the Philadelphia College of Pharmacy. He made sundry geological excursions into New Jersey, New York, and other interesting localities in the vicinity.

He removed, in company with Thomas Say, William Maclure and others, to New Harmony [Indiana,] in 1825, under the auspices of the then reputed philanthropist, Robert Owen. He soon became dissatisfied with Mr. Owen's impracticable novelties and peculiar social arrangements. He thence removed, with his family and mineral treasures, to Nashville in 1827. Here has been his quiet and pleasant home ever since.

He was appointed Professor of Chemistry, Geology and Mineralogy in the University of Nashville in 1828; and State Geologist in December, 1831. The latter appointment was renewed at every biennial session of the Legislature until the last:—when that very economical body abolished or discontinued the office.

1. State Geologist. How largely the State of Tennes-

see is indebted to him for geological surveys and learned reports—towards the discovery and development of her mineral wealth—cannot be conjectured, much less appreciated. And yet, how cheaply gained! How meagre the pittance doled out, by the representatives of the million, to the master mind employed to enrich them all! Several of our sister States have been more liberal, or rather, less unjust, towards their respective Geologists. Though none could boast of a more accomplished, or more faithful labourer, either in the field, or at the desk, or in the laboratory. A few centuries ago, the services of a public benefactor might have been undervalued or ignorantly denounced, without exciting surprise, and without the consciousness even of wrong-doing. A Roger Bacon, a Wickliffe, a Columbus, a Galileo, have conferred [an inglorious] immortality upon nations and ages of stolidity, barbarism, ingratitude and bigotry. But the illuminated NINETEENTH ought not to be equally tolerant of similar abuses.

Were I to indulge the sarcastic vein or give vent to an honest indignation, I might contrast the impudent, domineering, selfish, swaggering, successful career of the brazen-faced and iron-hearted popular demagogue, with the calm, subdued, patient, humble, retiring, modest carriage of the laborious philosophical pioneer, who is working out the great problem of human advancement, and expending the rarest and richest faculties in the gratuitous promotion of the welfare and prosperity of his brother man. I might tell of the sneers and scoffings and ridicule to which he is often subjected—to the neglect, poverty, suffering, privation and even positive persecution which await him—to the cold, heartless, calculating, mis-named economy, which crushes his spirit, and sometimes places upon his honoured head the crown of martyrdom. The Naturalist, even now is almost everywhere regarded, by the vulgar as a dreaming visionary or puerile enthusiast—without common sense or rational ambition. His priceless collections of stones, minerals, fossils, plants, animals, is gravely pronounced a *humbug:* and the office of State Geologist is incontinently voted a sinecure or nuisance.* But I forbear all such invidious comparisons and criminating insinuations.

* Of William Maclure, it is related that: "When travelling in some remote districts, the unlettered inhabitants seeing him engaged in breaking the rocks with his hammer, supposed him to be a lunatic who had escaped from confinement; and on one occasion, as he drew near a public house, the inmates, being informed of his approach, took refuge in doors, and closing the entrance held a parley from the windows, until they were at length convinced that the stranger could be safely admitted."

Incidents of this kind, and many others which occurred to him, appear to have influenced the following remarks in the Preface to his Geology: "All inquiry into the nature and properties of rocks, or the relative situation they occupy on the surface of the earth, has been much neglected. It is only since a few years that it has been thought worth the attention of either the learned or unlearned; and even now a great proportion of both treat such investigations with contempt, as beneath their notice. Why mankind should have so long neglected to acquire knowledge so useful to the progress of civilization—why the substances over which they have been daily stumbling, and without whose aid they could not exercise any one art or profession, should be the last to occupy their attention—is one of those problems perhaps only to be solved by an analysis of the nature and origin of the power of the few over the many." [Memoir of William Maclure, by Samuel George Morton, M.D., pp. 11, 12.]

Our late worthy friend was never friendless; nor was he ever the inmate of a debtor's prison or of the Holy Inquisitors' dungeon. He lived and died, esteemed and honoured and lamented by the wisest and best of his contemporaries.

2. College Professor. As a college professor, he was diligent, exemplary, punctual, and eminently instructive. He was always thoroughly prepared for lecture, experiment, and familiar illustration, at the appointed hour. Master of his theme, and felicitous in his manner of exhibiting the dry details and subtile mysteries of science, he could not fail to interest such of his pupils as were disposed to profit by his teachings. That the number of these should have been so exceedingly small, is matter of profound regret. He, indeed, spared no pains or efforts to awaken a spirit of inquiry and to create a proper enthusiasm in behalf of his favourite studies. The fruits of his labours are yet to be gathered by more fortunate successors. Learned foreigners and other strangers from the far-off East, when visiting the veteran sage and surveying his splendid, rare and costly museum, have expressed astonishment, that he was not daily surrounded by scores and hundreds of eager, attentive, devoted disciples. Here then is proof, if proof were needed, that unquestioned merit of the highest order, does not always and everywhere—not even among the enlightened fathers and chivalrous sons of Tennessee—command the reverence and patronage which might be justly claimed or reasonably anticipated. No college, within the wide range of the Mississippi Valley, I ven-

ture to assert, has ever provided such able and ample means of instruction in the natural and experimental sciences, as the University of Nashville has possessed and cheaply proffered to the public for more than twenty years past. Whatever may have been the defects or faults or vices of the institution in other respects—and for these I am no apologist—still, it has had no superior, no equal, in the grand departments of Chemistry, Mineralogy and Geology. How many youth have been attracted hither solely or chiefly with a view to proficiency in all or any of them? Probably not a dozen, or even the half of that number.* While devout pilgrims from distant lands have come to do homage to the renowned Professor, our own Western youth seem not to have been aware that a prophet was in their midst. By all the actual students of the University since 1828, and especially by the graduates, his memory will be reverently and affectionately cherished. Whatever considerations may have allured them to the University in the first instance, or however indifferent any of them may have been to his instructions, he will ever be gratefully associated with all their reminiscences of college life. He was so good, so kind, so patient, so indulgent, so fatherly—he can never be forgotten or cease to be honoured. However discouraging may have been the aspect of his little auditory, he performed his duty faithfully, generously, and even hopefully, to the last.

3. As a Philosopher. Let us view him, for a mo-

---

* Scarcely any students ever entered for the express purpose of cultivating the above sciences.

ment, as a philosopher; for such he truly was. As a devotee to science—as a successful student and interpreter of nature—as a discriminating, sagacious, indefatigable, cautious searcher after truth—he had few equals. He arrived at no crude or novel conclusions hastily. He did not generalize from doubtful or insufficient facts. He assumed no premises or *data* without proof. Anomalous or extraordinary phenomena did not startle him, or prompt the premature utterance of a new theory, or the claim to a grand discovery. He patiently revised, restudied, re-examined; analyzed and experimented; extended his inquiries and investigations; until he could speak to the public with a satisfied conviction of the certainty and value of his discoveries and deductions.

It would require a thorough and minute acquaintance with his favourite and habitual pursuits—such as I do not pretend to, and such as few possess—in order to specify, or to render intelligible, the character or amount of his attainments, or of his contributions to human knowledge and general philosophy. With the three great kingdoms of nature—animal, vegetable, mineral—he was more or less intimately conversant. He had read, I believe, every authority, book and treatise upon natural science; from those of Aristotle, Theophrastus and Pliny, down to the last elaborate volume of his old friend, the octogenarian Humboldt, and the latest lively *brochure* of his youthful correspondent, Agassiz.

He was, of course, *au fait* in the history of science. Familiar with all the stages and changes of its progress—with the conflicting theories, schools and systems—with the diverse modes of classification and nomenclature adopted and rejected—with all, indeed, that had been achieved in every field or department of natural or empirical philosophy. So that he could not be easily imposed on by any apparent novelty or by any pretended discovery. Not content, however, with learning what others could teach, he was constantly engaged in exploring unknown territory, for the extension and enlargement of human knowledge.

Of his published writings, I cannot furnish even an outline. They consist chiefly of translations, of communications to scientific journals and learned societies, or of occasional pamphlets and geological reports. The result of his latest researches was embodied in a monograph, carefully prepared for the press, and forwarded to the Smithsonian Institution, at Washington, for publication, only a few weeks before his death. It is a treatise upon the rare and hitherto undescribed *encrinites* of Tennessee—with accurate and beautiful drawings, executed by an accomplished artist of our city, from the original specimens in the Doctor's cabinet. This will prove a real acquisition to science; and will add much, it is believed, to the reputation of its author. This was his last labour of love in his chosen field: and in its elaboration, he expended the feeble remnant of his declining age and health. He gradually wasted away, still at his post—for he was at work in his laboratory only forty-eight hours before he ceased to breathe—with a mind unimpaired, though with physical strength scarcely adequate to the slightest exertion. He died almost pen in hand; and, we trust, with glorious visions of the beautiful world which its beneficent Creator had enabled him so long to study and admire, as the product and evidence of infinite wisdom, power and goodness.

He was a member—regular, honorary or corresponding—of most of the Scientific and Philosophical Societies in Europe and America. Numerous testimonials of the high estimation in which he was held by these learned associations and by the whole scientific world, might be readily furnished, were it necessary, or rather, not superfluous, on the present occasion.

As a philosopher, without arrogance, pride or pretension, he pursued the noiseless tenor of his way; free from envy, jealousy or ungenerous rivalry. He knew how to defend truth and to maintain his own opinions, without decending to personal controversy or wounding the *amour propre* of his opponents. He conceded to others the intellectual rights and immunities which he claimed for himself. He did full justice to the merits of his brethren, and rejoiced in their success and prosperity. He was ever ready to counsel, instruct and assist all sincere inquirers; and to mark out for them the road to fame and fortune. His very nature was so guileless and unselfish, that, occasionally perhaps, he was imposed on by the crafty and insidious, who craved his instructions for no very honourable purposes.

For every species of sciolism, quackery, and ignorant assumption or rude presumption, however, he manifested a dignified neglect or silent aversion. In extreme cases, he could administer a becomingly stern rebuke. He had no particular fancy for the schoolmaster or professor who could teach all languages, ancient and modern, together with all the sciences; and write newspaper plagiarisms upon lunar rainbows, and orthodox cosmogonies in accordance with the *dicta* of Moses, De Luc, and Cuvier.* He well understood, and could expose, the entire process of deception resorted to. How easy to make a pompous flourish and display before an assemblage of laughing little schoolgirls or mischievous dozy sophomores, by mouthing off, in sonorous style and with appropriate magisterial solemnity, any amount of foreign gibberish or technical jargon, borrowed from Babel or the lexicon, for that special purpose! How easy too, is it to astonish the natives by a newspaper column of geological *feldspar* and *horneblende,* stolen from Lyell or the Penny Cyclopædia! What a profound *Solomon* does not the writer speedily become in the estimation of his fellow villagers! He is forthwith the very man for State Geologist, or for the presidency of the new college, that is soon to eclipse all others in the Commonwealth! I have lately read, in one of our city papers, a school prospectus, heralded, as usual, by a half dozen editorial commendations, in which a single Yankee promises to teach more languages and sciences than any score of modest Newtons, Porsons, Davys, Bucklands or Brewsters would venture to attempt!

* The audience readily understood the allusion here made to certain advertisements and essays which had recently appeared in some of the Nashville gazettes.

Now our lamented friend could not countenance such egregious charlatanry, nor tolerate any specimen of the genus. He deplored the prevalence of this imposing and insolent superficiality, and argued no good to the cause of genuine science from its increasing popularity. Were a man to advertise himself as duly qualified and prepared to practise all the learned professions or a dozen or two of the mechanical trades, I suppose he would be pitied as a lunatic, or denounced as an impostor or vain braggart. But when he proclaims his competency to teach all that is known or knowable in science and literature, he is, without hesitation, taken by the hand, trusted, patronized and enriched by a credulous public—especially if warranted by the customary prepaid newspaper puff extraordinary—though he may not be master of his own vernacular or of vulgar arithmetic to the Rule of Three! Whether this be a disease or folly peculiar to the West, I have not inquired. The sooner we get rid of it, the better for us and our children. It is humiliating to see how cant, and twaddle, and bluster, and puffing, and effrontery, and ostentatious egotism abound and flourish and succeed amongst us.

It is the easiest thing in the world to get up a popular lecture *about* Geology or Chemistry or Mesmerism or Phrenology or Engineering or Magnetism or Electricity or Architecture, or *about* any other science, art or mystery; and that too, without the slightest acquaintance with the elements or first principles of one of them. This is done everywhere by travelling or occasional lecturers. Hundreds of this class would have triumphantly borne away the palm, by acclamation, from our late unpretending Professor, in the very departments of nature which he loved and cultivated beyond all fair rivalry or competition. He would have stood no chance of victory on trial with flippant, strutting, obtrusive, thievish, *jackdaw* impudence, arrayed in *peacock* finery, and all made up and rigged out for the exhibition, and for the especial divertisement of his most select auditory of fashionable ladies and gentlemen. Not he. He would have been voted a *bore*, or mere *proser*, by those who laud the other to the skies.

In these allusions, comparisons and contrasts, I am not digressing very far from my proper theme. It was in reference to such abuses and absurdities, that Dr. Troost seemed ever to be much excited, or to suffer the calm philosophical temperament of his kindly nature to be ruffled. Upon these, I have often heard him discourse strongly, freely, indignantly. Not because he fancied himself to be slighted or wronged: far from it. It was the injury, the insult, the opprobrium, thus inflicted upon science—sacred science—that roused his spirit and provoked his resentment.

This enormous system of swindling quackery might and ought to be put down by the omnipotent periodical press. Newspaper editors create and destroy at pleasure. They make our rulers, and rule them when made. They manufacture public opinion and individual reputation. They are the only recognized self-appointed guardians of the people's rights and of the people's conscience. They are *ex-officio* judges, critics, censors, of all public officers from the President to the town constable, of all authors from Homer to Carlyle, of all institutions and professions, of all discoveries and inventions, of all projects and enterprises. They are the arbiters of fashion, morals and manners—of taste, art, refinement, and all the proprieties of social life. They puff theatre, church, school or college; according to the dictates of purse or conscience—their conscience being understood to lie at the bottom of their purse. The Saturday night's inimitable "bright, particular star," and the Sunday morning's graceful popular preacher, share alike their disinterested and judicious favours. They are privileged, by common consent, to write about everybody and everything—*de omni scibili, et quibusdam aliis.* And their sentence of approval or reprobation is duly ratified by their grave and independent readers. Their utterances are deemed oracular, and worthy of implicit acceptation. They are *popes* all—and the only living popes whose *bulls* are never dishonoured,—though their *bills* often are! They are infallible in their judgments and edicts—as no Roman Pontiff ever was, is, or will be. That they should dogmatize stoutly, and affirm boldly, and decide promptly, and arrogate largely—is a matter of course. The editorial tripod is the seat of inspiration as well as of honour. And wo to the luckless wight, who shall become obnoxious to the frowns of a tribunal from which there lies no appeal.

I find no fault with this established *constitutional* preeminence and paramount authority or absolute supremacy of the press; or with its upright, impartial, all-knowing, dignified, conservative, accomplished and most liberal conductors. I make no complaint on this score. I concede omniscience and infallibility, however, to no other caste or clique or fraternity amongst us. And I now respectfully bespeak their seasonable and potent interposition to annihilate the claims and pretensions of all rival adventurers. Let the wordy pedant and the brainless pedagogue, the bullying empiric and smattering sciolist, and all others who profess to work miracles or to achieve impossibilities in the divine art of education, be made forthwith to know and to occupy their appropriate rank and sphere. Do this, gentlemen editors, and we will sing *pœans*, loud and long, in your praise and to your honour. And may you live and reign a thousand years! and still find upon your banners *esto perpetua* as bright and cheering as at this present most auspicious deliverance!!*

4. His Cabinets, Library, etc. A word about the Doctor's extensive and diversified cabinets for the illustration of Natural History, might be expected along with our notice of him as a philosopher and instructor. Any enumeration or description, however, would fail to be intelligible or satisfactory. It has often been asked, when, where, how, did he contrive to amass so choice a treasure of rare, curious and costly specimens both of nature and art? Such a collection, indeed, as can hardly be found in a half dozen of our largest cities or oldest universities? For he had accumulated specimens not only of the well-known minerals, rocks and fossils, but

* Scottice for delivery or utterance.

of numbers discovered by himself—of new species of *crinoidea* and other organic remains so abundant throughout the West, together with not a few hitherto undescribed birds, serpents, fishes, and especially the *testaceous mollusks* of our rivers—as well as anatomical and botanical preparations, in various forms, all well adapted to the purposes of the lecturer and teacher—to say nothing of his every-day chemical operations, for which he was amply supplied. His library was large and judiciously selected—abounding not only in the standard works on science in several languages, but also in valuable engravings, prints and lithographs. To account for such extraordinary results, we can only add, that his heart was in the work—that he spared neither labour, nor pains, nor expense, in the search and in the purchase—and that his whole life was steadily and sagaciously devoted to the object.* He commenced, after his arrival in this country, with small means: for like his illustrious masters, Hawy and Cuvier, he had to struggle with the *res angusta domi;* and like them he persevered manfully against all obstacles, from less to more, until in the progress of half a century, his few hundred native specimens had increased to many thousands—gathered from every locality on the globe which science had explored. An hour's careful inspection of his actual possessions, would give to the practised eye a far better idea of their rarity and opulence than any mere verbal description could convey. Many of you have visited his rooms:

* See Appendix.

and you were not less surprised at the variety and multitude of the curiosities which arrested your attention, than charmed with the graceful urbanity of "the old man eloquent," who delighted to tell you all about them. And probably, on taking leave, you were more impressed with the goodness of the latter than with the magnificence of the former.

Let us now contemplate the Doctor's character under other aspects, and in other relations.

1. His private life was a model of the domestic virtues. Though a genuine philosopher, he was no stoic. Though a most laborious student, he was not a recluse. Though devoted to science, and sedulously occupied in its solitary investigations, he was alive to all the endearments of social and domestic life. Cheerful, conversable, joyous, playful, in the little family circle about his own delightful fireside, he was there the centre of attraction, love and reverence. The best of husbands and fathers, his presence at home was always greeted with a welcome of smiles and gladness and affectionate attentions, which no mere conventional usage or prescriptive custom could have elicited. His grandchildren loved him, not merely as a parent, but as a friend and companion. He possessed true, simple, native dignity, without a particle of affectation or mock assumption. He never appeared to condescend, or to exhibit a patronizing air and manner, when conversing with inferiors in knowledge, age, or relative social position. He was so affable, so benevolent, so approachable, so good, that everybody was at ease and happy in his presence.

He was a man of the world—a perfectly well-bred gentlemen. He had travelled and seen much in various countries; and had been early and long familiar with the tone and atmosphere and *bienséances* of fashionable and intelligent society. He had none of the stiffness, formality, awkward diffidence, offensive pedantry, impracticable reserve, or *mauvaise honte*, which too often mark the mere scholar and render him unfit for the saloon or drawing-room. The *savans* of Paris, more than those of any other European metropolis perhaps, mingle on easy and equal terms with the most select and polished aristocratic circles of the city. From such a school, he came forth accomplished, as well in the art of pleasing, as in the science of the Academy. As courteous in his bearing, and as observant of etiquette, in all companies, as if he had spent his days in a palace, rather than in a college or in the museum of nature.

Even the urbanity of his manner was striking; because it was evidently more the result of sheer innate kindness than of artificial training. No one ever fancied that he had *studied* the art of pleasing or of being agreeable; but that he was so, because he couldn't help it. "Caput artis est decere—et celare artem." You never suspected him of acting a part, or of being made up for the occasion, or of any attempt at self-display or exhibition. He was as sincere in his manners as in his morals. And in both, he might serve as a model, worthy of all praise and of general imitation.

To say that he was an honest man, I suppose, would be regarded as but common-place among people who are all honest; and yet a shrewd ethical poet has declared that, an honest man is the noblest work of God. Dr. Troost was honest, in the full sense of the poet's sublime meaning. In all pecuniary transactions and dealings, he was, of course, punctual, exact, and faithful to engagements. More than this, he was honest, just and liberal in his feelings, sentiments and opinions, in his language and conduct, towards his professional brethren, as well as towards all other classes and individuals.

2. *Was he a genius?* The answer to this interrogatory will depend on the meaning which we assign to the term *genius.* If genius be a purely creative faculty, such as is commonly, though perhaps erroneously, awarded to Homer, Shakspeare, Milton, Scott, and Byron, I suppose it would not be conceded to our late Professor. But if we allow it a wider and more comprehensive scope, so as to include those who achieve great ends by the legitimate exercise of their intellectual powers; who enlarge the boundaries of science; penetrate, develope and explain the mysteries of nature; who, by persevering, indefatigable, well-directed industry, overcome all difficulties and obstacles; creating a pathway where circumstances seemed to forbid any progress; and reaching the goal in spite of all physical or conventional impediments;—then was he a man of genius. What was the genius of Demosthenes, of Aristotle, of Cicero, of Columbus, of Bacon, of Galileo, of Newton, of Franklin?—Unless it was the spirit or inspiration which impelled them to *work*, WORK, WORK, ever and always?—To struggle onward, until triumphant success had crowned their labours and their

names with a glorious immortality? What would *they* have achieved without labour—and such labour as genius alone would have submitted to or could have endured?

Having selected the proper field of action or enterprise, true genius goes right ahead, and never falters or despairs. Where ordinary men would be discouraged and give over the pursuit as impracticable, he plods along, slowly, surely, hopefully, until the faint rays of the distant sun begin to glimmer through the darkness and to assure him that broad daylight is at hand. *Impossible* has no place in his vocabulary. He is a man of strong faith, of unfailing self-reliance, of untiring patience, of indomitable moral courage.

But, without disputing about words, we may safely affirm, that Dr. Troost possessed a philosophical genius, or precisely the kind of intellect best adapted to philosophical pursuits. His was a well-balanced mind—vigorous, discriminating, sagacious, logical and enthusiastic. He exhibited a sound judgment, as well as an ardent zeal, in the study and interpretation of the grand volume of Nature. He loved truth, and eschewed all forms of hypocrisy. He was wise, without cunning or craftiness. He was all that he professed or claimed to be. He accomplished, in good faith, whatever he promised.

3. *Was he self-made?* He was as much a self-made man as any of his contemporaries or predecessors. Every man who has been or is eminent in any profession or vocation, was or is a self-made man. The University alone does not make great men, or even great scholars. It merely aids self-exertion, and enables the young aspi-

rant to start forth at an earlier period and with a better outfit, in the career which he has chosen: but every step in his progress onward and upward is his own voluntary act; or, in other words, he is all the while a self-making man.—True in every age and country. We call Socrates a self-made man. And yet, after he became the founder and president of the most renowned school or university in the world, and was attended by hundreds of admiring pupils, we find among them but one Plato and one Xenophon. And among the disciples of Plato, we hear of but one Aristotle, though multitudes had listened to his eloquent and most instructive lectures. Now Plato, Xenophon and Aristotle, with all their superior advantages, were as truly self-made men, as had been the great master, Socrates.

We justly admire the energy and heroism of the obscure friendless boy, who nobly struggles against poverty, neglect, privation and ignorance—like Heyné, Davy, Arkwright, and hundreds in Europe—like our own Franklin, Henry, Sherman, Fulton, and a goodly host of others, among the dead and the living—but even they had to use the same means and to labour in the same fashion as the most favoured and gifted sons of the university. There is no royal road to science or to the temple of fame. And no man has ever yet been distinguished for learning or usefulness without corresponding industry. I dwell on this point, not because it is either questioned or questionable among competent judges, but because the young, and especially college students, are prone to indulge the fatal heresy, that genius will command distinction without labour: and, what is worse, they often fancy that they may establish a title to genius by habitual idleness and an ostentatious neglect of text-books and professors. Just run over the catalogue of illustrious names, ancient and modern, and point out one exception, which you could honour as a model or would be ambitious to emulate.

Dr. Troost, I venture to say, laboured more assiduously to the last—even when broken down by age and infirmities—than any of his pupils. Had he relied on his genius, rather than his ability to labour, he would never have mastered the a, b, c, of nature, or contributed a single page towards its illustration.

4. *He was a good man.* So numerous and universal, so obvious and striking were the traits of goodness in his daily conversation and habitual deportment, that nothing which we can say, would add to the impression already made upon this entire community. Everybody knows that Dr. Troost was a good man: but, possibly, some of my hearers do not know that he was a peacemaker: that he manifested his good will to men by embracing every proper occasion to promote peace and kindly feeling among those who happened to be at variance with one another.* [Here certain letters were

* A single anecdote will sufficiently illustrate our meaning. Whoever visited Peale's Museum, while in its zenith of popular favour, must have noticed three remarkable portraits, suspended in a row upon the wall of the picture gallery, and looking down upon the spectator with a gracious and significant smile, as much as to say, hereby hangs a tale, or here is a legend worth your hearing; pray listen to your *ciceronê*—he will tell you about us three. Our guide begins:

read or referred to, and facts stated, illustrative of the Doctor's peace-making character.] If the tree is known by its fruits, if a man is to be judged by his actions, if right conduct is the outward manifestation of right principles, then will sentence of approbation be pronounced upon the moral character of Dr. Troost: namely, that he was an eminently good man.

5. As a religionist, he belonged, by birth, education and choice, to the sect or denomination known in Holland as Remonstrants—and elsewhere as Arminians, from their founder, James Arminius, who died in 1609. His followers included some of the first men in the re-

---

That, says he, is the portrait of the great Doctor A., and that is the portrait of the learned Doctor B., and between them is the portrait of the Peace-maker, the good Dr. Troost, whom everybody loves and honours. His two friends, Doctors A. and B., among the most eminent physicians of Philadelphia, were at deadly feud with each other: they not only were not on speaking terms, but a duel or street-fight was confidently anticipated by their, so called, mutual friends.—But this then scarcely known stranger amongst us—this worthy benevolent Dutchman, who had bravely fought, as a volunteer, in defence of his native country's independence—here in this city of brotherly love, contrived to effect what none of our citizens seemed ever to have thought of. In short, he made himself acquainted with all the grounds of misunderstanding and hostility; invited the belligerent parties to his house; made such explanations and representations as to bring about, not only a cessation of arms, but a perfect reconciliation. So that Doctors A. and B. became thenceforth more sincerely attached to each other and to their common friend, than is usual among the members of that faculty in any circumstances. The two reconciled Doctors, in commemoration of the happy event, procured these three portraits, placed that of Dr. Troost in the centre, and ever since he has been styled "the peace-maker." [We tell the tale as 'twas told to us—merely substituting A and B for real names.] "Blessed are the peacemakers: for they shall be called the children of God."—Matt. v. 9.

public at the time—as Barneveldt, Hoogerbeets, Grotius, etc. The doctrines of Arminius, under various modifications, prevail at this day, to a large extent, among churches usually esteemed orthodox and evangelical.—As in the English established church, and in the Wesleyan Methodist churches of all countries. I am not their advocate or apologist; nor do I judge or denounce any who believe them, and love their brother man.

6. He was a happy man. Of course, a truly good man must ever be a happy man. The *mens conscia recti* is indispensable to inward peace and habitual tranquillity. The man of a bad spirit, of bad principles, of bad conduct, is always discontented, irritable, and dissatisfied with himself and with the world around him. There is no peace to the wicked: and the way of [See Isaiah xlviii. 22; and lvii. 21. Also Proverbs xiii. 15.] transgressors is hard.—While virtue is its own best reward. A contented mind is a continual feast. A complaining, morose, murmuring, censorious, envious, covetous Christian is a solecism—a contradiction in terms. And yet, how often do we meet with men who make loud and ostentatious professions of Christian goodness, who nevertheless are perpetually talking of their troubles or privations or self-sacrifices, of their poor health and bodily ailments, of their family or personal wants, of harsh treatment by the brethren and by the world, and of the general wickedness of all mankind except themselves! Now our good Doctor had no affinity or sympathy with that large species of morbid self-tormenting, or proud phari-

saic humanity. The smile of contentment seemed ever fresh and vivid upon his benignant countenance.

He had wisely chosen a genial vocation. Much of human weal or wo depends on this very choice. To prosecute any calling or business, which is either useless or pernicious—however profitable—must be irksome and repulsive, and therefore a source of constant annoyance and self-reproach. Again, the most beneficial occupation, pursued only for gain—thereby mistaking the means for the end—is scarcely less wearisome and unsatisfactory. For example, to preach the gospel, merely for worldly honour or emolument, would contribute little to the preacher's happiness, however much it might enlarge his purse or his reputation.

In this affair of life-work, two or three things are to be looked after. 1. The work to be done, or the profession to be practised, must be honest, legal, useful. 2. It must be one suited to our capacity, taste and qualifications.—The best, indeed, that we are fit for. 3. It must be pursued with a benevolent purpose—with the hope and design of benefiting others as well as ourselves. These considerations do not preclude a proper regard to our own private or domestic interests. Every man is in duty bound to earn an independent livelihood.—And also, to support and cherish all whom Providence may have rendered dependent upon his labours. Thus teacheth Paul: "But if any provide not for his own, and specially for those of his own house, he hath denied the faith, and is worse than an infidel."—1 Tim. v. 8. Having fulfilled the demands of that charity which begins at home; having satisfied all the just and reasonable claims which family or station can fairly urge; our obligations on that score extend no further. To devote one's life to the single object of accumulating wealth, either for its own sake or for posterity, is sanctioned neither by religion nor philosophy. Such a life would hardly be pronounced wise, useful or happy. Extremes in this case, as in others, must be avoided. There is danger in both. "Give me neither poverty nor riches: feed me with food convenient for me: Lest I be full, and deny thee, and say, Who is the Lord? or lest I be poor, and steal, and take the name of my God in vain." Such was the prayer of a very sensible man.—Prov. xxx. 8, 9.

Now in reference to all these views, motives and ends, we think Dr. Troost was exceedingly judicious and fortunate. He chose a profession which enabled him to be constantly useful to others; which highly gratified his own peculiar taste; and furnished him the richest entertainment—the purest pleasure—a real feast of reason without alloy or abatement. And though but moderately rewarded by cash payments for his services, his frugal habits and philosophical self-command qualified him to enjoy with cheerful gratitude, and in the kindliest, most hospitable manner, the good things which his patient earnings could supply. He appeared always to have enough; and not to covet what was beyond his reach. At any rate, he did not complain, nor vex himself about what could not be helped. Upon the whole, I have seldom known a happier man. His daily vocation was his delight. It created the very atmosphere which he inhaled, and which never failed to exhilarate and fortify him for renewed exertions. Was there wisdom in such a choice? Might not the Doctor, with less labour and self-denial, have become rich and respectable in a different sphere or profession? Undoubtedly, he might: and that too, without losing *caste*, either in the land of his birth or adoption. For in both, fortune-making has ever been duly honoured: and the *millionaire* is everywhere "the observed of all observers."

I shall not stop to inquire what the largest opulence might have done for *him*, had he possessed it: but to most other men or their children, it has proved a curse rather than a blessing. This is so generally acknowledged, as to have become a matter of every day's observation, that but little of manly excellence is ever expected from the sons of wealthy parents. They want the usual motive or stimulus to exertion, enterprise and self-reliance. If they do not speedily become dissipated, wasteful, intemperate, reckless, profligate, gambling loafers and nuisances; they are, at best, mere drones, idlers, exquisites, and fashionable *do-nothings*. In this respect, our philosopher had the advantage. He lived to see his children better off, more respectably established, and more usefully employed, than most of their youthful associates, who commenced life in affluent circumstances. How few of the latter are now their equals either in fortune or reputation? To the heart of paternity, nothing is so grateful as the assurance that his children are virtuous, dutiful, industrious, respected and prosperous. This necessary ingredient in the cup of human felicity was therefore not wanting in his case. He lived and died with the soul-cheering conviction that his posterity promised to be all that he could desire; and that they would cherish and revere his memory. More than this, neither wealth, nor rank, nor station can purchase or command.*

Had he, in his solitary rambles among the rocks and groves of our wild mountains and valleys, chanced to stumble upon a mine of gold; and could he have appropriated millions to his own private coffers; he would have been hailed and caressed as the most fortunate and successful of adventurers. And, perhaps, even Geology would have been exalted in the popular estimation, and voted a very gainful and respectable science or profession. What then might have been the destiny and character of his children? Let the worshippers of Mammon *calculate* at their leisure.

But how did the Doctor contrive to get through his long life of more than threescore years and ten, in such laborious, and, apparently, thriftless, as well as repulsive drudgery? Could his be a life of pleasurable enjoyment? Let us see. To the curious and inquisitive, the pursuit and acquisition of knowledge, of some kind, must be always gratifying. The lover of history or astronomy delights to ponder over the records of by-gone ages, or to scan the heavens with his telescope: and we do not marvel at his folly or enthusiasm. Why then should we

* Dr. Troost left one son, *Lewis*, and one daughter, married to Albert G. Stein. Lewis Troost and A. G. Stein are among the most eminent civil engineers of the Southwest.

fancy that the history of the planet which we inhabit, as well as its structure and composition, might not be equally interesting to another class of curious inquirers? All real students love their books and their work. The book of nature, to the student of nature, becomes more and more fascinating, just in proportion to his ability to understand it: and the more thoroughly it is studied, the greater the intellectual satisfaction in the pursuit.

How far science may proceed in the discovery of the true history of our earth—of its various revolutions, changes, formations—of its adaptations to successive genera of animals and vegetables, before it was fitted up for the habitation of man and of its present living occupants—cannot be even conjectured. The geologist is labouring in this grand work: and he has already made good progress, and given evidence that he is in the right way of ultimately arriving at most satisfactory results. He has ever before him the cheering prospect of discovery: as had Columbus of discovering a new world, or of reaching the far off Orient by a new route. But even should he not succeed in the main object of compassing a complete or probable history of our globe; he has, at least, the constant satisfaction of increasing our acquaintance with the valuable materials of which it is composed; and thereby of adding largely to human wealth and general advancement in the useful arts. Simply then, as a utilitarian, his studies are not profitless; while, as a liberal contributor to liberal science, he scarcely has a superior or equal in the whole range of philosophical investigation.

These are studies, moreover, worthy not only of the loftiest intellect, but of the most devotional spirit. Moses, Job, David, Solomon, Paul—appear to have taken great pains and great pleasure in the study of the Almighty's wonderful works. For, says David, "The heavens declare the glory of God; and the firmament showeth his handywork."—Ps. xix. 1. And Paul: "For the invisible things of him [God] from the creation of the world are clearly seen, being understood by the things that are made; even his eternal power and Godhead; so that they are without excuse."—Rom. i. 20. Says Job: "Dead things are formed from under the waters, and the inhabitants thereof." "He stretcheth out the north over the empty place, and hangeth the earth upon nothing." "He bindeth up the waters in his thick clouds; and the cloud is not rent under them."—Job, xxvi. 5–8.

Solomon was not only very wise and learned, but also a zealous advocate of learning. "Every prudent man dealeth with knowledge: but a fool layeth open his folly."—Prov. xiii. 16. "Wise men lay up knowledge: but the mouth of the foolish is near destruction."—Prov. x. 14. "How much better is it to get wisdom than gold?"—Prov. xvi. 16. That his range of knowledge extended vastly beyond the mere ethical and literary, is evident from the historical record. "And he spake of trees, from the cedar-tree that is in Lebanon, even unto the hyssop that springeth out of the wall: he spake also of beasts, and of fowl, and of creeping things, and of fishes."—1 Kings, iv. 33.

These are good authorities at least, if any were needed,

for such sublime and elevating studies. And no man need hesitate to follow their example. "An undevout astronomer is mad"—not more so than an undevout naturalist—or than the *devout* oppugner of all natural science. Even the latter, when better informed, is constrained to acknowledge:

> "That what he views of beautiful or gran;
> In nature, from the broad majestic oak
> To the green blade that twinkles in the sun,
> Prompts with remembrance of a present God."

The study of nature does not prevent or impede the study of revelation, or of general literature. The more we learn of our earth's vicissitudes and revolutions, the more shall we be inclined to read what man has recorded of himself in all past time, and what God has taught us in his word of both. Why should there be jealousy, suspicion or hostility between the parties thus engaged in the same grand inquiry?—As if the Deity had given us two conflicting revelations, on purpose to bewilder and confound our intellectual vision, whenever we attempt to scrutinize his works. Not thus, reasoned the royal Psalmist, when he exclaimed: "O Lord, how manifold are thy works! in wisdom hast thou made them all: the earth is full of thy riches. So is this great and wide sea, wherein are things creeping innumerable, both small and great beasts."—Ps. civ. 24, 25. Nor would he have been less devoutly inspired, had all or any considerable portion of modern geology been patent to his contemplative eye. The evidences are everywhere present, of extinct races or species of animals and vegetables, wrought up, in the progress of unknown ages, into the very texture of the mountains and valleys of the earth's surface—still speaking of the wisdom and power of the infinite Eternal, as plainly as do the gigantic ruins of Thebes and Nineveh of the exertion of human skill and energy three thousand years ago.

Even in the limited sphere of operations allotted to the *encrini*, and which engaged so much of Dr. Troost's attention towards the close of life, we find marvels enough to astonish and amaze the most unimaginative mind. Says Buckland: "We may judge of the degree to which the individuals of these species multiplied among the first inhabitants of the sea, from the countless myriads of their petrified remains which fill so many limestone-beds of the transition formations, and compose vast strata of entrochal marble, extending over large tracts of country in Northern Europe and North America. The substance of this marble is often almost entirely made up of the petrified bones of encrinites. Man applies it to construct his palace and adorn his sepulchre; but there are few who know, and fewer still who duly appreciate, the surprising fact, that much of this marble is composed of the skeletons of millions of organized beings, once endowed with life, and susceptible of enjoyment, which, after performing the part that was for a while assigned to them in living nature, have contributed their remains towards the composition of the mountain masses of the earth."*—*Dr. Buckland's Bridgewater Treatise.*

* The improved compound microscope has become one of the most

Assuredly, studies like these can never cease to absorb and exalt the mind that is capable of pursuing them.

Dr. Troost was a scholar, in the good old English sense,

---

important instruments ever bestowed by art upon the investigator of nature. "In almost every department of science are we indebted to it for the extension of our knowledge, and the verification of previous observation." The chemist, the pharmacist, the physiologist, the pathologist, the physician, the botanist, the zoologist, have, by its assistance, already achieved the most wonderful discoveries. In the hands of the geologist, the microscope is an instrument of magic power; by means of which, from the inspection only of a bone or tooth, the habits of the animal to which it belonged are decided; the colossal reptiles of the ancient earth are revived in all the reality of life and being; and the early formations of our globe decked with their former inhabitants and the vegetation which clothed them long ere man was created the lord of all below.

"While the telescope enables us to see a system in every star, the microscope unfolds to us a world in every atom. The one instructs us that this mighty globe, with the whole burden of its people and its countries, is but a grain of sand in the vast field of immensity; the other, that every atom may harbour the tribes and families of a busy population. The one shows us the insignificance of the world we inhabit; the other redeems it from all its insignificance, for it tells us that in the leaves of every forest, in the flowers of every garden, in the waters of every rivulet, there are worlds teeming with life, and numberless as are the stars of the firmament. The one suggests to us, that, above and beyond all that is visible to man, there may be regions of creation which sweep immeasurably along, and carry the impress of the Almighty's hand to the remotest scenes of the universe; the other, that, within and beneath all the minuteness which the aided eye of man is able to explore, there may be a world of invisible beings; and that, could we draw aside the mysterious veil which shrouds it from our senses, we might behold a theatre of as many wonders as astronomy can unfold; a universe within the compass of a point, so small as to elude all the powers of the microscope, but where the Almighty Ruler of all things finds room for the exercise of His attributes, where He can raise another mechanism of worlds, and fill and animate them all with evidences of His glory!"—*Dr. Chambers.*

as well as a *savant* and philosopher. He was well acquainted with classic and general literature. He was master of several languages, ancient and modern; particularly, of the Latin, German, French, English, and his own vernacular of Holland. Few works, probably, on any branch of natural science, were extant in these languages, which he had not studied or examined.

This desultory sketch, with many claims upon your indulgence, must suffice for the present. With documents already promised, and with others very confidently expected, I may hereafter, when more at leisure, recast the rough materials at hand, and construct a memoir more worthy of the distinguished subject. Unless, indeed, the task shall be accomplished by some abler pen.

And now, fellow-citizens, what monument, more durable than brass or marble, shall we erect to his memory? Nothing occurs to me so appropriate to the occasion and the man, and so honourable to this community, as would be the purchase by the State of his entire collection, both of specimens and books, for the use of the public. If thus purchased, and deposited in a spacious apartment of your magnificent capitol when finished, it would constitute the greatest attraction within its walls to all scientific strangers and visitors. It would become a school for the young and inquisitive throughout the country. And it would perpetuate the name of the founder and the liberality of Tennessee. It would be known, in all future time, as the TROOST CABINET;—purchased of his heirs, and gratuitously offered to the public service.

Should the State decline the honour, then let the city

of Nashville secure the treasure, and have the whole credit of the munificent deed. This opulent and growing metropolis should not hesitate a moment about the purchase, if the State refuse. I do not urge this, either at the instance of the family of the deceased or for their especial benefit. I suggest it, because it would be disgraceful to allow such a cabinet to be removed from our midst; and because the few thousand dollars demanded for it, bear no proportion to its intrinsic or even commercial value.—To say nothing of the benefit which future generations would derive from its use and study.

"The Troost Cabinet" would be an invaluable acquisition and a glorious ornament to the classic halls of our new University, which is about to arise, Phœnix-like, from the ashes of the old, with all the splendour which architectural genius and artistic taste can impart.—Where liberal science and elegant letters, where sound morals and heroic virtue and stern patriotism, shall be cultivated and taught by high example and commanding talent. And where multitudes of ingenuous aspiring youth shall congregate, as to a pure fountain, to drink in wisdom and piety; and to learn to venerate the name of our illustrious TROOST, as the great and good benefactor of their loved and honoured ALMA MATER.

[It is proper to add that the author had resigned the presidency, and that this was the last day and the last act of his official connection with the University. It had already been decided to erect new college buildings, etc.]

APPENDIX.

NOTE A.—DR. TROOST was sent to Paris, for scientific pursuits, by Louis Napoleon, King of Holland.—His Passport was dated July 1, 1807. He had before this resided at Amsterdam and the Hague, probably as a Pharmacist. He had twice served in the army.—Was wounded in the thigh and also in the forehead. During his last term of service, he was an officer of health of the first class.

About 1809, he was commissioned by the King to visit Java, as a *savant*. He sailed in an American vessel, from a German port, to avoid the English, bound to the United States. Intending to take passage thence in an American ship to the East. He was soon after captured by a French privateer (which paid little respect to our neutral flag,) and carried into the port of Dunkirk.—Where he was deprived of his papers and detained as a prisoner. Being soon released (when his case was understood,) he proceeded to Paris.—Where he was elected a corresponding member of the Museum of Natural History of France. His diploma is dated March 21, 1810. He, soon after, sailed for America. His passport for the voyage is dated Paris, March 5,

1810,—authorizing him to sail in an American ship from Rochelle to Philadelphia.

[I have seen the diploma and passports referred to above. They were among the Doctor's papers, and shown to me by his son.]

Before this, he had travelled much in France, Italy, Germany, and Switzerland; and had collected a valuable cabinet of minerals, which he sold to the King of Holland. Or rather, as I suppose, he travelled and purchased as the King's agent and at his expense.

Subsequent European events induced him to settle in Philadelphia, where he married Margaret Tage in 1810. He there established a laboratory for the manufacture of drugs and various chemical preparations.

[The facts or incidents, mentioned above, were furnished by his son.]

His second wife was, at the time of his marriage with her, a widow, Mrs. O'Riley, and the mother of two children, a son and daughter. The son, after graduating at the University in 1835, and after serving several years as a civil engineer with every promise of eminence in his profession, died in ——, highly esteemed and lamented. The daughter is the wife of Thomas Crawford, Esq., of the Planters' Bank in Nashville.

Mrs. Troost, the Doctor's widow, is beloved and respected by all her acquaintance.

"He discovered the process of making alum from lignite, for which he obtained a patent." So says a paper handed me by his son. But there is probably some mistake about the matter.

Alum, however, is still manufactured from the ore found at Cape Sable, on the Magothy River, near Annapolis, in Maryland. "This ore, which was extensively worked during the late war under the superintendence of Dr. Troost, consists of lignite, clay, sulphuret of iron, and sand. It exists in beds of from six to ten feet in thickness, covered by a stratum of sand."—*Dispensatory of the United States*, Philadelphia, 1839, p. 70.

Dr. Troost's Cabinet contained specimens as follows:

1. Minerals—in number—13,582.
2. Fossil organic Remains—Paleontology—2851.
3. Geology—Rocks, etc. from granites to lavas, between 2000 and 3000.
4. Shells—not numbered.
5. Comparative Anatomy—mostly disposed of.
6. Zoology. Nearly all his birds, fishes, and other animals were sent to Europe a few years ago.
7. Botany.—Do.
8. Indian relics from ancient mounds—with dresses—ornaments—war-clubs and other weapons—arrow-heads—images, etc.

The following is a copy of the letter received from Charles T. Jackson, M.D., of Boston, Mass., respecting Dr. Troost. It came to hand September 28, 1850;

BOSTON, *Sept.* 19, 1850.

DR. PHILIP LINDSLEY,

President of Nashville University.

SIR:—With emotions of the deepest regret, I learned that my honoured scientific friend, Prof. Gerard Troost, had been removed by death. Your communication of 15th ultimo, just received, bears testimony to his worth as a good man and distinguished *savant.* I would, with your permission, add my testimony to yours, assuring you, and the late Dr. Troost's other friends, of the high appreciation in which his scientific services were held by American Geologists and Mineralogists, and of my own profound respect for him as a learned and excellent man. It was my good fortune to become somewhat intimately acquainted with Dr. Troost in 1825, while travelling in company with him and the late distinguished Geologists and Naturalists, Maclure, Say, and Le Sueur, during their scientific excursions through the counties of Sussex, N. J., and Orange, N. Y.; and I was struck with the unaffected simplicity of his manners, and his uniform kindness and courtesy, as well as with his prompt and scientific recognition of the minerals, and rocks, which it was our object to examine. He was an accurate and scientific mineralogist, and very correct crystallographer, remembering with the most remarkable fidelity the exact angles of known crystals of minerals, so that he readily distinguished rare and remarkable forms.

During the latter part of his life he devoted much of his attention to the study of Fossils; and had mastered the latest discoveries in paleontology. As State Geologist to Tennessee, he distinguished himself as a careful examiner of the economical Geology and Mineralogy of his State, and directed with ability the enterprise of those interested in mining.

The University of Nashville and your State have lost, in the death of Dr. Troost, a most valuable scientific man; and his friends, both in this country and in Europe, deplore the loss of an amiable and most worthy man, and an eminent *savant*.

With sentiments of high regard,
I have the honour to be
Your obedient servant,

(Signed,) CHARLES T. JACKSON, M.D.,
State Geologist to the States of Maine, New Hampshire, etc., and the United States; Chevalier de la Legion d'Honneur, etc.

[Copy of note from the Trustees, requesting the publication of the preceding Discourse, etc.]

NASHVILLE, *October* 23, 1850.

DEAR SIR:—The undersigned have been appointed a committee, by the Board of Trustees of the University of Nashville, to obtain the original manuscript, or a copy, (as you may choose to furnish either,) of your Discourse on the life and character of the late Dr. Troost, delivered at last Commencement. The object of the Board is, to have the same printed and published; in order that it may be preserved in a more durable form, and be more extensively circulated. In performing this duty assigned to the committee, they beg leave to express their opinion of the high merit of the Discourse, as a literary composition, and for the full, and just, and discriminating views which it presents of him who was the subject of it; which make it eminently worthy of a place in the archives of the University. The committee, therefore, respectfully request of you a compliance with the wishes of the Board, as herein communicated.

Very respectfully,

Signed,
THOS. WASHINGTON,
SAM'L D. MORGAN,
JOHN TRIMBLE,
Committee.

TO DR. LINDSLEY.

END OF FIRST VOL.

www.ingramcontent.com/pod-product-compliance
Lightning Source LLC
LaVergne TN
LVHW021224110826
845150LV00002B/243

* 9 7 8 1 4 2 5 5 6 4 2 7 8 *